Planning for Rites and Rituals

A Resource for Episcopal Worship, Year A, 2022–2023

Planning for Rites and Rituals

A Resource for Episcopal Worship, Year A, 2022–2023

CHURCH
PUBLISHING
INCORPORATED

Church Publishing Incorporated
19 East 34th Street
New York, NY 10016

Cover design by: Jennifer Kopec, 2 Pug Design
Typeset by: Linda Brooks

A record of this book is available from the Library of Congress.

ISBN: 978-1-64065-530-0 (pbk.)

Contents

Lent

Holy Week

Easter

Pentecost

Welcome

Welcome to Year A, 2022–2023 of *Planning for Rites and Rituals*. All of us at Church Publishing are pleased to bring you this resource for liturgical planning. CPI's editorial team (Milton Brasher-Cunningham and Nancy Bryan) were joined this year by **Joan Castagnone** in the task of creating this volume, still working with a diverse group of contributors to bring you a wide range of thought-provoking, creative options for Sundays and holy days throughout the liturgical year. Each section of the book opens with an overview of the liturgical calendar, as well as newly reviewed and expanded *Seasonal Rites* updated by **Di McCullough**, offering expansive ideas for worship in and outside the primary Sunday service. Specific suggestions for every Sunday and holy day follow, offering a variety of material for the liturgy as well as ideas for formation and community engagement within and beyond your church doors.

Dozens of individuals were part of the development of this year's all-in-one volume. Priests, educators, musicians, members of Altar Guilds, and many others are featured within these pages. They will give you lots to consider and incorporate into the worship and formation of your parish.

Here is a description of the areas to deepen themes of each Sunday and holy day, along with those who have contributed their creative ideas this year:

♦ "Preaching the Gospel for Year A" was written by **Peter Wallace**, executive producer and host of the popular *Day 1* program. The "Preparing for" seasonal overviews were written by **Marcus Halley**, college chaplain and Dean of Spiritual and Religious Life at Trinity College in Hartford, Connecticut. "Weekday Commemorations" are the work of **Martha Baker**, writer, editor, and educator in St. Louis, Missouri, drawing on the resources of *Lesser Feasts and Fasts 2018*.

♦ "Engaging All Ages" offers ideas for enriching all ages in their engagement with worship (children, youth, and adults). They include thoughts for the congregation to take home and discuss, things to notice or highlight during worship (colors, senses, symbols, gestures), and ideas for action. Contributors for these portions are: **Hillary Raining**, rector of St. Christopher's Church in Gladwyne, Pennsylvania; **Gray Temple**, a priest enjoying retirement between Atlanta and Western North Carolina; **Bryan Bliss**, the Assistant for Discipleship at St. Clement's Episcopal Church in St. Paul, Minnesota; and **Di McCullough**, an educator and writer in Columbus, Ohio.

♦ "Prayers of the People" are the offerings of **Jeremiah Williamson**, rector of Grace and St. Stephen's Episcopal Church in Colorado Springs, and first appeared as *Praying the Scriptures*, available from Church Publishing.

♦ "Ideas for the Day" approach the day and its text in preaching and worship, including contemporary issues, movies, technology and social media, literature, historical events, and figures related to the Sunday lections and season. Contributing these ideas are: **Becca Ehrlich**, Associate Dean for Community Life at General Theological Seminary in New York City; **Mark Francisco Bozzuti-Jones**, an Episcopal priest at Trinity Church Wall Street in New York City; **Heidi J.A. Carter**, Lay Minister Associate, St. Paul's Episcopal Church, Kansas City, Missouri; and **Sharon Ely Pearson**, a Christian educator from Norwalk, Connecticut.

♦ "Making Connections" offers insights into connecting our Episcopal tradition to each Sunday. This may take the form of referencing other areas of the Book of Common Prayer, our Baptismal Covenant, or faith in daily life. Contributors here are: **Barbara Crafton**, priest and writer, Metuchen, New Jersey; **Greg Garrett**, professor of English at Baylor University and Canon Theologian at the American Cathedral in Paris; **Lisa G. Fischbeck**, Launching Vicar Emeritus of the Church of the Advocate, Chapel Hill, North Carolina; **Paul Fromberg**, rector of St. Gregory of Nyssa Episcopal Church in San Francisco; **Jennifer Enriquez**, director of children and youth formation at St. Christopher's in Oak Park, Illinois; and **Heidi J.A. Carter**, Lay Minister Associate, St. Paul's Episcopal Church, Kansas City, Missouri.

♦ "Images in the Readings" tap into the metaphors, names, history, and theology that are found in the day's lections. **Gail Ramshaw**, well-known Lutheran scholar and author, is the source of those connections.

♦ "Hymns for the Day" are drawn from **Carl Daw Jr.** and **Thomas Pavlechko's** *Liturgical Music for the Revised Common Lectionary, Year A* (Church Publishing Incorporated, 2009). These compliment the theme and readings of the day and come from *Hymnal 1982*, *Lift Every Voice and Sing II*, and *Wonder, Love, and Praise*.

Your feedback and perspective, of course, continue to be important to us. Let us hear from you—what would you appreciate seeing? What was most helpful? Who are the writers you would recommend to us for future editions? We are also delighted to offer the digital resource RitePlanning, designed to work with the resources in this volume. A trial subscription is available through the Church Publishing website (https://www.churchpublishing.org/ riteplanning).

Thank you for the trust you put in Church Publishing Incorporated to provide liturgical planning tools for your parish use. We are grateful for the many ways in which you care for the church's worship and the opportunity to work with you in that venture.

Welcome

Preaching Matthew's Gospel

Because 2022 is an election year in the United States, we'll all be sick of polls soon, if not already. Nevertheless, I conducted a poll of my own to clergy and church people on social media: *Of the four gospels in the New Testament, which is your favorite— and why?* I was shocked by the lopsided results of my very unscientific poll, to which nearly a hundred people responded: Luke came out in front with 38 percent. Mark and John each had 27 percent approval. But Matthew came in dead last with only 8 percent of the vote—and two of those votes were cast by my son Matthew's girlfriend, who had decided to vote for his namesake rather than her true favorite (John), and by Matt's sister, my daughter, so that 8 percent may even be inflated.

Everyone offered good reasons for their gospel choice, though several balked and chose three or all four. One voter said he picked Matthew because it was the source of most of the lyrics of his favorite musical, "Godspell." But some comments about Matthew came perilously close to "cancel culture." One said he preferred "Mark (rapid journalism style), Luke (rich imagination, human touch), but NOT MATTHEW!!" Another wrote: "Mark is in my head. Luke is in my heart. John is in my soul. Matthew is . . . still working with me."

Based on my poll, therefore, the first gospel in the New Testament is not all that well liked. In many ways, though, I'm not surprised, as Matthew is not my favorite either (even though my son carries his name). And yet, we're about to spend a whole year with this troublesome gospel. Can Matthew be redeemed? What notes of grace can we tease out of its pages? What problematic issues can we see from different directions? Let's take a good look in hopes that we can move through a meaningful year of proclamation and ministry.

The Gospel Itself

Matthew's gospel may not be popular, but it is full of some of the most beloved sections of the Jesus story: a colorful account of his birth with otherwise unreported details. Vast swaths of his status-quo-shattering teaching, including the Sermon on the Mount and the version of the Lord's Prayer we use in worship. Beloved healing episodes. Memorable parables galore, many unique to Matthew. Not to mention (and let's not) the genealogies that launch his account—part of the argument Matthew puts forth to persuade readers that Jesus is the Messiah, fulfilling the prophecies of the Hebrew scriptures.

With Mark and Luke, Matthew is one of the synoptic gospels, which means they share similar bones, whereas John seems to take us to a different spiritual plane altogether. Matthew is the first of the four gospels in our Bibles, but why? Scholars consistently date Mark as the earliest written and say Matthew drew deeply from it, so shouldn't Mark be first? Some scholars suggest that the fourth-century church councils that set the New Testament canon placed Matthew first because of its emphasis on Jewish themes; the argument goes that it therefore serves as a thematic bridge between the Old and New Testaments.

So who wrote this gospel?

The Author and the Times

Matthew was one of the twelve apostles, a tax collector (9:9; 10:3) who assessed levies from fellow Jews for the despised Roman Empire, so he was likely unpopular among his Jewish neighbors in the imperial occupation. The gospel that bears his name was attributed by the early church divines to this apostle Matthew, also called Levi, with the assumption that it was written in the 60s CE. Scholars today largely support a composition date late in the first century, though still within mere decades of the events recorded. The unknown author expanded on the Gospel of Mark, along with other now lost sources, with the purpose of emphasizing Hebraic scriptural quotations and prophetic fulfillments in order to (1) persuade Jewish readers to believe in Jesus the Messiah, and (2) to encourage those Jews who had already become Christian, who doubtless faced internal and external tensions because of their new faith, and who therefore desperately needed inspiration.

The author was no doubt a Roman subject. The Empire was heavily commercialized with a nominal middle class; only the most powerful and wealthy men (yes, men) claimed positions of political and cultural power, and they were reinforced by government workers, the military, and other community and business leaders. The vast majority of the populace fell to the bottom of the pile, and this reality is apparent throughout the gospel: we see Jesus as a champion of this lower class, battling the Roman oppressors on their behalf. This conflict is especially evident during the last week of Jesus' life. John the Baptist was an early victim of the ruling hierarchy (14:1–12).

Frequently in Matthew, Jesus verbally wrestles with the Jewish religious leaders, questioning their authority as they do his, lambasting their hypocrisy and their hyper-focus on the minutiae of the law rather than on the glaring needs of God's people. This is a time of tumult and trouble, and the people are crying out for help—and for their Messiah.

Matthew is written principally for Jewish Christians who likely had broken away from or been thrown out of their synagogues and even their families—a circumstance many people face today because of their beliefs, gender identities and sexual orientations, or economic circumstances, those who have had to leave past relationships and even been thrown out of their homes. Keeping those parallels in mind can bear meaningful fruit.

Themes and Approaches

The Year A lectionary readings from Matthew will give you a wide range of opportunities to focus on recurring themes in order to make the message more meaningful to your parish. Here are just a few themes to dive into more deeply and carry through the year.

Kingdom of Heaven

In Matthew Jesus speaks often of the kingdom of heaven (for example, his first public words called for repentance, as the kingdom is coming, 4:17), which he holds as superior to the earthly Roman reign. In the coming of Jesus this kingdom is real and present now. "Kingdom" may be translated *rule, reign,* or even *empire.* With our understanding of those times under Roman dominion, we can relate aspects of our culture as mirroring Rome's deep divisions of economics, authority, and agency. What does Jesus say about wealth disparity, of serving the poor? Why does Matthew seem to prefer "kingdom of heaven"— a spatial, otherworldly description—to "kingdom of God" favored by other New Testament writers, which evokes a here-and-now reality? How does this kingdom make a difference in our expectations regarding following Jesus today? How is this reign not just for the future but also for the present, for the now and the not-yet? How did Jesus embody this kingdom in his miracles, his healings, and his radical teachings—and how can we follow him in that embodiment?

Jesus as Messiah

Beginning with the genealogy (not in the lectionary, mercifully), which starts with Abraham and moves through David, Matthew sees Jesus as a fulfillment of many Old Testament prophecies—as a great teacher like Moses, a healing Messiah, David's son, the Son of God, and the Son of Man of the last days. In all these roles Jesus fulfills the law and the prophets. Be sensitive to how this approach might come across today; some use these texts to support supercessionism and anti-Jewish sentiments by casting blame for

Jesus' death. While it is helpful to reveal Jesus as the Messiah in fulfillment of prophecy, let's be careful not to proclaim ourselves the winners and to perpetuate hateful rhetoric. So how might we, in positive and beneficial ways, connect the Old Testament with the work and life of Jesus? How can that connection deepen our faith in wholesome ways? How might we foster greater relationships with people of the Jewish and other faiths in our communities while holding on to our individual beliefs?

Teachings and Parables

One of the few poll respondents who chose Matthew did so because "it is the most thorough in recording and explaining the Sermon on the Mount." In fact, Matthew has five major teaching sections—look for "When Jesus had finished sayings these things," which marks the end of each (7:28, 11:1, 13:53, 19:1, 26:1). In his teachings, particularly the Beatitudes (5:3–12), Jesus often goes deeper inside or flips over various teachings and attitudes of the privileged religious leaders, and in so doing upends much of our own culture's views about who should be "blessed." Thirteen of Matthew's parables (of nearly two dozen) are found in Year A. Jesus' parables surprise us, move us, even confuse us. Many of them use agricultural or natural world examples, but we can find plenty of relatable commercial business activities, relationship drama, and even humor to give us fodder for understanding Jesus' way in our own times. How do these compelling short stories shine the light of God's reign and our part in it? What teachings challenge us, frustrate us, or call us to something more?

Church

Of the four gospels, Matthew alone uses the Greek word *ekklesia* ("a gathering of the summoned" or "a called assembly") and does so only twice (16:18; 18:17), but his intention seems clear: God's people are to live together as Jesus' disciples in community, so they must organize soundly, select leaders carefully, avoid false teachers vigilantly, and be encouraged by

Jesus' charge to them—because where two or three are gathered, he is there (18:20). How might your own church respond to the summons to be community as described in Matthew? How does this impact how your church is organized, led, and taught, and how your members respond to differences and divisions, even when they're interpersonal?

Good News

In Matthew, Jesus' final words call his followers to share the good news of God's reign (28:19). Matthew may see Jesus as the deliverer of good news to Israel, thus fulfilling the prophets, but Jesus does so in a surprising and unusual way by offering himself as God the Son, not simply to this one group of people as a way to overcome Roman dominion, but to the whole world as the means to ensure the eternal siblinghood of all with him. While sharing this good news can be fulfilled with words, how might we focus on sharing it this year through our deeds, our acts of kindness, our active support of justice, and our call to unity in diversity?

A Meaningful Year with Matthew

As you launch this new year of ministry in Matthew, why not poll your congregation on their favorite gospel? Your mileage may vary, but my guess is the majority won't pick Matthew, and their reasons are worth exploring. What are we avoiding? What about Matthew doesn't appeal to us? Those may be areas to dig into.

As you embrace this gospel account and relate its unique teachings and perspectives to your own community, I pray that this time around Matthew will yield fresh and unexpected insights and life-giving blessings for you and your people.

The Rev. Peter M. Wallace
Executive Producer and Host of *Day 1* and author/editor of fifteen books
Atlanta, Georgia

Advent

Preparing for Advent

The Season of Advent marks the beginning of the new church year (Advent I through the Last Sunday after Pentecost). As the Body of Christ, we begin with hope—hope for:

- Christ's apocalyptic coming,
- Christ's historic coming remembered on the feast of his Incarnation, and
- Christ's daily visitation.

While Advent is a season of penitence (albeit to a lesser degree than the Season of Lent), it is important to note that penitence is not an opportunity for self-harm or self-abasement; rather, seasons of penitence (Advent and Lent) represent opportunities to engage more deeply in spiritual practice that allows us to see and experience the love of Christ with great clarity and devotion.

Advent begins the Incarnation cycle of the Christian calendar, which includes Advent, Christmas, and the season after the Epiphany. These days, dependent on the central Feast of the Incarnation, all highlight the importance of the doctrine of the Incarnation to our understanding of what it means to be Christ. The Son of God took residence in colonized, brown, poor, Jewish flesh—flesh that would have been overlooked by the many in power and flesh that was repeatedly brutalized by the oppressive regime of Rome. Holding this reality against the hope that colors this season, we see a wrinkle developing—it might be true that what we hope for will arrive in a form we are tempted to overlook or even to look upon with contempt.

As James Farwell has noted (*Planning for Rites and Rituals, Year C, 2018–2019*), planning for this season draws a through line that connects the hopes of those in our faith communities and surrounding geographic communities with the mystery of the Incarnation and the surprising ways that God's continuous incarnation manifests itself in and around us.

It is also true that many congregations will be planning for Advent, Christmas, and the season after the Epiphany in the middle of an increasingly frantic schedule. As the secular holiday seasons approach, ministry volunteers are likely to find time increasingly limited even as the church calendar fills up with all sorts of events. Planning liturgy during this season takes patience and forward thinking that allows for worshipers and guests to experience the depth of the season without taxing the resources of the community beyond capacity.

Theological Themes that Might Shape Liturgy, Catechesis, and Education

Hope and anticipation are themes that readily come to mind during the Season of Advent. The Christian hope during Advent, hope for Christ, stands diametrically opposed to the secular hope of an increasingly secular season. Christian hope invites us to prepare for the manifestation of our hope through a season of penitence, which helps to deepen otherwise unsatisfactory expressions of hope. As the Collect for Advent IV names for us, we are to practice our faith in this season (and every season) in such a way that Jesus "at his coming, may find in us a mansion prepared for himself."

Liturgical Possibilities

Rites

Liturgy planners for the Season of Advent are at a marked advantage. Individuals and communities who normally ignore, or even hold in contempt, the message of the church are likely more open to hearing the message of the Gospel during this season. How we plan and execute our worship has the potential of modeling a different, more just, more reflective, more compassionate way of marking this season.

One of the ways that might distinguish a uniquely spiritual expression of hope is by beginning our liturgies with the Penitential Order. It has been said repeatedly, but Advent is a penitential season. Beginning by hearing God's commandments, reflecting on our need for grace in the face of failing to live up to those commandments, and then opening ourselves up to the need to daily rely on God's grace is a helpful way to reorient the season away from rampant consumerism.

In this season, and indeed all seasons, it might be a helpful practice to write Prayers of the People that are unique for the context of the worshiping community. Give hope an address. What are the hopes of your community? How might our prayers function not only to voice those prayers to God, but also to remind our communities of our duty to be the bringers of hope to those who are around us?

Space

Depending on the flexibility of your physical space, you might consider using it to mark the difference in the season. Lowering overhead light and using more candlelight (if you have adjustable lighting) and rearranging chairs (if you have moveable seating) are options.

Other Rituals and Resources

Advent lends itself to a variety of additional ritual acts. One of the more popular rituals is the lighting of the Advent wreath. Some congregations append a wreath-lighting liturgy to the beginning of the liturgy. Doing anything prior to the beginning of the actual liturgy feels like an unnecessary add-on. This is doubly problematic if you attempt to involve newer people, families, young children, and so on in the lighting because it can come across that their ministry really is not valuable enough to be included in the main liturgy. On the other hand, congregations that include an elaborate liturgy during the Entrance Rite can make the lighting of the Advent wreath more of a spectacle than it is meant to be, "gilding the lily" of a liturgy already saturated with more meaning than the average worshiper has room to absorb.

Congregations will make decisions about color (violet or blue) with each having its particular value. Some congregations will choose to observe "Gaudete Sunday" on Advent III. They will do this by altering the color to rose for that particular Sunday.

Particularly in a time when "regular attendance" is something like once month, disrupting the consistency of the season might be something worth challenging, particularly if its observance is not a long-standing or helpful practice of a particular community.

Many congregations observe a Lessons and Carols service of some kind during Advent. Some choose to alter the Liturgy of the Word in the Holy Eucharist to adopt a Lessons and Carols format while others will choose to hold an entirely separate liturgy (it should be noted that the former is not supported rubrically by the Book of Common Prayer). It might be worth exploring what it means to use a penitential season such as Advent to develop a culture that has the bandwidth to support an additional liturgy.

Through the Eyes of a Child

During Advent, we, along with our families and all who are the church, wait for the birth of the baby Jesus, who is a gift God gave to us and to all people because God loves us so much and has made us one big family. It is a time we prepare for when Jesus will come again to earth, and God will be in all and make all things new. During this season, we ask what we can give to others to celebrate the fact that in Jesus, God loves us so much his promise to be with us always is complete. In Advent, we tell stories of hope and promise and wonder how the light breaks through the darkness. The Advent wreath helps us to count the days and weeks toward Christmas, a circle of evergreen shows us that God's love never ends, and we light candles (one for each Sunday of Advent) to help us remember that Jesus brings the light into the world.

Through the Eyes of Youth

In Advent we advertise that we have faith in the birth of Jesus as well as faith that Christ will come again. We in the church prepare for the birth of Christ by giving the gift of ourselves as we wait in joy. It is a time of action: Hold on to the promise that Christ will come again by hosting an "alternative gift fair" such as an angel tree in which members of your community can provide gifts to those in your community who are in need. Pray, ask, and respond: Who are the people in our world who need the message of God's love? What are our hopes for how people today can receive the message of God's love? How do we help others know God's love?

Of all the Christian stories, the ones associated with Christmas seem to be the most ubiquitous. It is also true that the season leading up to Christmas is crowded with other, often mixed messages about the purpose of this season. It is important that the local church find ways to help our young people discern the spiritual reason behind this season. Preparing take-home kits to observe Advent at home by creating an Advent Wreath to help mark the days might be a great way to put Christian formation in the hands of parents and guardians.

Through the Eyes of Daily Life

Advent is a time of preparation, of patience, of remembering what grounds and sustains us. The function of Advent is to remind us who God is and who we are meant to be, as well. Advent is about the riches of emptiness. God coming as an infant without retinue or riches is the metaphor of a humility that requires us to remember how really small we are in the universe. In our secular culture, a tone of wanting more, spending more, and accumulating riches on earth surround us. As Christians, we long for our society to live up to God's vision, for the kingdom to come in its fullness outside of materialism. The cry of Advent, "Wake up! Be alert! Watch for his coming!" is difficult amidst the busyness of the season. We can practice some simple, but not easy, disciplines. We can fast from the media to become more alert to the still small voice of God. We can focus on the giving of ourselves to God. Plan to spend time apart from the busyness of the season each day so you can be alert to God in the silent, the small, and the simple.

The Church suggests that Advent is a preparatory time for Christmas wherein we hope for the coming of Christ. Secular society says that the season before Christmas (inaccurately and curiously mislabeled as the "Twelve Days of Christmas") is a preparatory time for Christmas wherein we buy all the gifts and attend all the parties we can. Planning liturgy during this time should aim to bear witness to the former without creating shame on behalf of the faithful. Preaching that points out spiritual practices that can be observed with little disruption might be helpful ways to create the bandwidth for deeper spiritual engagement. Modeling practices within the liturgy (silence and reflection, for example) might also be helpful.

Through the Eyes of Those Outside of the Church

People who normally ignore the church are more inclined to pay attention to how the church recognizes and marks this season. If our observance of Advent mirrors the anxiety and frantic nature with which secular society marks the days leading up to Christmas, we might be unwittingly communicating our own irrelevance. We are a people of hope and nowhere is that hope modeled more clearly than when a community holds vigil for the inbreaking of love into the world. We might think about leaning into the weirdness of the Christian story—apocalypses, prophesies, weirdly-clad-wild-haired-charismatic preachers—as opposed to making apologies for it.

Through the Eyes of the Global Community

Advent is a time of concern for God's judgment, particularly in reference to the coming kingdom. The power of this theme of judgment brings about a realization of the sinfulness of the present age. As Christians, we believe it is Jesus who bears this judgment through his life, death, and resurrection, revealing the reign of God to the church in every generation. Our Eucharistic Prayer reminds us that Christ will come again. This is the hope for Advent, and this is the hope we find in the Lord's Prayer in "thy will be done" and "thy kingdom come." These familiar words call us into a reality of the real presence of Christ in our lives as we look at our own response to today's world. The Collects of Advent remind us how we are living in the reality of Christ's presence that allows us to approach ethical, social justice, and global issues.

Advent

Advent Blessing

The following blessing may be used by a bishop or priest whenever a blessing is appropriate. It is a three-fold form, with an Amen at the end of each sentence, leading into a Trinitarian blessing.

May Almighty God, by whose providence our Savior Christ came among us in great humility, sanctify you with the light of his blessing and set you free from all sin. *Amen.*

May he whose second Coming in power and great glory we await, make you steadfast in faith, joyful in hope, and constant in love. *Amen.*

May you, who rejoice in the first Advent of our Redeemer, at his second Advent be rewarded with unending life. *Amen.*

And the blessing of God Almighty, the Father, the Son, and the Holy Spirit, be upon you and remain with you for ever. *Amen.*

A Prayer for Advent[1]

We are waiting, O God,
for the day of peace.
Give us the will to bring that day
through our own simple
goodness and hope.
Fill us with patient desire
that our work may be holy,
and our holiness bright,
through the Christ
for whose coming we long,
and the Spirit in whose
presence we live.
Amen.

Lighting the Advent Candles

A tradition in Advent is to create an Advent wreath made with evergreen branches fashioned into a circle with four candles, one for each of the weeks of Advent. The lighting of the candles reminds us of the coming of God's promised light into the darkness of the world. Each week, beginning on Sunday, light another Advent candle and watch the light grow as we get closer to celebrating the birth of Jesus.

First Week of Advent

Light one candle.
The people walking in darkness have seen a great light. On those living in a pitch-dark land, light has dawned.
— Isaiah 9:2

As we light the first candle of the Advent wreath,
we give thanks for the great light of the world,
    your Son, Jesus,
who is our light in the world so that we no longer walk in darkness.
May our lives be a light to others. *Amen.*

Second Week of Advent

Light two candles.
A man named John was sent from God. He came as a witness to testify concerning the light, so that through him everyone would believe in the light. —John 1:6–7

As we light the first two candles of the Advent wreath,
we welcome the prophets who shine your light
    in the world,
especially (*offer names*). Help us to get ready to welcome Jesus, once again. *Amen.*

1 Susan K. Bock, *Liturgy for the Whole World* (New York: Church Publishing, Inc., 2008), 17.

Third Week of Advent

Light three candles.
Jesus spoke to the people again, saying, "I am the light of the world. Whoever follows me won't walk in darkness but will have the light of life." — John 8:12

As we light the first three candles of the
Advent wreath,
we give thanks for your great love in Jesus, your Son.
Open our hearts to receive your love
and show us the way to give that love to others. *Amen.*

Fourth Week of Advent

Light four candles.
"My eyes have seen your salvation. You prepared this salvation in the presence of all peoples. It's a light for revelation to the Gentiles and a glory for your people Israel." — Luke 2:30–32

As we light all four candles of the Advent wreath,
we give thanks for your great love in Jesus, your Son.
Help us to make room in our hearts for your love
and live in our bodies, minds, and spirits. *Amen.*

Advent Festival of Lessons & Hymns

Nine lessons are customarily selected (but fewer may be used), interspersed with appropriate Advent hymns, canticles, and anthems. When possible, each Lesson should be read by a different lector, preferably voices of male and female readers as well as a variety of ages. The Lesson from the third chapter of Genesis is never omitted.

Genesis 2:4—9, 15–25
Genesis 3:1–22 *or* 3:1–15
Isaiah 40:1–11
Jeremiah 31:31–34
Isaiah 64:1–9a
Isaiah 6:1–11
Isaiah 35:1–10
Baruch 4:36–5:9
Isaiah 7:10–15
Micah 5:2–4
Isaiah 11:1–9
Zephaniah 3:14–18
Isaiah 65:17–25
Luke 1:5–25 *or* Luke 1:26–38 *or* Luke 1:26–56

The Celebration of Our Lady of Guadalupe

Sunday, December 12

The Feast of Our Lady of Guadalupe (Dia de Nuestra Señora de Guadalupe) is a celebration of the appearance of the Virgin Mary to an Aztec peasant during the first years of Spanish rule. Today it is both a national and religious holiday in Mexico. The festival begins on the eve of December 12, when conchero dancers gather in the atrium of the church.

In the Roman Catholic tradition, the liturgy includes a celebration of the Eucharist followed by a festive meal.

Readings

Zechariah 2:10–13 *or* Revelation 11:19a; 12:1–6a, 10
Luke 1:26–38 *or* Luke 1:39–47

O God of power and mercy, you blessed the Americas at Tepeyac with the presence of the Virgin Mary of Guadalupe. May her prayers help all men and women to accept each other as brothers and sisters. Through Your justice present in our hearts, may your peace reign in the world. We ask this through our Lord Jesus Christ, Your Son, who lives and reigns with you and the Holy Spirit, One God, forever and ever. *Amen.*

The Angelus (English)

Leader: The Angel of the Lord declared unto Mary

And she conceived by the Holy Ghost.

Leader: Hail Mary, full of grace: The Lord is with thee. Blessed art thou among women and blessed is the fruit of thy womb, Jesus. Holy Mary, Mother of God: Pray for us sinners now and at the hour of our death. *Amen.*

Leader: Behold, the handmaid of the Lord.

Be it done unto me according to thy word.

Leader: Hail Mary . . .

Holy Mary . . .

Leader: And the Word was made flesh

And dwelt among us.

Leader: Hail Mary . . .

Holy Mary . . .

Leader: Pray for us, O holy Mother of God,

That we may be made worthy of the promises of Christ.

Leader: Let us pray.

Pour forth, we beseech thee, O Lord, thy grace unto our hearts, that we, to whom the Incarnation of Christ, thy Son, was made known by the message of an Angel, may by His Passion and Cross be brought to the glory of His Resurrection, through the same Christ, our Lord, Amen.

El Angelus (Español)

Líder: El Angel del Señor anunció a María.

Y concibió por obra del Espíritu Santo.

Líder: Dios te salve, María. Llena eres de gracia: El Señor es contigo. Bendita tú eres entre todas las mujeres. Y bendito es el fruto de tu vientre: Jesús.

Santa María, Madre de Dios, ruega por nosotros pecadores, ahora y en la hora de nuestra muerte. Amén.

Líder: He aqui la esclava del Señor.

Hagase en mi segun Tu palabra.

Líder: Dios te salve María . . .

Santa María . . .

Líder: Y el Verbo se hizo carne.

Y habito entre nosotros.

Líder: Dios te salve María . . .

Santa María . . .

Líder: Ruega por nosotros, Santa Madre de Dios,

Para que seamos dignos de alcanzar las promesas de Jesucristo.

Todos: Derrama, Señor, Tu gracia en nuestros corazones; que habiendo conocido la Encarnación de Cristo, Tu Hijo, por la voz del Angel, por los meritos de Su Pasión y cruz seamos llevados a la gloria de la Resurrección. Por el mismo Cristo, Nuestro Señor. Amén.

Las Posadas

Las Posadas (Spanish for "the inn" or "lodgings") is a traditional Mexican festival which reenacts Joseph's search for room at the inn. Beginning on December 16 and continuing for nine days leading up to Christmas Eve worship, a procession carrying a doll representing the Christ Child and images of Joseph and Mary riding a burro walks through the community streets. The processional stops at a previously selected home and asks for lodging for the night. People are invited in to read Scriptures and sing Christmas carols. Refreshments are provided by the hosts. The doll is left at the chosen home and picked up the next night when the procession begins again.

Elements for the Procession

Invite participants to sing together a beloved Christmas carol, such as "O Little Town of Bethlehem" or the traditional Mexican song "Los Peregrinos" ("The Pilgrims").

The Collect

O God, you have caused this holy night to shine with brightness of the true Light: Grant that we, who have known the mystery of that Light on earth, may also enjoy him perfectly in heaven; where with you and the Holy Spirit he lives and reigns, one God, in glory everlasting. *Amen.*

The Phos Hilaron

O gracious Light, pure brightness of the everlasting Father in heaven, O Jesus Christ, holy and blessed!

Now as we come to the setting of the sun, and our eyes behold the vesper light, we sing your praises, O God: Father, Son, and Holy Spirit.

You are worthy at all times to be praised by happy voices, O Son of God, O Giver of life,

And to be glorified through all the worlds.

Advent

Advent

The Song of Mary, the *Magnificat*, Luke 1:46–55

And Mary said, "My soul magnifies the Lord, and my spirit rejoices in God my Savior, for he has looked with favor on the lowliness of his servant. Surely, from now on all generations will call me blessed; for the Mighty One has done great things for me, and holy is his name. His mercy is for those who fear him from generation to generation. He has shown strength with his arms; he has scattered the proud in the thoughts of their hearts. He has brought down the powerful from their thrones, and lifted up the lowly; he has filled the hungry with good things, and sent the rich away empty. He has helped his servant Israel, in remembrance of his mercy, according to the promise he made to our ancestors, to Abraham and to his descendants forever."

I Was a Stranger, and You Welcomed Me An Advent Prayer Vigil for All Seeking Refuge and Home [2]

OFFICIANT: Jesus said: "Come, you that are blessed by God, inherit the kingdom prepared for you from the foundation of the world; for I was hungry and you gave me food, I was thirsty and you gave me something to drink, I was a stranger and you welcomed me . . . " (Matthew 25:34–35)

ALL: We hold up in prayer the eighty million forcibly displaced persons in the world today.

OFFICIANT: Jesus said: "Come to me, all you that are weary and are carrying heavy burdens, and I will give you rest. Take my yoke upon you, and learn from me; for I am gentle and humble in heart, and you will find rest for your souls. For my yoke is easy, and my burden is light." (Matthew 11:28–30)

ALL: We hold up in prayer all of those who suffer due to the pandemic and its effects. We hold up in prayer our families, friends, and neighbors, our communities, healthcare workers, frontline workers, and decisionmakers, and all those whom we do not know but who are beloved by God.

OFFICIANT: We gather during a pandemic time. Millions have lost livelihoods and loved ones. Social safety nets have stretched beyond breaking and have been shown to be woefully inadequate. Millions have been left hungry and homeless, anxious and insecure. For these our kindred, for our families, for our communities, and for ourselves, let us pray to the Lord.

An Advent Litany of Darkness and Light [3]

Voice 1: We wait in the darkness, expectantly, longingly, anxiously, thoughtfully.

Voice 2: The darkness is our friend. In the darkness of the womb, we have all been nurtured and protected. In the darkness of the womb, the Christ-child was made ready for the journey into light.

> *You are with us, O God,*
> *in darkness and in light.*

Voice 1: It is only in the darkness that we can see the splendor of the universe—blankets of stars, the solitary glowings of distant planets.

Voice 2: It was the darkness that allowed the magi to find the star that guided them to where the Christ-child lay.

> *You are with us, O God,*
> *in darkness and in light.*

Voice 1: In the darkness of the night, desert people find relief from the cruel relentless heat of the sun.

Voice 2: In the blessed darkness, Mary and Joseph were able to flee with the infant Jesus to safety in Egypt.

> *You are with us, O God,*
> *in darkness and in light.*

Voice 1: In the darkness of sleep, we are soothed and restored, healed and renewed.

Voice 2: In the darkness of sleep, dreams rise up. God spoke to Jacob and Joseph through dreams. God is speaking still.

> *You are with us, O God,*
> *in darkness and in light.*

---

2 This litany was prepared by Episcopal Migration Ministries https://episcopalmigrationministries.org/wp-content/uploads/EMMRefugee-Prayer-Vigil-Advent-Blue-Christmas-style_editable.pdf; accessed January 14, 2022.

3 "An Advent Litany of Darkness and Light," from *The Wideness of God's Mercy: Litanies to Enlarge Our Prayers,* Jeffrey W. Rowthorn, editor (New York: Church Publishing, 2007), 65–66.

Voice 1: In the solitude of darkness, we sometimes remember those who need God's presence in a special way—the sick, the unemployed, the bereaved, the persecuted, the homeless; those who are demoralized and discouraged, those whose fear has turned to cynicism, those whose vulnerability has become bitterness.

Voice 2: Sometimes in the darkness, we remember those who are near to our hearts—colleagues, partners, parents, children, neighbors, friends. We thank God for their presence and ask God to bless and protect them in all that they do—at home, at school, as they travel, as they work, as they play.

> *You are with us, O God,*
> *in darkness and in light.*

Voice 1: Sometimes, in the solitude of darkness, our fears and concerns, our hopes and our visions rise to the surface. We come face to face with ourselves and with the road that lies ahead of us. And in that same darkness, we find companionship for the journey.

Voice 2: In that same darkness, we sometimes allow ourselves to wonder and worry whether the human race is going to make it at all.

> *We know you are with us, O God,*
> *yet we still await your coming.*
> *In the darkness that contains both*
> *our hopelessness and our expectancy,*
> *we watch for a sign of God's Hope.*
> *Amen.*

Advent

The First Sunday of Advent

November 27, 2022

The day will come when God's wisdom and presence will be fully revealed. God's people must live in readiness for that great day to come.

Color Violet or Blue

Preface Advent

Collect

Almighty God, give us grace to cast away the works of darkness, and put on the armor of light, now in the time of this mortal life in which your Son Jesus Christ came to visit us in great humility; that in the last day, when he shall come again in his glorious majesty to judge both the living and the dead, we may rise to the life immortal; through him who lives and reigns with you and the Holy Spirit, one God, now and forever. *Amen.*

Readings and Psalm

Isaiah 2:1–5

Today's passage looks forward to Jerusalem's restoration at the end of history. In Hebrew, the noun for word or message (v. 1) also means literally "thing"—a physical object. The word of the Lord is so concrete and objective a reality that the prophet sees rather than hears it. He foresees the time when Mt. Zion in Jerusalem will replace Mt. Sinai as the mountain of God's revelation. In the fulfillment of God's purpose at the end of time all peoples and nations will acknowledge and accept God's judgment, ushering in the era of peace.

Psalm 122

Psalms 120–134 are each titled "A Song of Ascents." This psalm was probably sung upon arrival in the city. The Holy City is acclaimed as the center for the Lord's worship and for the declaration of justice. The psalm ends with a prayer for its peace as emblematic of the welfare of the people.

Romans 13:11–14

Paul concludes a section of moral exhortation (chaps. 12–13) by presenting the general principle that underlies his specific directions: "Love one another" (v. 8). Paul asserts that the greatest motivation for the Christian's moral life lies in the future: Christ's second coming. The end of time is near at hand. The great day of salvation is coming.

Matthew 24:36–44

Chapters 24–25 are the last of the five major speeches that Jesus gives. Today's section focuses on the theme of preparedness. Jesus' coming will bring judgment, not upon sin, but upon one's state of readiness. The division made by God between the ready and the unready cuts across all human categories. The eternal choice may occur at any moment, therefore constant watchfulness is needed.

Advent

Prayers of the People

People of God, come, let us walk in the light of the Lord. Let us pray to the Lord saying, "Teach us your ways, O God, *that we may walk in your paths.*"

Wake from sleep, O God, your Church. Let us lay aside the works of darkness and put on the armor of light. Let us live honorably as salvation draws ever nearer.

Silence

Teach us your ways, O God,

> *That we may walk in your paths.*

Wake from sleep, O God, this nation. May we beat our swords into plowshares, and our spears into pruning hooks. May we learn war no more.

Silence

Teach us your ways, O God,

> *That we may walk in your paths.*

Wake from sleep, O God, your creation. May the mountains rise to meet you and the crops of the fields burst forth in praise.

Silence

Teach us your ways, O God,

> *That we may walk in your paths.*

Wake from sleep, O God, this city. May there be peace and prosperity within our walls. Make clear our paths that we may walk in your light.

Silence

Teach us your ways, O God,

> *That we may walk in your paths.*

Wake from sleep, O God, those in pain and sadness. Deliver them from their darkness that they may rejoice in your light. May all those waiting for healing find your salvation is near.

Invite the congregation to add their petitions and thanksgivings, followed by silence

Teach us your ways, O God,

> *That we may walk in your paths.*

Wake all your people from sleep, O God. Prepare your saints for that day when the Son of Man will return, with the saints at rest, to reign with us forever and ever.

Silence

Teach us your ways, O God,

> *That we may walk in your paths.*

Images in the Readings

The apocalyptic imagery of **the end of the world**, like the flood sweeping all things away, echoes from the Old Testament into the preaching of Jesus and continues in contemporary disaster movies and terrorist activity. For Christians, fear about the end always comes to rest in trust in the presence of God. When all is over, at our end, is God.

Today's readings expand and challenge our society's welcome of God arriving as only baby Jesus, for God comes as **judge** and calls us into a life of justice for all, evoking in us both anticipation and fear. Often in classical art, Justice is a towering, robed woman who judges right from wrong. Often in the Bible God meets with humankind on a **mountain**. In our language a "mountaintop experience" is one so overwhelming that it changes one's future. Sinai, Horeb, Jerusalem, the mount of Jesus' sermon, the Mount of Transfiguration, the Mount of Olives, Golgotha, Zion: all are superimposed on our church buildings, for the Christian mountain is wherever we receive the word and sacraments. In English, the phrase **"swords into plowshares"** indicates the hope for world peace, a hope for which Christians pray to God.

Ideas for the Day

♦ Advent is a baffling season: beginning with an end, ending with a beginning; remembering a birth that was millennia past while looking forward to a final coming sometime in the future. It is fitting then, that we begin the season with one of the prophets—quite mystifying figures themselves—who declares, "The word that Isaiah saw." That particular Hebrew verb describes a special way of seeing: a vision-of-the-future-replete-with-improbable-hope. Advent is an interrupter: it begins with a word that is seen, with visions of hope for a better future. Advent will end with a mother nurturing a child whose name is a promise: God-with-us.

♦ In this season of preparation and expectation, let us find active ways to express our faith, through areas of personal development, family development, and church community development. At the personal level, plant herbs, learn to notate music, write in a diary, create a Spotify playlist of twenty uplifting songs by various artists. At the family level, find ways to prepare meals together. At the church level, assist in planning an event for the community. These active ways of engaging our faith will allow us to ". . . cast off the works of darkness and put on the armor of light."

♦ We are offered a glimpse of God's ultimate vision for creation and humanity. We are challenged to set life goals around that vision. Advent invites the church to dream of what God's will being done fully "on earth as in heaven" might mean in light of Jesus' words and acts.

Making Connections

Advent is a time of preparation, and not just for Christmas. It is a time to prepare for the return of Jesus. Advent marks the beginning of a new year in the life of the Church, and the readings today are a collective invitation to turn over a new leaf, to live life in a new way. We can do that in two ways: by having joyful expectations and actively preparing, perhaps through prayer or other spiritual practices. Each of us can do something to prepare for Jesus and our thing is likely different from others'.

Engaging All Ages

"Swords into plowshares" is a theme often cited by groups working for peaceful solutions to the world's problems, including the Episcopal Peace Fellowship: http://www.epfnational.org/. How might their efforts and resources be used to engage children, youth, and adults in worship? How might your formation programming on this day speak about becoming voices of nonviolence in daily life?

Hymns for the Day

The Hymnal 1982
Blest be the King whose coming 74
Once he came in blessing 53
The King shall come when morning dawns 73
Christ is the world's true Light 542
Glorious things of thee are spoken 522, 523
Judge eternal, throned in splendor 596
O day of God, draw nigh 600, 601
Thy kingdom come, O God 613
"Thy kingdom come!" on bended knee 615
Awake, my soul, and with the sun 11
Awake, my soul, stretch every nerve 546
Awake, thou Spirit of the watchmen 540
Eternal Ruler of the ceaseless round 617
Hark! a thrilling voice is sounding 59
Jesus came, adored by angels 454
Lo! he comes, with clouds descending 57, 58
Rejoice! rejoice, believers 68
"Sleepers, wake!" A voice astounds us 61, 62

Lift Every Voice and Sing II
We're marching to Zion 12
Down by the riverside 210
Great day 5
Rockin' Jerusalem 17
Better be ready 4

Wonder, Love, and Praise

Advent

Advent

Weekday Commemorations

Thursday, December 1
Nicholas Ferrar, Deacon, 1637

Nicholas Ferrar was the founder of a religious community at Little Gidding, Huntingdonshire, England, which existed from 1626 to 1646. His family had been prominent in the affairs of the Virginia Company, but when that company was dissolved, he took deacon's orders and retired to the country. The community at Little Gidding became an important symbol for many Anglicans when religious orders began to be revived. Its life inspired T. S. Eliot, and he gave the title "Little Gidding" to the last of his *Four Quartets*, one of the great religious poems of the twentieth century.

Charles De Faoucauld, Monastic and Martyr, 1916

De Foucauld influenced revival of desert spirituality in the early twentieth century; he inspired the founding of new religious communities for women and men. Brother Charles of Jesus (b. 1858) mixed laxity with stubbornness as a young man. He served as an army officer before becoming an explorer in Morocco, where he encountered Muslims. Their faith inspired him to study his own: in 1886, he found God. He was ordained in 1901 and lived "a ministry of presence" in the Sahara. After being shot to death by bandits in 1916, he was beatified as a Roman Catholic martyr in 2005.

Friday, December 2
Channing Moore Williams, Bishop and Missionary, 1910

Bishop Williams was born in Richmond, Virginia, on July 18, 1829, and brought up in straitened circumstances by his widowed mother. He attended the College of William and Mary and the Virginia Theological Seminary. Ordained deacon in 1855, he offered himself for work in China; two years later he was sent to Japan and opened work in Nagasaki. Williams translated parts of the prayer book into Japanese; he was a close friend and warm supporter of Bishop Schereschewsky, his successor in China.

Saturday, December 3
Francis Xavier, Priest and Missionary, 1552

The Spaniard Francis Xavier (b. 1506) met Ignatius Loyola while studying in Paris. Francis and his companions bound themselves to serve God in 1534—thus, began the Society of Jesus (Jesuits). Xavier and Loyola were ordained together in 1537. Francis traveled to India, then on to Sri Lanka and Indonesia. In 1549, he moved to Japan and learned the language to prepare a catechism for his mission among peoples he came to respect. In 1551, he traveled to China, hoping to launch a new mission, but he died before he secured passage into China. Francis is buried in Goa, India.

The Second Sunday of Advent

December 4, 2022

John the Baptist proclaims the coming of Jesus and calls people into repentance through baptism.

Color   Violet or Blue

Preface   Advent

Collect

Merciful God, who sent your messengers the prophets to preach repentance and prepare the way for our salvation: Give us grace to heed their warnings and forsake our sins, that we may greet with joy the coming of Jesus Christ our Redeemer; who lives and reigns with you and the Holy Spirit, one God, now and forever. *Amen.*

Readings and Psalm

Isaiah 11:1–10

The hope associated with the kings of David's line was never really borne out by experience, yet it persisted. The picture painted here by the prophet Isaiah became even more meaningful to the exilic and postexilic generations, as shown by the quotation from it in Habakkuk 2:14. It formed the expectation of a messianic king embodying all the best qualities of the past and empowered with the Spirit of the Lord as was David, the son of Jesse. The king's wisdom issues in justice, especially for the poor. His reign restores the peaceful harmony of the created order.

Psalm 72:1–7, 18–19

This royal psalm was probably used as part of the enthronement ceremony for the Davidic kings. As God's representative, the king's dominion should extend to the whole world (vv. 8–11). His deliverance of the poor ensures power and prosperity for all (vv. 12–17), and his reign fulfills the promise to Abraham found in Genesis 12:2–3 (v. 17). After the end of the monarchy, this psalm was interpreted in reference to the coming Messiah.

Romans 15:4–13

At the beginning of today's reading, Paul justifies his use of the scriptures by pointing out their role in showing the continuity of God's activity and thus providing encouragement and hope to Christians. The example of Christ himself provides the model for imitation. Paul asserts that in Christ, God fulfills both the hope of the Jewish people for a Messiah and extended salvation to the Gentiles. A quotation from 2 Samuel 22:50 shows that the inclusion of the Gentiles had always been a part of God's purpose. Such encouragement in Christ and in the scriptures results in a divine hope that overflows in the believer's life.

Matthew 3:1–12

John the Baptist's clothing identifies him as a prophet. But he is more than a prophet, he is Elijah returned. He preaches the same message as Jesus, challenging the same opposition. Matthew also makes clear the distinction between John and Jesus. John calls his listeners to repent, to turn back to the covenant way of life, for the kingdom of heaven is spatially and temporally at hand in the person of Jesus. The kingdom stretches between present reality and future consummation.

Advent

Prayers of the People

Friends, may the God of hope fill you with all joy and peace in believing. Let us come before the Lord praying, "Blessed are you, Lord God; *May the earth be filled with your glory.*"

Grant your Church, O God of encouragement, to live in harmony with one another, in accordance with Christ Jesus, so that we may glorify you with one voice. Make us a people of repentance and bless us with your Holy Spirit and fire.

Silence

Blessed are you, Lord God;

May the earth be filled with your glory.

Grant this nation, O God of justice, the will to defend the needy and the poor. May we sincerely hope for that day when hurt and destruction are no more.

Silence

Blessed are you, Lord God;

May the earth be filled with your glory.

Grant your creation, O God of faithfulness, the hope of renewal. May we who are stewards of this earth, also live at peace with all you have created.

Silence

Blessed are you, Lord God;

May the earth be filled with your glory.

Grant this city, O God of understanding, prosperity. May all the people know and do justice. We ask that you teach us and our leaders the best ways to meet the needs of all our neighbors.

Silence

Blessed are you, Lord God;

May the earth be filled with your glory.

Grant all the needy, O God of steadfast love, your mercy. Prove yourself to be a God of righteousness and faithfulness. To all their pain and suffering bring your healing and peace. And with your winnowing fork clear from their lives all the forces of oppression.

Invite the congregation to add their petitions and thanksgivings, followed by silence

Blessed are you, Lord God;

May the earth be filled with your glory.

Grant to those who have died, O God of hope, eternal life in you. Bring the departed into your glorious dwelling where all their hope will be fulfilled in your Christ.

Silence

Blessed are you, Lord God;

May the earth be filled with your glory.

Images in the Readings

Ancient Near Eastern iconography often depicted the monarch as a **tree of life**, whose successful reign insured a vibrant life for the people. Both first and second readings rely on this ancient imagery when they refer to the "root of Jesse." In Israelite history, Jesse, the father of the legendary King David, is described as the root of the tree that was King David. John the Baptist warns that some trees will be cut down to make way for Christ, who is our tree of life. The gospel reading situates John the Baptist in the **wilderness**, baptizing in the Jordan River, the **river** that the Israelites crossed on their way into the Promised Land. Led by Jesus, our Joshua, who entered the wilderness of our lives, Christians too cross a river in baptism and so enter into the kingdom of God.

The lion and the lamb has become a beloved symbol of peace between natural enemies. The toddler is playing with the adder. In Christ is the promise of this extraordinary hope for the world.

Ideas for the Day

 ◆ Poet Anne Sexton claims that there are two things impossible to ignore: love and a cough. Let's add John the Baptizer, who crashes into our Christmas preparations this week and next like an irritating cough; beneath that rough exterior lies a man smitten with a passionate love for God and people. "Repent," he says. In the Bible, repentance, that turning around to take an honest look at ourselves, is something like a dance. It takes two: God and a newly aware "us." Think of John the B as the host at prom night. Our dance cards are full and it is God in whose arms we glide, God teaching us steps we thought we knew or thought we were too gawky to try.

 ◆ The beautiful imagery of all creation beginning at peace (Isaiah 11) has inspired poets and artists for generations. How might you share some poetry or paintings in your preaching, prayers, or focal installations during worship?

 ◆ How do we focus our voice to have the most impact in today's culture? There are many voices that call to us throughout the Bible. They ring out truth in times of tribulation. From the prophet Isaiah to John the Baptist to Jesus Christ, the message is loud and clear. Live your life in preparation for glory to come. The way of Christianity is not easy and we must find strength in the messages voices from the Bible have given us. These voices direct us in ways to live our lives properly. We can use these messages to empower our voice in our current age; whether it is through a blog, through activism, or through being a positive force to all of those we encounter, our voice must echo the voices of those who came before.

Making Connections

Christ is coming to fill all with the gifts of joy and peace. Christ is both Savior and Judge. We are loved and redeemed by God, no matter how many times we fall into sin. We are also held accountable for our actions. God is calling us to live out the Way of Love, to turn and to learn from our sins. God will forgive us and lift us up when we fall, but that does not mean we can give up or stop trying. We must always be seeking to follow the Way of Love more deeply.

Engaging All Ages

The story of John the Baptist, including the narrative details from the gospel of Luke (1:5–80) offer an opportunity for drama or storytelling in the liturgy. What objects can be shared (honey, locusts, camel's hair) to bring our senses to the person and message?

Hymns for the Day

The Hymnal 1982

Blessed be the God of Israel 444
Hail to the Lord's Anointed 616
God is working his purpose out 534
Lord, enthroned in heavenly splendor 307
O day of peace that dimly shines 597
Holy Father, great Creator 368
Redeemer of the nations, come 55
Savior of the nations, come 54
Comfort, comfort ye my people 67
Hark! a thrilling voice is sounding 59
Herald, sound the note of judgment 70
On Jordan's bank the Baptist's cry 76
Prepare the way, O Zion 65
There's a voice in the wilderness crying 75
What is the crying at Jordan? 69

Lift Every Voice and Sing II

Christ is coming 6

Wonder, Love, and Praise

Blessed be the God of Israel 889
Isaiah the prophet has written of old 723

Advent

Advent

Weekday Commemorations

Monday, December 5
Clement of Alexandria, Priest and Theologian, c. 210

Clement's liberal approach to secular knowledge laid the foundations of Christian humanism. Born mid-second century, Clement was a cultured Greek philosopher. He sought truth widely until he met Pantaenus, founder of the Christian Catechetical School at Alexandria. In 190, Clement succeeded Pantaenus as headmaster; Origen was Clement's most eminent pupil. Clement's learning and allegorical exegeses helped commend Christianity to intellectual circles of Alexandria during an age of Gnosticism. Clement dissented from the negative Gnostic view of the world, which denied free will. In *What Rich Man Will Be Saved?*, Clement sanctioned the "right use" of wealth and goods. Among his writings is the hymn "Master of eager youth." The time and place of his death are unknown.

Tuesday, December 6
Nicholas of Myra, Bishop, c. 342

Nicholas is the traditional patron saint of seafarers and sailors, archers, repentant thieves, brewers, pawn brokers, and, most important, children. He bore gifts to children. His name, Sinterklaas, was brought to America by Dutch colonists in New York, and from there, Saint Nicholas became known as Santa Claus. Because of many miracles attributed to his intercessions, Nicholas is also called the Wonderworker. Born in Patara, Lycia in Asia Minor (now Turkey) in 270, he traveled to Egypt and around Palestine and became the bishop of Myra. He was tortured and imprisoned during the persecution of Diocletian. After his release, he was possibly present at the First Ecumenical Council of Nicaea in 325.

Wednesday, December 7
Ambrose of Milan, Bishop and Theologian, 397

Ambrose was hastily baptized so he could become a bishop on December 7, 373, after the Milanese people demanded his election. He had been brought up in a Christian family; in 373, he succeeded his father as governor in Upper Italy. As bishop and a statesman of the Church, he soon won renown defending orthodoxy against Arianism. He was a skilled hymnodist, introducing antiphonal chanting to enrich liturgical texture; among hymns attributed to him is a series for the Little Hours. Ambrose, who was a fine educator in matters of doctrine, persuaded Augustine of Hippo to convert. He feared not to rebuke emperors, including the rageful Theodosius, made to perform public penance for slaughtering thousands of citizens.

The Third Sunday of Advent

December 11, 2022

The promised day of God is dawning. John is the herald of that day. Jesus proclaimed the kingdom of God by everything he said and did.

Color   Violet or Blue

Preface   Advent

Collect

Stir up your power, O Lord, and with great might come among us; and, because we are sorely hindered by our sins, let your bountiful grace and mercy speedily help and deliver us; through Jesus Christ our Lord, to whom, with you and the Holy Spirit, be honor and glory, now and forever. *Amen.*

Readings and Psalm

Isaiah 35:1–10

Chapter 35 is a hymn of praise to God for Zion's restoration. God will lead the people in a new exodus out of Babylon through the wilderness. Instead of being a place of trial and suffering, the desert will resemble paradise. God's coming will bring salvation and wholeness, especially to those who suffer in body or spirit. They will all be restored to Zion and worship there as the culminating act of God's redemptive work.

Psalm 146:4–9

The psalm calls for an unwavering trust in the Lord's goodness, power, and sovereign reign in the midst of outwardly dark and painful conditions. The psalmist is thankful that Yahweh is a God who cares for all who are most neglected by society.

or

Canticle 15 (Magnificat)

These excerpts from Mary's song of praise, the Magnificat, echo many gospel themes stressed by Luke: the joy of salvation, the reversal of this world's values, God's option for the poor and lowly and the fulfillment of the promises in the Hebrew Bible. This song of God's lowly handmaid is a foreshadowing of the way in which the kingdom of God will transform our world.

James 5:7–10

The early Church seems to have expected the Lord's return within the span of the first generation of believers and, as time went on, had to deal with the apparent delay. In contrast to the unbelieving rich, Christians have reason to look forward to his coming. They must, however, exercise self-restraint, as does the farmer waiting for the harvest. The imminence of judgment also colors the admonition against grumbling. A second exhortation to patience under persecution is based on the example of the prophets who often proclaimed God's message amidst the darkest circumstances.

Matthew 11:2–11

Jesus' words and works challenge people to a decision about the person of Jesus himself. Matthew, speaking for the Church, identifies Jesus as "the Messiah" (v. 2). John the Baptist asks if Jesus is indeed the "one who is to come" whom John announced. Jesus answers indirectly by referring to his own words and deeds, which point to God's action revealed through Jesus. Such miracles are not proofs but signs, for one may witness a miracle and react with doubt or rejection depending upon how one understands its significance.

Advent

Prayers of the People

Sisters and brothers, strengthen your hearts, for the coming of the Lord is near. Let us seek the Lord praying, "Let us see your glory, O Lord; *Come to us and save us!*"

Lord, save your Church from weakness of heart. Give us strength to prepare this world for the coming of your Christ. And give us patience when it seems Christ's kingdom does not come quickly enough.

Silence

Let us see your glory, O Lord;

Come to us and save us!

Lord, save this nation from disordered priorities and misplaced hope. May our values mirror your values. May we be a nation that gives justice to the oppressed, food to the hungry, and care to the stranger.

Silence

Let us see your glory, O Lord;

Come to us and save us!

Lord, save your creation from human misuse. Bless us to play a part in the redemption you have planned for all of creation.

Silence

Let us see your glory, O Lord;

Come to us and save us!

Lord, save this city from hopelessness. Give us a vision and a future. Raise up prophets who will speak hope and encouragement to the people of our region.

Silence

Let us see your glory, O Lord;

Come to us and save us!

Lord, save the sick and the sorrowful in the midst of their affliction. May they experience the healing work of their Messiah. Make happy all those who have you for their help.

Invite the congregation to add their petitions and thanksgivings, followed by silence

Let us see your glory, O Lord;

Come to us and save us!

Lord, bless all members of your heavenly kingdom. May they obtain eternal joy and gladness in your presence—where sorrow and sighing are no more.

Silence

Let us see your glory, O Lord;

Come to us and save us!

Images in the Readings

The **flowering wilderness** is the image presented in both the first reading and the gospel. Often the Bible uses imagery from nature to celebrate the presence of God. All of nature rejoices in God's continuing creation. We are called to ecological care for God's good earth, making literal the symbol of a flowering wilderness. The **healing of the blind and lame** is a recurring image in the Old Testament to describe the effect of the presence of God. The gospels say that Jesus healed the blind, the lame, the lepers, and the deaf; he raised the dead; and he preached to the poor—thus enacting all the miracles that are cited in the ancient poems. In the ancient Near East, conquerors built massive **highways** to allow for civic processions to display their power. The Bible cites and then transforms this image: there will be a highway on which the people will return in safety into their own city. Might is changed into right.

Ideas for the Day

"Are you the one?" John had the grit to ask the question. The biblical landscape is littered with questions starting with "Where are you?" in Genesis 3. Questions are most often directed to a second person, a "you," which invites overhearers and readers of the texts through the millennia to ponder the questions. John's query today, like Jesus', "Who do you say that I am?" of the Synoptics, bids us answer the questions for ourselves. Is the Jesus we meet in the gospels the One? Or are we looking for another Messiah, a comfier one, someone a little less disruptive and challenging?

It is in living out our Baptismal Covenant call that the church responds to the question raised by John, "Are you the one who is to come, or are we to wait for another?" (Matt. 11:3). The first reading and the gospel lection lie behind the church's call to be deeply involved in the ministry of service and justice. The church continues in the role of Jesus, pointing out God's coming reign in such actions.

Patience is a required virtue when we follow a Christian path. It is additionally important not to grumble against those around us. If we are constantly observing what others are not doing, then we are not devoting enough time and energy to what we are doing, working towards our own Christian walk. It has become so easy to post a negative comment on something we see online.

In fact, there are some people in our society whose entire lives are consumed with cutting down others in order to build themselves up. We must reject this path. The Christian path is one of constructivism. We must seek constantly to build relationships and never tear them down.

Making Connections

In all great stories, there comes a moment when characters cross a boundary, often with the help of a mentor figure, someone who inspires, offers life wisdom, or even offers practical suggestions about how we need to move forward in our lives. In the third Sunday of Advent we hear John, who baptized Jesus, wondering if he was right: Was Jesus the Anointed One of God he was expecting? Jesus' answer is instructive for us. Look at what is happening, Jesus says. Look at all the ways the kingdom of heaven is drawing near. It is John's story and Jesus' story, but it is also our story. We too are called to heal and to feed, to bring what was dead back to life, to carry the good news. Look for the figures in your lives who can inspire and instruct, and think about how we too can carry forward God's work.

Engaging All Ages

Do you wonder if John the Baptist died thinking he was a failure? We see him in this Gospel reading sending messengers to Jesus from prison asking if he is "the one." It wouldn't be long before John would be dead—another victim of empire, greed, and sin— the very things he railed against. He may not have felt like what he did mattered. The same may be true for us. We may not know what difference our efforts on behalf of the kingdom of God will make in the world—but we must have hope that God will magnify them in ways we could never imagine.

Hymns for the Day

The Hymnal 1982
Blessed be the God of Israel 444
Watchman, tell us of the night 640
O for a thousand tongues to sing 493
Come, thou long-expected Jesus 66
O heavenly Word, eternal Light 63, 64
The Lord will come and not be slow 462
"Thy kingdom come!" on bended knee 615
Hark! the glad sound! the Savior comes 71, 72
Herald, sound the note of judgment 70
O for a thousand tongues to sing 493
On Jordan's bank the Baptist's cry 76
Prepare the way, O Zion 65
There's a voice in the wilderness crying 75
Word of God, come down on earth 633

Lift Every Voice and Sing II

Wonder, Love, and Praise
Blessed be the God of Israel 889
The desert shall rejoice 722

Advent

Weekday Commemorations

Monday, December 12
Francis de Sales, Bishop, and Jane de Chantel, Vowed Religious, 1622 and 1641

Although Francis served as the Roman Catholic bishop of Geneva (1567–1622), he is better known for spiritual direction and for writing *Introduction to the Devout Life,* whose influence extended from Roman to Anglo-Catholics. A melancholy man, he was convinced he was predestined for hell; however, in 1587, in Paris, he found a loving God. That vision of God's mercy and love marked his writings forevermore. In addition to writing, Francis worked with Jane de Chantal to found the Congregation of the Visitation, a new women's order whose charism began with the sick but evolved toward contemplative life.

Tuesday, December 13
Lucy of Syracuse, Martyr, 304

Her name means "light." Lucy/Lucia is remembered for her purity and gentleness. For centuries, her feast day was the shortest of the year until Pope Gregory VIII shifted the calendar in 1582. On Lucy's Day, light returns as days lengthen. This signified greatly in Northern Europe, especially Sweden. Lucy's Day has long been a festival of light, observed both in churches and homes. A girl in the family dresses in white, dons a crown of lighted candles, and serves her family special foods. Lucy was martyred in Sicily during the Diocletian Persecution of 303–304 and buried in Syracuse.

Wednesday, December 14
John of the Cross, Mystic and Monastic Reformer, 1591

John (b. 1542 in Spain) has been dubbed "the poet's poet." He studied with the Jesuits, then entered a Carmelite Order. He completed his education in Salamanca and was ordained in 1567. Teresa of Avila recruited him to reform the Carmelite Order, which he thought had become careless. In 1568, he opened a monastery of "discalced" Carmelites, subject to strictness. The Calced Carmelites were not pleased. John was seized and imprisoned in the monastery, where he wrote poetry for comfort, including his masterpiece, *The Spiritual Canticle.* He inscribed the indelible phrase "dark night of the soul" in *The Dark Night.*

Thursday, December 15
Nino of Georgia, Missionary, c. 332

Nino, brought to Georgia in the fourth century as a captive from Cappadocia, was sold as a slave. A child was brought to Nino, who healed the girl with prayer. News of the miracle came to the queen, who, ill, was carried to the captive's cell and also healed through Nino's prayers. Nino preached the gospel of Christ to the queen, who asked to be baptized, so Nino performed the sacrament herself. As an act of worship to Christ, Nino exemplified pious, virtuous Christianity. She is known in Orthodox tradition as Equal to the Apostles and as Enlightener of Georgia.

Saturday, December 17
Dorothy L. Sayers, Apologist and Spiritual Writer, 1957

Sayers wrote not just detective stories about Lord Peter Wimsey and Harriet Vane. She was also a theologian, linguist, translator, and advocate for Christianity. Sayers (b. 1893), daughter of the chaplain of Christ Church, graduated from Oxford in 1915; she received her degree five years later when women were finally allowed such recognition. While a successful copywriter at the advertising company S. H. Benson Ltd., she wrote her first mystery, *Whose Body?* Sayers' religious writing began with the play *The Zeal of Thy House;* she upbraided the church for neglecting dogma and doctrine in *Creed or Chaos,* thus sealing her place as a Christian apologist.

The Fourth Sunday of Advent

December 18, 2022

Jesus' imminent birth is proclaimed in the scriptures; his continued presence in the world is proclaimed by the Church today.

Color   Violet or Blue

Preface   Advent

Collect

Purify our conscience, Almighty God, by your daily visitation, that your Son Jesus Christ, at his coming, may find in us a mansion prepared for himself; who lives and reigns with you, in the unity of the Holy Spirit, one God, now and forever. *Amen.*

Readings and Psalm

Isaiah 7:10–16

Today's reading carries two levels of meaning—one in the context of the politically troubled times in which it was written and the other in its use by Matthew in reference to the birth of Jesus. Through Isaiah, the Lord's word came to encourage Ahaz, the king of Judah, to remain calm in the face of the threats of the kings of Israel (Ephraim) and Syria. These kings hoped to force Judah to join their coalition against the Assyrian empire or, if Ahaz would not cooperate, to overthrow him and put another king on the throne.

Psalm 80:1–7, 16–18

This lament of the nation and cry for deliverance probably comes from the northern kingdom, whose tribes are enumerated (v. 2). The "Shepherd of Israel" (the only occurrence of this phrase in the psalms) is pictured as enthroned over the ark between the wings of the cherubim. The psalm's refrain (vv. 3, 7, 19) echoes the blessing given by Aaron in Numbers 6:24–26.

Romans 1:1–7

Paul introduces himself to the community in Rome by establishing his credentials. First, he asserts his authority as an apostle to the Gentiles and thus to them. He calls himself a "servant (or slave) of Jesus" (v. 1). The term "servant of God" was applied to such figures as Abraham, Moses and Joshua, but is now applicable to all Christians. Second, Paul goes on to show that he preaches the same gospel that the Roman church had heard proclaimed among them. He points out the role of the Hebrew Bible in showing the promises of God. Then he gives a brief creed-like statement (1:3–4), which may be a pre-Pauline credal summary known to the Roman Christians.

Matthew 1:18–25

Matthew describes neither the event of Jesus' conception nor of his birth, but rather the reactions and responses of others to these happenings. For Matthew, the significance of today's gospel lies first in Jesus' origin and second in Joseph's actions. The child's name, Jesus (the Greek form of the Hebrew name Joshua, meaning "Yahweh is salvation"), shows that "he will redeem Israel from all its iniquities" (Psalm 130:8). For the first of many times Matthew makes his announcement of fulfillment—the time of fulfillment is now begun in Jesus' birth. The name "Emmanuel . . . God with us" (v. 23) is for Matthew a central statement of Jesus' identity and his relationship to his people, the Church.

Advent

Prayers of the People

Grace to you and peace from God our Father and the Lord Jesus Christ. Let us appeal to the Lord praying, "Restore us, O God of hosts; *Show the light of your countenance, and we shall be saved.*"

We ask you, O God, to bless your Church. Give us your grace. Stir up your strength and come to help us even as we declare the gospel concerning your Son.

Silence

Restore us, O God of hosts;

> *Show the light of your countenance, and we shall be saved.*

We ask you, O God, to bless this nation. May our leaders not trust in their own strength but in you, O God of hosts. Teach us to refuse the evil and choose the good.

Silence

Restore us, O God of hosts;

> *Show the light of your countenance, and we shall be saved.*

We ask you, O God, to bless this planet. By your creative power bring forth new life in the places in which we have reaped too much or sown too little.

Silence

Restore us, O God of hosts;

> *Show the light of your countenance, and we shall be saved.*

We ask you, O God, to bless our city. Let your hand be upon us. Guide and strengthen all those who find themselves in difficult situations—especially young and single parents.

Silence

Restore us, O God of hosts;

> *Show the light of your countenance, and we shall be saved.*

We ask you, O God, to bless all those who are distressed. Hear their prayers, O Shepherd of the flock. May they take comfort in the knowledge that you are with them.

Invite the congregation to add their petitions and thanksgivings, followed by silence

Restore us, O God of hosts;

> *Show the light of your countenance, and we shall be saved.*

We ask you, O God, to bless all who have died. Welcome into your heavenly kingdom all who are called to be saints.

Silence

Restore us, O God of hosts;

> *Show the light of your countenance, and we shall be saved.*

Images in the Readings

In Matthew's narratives, an **angel** figures in the stories of Jesus' birth and resurrection. In our society, many depictions of angels are unfortunately quite cutesy, not very helpful as images of the might of God. The angel is the divine messenger, the extension of the power and mercy of God, and in the Bible often the way that believers encounter the Almighty. The **pregnant woman** can be a symbol of the life that comes from God. In the Bible, many women, from Eve in Genesis 4:1 on, conceive and bear children with the help of God. When we acclaim God as creator, we attest that God is continually creating life on this earth.

This Sunday it is **Joseph** who hears and receives the word of God. The history of art often depicted Joseph as an old man as a technique to convey that he was not instrumental in Mary's pregnancy. However, often in the scriptures a woman's pregnancy is seen as a gift from God. We are now Mary, and God is in us. We are now Joseph, receiving from God a gift we cannot have achieved on our own.

Ideas for the Day

♦ Even before we reach the actual feast toward which we've been leaning these four weeks, we get the news in today's gospel that Christmas *is*. Not just *was* a couple of thousand years ago, or *will be* in a Second Coming, but *is,* and *was* and *will be.* Immanuel, that name coined by Isaiah, is actually a sentence in Hebrew's nuanced grammar: "God *was/is/will be* with us." Christmas is timeless, or as poet U. A. Fanthorpe put it in the poem "BC:AD," "This was the moment when Before Turned into After, and the future's Uninvented timekeepers presented arms."

♦ Do we listen to the angels in our life? It can be perceived that our lives run at a hectic pace. The universe of the internet has fostered the illusion of the need to always be plugged in; know the latest news, watch the latest funny video, listen to the best new music, find ways to respond appropriately to twenty different emails, and so on. This constant need for updating and rapid-fire engagement with technology can be a distraction. The angels in our lives still speak through personal human contact. Are we prepared to listen to their message? Would we give up an hour of screen time to go visit a congregant who is shut in? The universe of human interaction is far more fascinating than anything the internet will ever be able to create.

♦ The role of the Christian congregation, and the individual Christian, is to reflect the presence of God in the world today. From the fourth Sunday of Advent through the Feast of the Epiphany, the church celebrates the Incarnation; God is present "in the flesh" of human life. God meets us in the midst of our human struggle.

Making Connections

Advent is a time of waiting—a time when we may also become conscious of the amount of waiting going on in our larger lives. It would be nice to receive daily signs that we are doing the right things, moving in the right direction, yet much of the time we have to wait to see how things play out. In the fourth Sunday of Advent, our readings revolve around God confirming that what is happening in this moment is God's plan, that faithful waiting can and will be rewarded. Maybe none of us will ever be visited by the archangel Gabriel, but all of us can watch and wait for confirmation that our faith and our actions will bear fruit, and all of us can embrace the promise that God is with us.

Engaging All Ages

Advent is the season of dreams. So many people in Jesus' story had dreams telling them to have faith and to take action. Dreams can still be powerful avenues for God's revelation to us if we take the time to "incubate" them. To incubate a dream, ask God to bless your time of rest each night. Perhaps make a commitment during Advent to leave all electronics off an hour before slumber. And keep some paper by your bed so you can write down any interesting dreams that you have at night. Sleep is the perfect space to invite God's spirit to dwell within you—healing you, shaping you, and inspiring you in ways that you could never imagine.

Hymns for the Day

The Hymnal 1982

God himself is with us 475
How bright appears the Morning Star 496, 497
O come, O come, Emmanuel 56
Come, thou long-expected Jesus 66
By the Creator, Joseph was appointed 261, 262
Come now, and praise the humble saint 260
Creator of the stars of night 60
Redeemer of the nations, come 55
Savior of the nations, come 54

Lift Every Voice and Sing II

Wonder, Love, and Praise

Advent

Advent

Weekday Commemorations

December 20
Katharina von Bora, Church Reformer, 1552

Although drawn to religious life, Katharina shifted her interest to ecclesiastical reform after noting the church's abuses. In 1523, she and eleven Cistercian sisters sought Martin Luther's help in escaping their convent. They were smuggled out but had nowhere to go—certainly not to their families. They found husbands in the reform community. Katharina found a husband in Luther himself. She became a model pastor's wife, raising their six children, providing hospitality, and assisting in his preaching and publishing. Encouraged by Luther, she actively participated in theological dialogues at her table, drawing on her impressive knowledge of scripture and Latin.

December 21
Saint Thomas the Apostle

John's gospel narrates incidents in Thomas' life. He was with Jesus when he went to Judea to visit friends at Bethany. At the Last Supper, Thomas questioned our Lord: "Lord, we do not know where you are going; how can we know the way?" Thomas questioned Christ's resurrection until Jesus himself showed Thomas his wounds. Thomas, a staunch friend, was skeptical but did not deserve to be reduced to "doubting Thomas": he did not dare believe; also, a doubter was needed for contrast in the story, and Thomas became the protagonist. According to tradition, Thomas evangelized Parthians, Syrian Christians, and Indians in Kerala. The Gospel of Thomas, an apocryphal writing, is attributed to Saint Thomas the Apostle.

Christmas

Preparing for Christmas

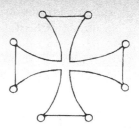

Theological Themes that Might Shape Liturgy, Catechesis, and Education

If the Season of Advent is all about hope and anticipation, then Christmastide is all about the fulfillment of that hope in the mystery of the Incarnation. It can be difficult to separate the distinctive qualities of Advent and Christmas from the franken-season of secular Christmas, but it is important to think about intentional ways to celebrate this season in ways that rise above the seasonal noise. This may mean intentionally eschewing the anxiety that accompanies performing the sacred traditions of the season that do little to convey the rich meaning of the season. As with any liturgy, but especially true during festival occasions, adding too many idiosyncratic elements to the liturgy might undermine the messages the occasion is meant to convey.

The Incarnation is the central theme of Christmas and not simply the incarnation of the Christ in the form of a newborn in a manger. It is important to draw direct connections between the physical body of Christ, expressed in the Christ-child, and the mystical body of Christ, the Church. The alternative is the liturgical fetishization of an aloof infant deity that does little to edify the assembly or equip the saints for the work of ministry.

Liturgical Possibilities

Rites

As the Holy Eucharist is "the principal act of Christian worship on the Lord's Day and other major Feasts," it is likely that, unless there are extenuating circumstances, your community will commemorate the Lord's incarnation by celebrating the Holy Eucharist. If prior planning has connected Christmas with the previous Season of Advent, it might be helpful to make the changes necessary to highlight the different qualities of this season. For example, if you have chosen to use the Penitential Order through Advent, you might consider returning to a regular Entrance Rite. This also has the added benefit of appealing to those who will visit our congregations, but aren't familiar with celebrations of the Eucharist that deviate from the typical form.

Depending on the worship life of your faith community, you might consider if and how you will observe the Feasts that immediately follow Christmas. J. Neil Alexander astutely observes that the Feast of the Holy Innocents (December 28) is the only one thematically associated with the Christmas season, the other two—St. Stephen (December 26) and St. John the Evangelist (December 27)—are only in the Christmas season by coincidence. All to say: one need not perform liturgical acrobatics either to mandate their commemoration if it isn't germane to a particular community or to force homiletical connections that do not actually exist.

Space, Other Rituals, and Resources

In spaces that feature adjustable lighting or flexible seating, it might be helpful to use the resources at our disposal to further highlight the difference of the season. Christmas is also an opportunity to involve more people in the celebration than usual, such as in the performance of a pageant. While creativity is to be celebrated, the warning still stands: the key portions of the liturgy should still be observed or else the message of the Incarnation gets lost.

Many communities will have at least one celebration of Christmas on the Eve and one celebration on Christmas Day. If possible, these services should be distinct, perhaps employing a different Entrance Rite on the Eve (taking advantage of the light in a way that is rubrically sound) and reverting to a traditional Entrance Rite for the celebration on Christmas Day. There are resources in the Book of Common Prayer and the *Book of Occasional Services* that can help with this planning. Think simple but meaningful.

Through the Eyes of a Child

At Christmas, we who are the church welcome Jesus and joyfully celebrate his birth. The church is often filled with greens and trees and lights. Something wonderful has happened and it is time to celebrate. We give thanks for God's greatest gift of love to us, the Son, Jesus Christ. We give to others in response to the gift that has been given to us. This is the time to blend family traditions—meals, visits, and activities—with an awareness of the birth of Jesus. The traditional crèche and manger need to have a prominent place for children to touch and re-enact the story of the birth of Jesus. Child-friendly pageants and Christmas plays that invite the children into telling and being a part of the story are critical, as well as doing something as a family, such as gathering up clothes that no longer fit to give to those in need, to teach and demonstrate ways to bring the light of Christ into the darkness. Music is also important; singing the beloved Christmas carols that announce the birth of Christ will offer the child a way to proclaim how the love of God breaks into the world in the birth of Jesus.

Young people are likely to be inundated with all sorts of messages surrounding the Christmas season, some less helpful and spiritually edifying than others. Their experience marking this season in worship can go a long way to pointing to the real meaning of this season. As with all liturgical and aesthetic differences throughout the year, it would be incredibly helpful to find ways of pointing out and explaining those differences to children (flash cards, notes in the bulletin, and so on). This has the added benefit both of explaining this meaning to adults who are often less apt to ask what they do not know and of empowering parents to bring Christian formation into their homes.

Through the Eyes of Youth

The Church is called to demonstrate how the birth of Jesus changes the whole world. This is the time for families to talk about God, for parents to share their faith with their teens, and particularly talk about their faith in regard to family traditions, which show (or "embody") Christ's presence through the way the family marks the change in seasons. To welcome all to the joy of the birth of Christ, encourage youth to invite friends to attend worship services, to sit at the dinner table, and to gather for sharing of gifts at the tree. Some of the sharing of gifts could include special reflections on gifts of faith, gifts of courage, gifts of sports, or intellectual gifts. Invite youth into the question, "Where is there need for peace in our country? In our world? What can one do? Jesus came to offer peace to all people, how can each one of us make a difference?" Choose a particular project to complete during the Christmas and Epiphany seasons.

Young people are often included in the additional aspects of the Christmas liturgies (acolyting, Christmas pageants, and so on). The danger with creating too much of a fuss during this season is that we simply teach young people to mimic the anxiety of the wider, secular society. Striking a balance is key.

Through the Eyes of Daily Life

Christmas is to be celebrated for twelve days. Reflect on how we can live the joy of Jesus' birth this and every day, knowing that the Spirit of Christ dwells in us and guides us so that we may be his witnesses in all that we say and do. How do you live your life, knowing that God's Word lives among us?

Given that the mystery of the Incarnation is inexhaustible, we might think about how to give people tools to further explore the meaning of the Incarnation at home. Preparing resources for worshipers to take home with them might be a wonderful way to think about a church Christmas gift (the gift that keeps on giving . . . for twelve days).

Through the Eyes of Those Outside of the Church

Because many outside of the Church will be unclear about the distinction of Advent and Christmas, how we celebrate Christmas is an opportunity to proclaim the relevance of the mystery of the Incarnation for the world. This season presents a great opportunity to empower regular worshipers with resources to invite their family, friends, and others to attend worship.

Christmas should also be observed in a manner that conveys its gravity. A poorly executed liturgy might unintentionally convey a message that undermines the magnitude of the Incarnation. Consider a rehearsal that not only helps to tighten up the liturgy, but also helps to convey the message to the liturgical ministers who then, by their liturgical performance, will convey that meaning to the gathered community.

Through the Eyes of the Global Community

Christmas is the perfect time to offer opportunities for seeing the Season of Christmas from the perspective of children from around the world. While the tradition of the 1979 prayer book centers us on the incarnation, it is vitally important that we look at the state of children from a global perspective. Holy Innocents (December 28) is often overlooked; this is a time to learn of those places where children are persecuted and the places where children have no hope. Expand the vision of mission during Christmas to respond to those who are most vulnerable, which includes the children of our world. The United Nations and the Children's Defense Fund offer current statistics and initiatives that a congregation can learn from and discuss as a way to discern possible mission initiatives for the New Year.

Christmas

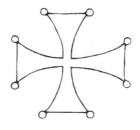

Seasonal Rites for Christmas

Christmas Blessing[1]

The following blessing may be used by a bishop or priest whenever a blessing is appropriate. It is a three-fold form, with an Amen at the end of each sentence, leading into a Trinitarian blessing.

May Almighty God, who sent his Son to take our nature upon him, bless you in this holy season, scatter the darkness of sin, and brighten your heart with the light of his holiness. *Amen.*

May God, who sent his angels to proclaim the glad news of the Savior's birth, fill you with joy, and make you heralds of the gospel. *Amen.*

May God, who in the Word made flesh joined heaven to earth and earth to heaven, give you his peace and favor. *Amen.*

And the blessing of God Almighty, the Father, the Son, and the Holy Spirit, be upon you and remain with you for ever. *Amen.*

Christmas Prayer[2]

Gift-giving God,
    of angels and stars,
    magi and shepherds,
    promise and hope,
    journeys and longing;
God who calls and sends,
    blesses and guards,
    hides and reveals,
    asks and waits,
    ancient love,
    that is always new;
God of Christmas,
God of our hearts;
    may we bear the Christ
    to all who need him,
    and allow his birth
    in us again.
    Amen.

The Christmas Crèche[3]

At their entry into the church for the celebration of the Holy Eucharist, the Celebrant (and other ministers) may make a station at a Christmas Crèche. The figure of the Christ Child may be carried in the procession and placed in the Crèche. Other figures may also be brought in if desired.

A versicle may be said, followed by a prayer.

V. The word was made flesh and dwelt among us.
R. And we beheld his glory.

Most merciful and loving God, you have made this day holy by the incarnation of your Son Jesus Christ, and by the child-bearing of the Blessed Virgin Mary: Grant that we your people may enter with joy into the celebration of this day, and may also rejoice for ever as your adopted sons and daughters; through Jesus Christ our Lord. *Amen.*

Blessing of a Christmas Tree[4]

For centuries, in the northern hemisphere, evergreen trees have been brought into homes during the cold, dark winter in anticipation of spring. Today, may households decorate trees in festive anticipation of the gift of Jesus, born on Christmas Day. Consider waiting to light the tree until Christmas Eve with this blessing:

Creator God, we gather around this evergreen tree in thanksgiving for creation and your love. We wait with joy for the coming of your Son, Jesus. Bless this tree of light, that it may brighten our night and remind us that Jesus is a light for all people. Bless us also, that we may give the gift of light to others. *Amen.*

---

1 "An Advent Litany of Darkness and Light" in *The Wideness of God's Mercy: Litanies to Enlarge Our Prayers*, ed. Jeffrey W. Rowthorn (New York: Church Publishing, Inc., 2007), 23.
2 Susan K. Bock, *Liturgy for the Whole Church* (New York: Church Publishing, Inc., 2008), 41.
3 *Book of Occasional Services* 2003 (New York: Church Publishing, 2004), 36.
4 Jenifer Gamber and Timothy J. S. Seamans, *Common Prayer for Children and Families* (New York: Church Publishing, Inc., 2019), 56.

Christmas Festival of Lessons & Music

Nine Lessons are customarily selected (but fewer may be used), interspersed with appropriate carols, hymns, canticles, and anthems during this service, which can take place within the twelve days of Christmas. When possible, each Lesson should be read by a different lector, preferably voices of male and female readers as well as a variety of ages. The Lesson from the third chapter of Genesis is never omitted.

Genesis 2:4b–9, 15–25
Genesis 3:1–23 *or* 3:1–5
Isaiah 40:1–11
Isaiah 35:1–10
Isaiah 7:10–15
Luke 1:5–25
Luke 1:26–58
Luke 1:39–46 *or* 1:39–56
Luke 1:57–80
Luke 2:1–20
Luke 2:21–36
Hebrews 1:1–12
John 1:1–18

On-the-Spot Christmas Pageant in Four Parts

Hold an impromptu Christmas pageant by inviting participants to act out with silent movements the Christmas story, as it is read. Makeshift costumes and props could be made available with part of the congregation assigned as the chorus, volunteers given the role as narrators/readers, and children (of all ages) being given the parts of Mary, Joseph, animals, shepherds, and angels.

Read: Luke 2:1–4
At that time Emperor Augustus ordered a census to be taken throughout the Roman Empire. When this first census took place, Quirinius was the governor of Syria. Everyone, then, went to register himself, each to his own hometown. Joseph went from the town of Nazareth in Galilee to the town of Bethlehem in Judea, the birthplace of King David. Joseph went there because he was a descendant of David.

Sing: "O, Little Town of Bethlehem"

Read: Luke 2:5–7
He went to register with Mary, who was promised in marriage to him. She was pregnant, and while they were in Bethlehem, the time came for her to have her baby. She gave birth to her first son, wrapped him in cloths and laid him in a manger—there was no room for them to stay in the inn.

Sing: "Silent Night, Holy Night"

Read: Luke 2:8–14
There were some shepherds in that part of the country who were spending the night in the fields, taking care of their flocks. An angel of the Lord appeared to them, and the glory of the Lord shone over them. They were terribly afraid, but the angel said to them, "Don't be afraid! I am here with good news for you, which will bring great joy to all the people. This very day in David's town your Savior was born—Christ the Lord! And this is what will prove it to you: you will find a baby wrapped in cloths and lying in a manger." Suddenly a great army of heaven's angels appeared with the angel, singing praises to God: "Glory to God in the highest heaven, and peace on earth to those with whom he is pleased!"

Sing: "Go, Tell It on the Mountain"

Read: Luke 2:15–20
When the angels went away from them back into heaven, the shepherds said to one another, "Let's go to Bethlehem and see this thing that has happened, which the Lord has told us." So they hurried off and found Mary and Joseph and saw the baby lying in the manger. When the shepherds saw him, they told them what the angel had said about the child. All who heard it were amazed at what the shepherds said. Mary remembered all these things and thought deeply about them. The shepherds went back, singing praises to God for all they had heard and seen; it had been just as the angel had told them.

Sing: "O Come, All Ye Faithful"

Feast of the Holy Innocents[5]

Wednesday, December 28

Psalm 124 is appointed for this day. Different individuals can read each portion with a refrain offered by all.

If you had not been on our side
when destructive powers rose up and barred our path,
if you had not been committed to our good,
like monsters they would have swallowed us alive.

Refrain: Praise to the God who is for us, and for all that is being created.

---

5 Jim Cotter, *Psalms for a Pilgrim People* (Harrisburg, PA: Morehouse Publishing, 1998), 282.

Their anger was kindled against us,
like the sweep of the forest fire.
Their fury bore down upon us,
like the raging torrent in flood,
the waters of chaos that know no limits,
trespassers that are hard to forgive. *Refrain.*

Thanks be to you, our deliverer,
you have not given us as prey to their teeth.
We escaped like a bird from the snare of the fowler:
the frame snapped and we have flown free. *Refrain.*

In the joy of deliverance we praise you, O God.
Our hearts expand in a new generosity:
we embody love with which you create.
Even the powers you do not destroy:
you redeem all our failures to live,
you are strong to bring good out of evil. *Refrain.*

Service for New Year's Eve[6]

During the evening of December 31, which is the eve of the Feast of the Holy Name and also the eve of the civil New Year, this service begins with the Service of Light (BCP, 109) and continues with readings, silence, and prayer.

The Hebrew Year
Exodus 23:9–16, 20–21
Psalm 111 *or* Psalm 119:1–8

O God our Creator, you have divided our life into days and seasons, and called us to acknowledge your providence year after year: Accept your people who come to offer their praises, and, in your mercy, receive their prayers; through Jesus Christ our Lord. *Amen.*

The Promised Land
Deuteronomy 11:8–12, 26–28
Psalm 36:5–10 *or* Psalm 89, Part I

Almighty God, the source of all life, giver of all blessing, and savior of all who turn to you: Have mercy upon this nation; deliver us from falsehood, malice, and disobedience; turn our feet into your paths; and grant that we may serve you in peace; through Jesus Christ our Lord. *Amen.*

A Season for All Things
Ecclesiastes 3:1–15
Psalm 90

In your wisdom, O Lord our God, you have made all things, and have allotted to each of us the days of our life: Grant that we may live in your presence, be guided by your Holy Spirit, and offer all our works to your honor and glory; through Jesus Christ our Lord. *Amen.*

Remember Your Creator
Ecclesiastes 12:1–8
Psalm 130

Immortal Lord God, you inhabit eternity, and have brought us your unworthy servants to the close of another year: Pardon, we entreat you, our transgressions of the past, and graciously abide with us all the days of our life; through Jesus Christ our Lord. *Amen.*

Marking the Times, and Winter
Ecclesiasticus 43:1–22
Psalm 19 *or* Psalm 148 *or* Psalm 74:11–22

Almighty Father, you give the sun for a light by day, and the moon and the stars by night: Graciously receive us, this night and always, into your favor and protection, defending us from all harm and governing us with your Holy Spirit, that every shadow of ignorance, every failure of faith or weakness of heart, every evil or wrong desire may be removed far from us; so that we, being justified in our Lord Jesus Christ, may be sanctified by your Spirit, and glorified by your infinite mercies in the day of the glorious appearing of our Lord and Savior Jesus Christ. *Amen.*

The Acceptable Time
2 Corinthians 5:17–6:2
Psalm 63:1–8 *or* Canticle 5 *or* Canticle 17

Most gracious and merciful God, you have reconciled us to yourself through Jesus Christ your Son, and called us to new life in him: Grant that we, who begin this year in his Name, may complete it to his honor and glory; who lives and reigns now and for ever. *Amen.*

---

6 Ibid, 43–45.

Christmas

While It Is Called Today

Hebrews 3:1–15 (16–4:13)

Psalm 95

O God, through your Son you have taught us to be watchful, and to await the sudden day of judgment: Strengthen us against Satan and his forces of wickedness, the evil powers of this world, and the sinful desires within us; and grant that, having served you all the days of our life, we may finally come to the dwelling place your Son has prepared for us; who lives and reigns for ever and ever. *Amen.*

New Heavens and New Earth

Revelation 21:1–14, 22–24

Canticle 19

Almighty and merciful God, through your well beloved Son Jesus Christ, the King of kings and Lord of lords, you have willed to make all things new: Grant that we may be renewed by your Holy Spirit, and may come at last to that heavenly country where your people hunger and thirst no more, and the tears are wiped away from every eye; through Jesus Christ our Lord. *Amen.*

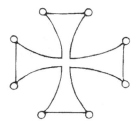

Christmas Eve

December 24, 2022

God came in Jesus of Nazareth to reveal the power of God's love and healing. In the birth of Jesus we realize that God shares life with us intimately. We meet God "in the flesh" of human struggle and most especially in the midst of human love. Christmas celebrates the incarnation of God; God "in the flesh of" human life.

Color   White

Preface   Of the Incarnation

Collect

O God, you have caused this holy night to shine with the brightness of the true Light: Grant that we, who have known the mystery of that Light on earth, may also enjoy him perfectly in heaven; where with you and the Holy Spirit he lives and reigns, one God, in glory everlasting. *Amen.*

Readings and Psalm

Isaiah 9:2–7

Isaiah describes God's grand reversal of human situations: the most despised will receive the greatest privilege; those living in spiritual darkness will enjoy the first glimmers of light. The results of God's glorious scheme will include freedom from enemies and the end of war.

Psalm 96

The Lord's appearance is described in terms that recall both God's manifestation at Sinai and on the coming day of the Lord. Then the psalmist describes the implications of the Lord's kingship over the world: all creation reveals God so that those who worship idols have no excuse.

Titus 2:11–14

This New Testament reading speaks of the two comings of Christ: first in his sacrificial ministry for all people and then in glory. He has enabled his disciples to free themselves from ways of evil. Disciplined and eager to do good, they look forward to the fulfillment of the hope God has given to the world in Jesus.

Luke 2:1–14 (15–20)

The good news of salvation is announced not to the mighty but to shepherds, suspected of being thieves and regarded as outcasts because their nomadic way of life made it difficult to keep the law. The "sign" (v. 12) to them is the child lying in a manger. This "thing that has taken place" (v. 1) is literally a word, a communication of significance. They respond, as Luke intends his readers to respond, by spreading the news and by praising God.

Prayers of the People

Come let us adore Christ, the Lord. Let us pray, "Glorious Lord, *grant us your peace.*"

Christ the Lord, we humbly adore you: make joyful our hearts. Strengthen your Church with humility and faith that we might triumph over the power of evil.

Silence

Glorious Lord,

Grant us your peace.

Christmas

Christ the Lord, we humbly adore you: you abhor neither the simple nor the lowly. Shine your light on all the world that the nations may look upon your truth and find their salvation.

Silence

Glorious Lord,

Grant us your peace.

Christ the Lord, we humbly adore you: may all of creation burst forth in songs of praise. May all the works of your hand glorify you.

Invite the congregation to add their thanksgivings, followed by silence

Glorious Lord,

Grant us your peace.

Christ the Lord, we humbly adore you: summon the people of the city to yourself. May all of the distractions and heartache of our lives fade away in the joy of your presence.

Silence

Glorious Lord,

Grant us your peace.

Christ the Lord, we humbly adore you: you love us so dearly. Grant your healing grace to sinners, to the poor, to those in need of love. Open your arms to the sick and the lonely.

Invite the congregation to add their petitions, followed by silence

Glorious Lord,

Grant us your peace.

Christ the Lord, we humbly adore you: all glory be given to you. You blessed our earthly bodies with your birth; and you promise to raise us to new life by your death and resurrection.

Silence

Glorious Lord,

Grant us your peace.

Images in the Readings

Luke writes that **angels**, messengers from heaven, a link between God and humankind, announce Christ and sing praise to God. It is a challenge to describe and, especially, to depict angels in a worthy manner. Contrary to popular notions, Christian doctrine does not teach that dead Christians become angels, but rather that angels are supernatural beings that signify and convey the power of God. In Luke, the angels proclaim the meaning of the incarnation. Recall that in Luke's telling of the annunciation to Mary, the angel is Gabriel, whom Jewish tradition identified as the one who proclaims the arrival of the eschaton.

Although in some places in the Bible cities are described as evil and filled with temptations, in Isaiah 62 the city **Jerusalem** symbolizes God's protection, God's very presence on earth. Throughout history, the church has used the image of Jerusalem as a picture of itself: we are like Jerusalem, a magnificent city, protected by the arms of God, thriving on word and sacrament. This imagery might not be clear to all worshipers, who might likely think that we are referring to the actual city of the twenty-first century: sometimes in our worship "Jerusalem" identifies first-century geography, sometimes it is a metaphor for the church, and sometimes it is the name of a current city filled with international religious conflict.

On a day that we think about the **birth** of Jesus, we recall also the water of our rebirth in baptism.

Ideas for the Day

- One of the reasons that Luke tells his story the way he does—quietly, unpretentiously, no one but the family and a few shepherds in attendance—is to remind us that the miraculous happens in the most unexpected places to the most unlikely of people who do what they can to make room for a God who risks so much, who dares to become one of us. God came among us in diapers once upon a time in backwater Bethlehem. And that God continues to come among us still, wherever and however we find ourselves, because God "so loved the world" not just once, but always, even when we can't believe it, even in the mess of our world, even now.

- Christmas is, period.

♦ "Sing to the Lord a new song." Create a melody tree. Take a sheet of ten staff manuscript paper. Cut it into strips so that each staff is separate, giving you ten single-line staves. Using the *Hymnal 1982* and four other hymn supplement resources, (for example *Wonder Love and Praise, Voices Found, Lift Every Voice and Sing*, and so on) find melodies of the Christmas season. Look particularly for music by composers who are still living. On each strip of manuscript paper, notate ten melodies. Include the words. Tape your melody strips to pipe cleaners. Affix them to a base to form a tree/plant like pattern. You could also take the melody strips and paste them in an artful way to poster boards. Sing, sing, sing.

♦ The kindness and grace-filled actions we experience every day from other people can give us hope. Regular practices of prayer and Sabbath—practices that allow our bodies, our minds, and our spirits time to rest and recharge—help us to keep our hope strong. All of these things point us to the source of all our hope. The actions of others inspire us and prayer and rest strengthen us because they deepen our connection to God. Our hope is found in God, in an eternal well, an eternal Way of Love and Blessing.

Making Connections

Christmas Eve is often the busiest night of the year for churches. The church is filled with worshippers—some familiar, others less so. Christmas Eve is a time to boldly proclaim the story of the Incarnation. Of course, we tell the story of Jesus' birth in Bethlehem. We also have the opportunity to share the good news of God's work with and through the Body of Christ here and now. How is God alive and at work in your community? How is the Spirit drawing your community into a new life? How might a visitor learn more and find a home in the common life of your community?

Making Connections

How shall we greet one another this night? At Easter, the Church gives guidance, allowing us to join with Christians throughout the millennia, saying, "The Lord is Risen!" "He is Risen indeed!" But for Christmas, we are left on our own. And most of us turn to the words of medieval England: "Merry Christmas!" It's fine, really, but other than Christmas, how often do we use the word "merry"? Probably not much. And truthfully, "merry" isn't what many feel. Consider a practice of using an alternative that more authentically expresses what you wish, what you pray, for those around you. "Comfort and joy" is likely more accurate. Joy carries echoes of faith and hope. Comfort is what many of us need. The French say *Joyeux Noel*, meaning joyful Christmas. Spanish speakers, Germans, and indeed many in England say the equivalent of "happy." What might you say?

Engaging All Ages

Assembling luminaria to be placed outside of a church on Christmas Eve is fun for all ages. All that is needed is a cup of sand placed in an open white paper bag, with a white votive candle resting in the sand. These can be assembled in advance and placed outside along the sidewalks, stone walls, or entrances to your sanctuary by many. Adults can then light them as darkness approaches, providing a welcoming light to all who enter (and pass by) throughout the evening.

Hymns for the Day

The Hymnal 1982

God himself is with us 475
How bright appears the Morning Star 496, 497
O come, O come, Emmanuel 56
Come, thou long-expected Jesus 66
How bright appears the Morning Star 496, 497
By the Creator, Joseph was appointed 261, 262
Come now, and praise the humble saint 260
Creator of the stars of night 60
How bright appears the Morning Star 496, 497
Redeemer of the nations, come 55
Savior of the nations, come 54

Lift Every Voice and Sing II

Wonder, Love, and Praise

Christmas

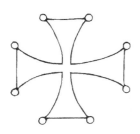

The Nativity of Our Lord Jesus Christ: Christmas Day

December 25, 2022

God came in Jesus of Nazareth to reveal the power of God's love and healing. Christmas celebrates the incarnation of God; God "in the flesh of" human life.

Color   White

Preface   Of the Incarnation

Collect

Almighty God, you have given your only-begotten Son to take our nature upon him, and to be born this day of a pure virgin: Grant that we, who have been born again and made your children by adoption and grace, may daily be renewed by your Holy Spirit; through our Lord Jesus Christ, to whom with you and the same Spirit be honor and glory, now and forever. *Amen.*

Readings and Psalm

Isaiah 52:7–10

This reading may have been written after the exiled Israelites had returned from Babylon. It heralds a time of great joy as the Lord saves the people and brings deliverance to Jerusalem. The long exile is at an end. The messenger proclaims the good news, "The Lord reigns." The watchmen of the city respond with shouts of triumph to see God's salvation.

Psalm 98

This psalm is closely related to Psalm 96. Its original setting may have been the enthronement festival of Yahweh, celebrated each year at the New Year's Feast of Tabernacles. In later times the psalm was interpreted to herald the Lord's final coming. It presents the Lord, in faithfulness to the covenant, acting in history for the salvation of God's people.

Hebrews 1:1–4 (5–12)

The author of Hebrews begins the letter by introducing its theme: Jesus is unique, the supreme voice and Word of God, the beginning of the universe and its final purpose. In his being, he is the fullness of God, and in his work, he is the expression of God.

John 1:1–14

John understands the incarnation as the presence of God among humanity, surpassing every other experience in history. In Jesus, God is with us more fully than ever before. The glory of the lord manifests itself clearly in Jesus through his ministry. Grace and truth, two weighty words in John's gospel, perfectly describe this incarnate Word. Grace describes the unmerited favor of God, which Jesus embodies and communicates to us. Truth becomes a refrain throughout the gospel. It describes the reality that lies behind all the confusion, misbelief, and ignorance of our lives. In Hebrew thought, truth only had meaning in relation to God's character. The reality of God provided the basis for truth, and God's name represented the integrity of truth. For John, Jesus does more than simply tell us the truth. Jesus is truth.

Prayers of the People

The Lord God is both sun and shield; God will give grace and glory. In the house of our God, let us pray, "Lord God of hosts, *hear our prayer.*"

We give thanks for your Church, O God. Bless it with every spiritual blessing in the heavenly places. May we be made happy in the knowledge of the hope to which we are called.

Invite the congregation to add their thanksgivings, followed by silence

Lord God of hosts,

Hear our prayer.

We give thanks for this nation, O God. Give to our leaders a spirit of wisdom. Deliver them from selfish ambition and give all the people a heart for your children, especially those little ones born into poverty.

Silence

Lord God of hosts;

Hear our prayer.

We give thanks for your creation, O God. Where there is desolation, bring forth springs of clean water. Where your creatures are without a place, may they find a place with you.

Silence

Lord God of hosts,

Hear our prayer.

We give thanks for this city, O God. Set us on a straight path where we shall not stumble. Bring new life to languishing areas.

Silence

Lord God of hosts,

Hear our prayer.

We give thanks for all those in our lives, O God. We pray especially for those who know weeping and tears. Turn their mourning into joy, comfort them and give them gladness for sorrow.

Invite the congregation to add their petitions, followed by silence

Lord God of hosts,

Hear our prayer.

We give thanks for the saints at rest, O God. Gather them into your great heavenly company. May they enjoy forever the riches of your glorious inheritance among the saints.

Silence

Lord God of hosts,

Hear our prayer.

Images in the Readings

Luke writes that **angels**, messengers from heaven, a link between God and humankind, announce Christ and sing praise to God. It is a challenge to describe and, especially, to depict angels in a worthy manner. Contrary to popular notions, Christian doctrine does not teach that dead Christians become angels, but rather that angels are supernatural beings that signify and convey the power of God. In Luke, the angels proclaim the meaning of the incarnation. Recall that in Luke's telling of the annunciation to Mary, the angel is Gabriel, whom Jewish tradition identified as the one who proclaims the arrival of the eschaton.

Although in some places in the Bible cities are described as evil and filled with temptations, in Isaiah 62 the city **Jerusalem** symbolizes God's protection, God's very presence on earth. Throughout history, the church has used the image of Jerusalem as a picture of itself: we are like Jerusalem, a magnificent city, protected by the arms of God, thriving on word and sacrament. This imagery might not be clear to all worshipers, who might likely think that we are referring to the actual city of the twenty-first century: sometimes in our worship "Jerusalem" identifies first-century geography, sometimes it is a metaphor for the church, and sometimes it is the name of a current city filled with international religious conflict. On a day that we think about the **birth** of Jesus, we recall also the water of our rebirth in baptism.

Ideas for the Day

+ The celebrant said "The Lord be with you," but instead of the expected response, what came back was "And I'll sit with you" from a four-year-old congregant. The kiddo had it right. In the magnificent opening of the fourth gospel, the verse translated "the Word became flesh and dwelt among us" is really something more like "the Word…pitched a tent in our campsite" in the Greek. Moved into our neighborhood. Wanted to hang out with us. "The Lord be with you." "And I'll sit with you." God did. This year, let's return the favor.

+ Luke's account of Jesus being placed in a manger at his birth because there was no room in the inn serves as a constant reminder to the Christian that God identifies with the weak, the poor, and the outcast.

+ In this season of birth/rebirth, let us be open to wonder. Babies have a natural ability for this. Observe how they react to something new. Sheer wonder envelopes their whole face. O how jaded we have become. Yet in many ways, our Christian perspective gives us the opportunity to see old things anew. We can infuse wonder into old traditions by adding, expanding, and updating. This can best be done by connecting with traditions that are not of our own particular culture. Christians around the world bring their own voices and approaches to living their faith. What can we learn by joining with others in new ways, engaging in our innate ability to wonder?

Making Connections

When God became a human being in Jesus, all of humanity was clothed in dignity and grace. How can we live into this faith? As a people who believe that we are formed by our actions, we can celebrate the Incarnation in part by giving with abundant generosity, not only to those we know and love, but to the strangers among us, too. Consider celebrating Christmas by practicing such abundance, perhaps tipping with extra generosity those who serve, giving dollar bills instead of coins to fellow human beings begging on the corner. Consider extending this practice for the whole twelve days of the season. Consider sharing stories of such encounters with others, not to brag, but to encourage. See in each action a celebration of God with us, God with us each and everyone.

Engaging All Ages

Plan in advance to invite congregants and families to bring and display their crèches in your nave, narthex, or parish hall. Invite individuals to share stories about their crèches, such as the history of the crèche and the traditions that they observe during the Christmas season. If your church has a traditional crèche with an interesting story, invite a long-standing member or leader to also share the story.

Hymns for the Day

The Hymnal 1982
Awake, thou Spirit of the watchmen 540
Surely it is God who saves me 678, 679
Good Christian friends, rejoice 107
Love came down at Christmas 84
Angels we have heard on high 96
Christians, awake, salute the happy morn 106
Go, tell it on the mountain 99
O come, all ye faithful 83
Once in royal David's city 102
Hark! the herald angels sing 87
'Twas in the moon of wintertime 114
While shepherds watched their flocks by night 94, 95

Lift Every Voice and Sing II
Go, tell it on the mountain 21
Rise up, shepherd, and follow 24

Wonder, Love, and Praise

Weekday Commemorations

Monday, December 26
Saint Stephen, Deacon and Martyr

Very probably a Hellenistic Jew, Stephen was one of the "seven men of good repute, full of the Spirit and of wisdom" (Acts 6:3), who were chosen by the apostles to relieve them of the administrative burden of "serving tables and caring for the widows." By this appointment, Stephen, the first named of those the New Testament calls "The Seven," became the first to do what the Church traditionally considers to be the work and ministry of a deacon.

Tuesday, December 27
Saint John, Apostle and Evangelist

John and James, sons of Zebedee, were fishers who became "fishers of men" as disciples. With Peter and James, John became one with the "inner circle" whom Jesus chose to witness his raising of Jairus' daughter, his Transfiguration, and his praying in the garden of Gethsemane. John and James were such angry males that Jesus called them "sons of thunder." Ambitious, they sought to sit next to Jesus at table; willing companions, they shared the communal cup of wine, little knowing the cost. Possibly, John held a special relationship as the "disciple whom Jesus loved," the one asked to care for his mother. It is said that John, alone of the twelve, lived long—no martyr he.

Wednesday, December 28
The Holy Innocents

The Holy Innocents were the baby boys ordered killed by Herod. Herod the Great, ruler of the Jews, was described by the historian Josephus as "a man of great barbarity towards everyone." Appointed by the Romans in 40 BCE, Herod kept peace in Palestine for thirty-seven years. Ruthless yet able, this Idumaean was married to the daughter of Hyrcanus, the last legal Hasmonean ruler, so Herod always feared losing his throne. According to the story, the Wise Ones' report of the birth of a King of the Jews scared him: he ordered the slaughter of all male children under two in Bethlehem. Although not recorded in secular history, the massacre of the innocents keeps to Herod's character.

Thursday, December 29
Thomas Becket

Thomas Becket was born in London in 1118 of a wealthy Norman family. Well educated, he was appointed archdeacon of Canterbury and later King Henry II's chancellor of England. As archbishop of Canterbury he defended the interests of the Church against those of his former friend and patron, the king. Taking the king's frustration with Becket as call to action, four barons struck Thomas down with their swords. His final words were, "Willingly I die for the name of Jesus and in the defense of the Church."

Saturday, December 30
Frances Joseph Gaudet, Educator and Prison Reformer, 1934

Gaudet (b. 1861) descended from African American and Native American bloodlines. While living in the South in 1894, Gaudet dedicated her life to prison reform. She started with prayer meetings for Black prisoners, then extending her prison ministry to white prisoners. She wrote prisoners' letters, delivered their messages, and clothed them. Doing so won her the respect of prison officials, city authorities, and the governor of Louisiana. She supported young offenders in Louisiana and rehabilitated young Blacks arrested for misdemeanors. She helped found the Juvenile Court. She also founded an industrial school and the Gaudet Episcopal Home for African American children.

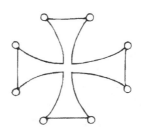

The Holy Name of Our Lord Jesus Christ

January 1, 2023

God's identity is revealed as "merciful and gracious" (Exodus 34:6). Jesus' name has significance: it is the Greek form of the Hebrew name Joshua, meaning "God saves."

Color   White

Preface   Of the Incarnation

Collect

Eternal Father, you gave to your incarnate Son the holy name of Jesus to be the sign of our salvation: Plant in every heart, we pray, the love of him who is the Savior of the world, our Lord Jesus Christ; who lives and reigns with you and the Holy Spirit, one God, in glory everlasting. *Amen.*

Readings and Psalm

Numbers 6:22–27

In this reading, God blesses the people. This benediction becomes an integral part of the temple liturgy and reveals God's intentions toward those who are willing and obedient. The Lord's shining face turned toward the people represents God's favor and loving attention. The peace (Hebrew: *shalom*) that the Lord offers includes both physical and spiritual well-being.

Psalm 8

This psalm is a hymn to God's glory and the God-given dignity of humans. The psalmist marvels at God's sovereignty, is awestruck at God's handiwork, and humbled by humanity's place within God's creation. As humanity fulfills this unexpected gift and privilege, God's glory is revealed.

Galatians 4:4–7

Those who believe in the Son are adopted as God's children, making possible not merely a new status but also a new relationship with God. Paul makes a direct appeal to the Galatians' experience of "the Spirit of his Son" (v. 6). Through the Spirit, the believer addresses God as Jesus himself did—as a child and thus an heir to the promises made to Abraham.

or

Philippians 2:5–11

Verses 6–11 are generally considered to be a pre-Pauline hymn to Christ that Paul adopts to make his own point. The hymn contains a summary of the Christian proclamation that includes divine preexistence (v. 6), incarnation (v. 7), death (v. 8), celestial exaltation (v. 9), heavenly adoration (v. 10), and Jesus' new title (v. 11). The first stanza (vv. 6–8) recounts Jesus' own action. His equality with God is not a prize to be exploited for his own advantage. The second stanza (vv. 9–11) stresses the response by God to bestow on Jesus the name lord (Greek, *kyrios*; Hebrew, *adonai*) and our response to honor him as God is honored.

Luke 2:15–21

The good news of salvation is announced not to the mighty but to shepherds, suspected of being thieves and regarded as outcasts because their nomadic way of life made it difficult to keep the law. The "sign" (v. 12) to them is the child lying in a manger. This "thing that has taken place" (v. 1) is literally a word, a communication of significance. They respond, as Luke intends his readers to respond, by spreading the news and by praising God.

Prayers of the People

Sisters and brothers, let the same mind be in you that was in Christ Jesus. With humble hearts let us say to the Lord, "Lord Jesus, *we bow our hearts at your name.*"

Jesus, we exalt your name in all the world! Bless your Church. Inspire us by the Holy Spirit to confess you as Lord over all we are, all we do, and all we hope to do.

Silence

Lord Jesus,

We bow our hearts at your name.

Jesus, we exalt your name in all the world! Bless the people of the world. May the whole world experience your peace.

Silence

Lord Jesus,

We bow our hearts at your name.

Jesus, we exalt your name in all the world! Bless our planet. Make us faithful stewards of all the works of your fingers. Forgive us when we fail to respect your creatures: the beasts of the field, the birds of the air, and the fish of the sea.

Silence

Lord Jesus,

We bow our hearts at your name.

Jesus, we exalt your name in all the world! Bless our city and our region. Give us renewed hope and purpose as we begin this new year.

Silence

Lord Jesus,

We bow our hearts at your name.

Jesus, we exalt your name in all the world! Bless the sick and the lonely and all those in great need. Make your face to shine on them and be gracious to them.

Invite the congregation to add their petitions and thanksgivings, followed by silence

Lord Jesus,

We bow our hearts at your name.

Jesus, we exalt your name in all the world! Bless the dying and the dead. We praise you, that through your death on the cross, you have earned for us everlasting life.

Silence

Lord Jesus,

We bow our hearts at your name.

Ideas for the Day

- The rabbis taught that engaging scripture was something like participating in a wrestling match (noting Jacob's bout in Genesis 32). As the NRSV describes it, Mary is "treasuring and pondering" the words that the shepherds had proclaimed. But the force of the Greek has Mary probing, struggling, prodding meaning from what has been said. And the force of the verbs has her continuing to do this over time, so that one wonders if she returned to these words and the ones that would describe her son in the future, again and again to make sense of his work in the world.

- Purchase loose-leaf paper. Number twenty pieces of paper. Using the internet, find twenty different song/hymn lyrics connected to the name of Jesus Christ. Once you find the lyrics, physically write the words on the pieces of paper. Feel free to come up with different designs for how you place the words on the page. Leave space for a picture somewhere on the page. Find twenty corresponding pictures and paste them to each page. On a separate sheet of paper write a two-verse hymn inspired by the lyrics you have researched. Take your papers and research different ways to bind the papers together. Your book will be specific to you, a reflection of your own personal view on the name of Jesus Christ.

- The naming of a person being baptized is an important element in the baptismal rite, as in scripture: "You shall be called by a new name that the mouth of the Lord will give" (Isaiah 62:2). In some traditions a child was literally named at baptism and given the name of a Christian saint. Whether or not the name is given at baptism, one's given name takes on new significance as one is adopted into the family of Christ.

Christmas

Making Connections

When you hear the name Jesus, what comes to mind? Take a minute to think about it. Perhaps make it a small group exercise with index cards or a large group exercise with newsprint. From that first day in the temple until now, the name has been used in a multitude of ways. Some bring us comfort, others make us cringe. When you hear the name Jesus, what comes to mind?

George Frederick Handel put the words of the prophet Isaiah to music in his choral masterpiece, *Messiah*: "His name shall be called Wonderful, Counsellor, the Mighty God, the Everlasting Father, the Prince of Peace." (Isaiah 9:6) The hauntingly beautiful Advent hymn also recalls Isaiah: "Look, the young woman is with child and shall bear a son, and shall name him Immanuel." (NRSV Isaiah 7:14) These words are echoed by the angel Gabriel in the Gospel of Matthew. Immanuel, God with us. What does the name Jesus mean to you?

Engaging All Ages

In scripture, Jesus is given many names. We may see these symbols at our churches and even on bumper stickers, but do we know what they mean or where they come from? Explore the meanings and origins of names associated with Jesus from birth to resurrection: *Chi Rho* (the first two letters of the Greek spelling of Christ); *Alpha* and *Omega* (Rev. 1:8 and 22:13); *INRI* (the Latin inscription on the cross of Calgary—John 19:19—meaning "Jesus of Nazareth, King of the Jews"); *IHS* (monogram derived from first three letters in Greek spelling of "Jesus"—Matt. 1:21); *Ichthus* (Greek letters spell "fish" and make a rebus, "Jesus Christ, God's Son, Savior"); and *Agnus Dei* (Lamb of God—Rev. 5:12–14).

Hymns for the Day

The Hymnal 1982
Jesus, the very thought of thee 642
How sweet the Name of Jesus sounds 644
Now greet the swiftly changing year 250
O for a thousand tongues to sing 493
To the Name of our salvation 248, 249
Sing praise to our Creator 295
A stable lamp is lighted 104
All hail the power of Jesus' Name! 450, 451
All praise to thee, for thou, O King divine 477
At the name of Jesus 435
From east to west, from shore to shore 77
Jesus! Name of wondrous love! 252

Lift Every Voice and Sing II
Blessed be the name 78
Glorious is the name of Jesus 63
O how I love Jesus 95
There's something about that name 107
God be with you 234
A choral benediction 231

Wonder, Love, and Praise
God be with you till we meet again 801
You're called by name, forever loved 766

Weekday Commemorations

Wednesday, January 4
Elizabeth Ann Seton, Vowed Religious and Educator, 1821
Mother Seton founded the Sisters of Charity, the first community of sisters in the United States. Raised an Episcopalian, she converted to Roman Catholicism in 1805; a year later, she patterned a congregation of seven women religious after the French Daughters of Charity of Saint Vincent de Paul. The sisters' charism plaited social ministry, education, and religious formation. In Maryland in 1810, they opened St. Joseph's Free School for needy girls. Until her death, Elizabeth Seton remained the superior of the Sisters of Charity on which the earliest Anglican religious orders for women rested their rules.

Thursday, January 5
Sarah, Theodora, and Syncletica of Egypt, Desert Mothers, 4th–5th century
The forty-seven sayings of these three *ammas* are included with those of the desert fathers in the fifth-century *Apophthegmata Patrum*. They were consulted by many: Sarah for her spiritual advice ("...I shall rather pray that my heart may be pure towards all"); Theodora for her wisdom on prayer ("Clearly I am very near death, and so I should get up and pray right now before I die!"); and Syncletica for her model of living a spiritual life within a secular society. She wrote: "...it is also possible for a monastic to live in a crowd amidst her own thoughts."

Epiphany

Preparing for Epiphany

Theological Themes that Might Shape Liturgy, Catechesis, and Education

In previous "Preparing for . . . " sections, we highlighted the importance of planning a through line that connects the seasons of Advent, Christmas, and the Epiphany. The theme of revelation, light, and illumination that characterizes the season after the Epiphany is built upon the incarnation of Jesus Christ and the inception of his movement in Christmas, which itself hinges on the yearning and anticipation of the Advent season. We hope, we receive, we share. If underscored in this manner, we develop the capacity to build out a more fulsome expression of the Christian witness than might otherwise be possible if we simply acquiesce to the secular commemorations of the season.

Throughout this season, we hear how Jesus' ministry is manifested throughout this context, beginning with the Feast of the Epiphany where the power of Jesus is confirmed by the presence of non-Jewish visitors from afar. The message from the start seems to be clear—Jesus is for all people, and all means all.

Liturgical Possibilities

Rites

As its name might suggest, the season after the Epiphany begins on the Feast of the Epiphany—January 6. Epiphany is not a transferable feast for the majority of congregations. Contrary to what we might like to think, clergy are not Time Lords (obscure Dr. Who reference). Abiding by the framework of the Church calendar presents congregations with an opportunity to add additional worship opportunities for their congregations and, because it will likely not be a principal liturgy, gives a little more room for experimentation and innovation. What might

a midweek liturgy look like that is inclusive of families and other non-regular worshipers from the community? A Saint Lydia's style dinner church? A liturgy with experiential prayers of the people?

It is important not to simply transfer the Feast of the Epiphany because the first few Sundays mark important, building moments in the life of Jesus. The first Sunday after the Epiphany is the Baptism of our Lord which marks a pivotal moment in the life of Jesus as he immediately goes into the wilderness before beginning his public ministry. The beginning of that ministry is marked in Year A and B with the calling of his disciples, which makes an important statement about the nature of the Jesus Movement. These stories might be as dramatic as some of the creative ways we find to tell the story of the Visit of the Magi (though an argument can be made about doves and disembodied voices being incredibly dramatic), they represent concepts that are foundationally important to the Jesus Movement, concepts that will be further developed through the season.

The Season after the Epiphany, unlike the Season after Pentecost (which will be explored later), has a particular character. Prayers of the People, Eucharistic Prayers, and other adjustable portions of the liturgy should be adapted to reflect this character. The celebration of the Epiphany (January 6) should be further differentiated from the season that follows, as it is a major feast.

Another feast that pops up during this season is the Presentation of our Lord Jesus Christ, which, like the Epiphany, is non-transferable. This feast, which some confuse for the Feast of the Circumcision (which occurs on January 1), marks the occasion where Mary and Joseph present the infant Jesus to Simeon the priest and Anna the prophet in fulfillment of the ancient Jewish custom. Candlemas, as the feast is also known, directly appeals to the themes of light and illumination, and presents another opportunity to develop an innovative, attractive liturgy.

Space

What better season to experiment with different kinds of light than the season that follows the Epiphany? Where might additional candles add depth of meaning? How might artificial light be adjusted to create a different experience?

Other Rituals and Resources

As with most seasons, there are other, smaller but meaningful ways to observe the season. A community might observe the burning of the greens, burning of the palms (on the last Sunday after the Epiphany), baptisms, or the blessing of homes. Some resources can be found in the *Book of Occasional Services* or by simply doing a web search.

Through the Eyes of a Child

What Jesus did and said helps us to know who God is and what God is doing for us: On the night of Jesus' birth, the giant comet star let the world know that God is with us; magi from far away saw the star and journeyed to visit Jesus. Jesus called his friends to be with him and to help him in his work. Jesus said and did amazing and wonderful things that no one else could do. He healed many people to show how much God loved them. Jesus, the gift of love, came for all the people of the world. Jesus is like a light, helping us to see better. We are a part of Jesus, and in Jesus we are baptized into God's family, the Church. The wonder and mystery of the magi invite us to wonder about the mystery. Jesus, who are you really?

When it comes to young people, indeed all people, it is important to keep formation as a key principal. Epiphany is filled with opportunities for community to live into traditions that they find important, but has that meaning been conveyed to a younger audience? If you are burning the Advent and Christmas greens, have you explained why that is so and why they aren't merely discarded? If you are blessing homes, have you explained what it is about this season that makes this a particularly appropriate time to do so?

Epiphany is also an opportunity to make worship more sensory by deploying light (sight) and incense (smell) in ways that contribute to deeper worship experience. Even if incense isn't used in worship, how might we teach our children what frankincense and myrrh are in ways that expand their spiritual and liturgical experience?

Through the Eyes of Youth

The Church is called to reveal Jesus to the world, and to reaffirm baptismal vows strengthening the ways to seek Christ in all persons, and to continue in the apostles' teachings, breaking of bread, and the prayers. Epiphany is a time to celebrate the mystery of the visit of the magi to the infant Jesus. Epiphany is the sudden realization or comprehension of the essence or meaning of something sacred. Invite the youth to read God's Word every morning; use the lectionary and follow the stories for the Season of Epiphany. This is a wonderful season to take each sentence of the Baptismal Covenant and invite the teens to determine how to put it into action, not only for themselves, but for the community.

Through the Eyes of Daily Life

Epiphany is a time to bless the homes of Christians with holy water, incense, and prayers, that those who abide in the home may be empowered to live lives that are an epiphany of God's coming among us in Jesus, into whose body we have been incorporated at our baptism. (See *The Book of Occasional Services*.)

Through the Eyes of Those Outside of the Church

If the Epiphany is about the light of Christ being manifested to the world, it would follow that this is a great opportunity for the local faith community to make some kind of effort to reach out to the community in new ways. If the Epiphany and Candlemas are observed as non-Sunday liturgies, it might be worthwhile to engage them as seeker-friendly liturgies, playing into the spiritual themes that resonate across religious experience—light and illumination.

Through the Eyes of the Global Community

Many of the collects during this season speak of covenants and commandments. The Baptismal Covenant calls Christians to strive for justice and peace among all people, and to respect the dignity of every human being (BCP 305). Six of the Ten Commandments, which summarize the 613 commandments of the Torah, remind us that to honor God is to love others as we love ourselves. Many of the commandments of the Torah deal with proper treatment of the poor, the stranger, and the disadvantaged in society, as well as ethical business practices. Jesus' "new Law" outlined in the Sermon on the Mount calls the Christian to an even higher standard: reconciliation in all relationships; truthfulness in business, personal, and political matters; justice and respect for human rights; and love for all people, even those perceived to be enemies. In 1997, the General Convention of the Episcopal Church designated the Last Sunday of Epiphany as World Mission Sunday to increase awareness of and participation in the wider global mission of the Church.

Epiphany

Seasonal Rites for Epiphany

Epiphany Blessing[1]

The following blessing may be used by a bishop or priest whenever a blessing is appropriate. It is a three-fold form with an Amen at the end of each sentence, leading into a Trinitarian blessing. This may be used from the feast of the Epiphany through the following Sunday.

May Almighty God, who led the Wise Men by the shining of a star to find the Christ, the Light from Light, lead you also, in your pilgrimage, to find the Lord. *Amen.*

May God, who sent the Holy Spirit to rest upon the Only-begotten at his baptism in the Jordan River, pour out that Spirit on you who have come to the waters of new birth. *Amen.*

May God, by the power that turned water into wine at the wedding feast at Cana, transform your lives and make glad your hearts. *Amen.*

And the blessing of God Almighty, the Father, the Son, and the Holy Spirit, be upon you and remain with you for ever. *Amen.*

The Blessing of the Home

From the time of the Middle Ages it has been a tradition that on the Feast of the Epiphany we pray for God's blessing on our dwelling places, marking the entrance to our homes with chalk. Chalk is used as a tangible reminder of the dust of the earth from which we are all made.

We mark the main door of our home with the initials of the magi and the numerals of the new year. The initials remind us of the names of the magi— Caspar, Melchior, and Balthasar—and also stand for the Latin motto: *Christus mansionem benedicat,* "May Christ bless this house." We connect the initials and the numerals with crosses as a sign that we have invited God's presence and blessing into our homes.

Gather everyone to bless the chalk. Then invite everyone to take the chalk home to bless their homes after your gathering with a "The Blessing of a Home"[2] liturgy.

The Blessing of the Chalk

Participants gather around a basket containing pieces of ordinary white or colored chalk.

The Blessing

Leader: God dwells in you.

Participants: And also with you.

Leader: Let us pray. Bless, O Lord, this chalk that it may be a sign of your blessing upon the homes of your people. We pray that, like wise men and women of old, we may serve him as our only King, worship him as the one true God, and honor him with lives of sacrifice and praise, who lives and reigns with you and the Holy Spirit, one God, for ever and ever. *Amen.*

The Blessing of the Home

The blessing of the house begins with all members of the household at the entrance of the home. A member of the family leads the blessing.

Leader: Peace be to this house.

Participants: And to all who enter here.

The Leader speaks the following while marking the doorway with the chalk as indicated:

Leader: Wise ones came to honor the Savior and offer him gifts.

C Caspar,

M Melchior,

B and Balthasar followed the star of God's Son who became human two thousand and twenty years ago.

---

1 *Book of Occasional Services 2003* (New York: Church Publishing, 2004), 24.

2 This is available as a download at www.churchpublishing.org/ faithfulcelebrations3 and is adapted from *Faithful Celebrations: Making Time for God from Advent through Epiphany* edited by Sharon Ely Pearson (New York: Church Publishing, Inc., 2018), 129–130.

++ May Christ bless our home and all who join us here,

++ and remain with us throughout the new year. *Amen.*

20 + C + M + B + 19

All: May this Epiphany blessing be a reminder of Christ's presence among us and a symbol of God's love and care as we share the blessings and burdens of our daily lives. *Amen.*

Candlemas

Thursday, February 2

THE FEAST OF THE PRESENTATION[3]
A Tableau Vivant

The beauties of a tableau vivant are that they are easy and quick to prepare, they can use actors of all ages, and the group of actors can come up with its own choreography, although some suggestions follow. In a tableau, worshipers close their eyes and the reading begins. While the reader is reading, the actors are creating a scene. They freeze, a bell is rung, the worshipers open their eyes and view the scene, in silence, for about ten seconds. The bell is rung again, the worshipers close their eyes again, the reader continues, and the actors get into their next scene, and so on.

The more variety there is in terms of age, gender, posture, height, facial expression, arm positions, and placement of bodies, the more interesting and "real" will be the scene. Even a ladder works well for adding height dimension. Big facial expressions and creative use of hands add interest; you can't overdo it! Quiet music may be played during the tableau.

Ring the bell, have worshipers close their eyes. The reader begins while the actors arrange themselves in the scene.

SCENE ONE

When the time came for their purification according to the law of Moses, they brought him up to Jerusalem to present him to the Lord (as it is written in the law of the Lord, "Every firstborn male shall be designated as holy to the Lord"), and they offered a sacrifice according to what is stated in the law of the Lord, "a pair of turtledoves or two young pigeons."

Here, actors should set a scene in Jerusalem, outside the temple. Mary and Joseph, tenderly holding a baby (just mimed!), should be on their way up to the altar. There could be merchants hawking their wares, kids playing with marbles, people gossiping. Go wild!

---

3 Susan K. Bock, *Liturgy for the Whole Church* (New York: Church Publishing, Inc., 2008), 66–68.

Make it seem alive. Mary and Joseph are probably feeling a mixture of elation and intimidation. Anna, who shows up later ("who never left the temple") should be in the back, praying.

Actors freeze, the bell is rung, and worshipers view the scene. The bell is rung, worshipers close their eyes; the reader and actors proceed as before.

SCENE TWO

Now there was a man in Jerusalem whose name was Simeon; this man was righteous and devout, looking forward to the consolation of Israel, and the Holy Spirit rested on him. It had been revealed to him by the Holy Spirit that he would not see death before he had seen the Lord's Messiah. Guided by the Spirit, Simeon came into the temple; and when the parents brought in the child Jesus, to do for him what was customary under the law, Simeon took him in his arms and praised God, saying, "Master, now you are dismissing your servant in peace, according to your word; for my eyes have seen your salvation, which you have prepared in the presence of all peoples, a light for revelation to the Gentiles and for glory to your people Israel."

Here, Mary, Joseph, and the baby would be up nearer the altar, with Simeon, perhaps, behind it. Simeon and Mary could be reaching across the altar, each holding or touching the baby, and Simeon is ecstatic, with one hand up, praising God. Joseph could be bewildered and guarded. Have Anna creep out of the corner, and starting to see what's going on. Change the street scene below, with perhaps some people, having heard the commotion, peering into the temple.

Actors freeze, the bell is rung, and worshipers view the scene. The bell is rung, worshipers close their eyes; the reader and actors proceed as before.

SCENE THREE

And the child's father and mother were amazed at what was being said about him. Then Simeon blessed them and said to his mother Mary, "This child is destined for the falling and the rising of many in Israel, and to be a sign that will be opposed so that the inner thoughts of many will be revealed—and a sword will pierce your own soul too."

Here, Mary could be crouching down and holding her baby protectively, with Joseph between her and Simeon. The scene is sad, darkening the joy of the day. Add your own interpretation. Again, change the crowd, perhaps by having them near and some reaching for the baby, foreshadowing the need many would have of Jesus.

Actors freeze, the bell is rung, and worshipers view the scene. The bell is rung, worshipers close their eyes; the reader and actors proceed as before.

SCENE FOUR

There was also a prophet, Anna the daughter of Phanuel, of the tribe of Asher. She was of a great age, having lived with her husband seven years after her marriage, then as a widow to the age of eighty-four. She never left the temple but worshiped there with fasting and prayer night and day. At that moment she came and began to praise God and to speak about the child to all who were looking for the redemption of Jerusalem. When they had finished everything required by the law of the Lord, they returned to Galilee, to their own town of Nazareth. The child grew and became strong, filled with wisdom; and the favor of God was upon him.

For this scene, Mary and Joseph could be in the aisle, heading back home, and Anna could be standing on the chancel steps, preaching to a small crowd of amazed and curious people. She could be pointing at the Holy Family, with Mary looking serious, engrossed in the baby, and Joseph looking back over his shoulder, warily.

The bell rings, and there is a brief silence for contemplation. The actors should quickly and quietly disappear. The reader says, "The Gospel of the Lord," the bell is rung, and the worshipers open their eyes to a cleared "stage."

Other Notable Days during the Epiphany Season

Martin Luther King Jr. Day

January 16

> *A federal holiday, this day will fall on Monday, January 16, 2023. Some schools celebrate the day by teaching their pupils or students about the work and ministry of Martin Luther King and the struggle against racial segregation and racism. It has also become a day where Americans give some of their time on this day as volunteers in action in their communities. For congregations, Sunday, January 15 can be a day of focused prayer, preaching, and education on the legacy Dr. King entrusted to us. Resources can be found at http://www.thekingcenter.org/king-holiday and https://www.serve.gov/site-page/mlkday*

Lord our God, see how oppression and violence are our sad inheritance, one generation to the next. We look for you where the lowly are raised up, where the mighty are brought down. We find you there in your servants and we give you thanks this day for

your preacher and witness, Martin Luther King Jr. Fill us with your spirit: where our human community is divided by racism, torn by repression, saddened by fear and ignorance, may we give ourselves to your work of healing. Grant this through Christ our Lord. Amen.[4]

Week of Prayer for Christian Unity[5]

January 18–25

Deacon or other leader

Gracious God, who knit our inmost parts before we were born, and who shelters us with a strong hand, in our gratitude receive the prayers we offer as we respond to each petition by saying, "Kyrie eleison."

In thanksgiving for the unity we share through our death and resurrection in Jesus Christ, that we who have been entrusted with the fight of new life, may bring life to the world and renewed hope to our Church; for this we pray.

Kyrie eleison

For the courage to hold fast to the high ideals of our calling, bringing the lamp of charity to those who live in despair and desperation, and through their cries receive the saving grace that enlightens our ministry; for this we pray.

Kyrie eleison.

For a renewed sense of the Body of Christ, the Church, that together with our Presiding Bishop, our bishop(s), and all other ministers, we may rededicate ourselves in the unity of the Triune God; for this we pray.

Kyrie eleison.

For the urgency to seek peace before the battle breaks, and economic justice before the weight of poverty fractures the will of nations; for this we pray.

Kyrie eleison.

For the forgiveness of our sins, that the wounds that we inflict on one another in the name of righteousness may be healed by the Divine Life that overcomes human frailty; for this we pray.

Kyrie eleison.

---

4 Christopher L. Webber, ed. *An American Prayer Book* (Harrisburg, PA: Morehouse Publishing, 2008), 124.

5 Rt. Reverend Geralyn Wolf, "For Unity in the Church," in *Women's Uncommon Prayers* (Harrisburg, PA: Morehouse Publishing, 2000), 333.

Epiphany

For those whose lives are approaching death, and for those who have died, remembering especially _____, that they and their loved ones may receive the comfort of the Holy Spirit; for this we pray.

Kyrie eleison.

In Christ, who baptized us with fire and water and called us to be a baptizing community, we continue our prayers either silently or aloud.

Theological Education Sunday

February 5

Theological Education Sunday (TES) is officially recognized on the first Sunday in February. It is a day parishioners set aside to pray and give for all laity and clergy whose ministry is Christian education, wherever that ministry happens—in the home, preschool programs, parishes, colleges, universities, and seminaries. Established in 1999 by the Episcopal Church, this Sunday on the church calendar is an occasion for all parishioners to focus on education as a key aspect of mission. Guest preachers and seminarians sponsored by the congregation are often invited to preach.

O God of truth, ever beckoning us to loftier understanding and deeper wisdom, we seek your will and implore your grace for all who share the life of divinity schools and seminaries in our day, knowing that, unless you build among us, we who teach and learn will labor but in vain.

Silence

For the men and women who teach, that they may together bring fire and vision to a common task, knowing one field yet eager to relate it to all others; just in their academic demands, yet seeing each student as a child of God; fitted to teach not only by great learning but by great faith in humankind and in you, their God:

In them and in us, O God, kindle your saving truth.

Silence

For deans and presidents, trustees and development officers, and all others who point the way for theological education in our day, that their chief concern be not budgets and buildings and prestige, but men and women freed to know your whole will and roused to serve you in your Church:

In them and in us, O God, kindle your saving truth.

Silence

For janitors and maids, for cooks and keepers of the grounds, for those who prepare our food and wash our dishes, and for the host of other workers and suppliers whose faithfulness ministers to our common life:

In them and in us, O God, kindle your saving truth.

Silence

For parents and givers of scholarships, who support theological students, that they may not desire for them more income, or social acceptance, or glory of family or of donor, but look rather for new breadth of intelligence, the spirit made whole, and devoted Christian service in life:

In them and in us, O God, kindle your saving truth.

Silence

For the students themselves, that their confusion may be brief, their perspective constantly enlarged, and their minds and spirits alert to all that chapel and classroom, library and fieldwork assignment can mean in their lives:

In them and in us, O God, kindle your saving truth.

Silence

For every member of this community of learning and service, that with them we may be aware of your Holy Spirit leading us all into truth, and may grasp here your special intention for all our learning and striving:

In them and in us, O God, kindle your saving truth.

Silence

We know, O heavenly Father, that a seminary education is but the willing and planning of many men and women, each sought by your great love. Grant that we who would earnestly serve you may witness in the world to the reality of your gospel, as it is shown forth in Christ Jesus our Lord. Amen.[6]

6 John Oliver Nelson, "For Theological Seminaries," in *The Wideness of God's Mercy: Litanies to Enlarge Our Prayer* ed. Jeffrey W. Rowthorn (New York: Church Publishing, Inc., 2007), 165–166.

Super Bowl Sunday: Souper Bowl of Caring

February 12

The Souper Bowl of Caring is a national movement of young people working to fight hunger and poverty in their own communities around the time of the Super Bowl football game. In the weeks leading up to or on Super Bowl Sunday, young people take up a collection (many use a soup pot), asking for one dollar or one item of food for people in need. They give 100 percent of their donation directly to the local hunger-relief charity of their choice. Learn more at https://souperbowl.org/welcome

We have seen your hand of mercy in the service of those who spread food, shelter, hope, and faith to suffering humankind. Plant more seeds in the bellies of the full, to burst forth in joy, to explode like the ripened grain with life-giving bread. Give us, we beseech you, in the bosoms of our souls, a passion for the powerless and a commitment to place all poverty in the past. *Amen.*[7]

President's Day

Monday, February 20

O Lord our Governor, whose glory is in all the world: We commend this nation to thy merciful care, that, being guided by your Providence, we may dwell secure in your peace. Grant to the President of the United States, the Governor of this State, and to all in authority, wisdom and strength to know and to do thy will. Fill them with the love of truth and righteousness, and make them ever mindful of their calling to serve this people in your fear; through Jesus Christ our Lord, who lives and reigns with you and the Holy Spirit, one God, world without end. *Amen.* (BCP, 820)

Preparing for Lent

The last Sunday of the season of the Epiphany features the story of the Transfiguration in the Gospel reading. This is also the last Sunday the word "Hallelujah" will be used in liturgy and preparations begin for the coming week's Ash Wednesday liturgy as well as the solemn season that follows.

Here are two traditions for making the transition from Epiphany to Lent.

Burying the Alleluia

As we keep the ancient practice of fasting from singing or speaking "hallelujah" through the forty days of Lent, you may consider the practice of "burying" the hallelujah at the end of the liturgy on the last Sunday before Ash Wednesday. This might mean simply singing an appropriate song at the end of the service or including the actual lowering of a visual hallelujah banner (perhaps created by children) while singing. You could bury it in your churchyard or hide it away in a dark place (but remember where you put it!). Bring the hallelujah back as part of the first hallelujah at the Great Vigil of Easter or your Easter Festive Eucharist.

Farewell to Alleluia

Leader: O God, make speed to save us, hallelujah, hallelujah.

> *O Lord, make haste to help us, hallelujah, hallelujah.*

All: (Sing a Hallelujah hymn such as #178, #460 in The Hymnal 1982 *or #41 from* Lift Every Voice and Sing II)

Reading I

Leader: After this I heard what seemed to be the loud voice of a great multitude in heaven, saying, "Hallelujah! Salvation and glory and power belong to our God. . . ."

And the twenty-four elders and the four living creatures fell down and worshiped God who is seated on the throne, saying, "Amen. Hallelujah!" And from the throne there came a voice saying, "Praise our God, all you his servants, and all who fear him, small and great."

> *Then I heard what seemed to be the voice of a great multitude, like the sound of many waters and like the sound of mighty thunderpeals, crying out, "Hallelujah! For the Lord our God the Almighty reigns" (Revelation 19:1, 4–6).*

Procession *(Carry the hallelujah banner to its resting place for Lent.)*

Reading II

Leader: Let us pray, reading aloud Psalm 137:1–6.

All: **By the rivers of Babylon—**
> there we sat down and there we wept,
> when we remembered Zion.
> On the willows there
> we hung up our harps.
> For there our captors
> asked us for songs,

---

7 Marcia King, "For An End to Poverty" in *Lifting Women's Voices: Prayers to Change the World,* Margaret Rose, Jenny Te Paa, Jeanne Person, and Abagail Nelson, editors (Harrisburg, PA: Morehouse Publishing, 2009), 6.

Epiphany

and our tormentors called for mirth, saying,
   "Sing us one of the songs of Zion!"
How could we sing the Lord's song
   in a foreign land?
If I forget you, O Jerusalem,
   let my right hand wither!
Let my tongue cling to the roof of my mouth,
   if I do not remember you,
   if I do not set Jerusalem
   above my highest joy.

Farewell to Alleluia *(Silently put away or veil the hallelujah banner.)*

Prayer

Leader: Let us pray.

All: (Pray the Lord's Prayer in unison.)

Leader: God, you teach us to sing in praise. You teach us to pray in silence. Help us who prepare for the season of Lent to come with joy to the celebration of Easter, through Jesus Christ our Lord. *Amen.*

Dismissal *(Depart in silence at the conclusion of this service.)*

Shrove Tuesday

The day before Ash Wednesday was the day all households were to use up all milk, eggs, and fat to prepare for the strict fasting of Lent. These ingredients were made into pancakes, a meal which came to symbolize preparation for the discipline of Lent, from the English tradition. "Shrove" comes from the verb "to shrive" (to confess and receive absolution) prior to the start of the Lenten season. Other names for this day include Carnival (farewell to meat) and Mardi Gras (Fat Tuesday of the French tradition). Thus, many congregations have Shrove Tuesday pancake suppers.

O Lord, as we prepare our hearts for our Lenten journey, bless these pancakes we are about to share. As they remind us of the rich ingredients from our kitchens that fill our bellies with satisfaction, may we also remember your time in the wilderness when you did not even have bread or water. Be present with us as we get ready to begin the holy Season of Lent, strengthening us to be ready to serve you in the days and weeks to come. *Amen.*

Making Pretzels

The pretzel has been used during Lent for over 1500 years. It is thought that originally pretzels were made by monks to resemble arms crossed in prayer. These breads were called "little arms." This can have deep spiritual meaning for us during Lent. Since basically only flour and water are used, pretzels can remind us of fasting.

Heavenly Father, we ask you to bless these little breads. Each time we eat them may we be reminded of the special season we are in and that through prayer we will become better people to each other. Let us not forget those who are in need of our prayers daily. Keep your loving arms around us, O Father, to protect us always. *Amen.*

The Epiphany

January 6, 2023

The significance of Jesus's birth is revealed to the world beyond Judea.

Color   White

Preface   Of the Epiphany

Collect

O God, by the leading of a star you manifested your only Son to the peoples of the earth: Lead us, who know you now by faith, to your presence, where we may see your glory face to face; through Jesus Christ our Lord, who lives and reigns with you and the Holy Spirit, one God, now and for ever. *Amen.*

Readings and Psalm

Isaiah 60:1–6

The prophet envisions the end of exile and the glorious restoration of Jerusalem. Although darkness covers the earth, the Lord will be a light making God's people shine. To this radiance shall come the nations. Rich treasures will be brought from afar to honor God.

Psalm 72:1–7, 10–14

The psalm asks that God endow the king with compassionate justice and righteousness, and that his reign may extend over all nations and throughout all generations.

Ephesians 3:1–12

The great theme of Paul's apostolic commission is this: the revealed mystery that Christ's salvation extends beyond Judaism to include all peoples. The apostle is near the end of his ministry and in prison at the time of the writing of this letter. Now it is recognized as God's eternal purpose that the Gentiles are to be members of the same body. The wisdom of God is made known through the Church even in transcendental realms.

Matthew 2:1–12

Our gospel is the story of the wise men from the east, who, guided by a star, come to worship the child born to be king. Despite the wicked plotting of Herod, the Magi are able to bring their gifts to Jesus without betraying his exact location. Early Christians found in the rich symbolism and motifs of the story the fulfillment of both Hebrew scripture prophecy and the dreams of many peoples. The meaning of this birth, amid terrifyingly human circumstances, enlightens and transcends human history.

Prayers of the People

Arise, shine; for your light has come, and the glory of the Lord has risen upon you.

We pray as pilgrims, "Lead us to your presence; *let us see your glory!"*

Almighty God, grant to your Church wisdom. Work through us that we might lead many to the knowledge and love of you.

Silence

Lead us to your presence;

Let us see your glory.

Defend the needy, Lord Christ. Rescue the poor and thwart all the ways of oppression.

Silence

Lead us to your presence;

Let us see your glory.

The heavens reveal your wonders, O God. Give us eyes to see, hearts to follow, and lives that pay you homage.

Invite the congregation to add their thanksgivings, followed by silence

Lead us to your presence;

Let us see your glory.

Epiphany

Bless all students as they return to school and university. May they find wisdom as well as knowledge; give them a hunger for your truth.

Silence

Lead us to your presence;

Let us see your glory.

Loving God, you are the help of the helpless and the deliverer of those in distress: bless and heal all those in need.

Invite the congregation to add their petitions, followed by silence

Lead us to your presence;

Let us see your glory.

Great redeemer, you have guided us to your presence; you have shown us your glory.

Grant us, that we might at last, see you face to face.

Silence

Lead us to your presence;

Let us see your glory.

Images in the Readings

The main image is **light**. The star symbolizes a new light in the cosmos. The dawn pierces the thick darkness that has obscured our vision. During January, the northern hemisphere is experiencing a gradual lightening of the darkest time of the year, an appropriate time for the church to praise Christ as the light. This light shines again in the night of the Easter Vigil.

Made popular in hymns, pageants, and crèche sets are the gifts of the magi: **gold, frankincense, and myrrh**. Gold denotes Jesus as a king. Frankincense and myrrh are sweet-smelling resins that were used in offerings to a god and at status burials. These are symbolic gifts for the divine king who has come to die. The birth narratives contain in them the death of Christ.

The ancient political idea was that monarchs were supposed to ensure safety for their subjects. Christ, not Herod, is the true **king** who gives life, rather than death, to the people.

Ideas for the Day

- ◆ "Epiphany" comes from a Greek word that has at its core the meaning of manifestation, showing, and revelation. As with anything with God, this experience is a two-way experience. Epiphany is always a covenant in which God seeks to be our God and invites us to be God's people. Divine epiphany requires human epiphany—God's manifestation seeks human manifestation. God in the wisdom of God draws near and manifests to human beings all the time. We exist to manifest ourselves to God and to show forth the glory of God to every human being.

- ◆ In the poem "Sweet Darkness," David Whyte writes, "anything or anyone/ that does not bring you alive/ is too small for you." One way of considering the Season of Epiphany is to claim that Epiphany is the season meant to "bring us alive." The Epiphany readings use light, stars in the heavens, and visitors guided by heavenly beings to remind us that God seeks to be revealed in and for us, every single day. On closer examination, we uncover a deeper truth: God's revelation, God's epiphany has always been meant for the nations, for all of humanity. In truth, the Season of Epiphany reminds us that God is a God of "epiphanies." The spiritual life is a life of "revelation" and "showing." The Church invites us to pay attention and to reveal our lives in order to bring the world alive. If Epiphany does not bring you alive, it is too small for you.

- ◆ In the activity of the Magi, we see an implicit invitation for us to move towards something that we may not already know. They were willing to make a journey. Curiosity and discovery are essential elements of the spiritual life. The evangelists have Jesus repeatedly ask this question, "What are you looking for?" Knowing this is an important question for Jesus gives us a sense of what is needed in the spiritual life: We are called to seek God with all our hearts. "You shall seek me and find when you search for me with all your heart" (Jeremiah 29:13.) What if, in this Epiphany season, we sought to see or understand more broadly—perhaps to encounter something from a different culture, different religion, or different journey? Epiphany invites us to pay attention to the things around us we might not notice or pay attention to daily. What if this Epiphany you read or listened to a book, music, sermon, or poem outside the comfortable genres or styles you would normally choose?

Making Connections

Use all your senses to pay attention to things around you. The stars may be calling you to make a journey. Make the journey. The Christian path ever invites us to journey, to go places, to seek out revelation. When was the last night we made a new journey "led by the Spirit"? When you are lost, ask directions. The Magi getting lost and visiting Herod's courts remind us that we sometimes get lost. It is fair to imagine the Magi considering return to the courts of Herod, in contrast to the invitation of the child in the manger. Do we take time to reflect on what has brought us alive or on the lessons learned while we were lost? The journey of the Magi reminds us to listen carefully and deeply in discerning ways. The story turned out differently because the Magi chose to follow their awakened hearts. Think for a moment, how this story invites us to listen to God over the political, cultural, and powerful warnings.

Engaging All Ages

How do we discern which is the more important or urgent voice among the messages we are hearing? Do we listen to Herod or to the angels?

Epiphany reminds us that when we meet Jesus, it is not once and for all. And we are not the same at all. We are surrounded by revelations of God's love—day in and day out—if we would only sharpen our seeing with the eyes of gratitude.

Notice how, after the Magi meet Jesus, we never hear from them again. And yet we trust that they would never journey alone, from that time on.

Epiphany follows Christmastide to remind us of the dance between life and death and darkness and light. How are we paying attention to the daily experience of life and death and darkness and light? Can we join in the dance, holding the tension, setting our eyes on God's unceasing revelation?

Hymns for the Day

The Hymnal 1982

Hail to the Lord's Anointed 616
How bright appears the Morning Star 496, 497
Now the silence 333
Arise, shine, for your light has come S223ff
O very God of very God 672
O Zion, tune thy voice 543
Now, my tongue, the mystery telling 329, 331
Our God, to whom we turn 681
As with gladness men of old 119
Brightest and best of the stars of the morning 117, 118
Duérmete, Niño lindo / Oh, sleep now, holy baby 113
Earth has many a noble city 127
Father eternal, Ruler of creation 573
On this day earth shall ring 92
Songs of thankfulness and praise 135
Unto us a boy is born! 98
The first Nowell the angel did say 109
We three kings of Orient are 128
What star is this, with beams so bright 124
When Christ's appearing was
    made known (vs. 1, 2, 5) 131, 132
Where is this stupendous stranger? 491

Lift Every Voice and Sing II

Wonder, Love, and Praise

Where is this stupendous stranger? 726
Arise, shine, for your light has come 883

Epiphany

The First Sunday after the Epiphany: The Baptism of Our Lord Jesus Christ

January 8, 2023

The baptism of Jesus.

Epiphany

Color   White

Preface   Of the Epiphany

Collect

Father in heaven, who at the baptism of Jesus in the River Jordan proclaimed him your beloved Son and anointed him with the Holy Spirit: Grant that all who are baptized into his Name may keep the covenant they have made, and boldly confess him as Lord and Savior; who with you and the Holy Spirit lives and reigns, one God, in glory everlasting. *Amen.*

Readings and Psalm

Isaiah 42:1–9

This song is written in the recognized formula for the king's designation of a court official. The servant is presented, his power is attested, his mission and manner of accomplishing it are defined. With gentleness he will "bring forth justice to the nations" (v. 1), that is, bring all people into the covenant relationship with God and one another. Verses 5–9 are the first part of a response to this servant song, describing the servant's mission more fully. Speaking to the servant, God designates him as the means whereby the covenant will be extended to all.

Psalm 29

Psalm 29 is a hymn to Yahweh as the God of storm. It may have been written as an objection to the pagan assertion of Baal as the thunder-god. The "glory of the Lord" gives God dominion over nature and over all gods. Thus Yahweh alone is the source of strength and blessing for the people.

Acts 10:34–43

Today's reading is a part of Peter's missionary speech to the Gentile centurion Cornelius and his household. The conversion of Cornelius marks an important turning point in the outreach of the Church. Some Jewish Christians rejected and feared the possible inclusion of Gentiles in the Church, but Luke shows that Peter began the mission to the Gentiles under the direction of the Holy Spirit. Peter's sermon to the new converts is a summarized example of the basic preaching of the early Church.

Matthew 3:13–17

The baptism of Jesus is a central event in Matthew's revelation of God in and through the incarnate Son. Matthew examines both Jesus' role and John's to answer questions raised by the baptism: (1) Does this mean that Jesus is sinful? (2) Does it imply that Jesus is somehow subordinate to John? Both concerns are met by Jesus' reply in verse 15. Though sinless, he identifies himself with sinful humanity. He also emphasizes his obedience to and fulfillment of prophetic expectations.

Prayers of the People

Ascribe to the Lord the glory due God's name; worship the Lord in the beauty of holiness. Let us pray to the Lord saying, "In the house of the Lord all are crying, '*Glory.*'"

Lord, give your Church the blessing of peace. Give us the power to testify about your Son, Jesus. Give us your Spirit that we may live fully into your righteous calling.

Silence

> ***In the house of the Lord all are crying, "Glory."***

Lord, give this nation the blessing of peace. Make our hearts understand that you show no partiality, but know that in every nation you accept anyone who does what is right.

Silence

> ***In the house of the Lord all are crying, "Glory."***

Lord, give your creation the blessing of peace. You make yourself known to us in your works. You created the heavens and stretched them out; you spread out the earth and what comes from it. You are upon the mighty waters. May we witness your presence all around us.

Silence

> ***In the house of the Lord all are crying, "Glory."***

Lord, give this region the blessing of peace. May we not grow faint until your justice has been established in our hearts and lives.

Silence

> ***In the house of the Lord all are crying, "Glory."***

Lord, give to our friends and family the blessing of peace. Bring your light to those who sit in darkness. In their places of hurt, pain, and death, declare new things and spring forth new life.

Invite the congregation to add their petitions and thanksgivings, followed by silence

> ***In the house of the Lord all are crying, "Glory."***

Lord, give to those who have died the blessing of everlasting peace. May those who ate and drank of the body and blood of Christ in this life also know his resurrection life.

Silence

> ***In the house of the Lord all are crying, "Glory."***

Images in the Readings

There can be no life as we know it without **water**. Christians see in the waters of baptism the matrix of our new life in Christ. The font is like the Jordan, a river of water that leads us to the new land of promise. The **dove** functions in several biblical stories as a symbol of the presence of God's Holy Spirit. The white color matches the baptismal garment. Secular culture connects the dove especially with peace, which Acts cites as the message of Jesus' preaching.

The gospel reading uses the image of **Son** to describe Jesus' identity: the first reading uses the image of **servant**, and the second reading speaks of Jesus as **the anointed one**. Each of these images conveys something of the meaning of Jesus for believers. It is instructive to think about Son and Christ as metaphors before these words became literalized as part of Jesus' name.

Once again **light** is an image for the power of God. Early Christians referred to baptism as enlightenment.

Epiphany

Epiphany

Ideas for the Day

♦ Although the lectionary editors have divided the stories, the narrative of Jesus' baptism is immediately followed by the testing in the wilderness. Jesus sets off, still wet from the water of his baptism to face his first ordeal, the test that asked "What kind of Son of God will you be?" And he went with those words "My Son, the Beloved" ringing in his ears. With that claim and that love pronounced on him, and the commissioning it implies calling him forward, Jesus steps into his ministry, but he does not go alone. He goes armed with the love and the promise of the One who had sent him.

♦ The words of calling and anointing for ministry heard in connection with Jesus' baptism are the words that frame the church's ministry of all the baptized today: "You are my Beloved; with you I am well pleased." The radical nature of our calling is to bring justice and to serve the cause of right, to be part of God's own mission of liberating the suffering, the oppressed, and the hungry.

♦ Today, let us go for a hike. Leave the car at the parking lot and begin walking down your selected path. Smell the air that trees are making clean. Breathe in deeply and walk slowly. Engage in the environment away from cars, buildings, and computers. Listen to how the breeze rustles the trees' leaves and branches. Hear the melody that God is creating. Follow the path to the water. Take in the sight of the waterfall flowing in constant renewal. Touch the water. Feel its cold, brisk temperature. Water is life. Life is spirit. It is through baptism that these two are joined. Let the touch of water renew in you that which you already know.

Making Connections

This day is an opportunity for us to reflect on what it means to be a follower of Jesus and how we might deepen and strengthen the covenant we make at baptism. Being a Christian is about believing in God, in Christ, in the Holy Spirit, about believing God's promises, and it is about living in such a way that we share the abiding love of God with the world. Our Baptismal Covenant reminds us to share our stories and to do our part to help make this a world a place where the dignity of every human being is respected.

Engaging All Ages

If you are celebrating baptisms on this day—this Sunday is one of the five most appropriate times for baptism in the church (BCP, 312)—invite children to surround the font with perhaps a sibling of someone being baptized invited to pour the water in the font. Invite a teen to light a baptism candle from the Pascal candle, giving it to a godparent. This is a sacramental moment that easily involves all ages in the "action" and welcome of new members into the Body of Christ.

Hymns for the Day

The Hymnal 1982
Songs of thankfulness and praise 135
Blessed be the God of Israel 444
Thy strong word did cleave the darkness 381
In Christ there is no East or West 529
Christ, when for us you were baptized 121
From God Christ's deity came forth 443
"I come," the great Redeemer cries 116
O love, how deep, how broad, how high
    (vs. 1–3, 6) 448, 449
The sinless one to Jordan came 120
When Christ's appearing was made known
    (vs. 1, 3, 5) 131, 132
When Jesus went to Jordan's stream 139

Lift Every Voice and Sing II
Take me to the water 134
In Christ there is no East or West 62

Wonder, Love, and Praise
Blessed be the God of Israel 889

Weekday Commemorations

Monday, January 9
Julia Chester Emery, Lay Leader and Missionary, 1922

Born in 1852 in Dorchester, Massachusetts, Emery served the Episcopal Church's Board of Missions with loyalty, efficiency, and dedication for forty years. At twenty-two, she became editor of *The Young Christian Soldier*, a missionary publication of the Woman's Auxiliary of the Board. At first, the Auxiliary assembled and distributed "missionary boxes" to supplement salaries of missionaries; Emery's last report in 1916 recorded branches in two-thirds of the church's missions and parishes with receipts of $500,000. Emery traveled extensively for the church, including, in 1908, attending the Lambeth Conference in London. In retirement, Emery wrote *A Century of Endeavor*, her history of the Domestic and Foreign Missionary Society.

Tuesday, January 10
William Laud, Archbishop of Canterbury, 1645

Laud, born in 1573, was beheaded in 1645 after impeachment for treason. He was seen through his life—and ever since—as either a martyr or a bigot, either compassionate toward commoners against landowners or dispassionate, even murderous, toward "puritans." Made archbishop of Canterbury in 1635, he emphasized the marriage of church and state, headed by royalty as a divine right; raised up the priesthood and sacraments, especially the Eucharist; and demanded reverencing of the altar, which he returned to the eastern wall and fenced in. Laud, who headed the courts of High Commission and the Star Chamber, was fiercely loyal to the Church of England.

Friday, January 13
Hilary, Bishop of Poitiers, 367

Hilary was born about 315 in Poitiers in Gaul into a wealthy and pagan family. He wrote of his spiritual journey from unbelief to baptism (at about age thirty) to bishop in 350, a job he never sought but that he executed with skill and courage. His bravery was tested about 355, when Emperor Constantius ordered all bishops to condemn Athanasius; Hilary refused and was exiled to Phrygia. Uncomplaining, Hilary used those three years to write *On the Trinity*, his principal work. In 360, after great churchly agitation, Hilary returned to his see, where he continued to fight against heresy and to care for his diocese.

Saturday, January 14
Richard Meux Benson, Priest, and Charles Gore, Bishop, 1915 and 1932

Benson and Gore played roles in the revival of Anglican monasticism in the nineteenth century. Born in London in 1824, Benson studied under Edward Pusey and became well known for conducting silent retreats. In 1865, Fr. Benson helped establish the Mission Priests of St. John the Evangelist, the first community of men in the Church of England since the Reformation. Gore, ordained in 1876, founded the Community of the Resurrection, which combined traditional religious life with modern demands of ministry. Gore, a principal progenitor of liberal Anglo-Catholicism, believed in making biblical scholarship available to the church and pricking the conscience of the church to engage in social justice.

Epiphany

The Second Sunday after the Epiphany

January 15, 2023

Responding to God's call to be a "light to all nations."

Color Green

Preface Of the Epiphany or of the Lord's Day

Collect

Almighty God, whose Son our Savior Jesus Christ is the light of the world: Grant that your people, illumined by your Word and Sacraments, may shine with the radiance of Christ's glory, that he may be known, worshiped, and obeyed to the ends of the earth; through Jesus Christ our Lord, who with you and the Holy Spirit lives and reigns, one God, now and forever. *Amen.*

Readings and Psalm

Isaiah 49:1–7

Today's reading is the second of the four servant songs. In this song, the servant is the speaker. He testifies that his vocation was established before birth, and that his mission is not to Israel alone, but to the Gentile nations as well. This sense of the new Israel was appropriated by the Church (Acts 13:47, 26:23).

Psalm 40:1–12

This section of this psalm is a thanksgiving recording the psalmist's deliverance by God and his remembrance of all God's mighty acts in history for Israel. Verse 6 is a reminder that self-offering and obedience to the Lord's will are the interior disposition of which the sacrifice is intended to be a sign.

1 Corinthians 1:1–9

This reading is the first in a sequence of readings from this letter on the Sundays after the Epiphany. Paul uses the standard introductory form of ancient letters when he identifies the sender and the recipients, followed by a greeting and thanksgiving. In the thanksgiving, Paul sets forth the themes of the letter. He gives thanks for the spiritual gifts, "speech" and "knowledge" (v. 5), that were causing so much division and dissension in the Corinthian community. He will later deal with the misunderstanding and misuse of these gifts (in chapters 12 and 14), but they are undoubtedly God-given, the confirmation of "the testimony of Christ" (v. 6), that is, the preaching of the gospel.

John 1:29–42

Today's reading represents the fourth gospel's version of the baptism of Jesus and the calling of the first disciples, with an emphasis on the meaning of the events. John witnesses to Jesus by conferring on him a set of titles, the first being "the Lamb of God" (v. 29). For the author, this term points to the suffering servant of Isaiah and to the Passover lamb as a symbol for the death of Christ. In submitting to baptism, Jesus marks his vocation to an atoning death. In this story of the calling of the first disciples, Jesus takes the initiative by turning and asking the two disciples what they are searching for. They reply by asking for the abiding place, the permanence, they cannot find elsewhere. He responds with the surprising invitation that we also long to hear, "Come and see" (v. 39).

Prayers of the People

Brothers and sisters, grace to you and peace from God our Father and the Lord Jesus Christ. I bid you to, "Come and see the great things God has done. *Behold, we come.*"

We pray for your Church. Give us as a light to the nations. Sanctify us in Christ Jesus, call us to be saints and strengthen us to follow Jesus to the end.

Silence

Come and see the great things God has done.

Behold, we come.

We pray for this nation and the world. May your salvation, O God, reach to the ends of the earth. May all the peoples know of your faithfulness and your deliverance.

Silence

Come and see the great things God has done.

Behold, we come.

We pray for all of creation. Give us a sense of awe as we consider all of the works of your hands.

Invite the congregation to add thanksgivings, followed by silence

Come and see the great things God has done.

Behold, we come.

We pray for our local community. Make our footing sure. May our future be secured by your love and faithfulness.

Silence

Come and see the great things God has done.

Behold, we come.

We pray for all those in need of your healing and strength. Lift them out of the desolate pit. Put in their mouths a new song, a song of praise. May they know just how great for them are your wonders and your plans.

Allow the congregation to add their petitions, followed by silence

Come and see the great things God has done.

Behold, we come.

We pray for those who have died. In your great faithfulness, keep them blameless for the day of our Lord Jesus Christ. Honor them in your sight forever.

Silence

Come and see the great things God has done.

Behold, we come.

Images in the Readings

Once again we are given images of **water, light,** and **dove** (see Baptism of Our Lord).

The fourth gospel refers to Jesus as the **Lamb** of God. Several New Testament writers used this image to give salvific meaning to Jesus' execution. The lamb as apocalyptic conqueror, the lamb as suffering servant, and the paschal lamb are all possibilities of what the earliest Christians meant by the image. The medieval church stressed Christ as sacrificial lamb, whose blood takes away sin. God calls. The scriptures include many **call** narratives, in testifying that this God is the kind of deity who knows us by name and who calls us into a new identity. All three readings refer to such a call. In the poem from Second Isaiah, the call comes to the prophet even before birth. The church has described baptism as our call to servanthood, and many churches use the imagery of the call in descriptions of their clergy.

Epiphany

Ideas for the Day

♦ At the center of this story of the first disciples is a verb of some significance to the fourth Gospel; variously translated "remain," "stay," or "abide," it is a key to the process of discipling. We don't know what transpired between those two and Jesus that first afternoon and evening, but we do know that their "abiding" with him and he with them changed their lives. During his ministry, Jesus periodically carves out time to "abide" with his followers. In his last speech to them on the night before he dies, Jesus explains the import of the intimacy of abiding in his extended metaphor of the vine and the branches immediately followed by the command to "love one another" (John 15).

♦ This Sunday begins a serialized reading of 1 Corinthians 1–4; therefore, the epistle reading will not usually be in thematic harmony with the other lections. However, it provides an opportunity to dig into Paul's first letter to the Christians in Corinth as a sermon series or Bible study.

♦ Let us live our lives in ways that will be a legacy for those who come after us. The Bible is filled with ordinary people who lived extraordinary lives through their acceptance of a holy path. It is important that we not get caught up in the day-to-day. There will always be people who will doubt us. People who might make us think silly for having such a steadfast faith. It is important that we persevere. Use the examples shown to us in the Bible to reassure our intentions. We must think and plan ahead. We have to be good stewards today, in order to better stewards tomorrow.

Making Connections

Archbishop Rowan Williams has an interesting take on holiness. He does not see it as an exalted status for those select few who seem to lead ideal and exemplary lives. Holiness is about living lives with holes in them. Being holy is not about getting it all right. It is about leaving holes in your life that the light of Christ can shine through. What better way to do this than by being open and vulnerable? Just as Isaiah was called, we too have been called, to share God's light with the world.

Engaging All Ages

The star guided the Magi to Jesus, and stars were used for navigation and by travelers for thousands of years. The constellations guided runaway slaves in the United States from slavery to freedom. Read *Follow the Drinking Gourd* (Scholastic, 1992) by Jeanette Winter based on an American folksong first published in 1928. The "drinking gourd" refers to the hollowed-out gourd used by slaves (and other rural Americans) as a water dipper. But here it is used as a code name for the Big Dipper star formation, which points to Polaris, the Pole Star, and north. What (or who) do we follow when we have hopes for a better life? How does the light of Christ lead the way for us?

Hymns for the Day

The Hymnal 1982
Christ is the world's true Light 542
Christ, whose glory fills the skies 6, 7
God of mercy, God of grace 538
How wondrous and great thy works,
    God of praise! 532, 533
O Zion, tune thy voice 543
Strengthen for service, Lord, the hands 312
We the Lord's people, heart and voice uniting 51
By all your saints still striving (St. Andrew) 231, 232
In your mercy, Lord, you called me 706
Jesus calls us; o'er the tumult 549, 550
Lord, enthroned in heavenly splendor 307
What wondrous love is this 439
Ye servants of God, your Master proclaim 535

Lift Every Voice and Sing II
I have decided to follow Jesus 136

Wonder, Love, and Praise
Will you come and follow me 757

Weekday Commemorations

Tuesday, January 17
Antony, Abbot in Egypt, 356

Athanasius queried this regarding Antony: ". . . who met him grieving and did not go away rejoicing?" Antony, born in Egypt to Christians, exemplified the movement of the third century toward monasticism. He followed Christ's invitation to sell all his possessions, and he became an anchorite, or solitary ascetic. Antony dwelt alone for two decades: he prayed, he read, and he worked with his hands. In 305, he walked out of his mountain cave across the Nile and founded a monastery, its cells filled with monks living together in love and peace. He spent his remaining days in the mountains of Egypt, fighting against dissenters through preaching, converting, and performing miracles.

Wednesday, January 18
The Confession of Saint Peter the Apostle

Simon Bar-Jona, a boisterous fisher, confessed to Jesus: "You are the Christ." Jesus renamed him Peter, the "rock," on which Jesus built his church. Peter and his brother Andrew were the first disciples; thus, Peter figures keenly in the gospels despite his ill manners. Peter tried to walk on water; Peter wished to build three tabernacles. Peter thrice denied knowing Christ. On the other hand, Peter courageously risked his life to be a disciple, openly declaring his belief in Jesus as the Christ, and he courageously headed the young church's missions. Peter transformed from ordinary Simon, over-bearing and impetuous, to an extraordinary church leader, filled with the Holy Spirit.

Thursday, January 19
Wulfstan, Bishop of Worcester, 1095

Wulfstan lived through perilous political times, including the Norman Conquest. Perhaps because Wulfstan was admired for his courage and generosity, he numbered among the handful of Anglo-Saxon bishops to retain his see after 1066. He was born in Warwickshire (about 1008) and schooled by the Benedictines. Wulfstan, who first lived at the cathedral in Worcester as a monk, rose to be bishop, which he did not want but which he executed efficiently and lovingly for thirty years. During his bishopric, Wulfstan weathered the vicissitudes of politics and war, including submitting to William the Conqueror, to become the only English-born bishop among the Normans. He helped compile the Domesday Book.

Friday, January 20
Fabian, Bishop and Martyr of Rome, 250

Although he was not among the candidates for pope in 236, Fabian, a stranger to Rome and a layman, was elected without opposition after a dove alighted on his head. He served for fourteen years, reforming the office by developing structure among the churches. He set a custom of venerating martyrs at their shrines, and he appointed a committee to record their lives for posterity. He himself became a holy, exemplary martyr when Emperor Decius demanded persecution of the Church across the empire about 240. The Church Fabian had served diligently and with humility stood fast through this time of trouble.

Saturday, January 21
Agnes (and Cecilia) of Rome, Martyrs, 304 and c.230

Agnes and Cecilia, two highly venerated early Christians, were martyred during persecutions in Rome. Men propositioned Agnes ("lamb" in Latin) as a girl; when she rejected them, they denounced her as a Christian. She refused to sacrifice to Roman gods so was tortured and executed. A Roman basilica, oft visited by pilgrims, bears her name. Cecilia, patron saint of musicians, supported the conversions of her fiancé Valerian and her brother Tiburtius; after they, too, were martyred, Cecilia was arrested as she buried her beloveds. Cecilia was known to passionately sing praises to God; thus, many music schools, societies, and concert series honor her name.

Epiphany

The Third Sunday after the Epiphany

January 22, 2023

The calling of the disciples, yesterday and today.

Color   Green

Preface   Of the Epiphany

Collect

Give us grace, O Lord, to answer readily the call of our Savior Jesus Christ and proclaim to all people the Good News of his salvation, that we and the whole world may perceive the glory of his marvelous works; who lives and reigns with you and the Holy Spirit, one God, for ever and ever. *Amen.*

Readings and Psalm

Isaiah 9:1–4

Isaiah describes God's grand reversal of human situations: the most despised will receive the greatest privilege; those living in spiritual darkness will enjoy the first glimmers of light. The results of God's glorious scheme will include freedom from enemies and the end of war.

Psalm 27:1, 4–9

The first part (vv. 1–6) of Psalm 27 is a song of trust that speaks of Yahweh in the third person. The second section (vv. 7–14) is a lament addressed to Yahweh in the second person. This latter section presents the situation of someone, unjustly accused, who is coming to the temple to seek God's decision and offer sacrifice. They believe that the Lord's goodness will be made known in this life. The final verse of assurance is probably the priest's reply, speaking as an oracle of the Lord.

1 Corinthians 1:10–18

Paul takes up the first item on his agenda: the dissension in the Corinthian community and its manifestation in cliques. He appeals to the Corinthians to be of one mind and judgment, rather than divided into groups, each with its own label. Paul tactfully centers his criticisms on his own partisans. They have not been baptized in the name of Paul but in the name of Jesus Christ, to which name Paul has already appealed as the grounds for unity.

Matthew 4:12–23

Matthew's account of the beginning of Jesus' ministry includes his journey into Galilee, a statement of the meaning of his ministry, the call of the first disciples and a summary of his activity. The Isaiah citation in verses 15–16 was originally written in a context of messianic hope as Galilee faced conquest by the Assyrians in 732 BCE. This defeat for Israel meant that the native Israelites were exiled and foreign populations resettled there, thus allowing the region to be described as "Galilee of the Gentiles" (v. 4). In Jesus' time it was heavily influenced by non-Jewish culture and religion. Here Jesus announces that the long period of expectation is completed. The reign of God is a present reality but will only be realized fully in the age to come. The response he expects is repentance, literally turning around, and so a description of the entire reorientation of one's whole being as illustrated by the call of the first disciples.

Prayers of the People

Prayers of the People—*Epiphany 3A*

Friends, it is the Lord who speaks in our hearts, who says, "Seek my face." With humble hearts let us come before the Lord saying, "When we call, O Lord, *Hearken to our voice.*"

God, help your Church. Heal her divisions. Increase her joy. Unite her members that we might have a common purpose: to proclaim the gospel.

Silence

When we call, O Lord,

Hearken to our voice.

God, help this nation and the world. Where there are heavy burdens, where oppression reigns, show the strength of your arm and set your people free. May the coming of your kingdom be ever nearer.

Silence

When we call, O Lord,

Hearken to our voice.

God, help your creation. You make glorious the way of the sea; you bring us joy at the harvest. Teach us to live in harmony with all you have made.

Invite the congregation to add their thanksgivings, followed by silence

When we call, O Lord,

Hearken to our voice.

God, help our local community. May your great light drive away all of the shadows that darken our region. Even now lift up the heads of the downcast.

When we call, O Lord,

Hearken to our voice.

God, help the sick and suffering. Do not forsake them but show yourself to be the strength of their lives and their salvation. May Jesus be the healer of every disease and sickness among the people.

Allow the congregation to add their petitions, followed by silence

When we call, O Lord,

Hearken to our voice.

God, help the dying and the dead. Hide them in the secrecy of your dwelling. May all those being saved say with boldness, "I belong to Christ. Forever."

Silence

When we call, O Lord,

Hearken to our voice.

Images in the Readings

The gospel describes the first disciples as fishermen. This may be a memory of the profession of some in the Jesus movement. As well, it grounds the early Christian imagery of baptism as water, believers as water-dwellers, the net as the gospel, and the boat as the church. The Greek of the early Christian creed, "Jesus [i] Christ [**ch**], God's [**th**] Son [**u**], Savior, [**s**]" produces the acronym *ichthus*, fish, and fish show up in much Christian iconography.

The gospel introduces the image of "the **kingdom of heaven.**" Arguably the most important image in the New Testament, the kingdom invoked Israelite memory of a time of political independence. Yet this kingdom is, according to Matthew, "of heaven," that is, of a realm beyond this earth and was probably, in accord with Jewish sensibilities, a circumlocution for God. The designation of Jesus as Christ, that is, the one anointed by God for power to reign, relies on the kingdom imagery. It is not an image easily accessible for twenty-first century believers. In the New Testament, *basileia* is not solely a reference to either the church or an afterlife.

The poem in Isaiah mentions **Midian.** Israel remembered its oppression by the Midianites and then under the leadership of Gideon its victory over them. Invoking this memory, first Isaiah likens God's coming salvation to the military victory that set them free. Even the archetypal practice of warriors **plundering** the vanquished is offered as a positive image.

Epiphany

Ideas for the Day

♦ Immediately after the testing in the wilderness (4:1–11) Jesus begins his ministry in Galilee where he calls his first disciples to "Come, follow me." He will close his ministry twenty-four chapters later, again in Galilee, with the "Go, baptize" command. Between that coming and going, the disciples will have on-the-job training, not only to say the sorts of things Jesus said in his time with them, but to do the sorts of things he did with all sorts of people and to teach others to do the same. In some sense the Church is born in that time between the "Come" and the "Go."

♦ We begin to focus on mission, ministry, and discipleship in our readings today. Just as Jesus called his disciples (followers) who became his apostles (ambassadors) after the resurrection, he calls us to be his followers. In our baptism we too are called by the Lord to point beyond ourselves to God's eternal presence in creation.

♦ What things in our daily lives do we need to cast down and set aside so that we can more intently follow our given Christian path? Understanding the dynamics within society regarding financial self-sufficiency, is there something that we can let go of, in order to become a more faithful follower? Is there something that we fear that we can finally let go of? So many steps we refuse to take because we fear a particular outcome, yet faith provides the safety net we need to overcome anything we might face. Brothers Andrew and Simon Peter did not know what lay ahead of them, when Jesus called them to discipleship, yet they accepted the challenge, leaving their lives to the will of God.

Making Connections

The call to follow Jesus deserves a love and desire that jumps in with our whole selves, and it deserves the careful consideration of what it means. The secular world tells us our lives would be easier without Jesus. Being a Christian is a lot of work and completely worth it. Because it means holding to beliefs about how every human being is worthy of our care and respect, and about how there is always hope, even in the midst of great darkness. These beliefs matter, and they have the power to help us make a difference in the world.

Engaging All Ages

Today might be a good day to hold a ministry and mission "fair" for the congregation. Invite the ministries within your church (altar guild, youth group, teaching, and so on) and those who connect your church outside into the community (social justice, soup kitchen, pastoral care, mission trips, and so on) to set up a display in your parish hall during coffee hour for all ages to visit and learn how they might be called to a new ministry in the name of Christ. Make sure there are opportunities for all ages, not just adults, to be involved.

Hymns for the Day

The Hymnal 1982
How wondrous and great thy works, God of praise! 532, 533
My God, thy table now is spread 321
Spread, O spread, thou mighty word 530
Singing songs of expectation 527
The people who in darkness walked 125, 126
Thy strong word did cleave the darkness 381
God is Love, and where true love is 576, 577
I come with joy to meet my Lord 304
Where charity and love prevail 581
Where true charity and love dwell 606
Jesus calls us, o'er the tumult 549, 550
They cast their nets in Galilee 661

Lift Every Voice and Sing II

Wonder, Love, and Praise
Ubi caritas et amor 831
As we gather at your Table 763
Will you come and follow me 757
Put down your nets and follow me 807
Tú has venido a la orilla / You have come down to the lakeshore 758

Weekday Commemorations

Monday, January 23
Phillips Brooks, Bishop, 1893
Writer of songs ("O little town of Bethlehem") and sermons ("Remember the nearness of God to each one of us"), builder of churches in body and building (Trinity-Boston), innovator, youth leader, and bishop, Brooks was a tender friend and pastor. He spent ten years serving in Philadelphia before returning to Boston, where he had been born in 1835. He was appointed rector of Trinity, but three years later, the church building burned; Brooks oversaw its rebuilt altar placed daringly in the center of the chancel, "a symbol of unity." He was elected bishop in 1891, and through the force of his personality and preaching, he provided the spiritual leadership the diocese needed for that time.

Tuesday, January 24
Florence Li Tim-Oi, Priest, 1992
Named by her father "much beloved daughter," Li Tim-Oi was born in Hong Kong in 1907. When she was baptized as a student, she chose the name of Florence in honor of Florence Nightingale. Ordained deaconess in May 1941, Florence worked in Macao even after Hong Kong fell to Japanese invaders and priests could not travel to Macao to celebrate the Eucharist. Her work came to the attention of Bishop Ronald Hall, who decided that "God's work would reap better results if she had the proper title" of priest. She was ordained on January 25, 1944, the Feast of the Conversion of St. Paul, the first woman to be ordained priest in the Anglican Communion.

Wednesday, January 25
The Conversion of Saint Paul the Apostle
Saul, an orthodox Jew, studied under the famous rabbi Gamaliel, but soon after Jesus died, Saul connected to the Christian movement. He determined to crush it as heresy. On his way to Damascus to persecute Christians, Saul converted dramatically, becoming Paul and dedicating himself to Jesus. He planted Christian congregations bordering the eastern Mediterranean. His letters manifest his alignment with the mind of Christ, thereby founding Christian theology. Although rather frail physically, he was strong spiritually: "I will all the more gladly boast of my weaknesses that the power of Christ may rest upon me." His martyrdom is believed to have occurred in 64 under Nero.

Thursday, January 26
Timothy and Titus, Companions of Saint Paul
Timothy, born in Lystra in Asia Minor, and Titus, a Greek, accompanied Paul on his missions. Timothy's missions included encouraging Thessalonians to withstand persecution and Corinthians to strengthen converts' faith; he also represented Paul at Ephesus, becoming, according to Eusebius, the first bishop there. Titus accompanied Paul and Barnabas to Jerusalem for the apostolic council. On Paul's third mission, Titus was commissioned urgently to Corinth; later, Titus was entrusted to organize the church in Crete, becoming, according to Eusebius, the first bishop there. Though young, both bore tremendous responsibilities. As they shared a mission with Paul, Titus and Timothy share a commemoration close to the festal day of Paul's conversion.

Friday, January 27
John Chrysostom, Bishop and Theologian, 407
John was dubbed "Chrysostom" due to his "golden mouth," an apt description of this legendary preacher, one of the great saints of the Eastern Church. Born about 354 in Antioch, Syria, John followed a call to desert monasticism, but the desert compromised his health. Upon return to Antioch, he was ordained a presbyter; in 397, he became Patriarch of Constantinople, but his ascetic episcopate led to two banishments. He died September 14, 407, during his second exile. John, the patron saint of preachers, believed, "Preaching improves me." His sermons shed light on liturgy and emphasized the voice of the *laos* (the people). A Prayer of St. Chrysostom speaks significantly in the Book of Common Prayer at the end of Morning and Evening Prayer.

Saturday January 28
Thomas Aquinas, Friar and Theologian, 1274
Thomas is the greatest theologian of his time (the high Middle Ages—) and, perhaps, of all time. Born (probably in 1225) to a noble Italian family, he joined the new Dominican Order of Preachers. Teaching in a time of intellectual ferment, he ordered his thinking in the light of the recent rediscovery of Aristotle's works and their effect on Roman Catholic doctrine. Thomas asserted that reason and revelation harmonize: "Grace is not the denial of nature," he wrote. He understood that God's name in Exodus, "I Am Who I Am," means that God is Being from which everything else derives. Thomas died in 1274; his remains were removed to Toulouse on January 28, 1369.

Epiphany

The Fourth Sunday after the Epiphany

January 29, 2023

The Sermon on the Mount: God's word is revealed. God's way is proclaimed.

Color Green

Preface Of the Epiphany, or of the Lord's Day

Collect

Almighty and everlasting God, you govern all things both in heaven and on earth: Mercifully hear the supplications of your people, and in our time grant us your peace; through Jesus Christ our Lord, who lives and reigns with you and the Holy Spirit, one God, for ever and ever. *Amen.*

Readings and Psalm

Micah 6:1–8

Micah prophesied about the same time as Isaiah, at the end of the eighth century BCE. He focused particularly upon the social injustices of a period turbulent with political upheaval. The setting of today's reading is that of a law court; the Lord has a case to put against the people. God calls the created world as witness to God's steadfast adherence to the covenant bond. The reply expresses the criticism of the sacrificial system made by the eighth-century prophets. Sacrifice should be the external sign of an internal desire for obedience and self-offering.

Psalm 15

This psalm presents a brief entrance rite for someone desiring to enter the temple for worship. The pilgrim's question about who can enter (v. 1) receives a response from the temple personnel describing the attitudes and behavior required for worship. This portrait of an ideal worshipper can still act as a guideline for our approach to the altar of the Lord today.

1 Corinthians 1:18–31

In the verses immediately preceding today's reading (1:18–25), Paul sets forth the general principle that the wisdom of God, as manifested in the cross, appears to be folly to the worldly wise, while to those in the process of salvation, it reveals the true power of God. God's act of "foolishness" and "weakness" (v. 25) confounds both what the Jews expected of the Messiah and what non-Jews (Greeks, Gentiles) believed about God's power and wisdom. This principle of reversal is illustrated by the Corinthian community itself. Most of its members were not from the intellectual, political, or social elite. But God chose what the world counts worthless to overturn the world's expectations.

Matthew 5:1–12

Matthew gathers the teaching of Jesus into five great discourses and balances them with narratives of Jesus' deeds. Today's reading is the first of a series drawn from the first discourse, the Sermon on the Mount. The first four beatitudes reflect attitudes that climax with an unceasing hunger for a right relationship with God—both personally and communally. The second four reflect the actions and lifestyles of those who hunger in this way. In verse 10, Jesus teaches that those who live the Beatitudes will face persecution, for this way is contrary to all that the world espouses.

Prayers of the People

God's foolishness is wiser than human wisdom, and God's weakness is stronger than human strength. So let us pray to the Lord, saying, "For your blessing and guidance, *we give you thanks.*"

God, bless your Church. May our souls hunger and thirst for righteousness. Give us the grace to do those things you require of us: to do justice, and to love kindness, and to walk humbly with you.

Silence

For your blessing and guidance,

We give you thanks.

God, bless the people of this and every nation. You make foolish the wisdom of the world; we pray that our leaders find their wisdom in you. Teach us to be merciful and open us to receive mercy from others.

Silence

For your blessing and guidance,

We give you thanks.

God, bless your creation. Your mighty, creative voice echoes through the mountains. We offer back to you all the many gifts that spring forth from this earth.

Silence

For your blessing and guidance,

We give you thanks.

God, bless our local community. May we be a people who do no evil to our friends, who heap no contempt upon our neighbors.

Silence

For your blessing and guidance,

We give you thanks.

God, bless the poor in spirit with the inheritance of your kingdom. You choose what is weak in this world to shame the strong. Be the source of life for all those suffering and sick.

Invite the congregation to add their petitions and thanksgivings, followed by silence

For your blessing and guidance,

We give you thanks.

God, bless the dying and the dead. May their reward be great in heaven. Give to those who now mourn the blessing of your comfort.

Silence

For your blessing and guidance,

We give you thanks.

Images in the Readings

In the ancient Near East, some religious practice required parents to sacrifice their firstborn child to the deities, who would then reward the parents with many healthy children. Numbers 18:16 stipulates that instead parents should provide for the sacrifice of animals, the slaughter of which **redeems** the infant.

This practice, so alien to us, is fundamental to the New Testament's explanation of the purpose behind the crucifixion of Christ. Kept alive as an infant— recall also Matthew's story of Jesus escaping Herod's slaughter of the innocents—Jesus as an adult will die as a sacrificed lamb in order to redeem us all. Thus the festival of the Presentation is really a meditation on Good Friday.

Simeon's poem about Christ being **light** to the Gentiles—that is, to most of us—led to the medieval practice of people bringing to the church on this day their year's supply of candles to be blessed: thus the popular naming of this day as Candlemas. Perhaps you can use up the remainder of your Christmas candles by having all worshipers hold their lighted candles during the reading of this day's gospel. These tiny lights remind us of the refiner's fire that Malachi anticipates.

The white robe of baptism, like the vestment we call an alb, is a sign of our joy in the presence of God. We are to shine with the light of God.

Martin Luther says of Anna's being **eighty-four years** old that since 84 is 12 times 7, Anna's age combines all the meanings of twelve and of seven in the Bible. Thus her age can be seen as signifying the completion of the Old Testament in Christ.

The book of Hebrews expands the metaphor of Jesus being the sacrifice by naming him as the **high priest** who does the sacrificing of the lamb. This reminds us that no image of Christ is profound enough, and so we sometimes turn the image around and use it upside down. Here is part of today's gospel: that according to the oracle from Malachi, we become like **gold and silver**, precious, shining with the beauty of God.

Epiphany

Ideas for the Day

- A slip of the tongue turns Beatitudes into Attitudes. In a way, attitudes are what the Beatitudes are lauding. The familiar "Blessed are" or "Happy are" are the English versions of a Greek (and earlier) Hebrew expression that means something more like: "Congratulations, you've arrived!" It should come as no surprise to Matthew's hearers that the subjects of the plaudits are those whose attitudes are not the norm. The God of Israel had been famous for overturning preconceptions for millennia; the Son's inaugural teaching is an extension of the same and meant to be as provocative.

- "What does the Lord require of you but to do justice, and to love kindness and to walk with your God?" It is the compassion God shows us that should empower us to show compassion to others. Working towards justice in our community allows us to strengthen our resolve as we walk on our chosen Christian path. Expressing kindness in a variety of ways in different aspects of our life is yet another form of engaging in our faith. In the midst of injustice and people who are unkind, we must remain steadfast. We must be ambassadors of kindness in the world. We never know the impact a single act of kindness can have on the person who receives it.

Making Connections

At the heart of Micah's words is a question that is important for all of us to hear. What does our faith look like? Is the love of God that has been so generously given to us made manifest through our actions? As we look ahead to Lent, might we consider fasting in such a way as to make a difference in the lives of others? Might we seek to smile more, do more small acts of kindness and generosity, so that our lives show God's reconciling Way of Love to the world?

Engaging All Ages

Try an exercise of having the congregation look at the worship bulletin (or Book of Common Prayer) to visually see (and experience) how our liturgy envisions the reign of God. In worship we: (1) gather in God's name; (2) hear God's radical Word; (3) respond in prayer and thanksgiving; (4) offer ourselves to God through our offerings; (5) share a foretaste of the heavenly banquet through communion; and (g) go forth to love and serve.

Hymns for the Day

The Hymnal 1982
How lovely is thy dwelling-place 517
Angels, from the realms of glory 93
Love divine, all loves excelling 657
How bright appears the Morning Star 496, 497
Sing of Mary, pure and lowly 277
The great Creator of the worlds (vs. 1–4) 489
Blest are the pure in heart 656
Christ, whose glory fills the skies 6, 7
Hail to the Lord who comes 259
Let all mortal flesh keep silence 324
Lord God, you now have set your servant free 499
Sing we of the blessed Mother 278
Virgin-born, we bow before thee 258

Lift Every Voice and Sing II

Wonder, Love, and Praise
Lord, you have fulfilled your word 891

Weekday Commemorations

Tuesday, January 31
Marcella of Rome, Monastic and Scholar, 410

Born in 325, as a child Marcella studied with Athanasius of Alexandria. As a young widow, she traded richness for asceticism. Marcella made her dwelling a house of prayer, setting an example for a community of women devoted to fasting and serving the poor. With Paula (September 28), Marcella stands as a mother of Roman monasticism. In 382, with Paula, Marcella hosted Jerome at her estate; the three formed a friendship that encouraged Jerome's Latin translation of the scriptures into the Vulgate. Scholars sought Marcella's insight on the Greek and Hebrew scriptures. She died at the hands of Visigoths.

Wednesday, February 1
Brigid (Bride), Monastic, c523

As Irish as Patrick, and as beloved, Brigid was born to a Druid household in the mid-fifth century. She chose early to dedicate her life to Christ as a nun; in 470, she founded a nunnery in Kildare. To secure the sacraments, Brigid persuaded an anchorite to receive episcopal ordination and escort his community to Kildare, thus establishing the only known double Irish monastery. She effected policy at church conventions and may have received episcopal orders herself. Stories of her care for the poor include the healing of a leper woman and the taming of a wolf. Her feast day shares sacredness with Imbolg, the Celtic festival of spring.

Thursday, February 2
The Presentation of Our Lord Jesus Christ in the Temple

Variously known as the Purification of Saint Mary the Virgin and as Candlemas, in the Orthodox Church February 2 also is called the Meeting of Christ with Simeon. These names testify to the wealth of spiritual meanings conjoined to this incident. The "presentation" harkens to the Jewish law that every firstborn son had to be dedicated to God in memory of the Israelites' deliverance from Egypt. When Mary placed her Babe in the arms of Simeon, the Old and New Dispensations married: the old oblations were dismissed; the new, perfect offering had entered the temple. The offering was to be made once for all on the cross.

Friday, February 3
Anskar, Bishop and Missionary, 865

As archbishop of Hamburg, Anskar was papal legate for missionary work among the Scandinavians. The immediate result of his devoted and perilous labors was slight: two churches established on the border of Denmark and one priest settled in Sweden. He also participated in the consecration of Gotbert, first bishop in Sweden. While still a young man, Anskar was consecrated archbishop of Hamburg in 831, and continued his work among the Scandinavians until 848, when he retired to the See of Bremen and died in 865. The seeds of his efforts were not to bear fruit until over one hundred years later, when Viking devastation, weakness in the Frankish Church, and the lowest ebb of missionary enthusiasm came to an end. The rich harvest of conversion was three generations away. Nevertheless, Anskar is looked upon by Scandinavians as their apostle.

Saturday, February 4
Manche Masemola, Martyr, 1928

Born in Marishane, South Africa (1913?), into a non-Christian farm family, Masemola worshipped with the Anglican Community of the Resurrection as a girl, but her parents forbade her baptism, beating her as dissuasion. She prophesied that she would die at her parents' hand and be baptized in her own blood. On February 4, 1928, Masemola's parents indeed killed her. Although she had not been baptized, the church recognized her baptism by her desire for same. In 1935, a small band of pilgrims came to her grave; now hundreds visit every August. Her statue stands at Westminster Abbey.

Saturday, February 4
Cornelius the Centurion

The sum total of knowledge about Cornelius comes in chapters 10 and 11 in the Acts of the Apostles. Born a Gentile, he was the first convert to Christianity in his household. The writer of Acts credited Cornelius' conversion with affecting Christianity as it influenced the apostolic council of Jerusalem, held a few years later, to admit Gentiles to full partnership with Jewish converts. As a centurion, Cornelius commanded a company of a hundred soldiers in the Roman army; he took responsibility for their discipline, on the battlefield as well as in camp. Some centurions, like Cornelius, were men of deep religious piety. Tradition holds that Cornelius was the second Bishop of Caesarea.

Epiphany

The Fifth Sunday after the Epiphany

February 5, 2023

The Sermon on the Mount: God's people are to give witness to God's grace and power by leading righteous lives.

Color   Green

Preface   Of the Epiphany, or of the Lord's Day

Collect

Set us free, O God, from the bondage of our sins, and give us the liberty of that abundant life which you have made known to us in your Son our Savior Jesus Christ; who lives and reigns with you, in the unity of the Holy Spirit, one God, now and forever. *Amen.*

Readings and Psalm

Isaiah 58:1–9a (9b–12)

In today's verses, God redefines the role of fasting. An expression of humility, fasting offers the people an opportunity to do for others what God has already done for them. God had chosen to free the captives (52:1–3), feed the hungry (55:1–2), and bring Israel's homeless back to their homeland (49:8–12). The attitude of the heart and use of the tongue must also reflect charity. The people must give more than food, clothing, or shelter: they must give themselves. Instead of seeking their own pleasure, they must first satisfy the desires of the needy, finding their own desires satisfied by God (58:11).

Psalm 112:1–9 (10)

This is an acrostic psalm, each line beginning with a successive letter of the twenty-two letter Hebrew alphabet. It highlights the many blessing that come to those who remain faithful to God's law. The blessings are not only spiritual but include children (v. 2) and wealth that can be used to help others (vv. 3, 5, 9). These blessed faithful contrast with the wicked whose "desires come to nothing" (v. 10).

1 Corinthians 2:1–12 (13–16)

Paul develops the principle that "God's weakness is stronger than human strength" (1:18–25) by using himself as an example. Both his presentation and his physical unimpressiveness (2 Corinthians 10:10) show that the "demonstration of the Spirit and of power" was not his doing but resulted from God's power. Yet, despite the negative meanings of wisdom that Paul has argued against—that is, wisdom as oratorical technique (1:20, 2:4) or as human standards of judgment (1:21–26)—he can speak of a wisdom for the "mature" or perfect. This wisdom is the full significance of "Christ . . . the wisdom of God" (1:24) in the plan of salvation hidden for ages but not revealed.

Matthew 5:13–20

Matthew follows the Beatitudes with two sayings, one on salt and one on light. Salt was used as a purifier of sacrifices (Ezekiel 43:24). The images of both salt and light also described the law. Light also referred to God and to the restored Israel after the exile. Verses 17–20 explain Jesus' relationship to the law. Because of the destruction of the temple, the central authority for Judaism during the period in which Matthew was written was the law, and Jesus was to be evaluated in relationship to it.

Prayers of the People

Sisters and brothers, let your light shine before others, so that they may see your good works and give glory to God. Let us pray, "Lord, hear our call, *and answer us.*"

Establish your Church, O God, as a light to the world. Shine your Holy Spirit through us, and all for your glory and the welfare of your people.

Silence

Lord, hear our call,

And answer us.

Righteous God, you delight in justice and mercy: Loose the bonds of injustice and let the oppressed go free. Raise up leaders who care for the poor.

Silence

Lord, hear our call,

And answer us.

We thank you, O God, for the gift of light. By it you cause plants to grow; by it you generate warmth; by it you open our eyes to see the beauty of all you have made.

Invite the congregation to add their thanksgivings, followed by silence

Lord, hear our call,

And answer us.

In our own city, Great God, be the restorer of streets. Rebuild our ruined places. May all the people of this community live in security and peace.

Silence

Lord, hear our call,

And answer us.

Be present to all those who cry for help, O Holy One. We pray your healing will spring up quickly for those in need.

Invite the congregation to add their petitions, followed by silence

Lord, hear our call,

And answer us.

The human heart fails to conceive all the good you have prepared for your beloved ones, Heavenly Parent. We trust to you our dying and our dead, believing that you are good and faithful.

Silence

Lord, hear our call,

And answer us.

Images in the Readings

Light is an image on many Sundays. The Sermon on the Mount speaks also of the **lampstand**. Paul would remind us that, contrary to the wisdom of the world, our lampstand is the cross.

Salt is necessary for human life. In recollection of this passage, some early Christian communities placed salt on the tongue of the newly baptized. In the early twentieth century, the British placed an embargo on salt, requiring the Indian people to purchase salt from them, and Gandhi's Salt March became a symbol of the right of Indians to manage their own survival.

The passage from Isaiah speaks about a **fast**. In many religious traditions, people limit or refrain from some necessary human activity as a symbol that their truest life comes only from the divine. In both the Jewish and Christian traditions, fasting must be accompanied with justice for the poor for God to acknowledge its value.

Ideas for the Day

♦ The lectionary editors have it precisely right in their paring of this gospel portion with Isaiah's good news. Being "salt of the earth" or "light of the world" *is* "the fast" that Isaiah delineates. These actions—freeing captives and undoing oppression and feeding the hungry and clothing the naked—are not behaviors at a remove, but immediate, risky, hands-on interventions done for the sake of another, whoever that other may be. In fact, these are just the sorts of things that Jesus did and that he commends to his hearers in his final encouragement concerning the sheep and the goats at Matthew 25.31ff.

♦ Ministry is bringing Christ's light into the world in the daily life of each Christian and in the corporate witness of the Church.

♦ What can God reveal to us through the Spirit? We like to think we have things so well figured out. In fact, our desire to pinpoint and control every waking moment of our life may be blocking what the Spirit has to say to us. Spirit moves through people. Being active in our church provides opportunities for us hear what the Spirit is saying in our lives. Active participation in a Sunday service gives you the chance to listen to the Spirit. Sing the hymns with gusto, read the prayers with intention, greet your fellow congregants with energy and a smile.

Epiphany

Making Connections

The Gospel reading today is meant for any of us who have ever felt "less than." Jesus preaches a message that each of us matters, that each one of us is a beloved child of God. We are the light of the world, and the world needs our light. We are not meant to put it under a bushel basket. We are not meant to hide it away or give into those messages that we are less than. We are to cultivate shame resilience. Episcopalian Brené Brown believes that we do this by: "understanding our vulnerabilities and cultivating empathy, courage, and compassion."

Engaging All Ages

Jesus gives us a New Covenant, setting a higher standard than the basis of the Old Testament law. Christians respond to moral problems with the light of Christ rather than relying on guidelines for merely avoiding sinful behavior. For the Christian it is not so much what I must do to keep out of trouble, but what I will do to spread the light of Christ in the world. What guides our behaviors and interactions with others?

Hymns for the Day

The Hymnal 1982
Thy strong word did cleave the darkness 381
Lord, whose love through humble service 610
Now quit your care (vs. 3–5) 145
O day of God, draw nigh 600, 601
Lord, make us servants of your peace 593
Praise to the living God! 372

Lift Every Voice and Sing II
Out in the highways and byways of life
   (Make me a blessing) 158
This little light of mine 160, 221

Wonder, Love, and Praise
The church of Christ in every age 779
Gracious Spirit, give your servants 782
We are marching in the light of God 787

Weekday Commemorations

Wednesday, February 8
Bakhita (Josephine Margaret Bakhita), Monastic, 1947

Born in Sudan, Bakhita's enslavement at seven traumatized her so badly that she forgot her name. The slavers named her "Bakhita," "fortunate one." She remained a slave for twelve years. Finally in 1883, she was sold to the Italian consul in Khartoum, who gave her to his friend, with whom she traveled to Italy. As a nanny, Bakhita attended a Christian institute with her charge. There, she was baptized as Josephine. She became a Canossian Daughter of Charity in 1896. She said she found God in her heart without ever being evangelized. Bakhita stands as inspiration for all the victimized.

Friday, February 10
Scholastica, Monastic, 543

The patron saint of nuns is twin to Benedict, who founded the Benedictine order. Gregory the Great's *Dialogues* tell Scholastica's story. With a few other women religious, she lived in a small hermitage in Plumbariola, near her brother's monastery at Monte Cassino. The siblings often discussed scriptures and spiritual matters. Near death, she begged her brother to stay with her. He said no. She prayed to God and credited her Lord with the storm that kept her brother by her side that night. She died three days later. Brother and sister are buried together.

Saturday, February 11
Theodora, Empress, c. 867

This ninth-century Byzantine empress gained credit as a saint in Orthodox churches for her role in restoring icons to objects of veneration. She was married in 830 to Theophilos. Though Christian, he believed that venerating icons was idolatry. They had seven children, but at only twenty-nine, he died. Theodora ruled for their son, the emperor, as his regent from 842 to 855. In that role, she formed a synod to study iconoclasm; the gathering ended with members bearing icons back into Hagia Sophia. Theodora is also remembered for the gentle way she treated her theological opponents.

The Sixth Sunday after the Epiphany

February 12, 2023

The Sermon on the Mount: Jesus' commandments call for a profound commitment, leading the Christian to witness to a distinctive way of life.

Color   Green

Preface   Of the Epiphany, or of the Lord's Day

Collect

O God, the strength of all who put their trust in you: Mercifully accept our prayers; and because in our weakness we can do nothing good without you, give us the help of your grace, that in keeping your commandments we may please you both in will and deed; through Jesus Christ our Lord, who lives and reigns with you and the Holy Spirit, one God, for ever and ever. *Amen.*

Readings and Psalm

Jeremiah 17:5–10

Deuteronomy 30:15–20

This reading comes from Moses' third address (chaps. 29–30) and challenges the people to decide between two ways of living. The format reflects ancient treaties that concluded with a call to the gods to act as witnesses to the treaty. Here the whole created universe is called to witness the covenant (31:28). The people are urged to "choose life," not merely a prolongation of days but the fullness received in love, obedience, and faithfulness to God.

or

Sirach 15:15–20

The Wisdom of Jesus ben Sirach was written about 180 BCE. Sirach (50:27) seems to have been a teacher, the head of an academy in Jerusalem (51:23). In today's reading, he addresses the question of free will and the responsibility for sin. His interest is not in how humanity as a whole came to be sinful (as in Genesis), but rather in the actions of individuals. His intent is to exonerate God from complicity in human sin, in contrast to the idea that God is the primary cause of all activity. Although innocent of human sin, God is not ignorant or indifferent to it. Rather, a clear choice is presented, and God longs to pour out blessing.

Psalm 119:1–8

This psalm is an acrostic psalm, in which the first line of each of its twenty-two eight-line stanzas begins with a successive letter of the Hebrew alphabet. It is the longest in the Bible. In this reading, the psalmist describes those who are blessed because of their fidelity to God's commands and asks God to give wisdom and discernment for keeping them.

1 Corinthians 3:1–9

In addition to adopting party designations (1:12), the Corinthians seem to have enjoyed categorizing one another's spiritual maturity. Paul informs the Corinthians that they are far from being as spiritually mature (2:6) as they think. Although they have received the Spirit in baptism and are thus implicitly "spiritual," their strife shows that they are not living out their true status. Instead they are living in the "flesh," like mere human beings. Flesh, for Paul, is not the opposite of spirit; rather, flesh is what is human, weak, mortal, liable to sin. Far from acting as if their lives were determined by the Spirit, the Corinthians' parties and labels show that they are determined by individual or human considerations.

Matthew 5:21–37

Today's and next Sunday's gospels come from the section called "the six antitheses" (5:21–48), so named from the repeated phrase "it was said . . . but I say . . . ." Fundamentally, the antitheses are a statement about who Jesus is and what authority he bears (7:28–29). They also illustrate how Jesus fulfills the law (5:17). He does not pit his teaching against the law, but against the rabbinic interpretations and traditions. Jesus reveals the spirit of the law in a new standard of righteousness. These antitheses reach back past the Mosaic law to the original or "creation will" of God. This means that in some cases (murder, adultery, love of enemy) the law has been strengthened; Jesus' command is "not only . . . but also." Attention is shifted from external action to internal intention. In other cases (divorce, oaths, retaliation), the law as practiced is abrogated and external performance is altered.

Prayers of the People

Happy are they who walk in the law of the Lord! So let us come before the Lord, saying, "Righteous God, *direct our ways.*"

Lord our God, bless your Church. May those who plant and those who water recognize their common purpose. Give abundant growth where your Church labors faithfully.

Silence

Righteous God,

Direct our ways.

Lord our God, bless the people of this and every nation. Draw nations and leaders to choose those ways that promote life and not death.

Silence

Righteous God,

Direct our ways.

Lord our God, bless this planet—your very footstool. Give us the wisdom and will to allow the earth to prosper as you have intended—naturally bringing forth growth and prosperity.

Silence

Righteous God,

Direct our ways.

Lord our God, bless our city. Give us those things we need to live together as neighbors. Remove from our hearts anger, discord, and lust.

Silence

Righteous God,

Direct our ways.

Lord our God, bless the sick and the struggling. May they find life in relationship with you. Make them happy as they seek you with all their hearts.

Invite the congregation to add their petitions and thanksgivings, followed by silence

Righteous God,

Direct our ways.

Lord our God, bless the dying and the dead. May they find peace and comfort at the foot of your heavenly throne.

Silence

Righteous God,

Direct our ways.

Images in the Readings

According to Matthew, Jesus threatened immoral people with **hell**. The idea that God will punish sinners with eternal fire came into intertestamental Jewish tradition from their Zoroastrian neighbors and is included in some New Testament books. Matthew's literalism is seen in the phrases that one's "whole body . . . be thrown into hell." Fear of hell was apparently a central religious motivation during some pieties and periods of the Church, and lurid descriptions of torment extended far beyond what many theologians propose: that hell is self-willed distance from God, through life and beyond death. From the second century to the present, some Christians have maintained that eternal punishment contradicts the primary description of a merciful God. The Apostles' and Nicene creeds speak only of judgment and an everlasting life of the world to come, although according to the later Athanasian Creed, "those who have done evil will enter eternal fire."

The word of God is **milk** to us, who are infants. As nursing mothers know, both the infant and the mother need the times of feeding. It is as if God needs to give us the milk we need. The passage from Deuteronomy evokes the classic *The Pilgrim's Progress*, by John Bunyan, in which the Christian life is described as one **choice** after another. It is God's Spirit who inspires us to choose what God has already chosen for us: in Paul's words, life in God's field, God's building.

Ideas for the Day

♦ Jesus had insisted that he didn't come to change any part of the law (5:17), but like the best of the Pharisees, he knew that ancient practices, no matter how sacred, must always be nimble enough to be adapted for new generations whose needs and ethos reflected a different time. So his long initial speech in Matthew—the Sermon on the Mount—is a conscious return to Mosaic teaching on another mountain in the distant past, but a refreshing of that early covenant for a new generation that will usher in a new covenant and a new Way of being People of God.

♦ "I planted, Apollos watered, but God gave growth. So neither he who plants, nor he who waters is anything, but only God who gives growth." It is important to stay out of God's way when it comes to growth. We must find ways to facilitate spiritual growth in ourselves. We do this by engaging in our faith actions, seeking ways to participate in our larger community. We must balance self-care with care for others so that God can find expression through us. It important to recognize and respect others for their current level of spiritual growth. It is not for us to judge, but to facilitate spiritual growth by providing space, allowing them to freely walk on their own Christian path.

Making Connections

Choose life. We are called to follow in the way of Jesus, the Way of Love. Sometimes the loving, life-giving, liberating choice is not easy. It means saying no to other things. Yes to exercise and time with our families means resisting the temptation to stay in bed longer or work more. Yes to caring for ourselves and those we love means no to relationships that are toxic or destructive. Choosing life means engaging deeply with those around us, and that means taking the risk that we will have our hearts broken or we will lose someone for whom we care deeply.

Engaging All Ages

Two actions occur during our liturgy that give us examples as to how to follow Jesus' commandments. The passing of the peace expresses the command of Jesus to leave one's gift at the altar and be reconciled with one's sibling and then offer the gift. Since it follows the confession and absolution, the peace is an acting-out of the need to forgive as we have been forgiven. The offertory at the Eucharist continues the ancient temple practice of offering gifts at the altar as an act of commitment to and reconciliation with God. How do we raise awareness of these actions instead of seeing them as a chance to say "hello" to a neighbor or "pass the plate" in our worship?

Hymns for the Day

If thou but trust in God to guide thee 635
Come, gracious Spirit, heavenly Dove 512
God of grace and God of glory 594, 595
Lord, be thy word my rule 626
Now that the daylight fills the sky 3, 4
Praise to the living God! 372
I come with joy to meet my Lord 304
Lord, make us servants of your peace 593
Where charity and love prevail 581
Blessed Jesus, at thy word 440
"Forgive our sins as we forgive" 674
Go forth for God; go to the world in peace 347
Strengthen for service, Lord 312

Lift Every Voice and Sing II
I will trust in the Lord 193

Wonder, Love, and Praise
Come now, O Prince of peace 795
Ubi caritas et amor 831

Epiphany

Epiphany

Weekday Commemorations

Monday, February 13
Absalom Jones, Priest, 1818

Born a slave in 1746 in Delaware, Jones taught himself to read from the Old Testament. He bought his freedom in 1784 after buying his wife's. He served as a lay minister at St. George's Methodist Episcopal Church, evangelizing alongside his friend Richard Allen. The resulting numbers of Black people at St. George's caused the fearful vestry to segregate them into an upper gallery; the Black members indignantly left the building as one body. Jones and Allen were elected overseers of the Free African Society of Black Christians in 1787. They worked ceaselessly for Black people to be included within the Episcopal Church, into which Jones was ordained a priest on September 21, 1802.

Tuesday, February 14
Cyril, Monk, and Methodius, Bishop, Missionaries to the Slavs, 869, 885

These brothers by blood and mission served as apostles to the southern Slavs against mighty barriers from Germany but with equally mighty support from Rome. In 862, the Moravian king asked for missionaries to teach his people in their native tongue; both learned brothers knew Slavonic and accepted the mission, Cyril to the point that he invented an alphabet for transcription. He died in Rome in 869, but Methodius continued despite enmity among Germans and Moravians. While continuing his mission, Methodius translated the Bible into the Slavonic tongue; his funeral, attended by masses, was conducted in Greek, Latin, and Slavonic.

Wednesday, February 15
Thomas Bray, Priest and Missionary, 1730

As overseer for the church in Maryland, Bray, an English country parson, visited the colony in 1702 for the first and only time, but from that visit, Bray gained his *foci*: he felt deep concern over the state of the American churches; over the need for education among clergy and laity, adults and children; for Native Americans and African Americans. He founded thirty-nine lending libraries, raised funds for missions, and encouraged young English priests to emigrate to America. He founded societies for Promoting Christian Knowledge and for the Propagation of the Gospel. For his own country and for the colony of Georgia, he championed prison reforms.

Friday, February 17
Janani Luwum, Archbishop and Martyr, 1977

In 1969 Janani Luwum became Bishop of Northern Uganda, where he was a faithful visitor to his parishes as well as a growing influence at international gatherings of the Anglican Communion. In 1974, as archbishop of the Church of Uganda, Rwanda, Burundi, and Bog-Zaire, he had contact and confrontation with the Ugandan military dictator, Idi Amin. By early February 1977 the archbishop's residence was searched for arms by government security forces; on the 15th, he was summoned to the palace. He said to the bishops and others accompanying him, "They are going to kill me. I am not afraid." He was never seen alive again.

Saturday, February 18
Martin Luther, Pastor and Church Reformer, 1546

Martin Luther was born November 10, 1483, at Eisleben, in Germany. His intellectual abilities were evident early, and his father planned a career for him in law. Luther's real interest lay elsewhere, however, and in 1505 he entered the local Augustinian monastery. He was ordained a priest on April 3, 1507. In October 1512, Luther received his doctorate in theology, and shortly afterward he was installed as a professor of biblical studies at the University of Wittenberg. His lectures on the Bible were popular, and within a few years he made the university a center for biblical humanism. As a result of his theological and biblical studies, he called into question the practice of selling indulgences. On the eve of All Saints' Day, October 31, 1517, he posted on the door of the castle church in Wittenberg the notice of an academic debate on indulgences, listing ninety-five theses for discussion. As the effects of the theses became evident, the pope called upon the Augustinian order to discipline their member. After a series of meetings, political maneuvers, and attempts at reconciliation, Luther, at a meeting with the papal legate in 1518, refused to recant. Luther was excommunicated on January 3, 1521. Luther translated the New Testament into German and began the translation of the Old Testament. He then turned his attention to the organization of worship and education. He introduced congregational singing of hymns, composing many himself, and issued model orders of services. He published his large and small catechisms for instruction in the faith. During the years from 1522 to his death, Luther wrote a prodigious quantity of books, letters, sermons, and tracts. Luther died at Eisleben on February 18, 1546.

The Last Sunday after the Epiphany

February 19, 2023

The Transfiguration of our Lord.

Color   White

Preface   Of the Epiphany

Collect:

O God, who before the passion of your only-begotten Son revealed his glory upon the holy mountain: Grant to us that we, beholding by faith the light of his countenance, may be strengthened to bear our cross, and be changed into his likeness from glory to glory; through Jesus Christ our Lord, who lives and reigns with you and the Holy Spirit, one God, for ever and ever. *Amen.*

Readings and Psalm

Exodus 24:12–18

Many scholars today believe that Exodus, traditionally attributed to Moses, is a composite of the work of several different sources. The tablets God promises will record the commandments. Keeping these commandments was the condition of the covenant, under which God pledged providence and protection. Moses ascends a mountain top covered in cloud, a symbol of God's glory. His faithful vigil there brings the gift of the law to God's people.

Psalm 2

This psalm is a divine affirmation of the Jewish king. Amidst the rebellion of other kings (vv. 1–3), God reaffirms the choice (vv. 4–6) and adoption of the king as God's son (v. 7) in order to establish God's rule over the nations (vv. 8–9). The psalm ends with a warning to the kings of the nations to submit to God and "serve the Lord" or expect God's wrath (vv. 10–11). Christians have applied this psalm to Christ, the "anointed" one of God (v. 2).

or

Psalm 99

Psalm 99 is a hymn celebrating God's kingship. Each of its three stanzas closes with a refrain about God's holiness (vv. 3, 5, 9). The first stanza (vv. 1–3) celebrates this holiness as revealed by God's kingship, the second (vv. 4–5) as revealed by God's justice, and the third (vv. 6–9) as revealed by God's faithfulness in history.

2 Peter 1:16–21

The author writes in response to anxieties about different teachings in the community and about the delay of the second coming. He appeals to the tradition of apostolic testimony, particularly to his experience as a witness to the transfiguration. The transfiguration manifests Christ in his power, confirming the messianic prophecies of the Hebrew Bible and pointing toward his return in glory.

Matthew 17:1–9

Matthew's account, marked by allusions to Moses' own mountaintop encounter with God, links the transfiguration to the final coming of the Messiah as prefigured in the Church. As Matthew tells it, Jesus' transfiguration is primarily a manifestation of who Jesus really is. The promise of his return receives the beginning of its fulfillment in the event of Jesus' death, resurrection, and appearance to the disciples. Peter, overwhelmed by the presence of those most intimately acquainted with God's ways—Moses and Elijah—wishes to enshrine the three and thus capture the revelation. But the voice from heaven redirects their attention to a living, breathing, active person—Jesus. Relationship with God cannot be a static experience of localized worship but must be as dynamic as attending to the voice of One they love. Moses and Elijah vanish, for the law and the prophets have been fulfilled in what Jesus has done, and Jesus alone remains with them always.

Epiphany

Prayers of the People

When we call upon the Lord, God will answer us. So let us come before the Lord in prayer, saying, "Majestic God, *Show us your glory.*"

Lord our God, move your Church by your Holy Spirit. May we proclaim your greatness in the world. Inspire in us a prophetic message and let us not be overcome by fear.

Silence

Majestic God,

Show us your glory.

We pray especially today for our Bishop, _____. May (s)he, like your servant Moses, lead your people into a deeper experience of you.

Silence

Majestic God,

Show us your glory.

O mighty King, lover of justice, may this and every nation, strive for justice and peace. We pray that the leaders of the nations trust and care for those in their charge.

Silence

Majestic God,

Show us your glory.

Holy One, you have chosen to wear the clouds and meet our forebears on the mountains. In doing so, you remind us that you created all things good and continue to manifest your glory through those things you have created. Remind us to also honor your creation.

Invite the congregation to add their thanksgivings, followed by silence

Majestic God,

Show us your glory.

O Lord, after they witnessed your majesty, Jesus led his disciples back down the mountain to minister to the people. Lead us to proclaim the Good News of God in Christ to our neighbors—to be your lamps shining in dark places.

Silence

Majestic God,

Show us your glory.

God our Father, touch those who are overcome by fear, sickness or any other adversity. Overshadow them with the healing power of your love.

Invite the congregation to add their petitions, followed by silence

Majestic God,

Show us your glory.

God of Light, we pray for the dying and the dead. May all those who experience death also come to know the new day of resurrection that comes through your Risen Son.

Silence

Majestic God,

Show us your glory.

Images in the Readings

Once again the readings include the central biblical images of **light** and **mountain**. Yet God is not only brilliant light: important for the readings is the image of the **cloud**. Although contemporary people tend to think of clouds as relating to weather conditions, in the Bible the cloud is a sign of the presence of God. It is as if God covers the earth, brings life, effecting much yet suddenly vanishing. Christians can add that from God as cloud rains down the waters of baptism.

We are so accustomed to the language of being children of a God who is like a Father that we miss the astonishment of the early Church, when this imagery was a religious surprise. Christ is to God as a **son** is to a father, and we are not pitiful creatures struggling to live in a hostile environment but rather children cared for by a beneficent God. "Son of man," on the other hand, is the biblical name for the apocalyptic judge, thus only paradoxically the beloved Son of God.

Ideas for the Day

- As we began the season after the Epiphany, so we draw it to a close. Back then, at his Baptism, at the beginning of his ministry, a voice from heaven had declared, "This is my Son, the Beloved, with whom I am well pleased" (3:17). Now, as that season ends and just before we bend our way into Lent, we hear the same declaration from that same voice with the added proviso: "Listen to him." In the gospel, Jesus is now turning his steps and his attention toward Jerusalem where suffering and death and final victory await. Perhaps this is the disciples'—and our—final encouragement before their own trial begins.

- The Sundays after the Epiphany are framed both by the Feast of the Epiphany, with its star in the heavens, and Jesus' face shining like the sun at the Transfiguration. The light of God's revelation in Jesus becomes clearer in the ensuing weeks as disciples are called and his word is proclaimed.

- What are the ways God reveals God's self to us? Create a list of seven things that bring you personal joy such as hiking, biking, reading novels, writing music, aerobics, painting, sculpting, singing, writing poetry, teaching, among many other possibilities. Thinking of your church community, create a list of seven ways that you can bring joy to others. Pick a week in the future. Assign a personal "joy" and a community "joy" to each day of the week and find a way to achieve those moments. God is joy, God is love, God is peace.

Making Connections

"Get up and do not be afraid." Our communities are not going to change themselves. Transformation happens because we are engaged participants. It happens when we are in relationship, seeking to join with God's restoring and reconciling work in the world. Transformation happens when the hungry are fed, the naked are clothed, when the stranger is welcomed and we love our neighbors. Transformation happens when we strive for peace and justice, when we respect the dignity of every human being, when we strive to follow the Way of Love even more faithfully in all the facets of our lives.

Engaging all Ages

Like Moses, Elijah, and Jesus, it is in those mountaintop, seeing-the-light experiences that we begin to understand what the Lord is calling us to do in our covenant relationship. Martin Luther King Jr.'s "I Have a Dream" speech could be called a contemporary mountaintop experience. What does it take to have a mountaintop experience? Are there times in our lives when we have been changed by an experience or have seen life in a new way? How can we be open to seeing the face of God?

Hymns for the Day

The Hymnal 1982
Songs of thankfulness and praise 135
Alleluia, song of gladness 122, 123
We sing of God, the mighty source of all things 386, 387
Christ is the world's true Light 542
Christ, whose glory fills the skies 6, 7
From God Christ's deity came forth 443
Christ upon the mountain peak 129, 130
O light of Light, Love given birth 133, 134
O wondrous type! O vision fair 136, 137

Lift Every Voice and Sing II
I love to tell the story 64

Wonder, Love, and Praise

Weekday Commemorations

Monday, February 20
Frederick Douglass, Social Reformer, 1895
Born a slave in 1818, Douglass broke the law by teaching himself to read. At fourteen, he converted to Christianity in the African Methodist Episcopal Church, whose music bolstered his struggle for freedom. Douglass spoke on tours in the North sponsored by the American Anti-slavery Society, but his renown as an orator magnified his fear of capture. When Douglass fled to England, his American friends bought his freedom so he could return to America, where he edited *The North Star*, a pro-abolition journal. Douglass championed the rights of African Americans and of all women and children.

Thursday. February 23
Polycarp, Bishop and Martyr of Smyrna, 156

Polycarp died at eighty-six, a martyr, burned at the stake. He had filled his life with service to Jesus. He was one of the church leaders who carried on the tradition of the apostles through the Gnostic heresies of the second century. Polycarp, according to Irenaeus, was a pupil of John and had been appointed a bishop by "apostles in Asia." His letter to the Church in Philippi reveals his adhesion to the faith and his concern for fellow Christians. On the day of his martyrdom, probably in 156, Polycarp was ordered to curse Christ. He refused, declaring, ". . . he never did me any wrong." The mob clamored for him to be thrown to the hungry beasts.

Friday, February 24
Saint Matthias the Apostle

Little is known of Matthias beyond his selection as a disciple. In the nine days between Jesus' ascension and the day of Pentecost, the disciples gathered in prayer. Peter reminded them that the defection and death of Judas had left the fellowship with a vacancy. The Acts of the Apostles records Peter's suggestion that one of the followers from the time of Jesus' baptism until his crucifixion "must become with us a witness to his resurrection." After prayer, the disciples cast lots between nominees Barsabbas Justus and Matthias; the lot fell to Matthias. Tradition holds him as exemplary, a suitable witness to the resurrection, but his service is unheralded by history and unsung by psalms.

Saturday, February 25
Emily Malbone Morgan, Lay Leader and Contemplative, 1937

Morgan was born in 1862 in a prominent Anglican family in Hartford, Connecticut, where Adelyn Howard inspired her. Homebound, Howard sought spiritual companionship and offered intercessory prayer. Morgan responded by gathering together the women who formed the Society of the Companions of the Holy Cross in 1884. The community of Episcopal laywomen was devoted to prayer, discipleship, and social justice. Morgan, concerned about working women who had no hope of a break, developed vacation houses in the Northeast for these tired women and their daughters. In 1901, the Society established Adelynrood, a permanent home in Byfield, Massachusetts.

Lent

Preparing for Lent

Theological Themes that Might Shape Liturgy, Catechesis, and Education

Just as Advent, Christmas, and the season after the Epiphany should be thought of and planned with a through line in mind, Lent, Holy Week, and Easter should be as well. These three portions of the church year represent the Paschal cycle (as opposed to the Incarnation cycle) and are moveable (as opposed to fixed).

Lent is our time of intentional preparation to receive with freshness and renewed vitality the mystery of the resurrection of Christ. It is during this forty day period (forty-six including the Sundays) that we contemplate the suffering of Jesus Christ and that suffering makes the resurrection not only possible, but powerful.

The way we prepare to receive the mystery is by observing a period of penitence. Penitence is an opportunity to reflect on how far we have wandered from grace, how much we stand in need of God's forgiveness, and then how we might live a life more closely aligned with God's desires for us. The danger in our Lenten penitence is that, if not carefully observed, this season can quickly devolve into a competition of works-righteousness. Grace must remain at the heart of our Lenten practice and devotion. It is the grace of God that leads us to return to God once we have wandered away.

Because Lenten practice can be so countercultural, this is a great opportunity to engage in some intentional formation around Lent. Exploring the concepts of prayer and reflection, fasting and abstinence, almsgiving and charity can really support and strengthen the spirituality of our faith communities. There are also opportunities to engage in some formation around the specific rites that occur during this season only, particularly during Holy Week. Simply holding a liturgy and expecting people to gather its meaning without any type of context or framework can no longer be taken for granted. These liturgies are layered with meaning. We owe it to those who will come to worship to help them explore the depths of this season.

Liturgical Possibilities

Rites

Lent begins with the Proper Liturgy for Ash Wednesday, which, after reading the portion of Matthew's gospel that prohibits the outward showiness of religion, invites the congregation to be marked with an ashen cross as a sign of their mortality and penitence. I have found it right for these two portions of the liturgy to stand in a creative tension, asking the penitent listener to critically examine the spiritual efficacy of their Lenten practice.

As far as the Sundays in Lent are concerned, there are many options to make the liturgy reflect the penitential nature of the season. Observing the Great Litany is an appropriate way to open the season on Lent I (Book of Common Prayer and *Enriching Our Worship*). A community might also choose to open their liturgy with the Penitential Order. If the Penitential Order is included, it might also be helpful to include the Decalogue—God's commandments—as a way to further explore the ways we have failed to live up to the love of God and our need for God's forgiving grace.

Lenten liturgy should be simpler, solemn, but not overly sad. Lent is a season of nuance where we hold in tandem both our sinfulness and God's grace-filledness. Our Orthodox siblings refer to this tension as "luminous sadness." Altering the adjustable portions of the liturgy to reflect this might help to draw more of our focus into this tension.

It is also important to allow Lent to speak to the truths of our faith in ways that allow us to enter them differently. This might be a wonderful opportunity for a congregation to explore liturgical resources from another, minority community, not only as a way to repent for the sin of cultural superiority, but also to open the eyes of our hearts to see God at work in worlds we don't know about.

Adult baptism is most appropriately observed during Easter, so utilizing the Season of Lent as a time to prepare adult catechumens is especially appropriate. The *Book of Occasional Services* is filled with wonderful resources that can help to make this moment really meaning both for the congregation and the individual catechumens.

Space

As with Advent, adjusting the space where possible can help to dial up the distinctiveness of this season. Veiling crosses and other religious imagery (statuary, iconography, and so on) might also help to draw our focus to the way that sin prevents us from seeing God with greater clarity. The point is to draw a contrast between Lent and the Season of Easter that is to follow.

Other Rituals and Resource

A community might opt to observe Stations of the Cross during Lent. There are resources for this in the *Book of Occasional Services* as well as *Saint Augustine's Prayer Book*. Given that this service has so much flexibility, a nod towards creativity and innovation might help to make this service take on fresh meaning for a new community. It is also appropriate to more intentionally offer the Sacrament of Reconciliation to the community.

Through the Eyes of a Child

It can be tempting to want to shield younger people from the message of Lent; however, this would be unwise. Children are capable of engaging difficult topics and often the refusal to allow them to engage and wonder about tough topics speaks more to an insecurity on behalf of their guardians. Teaching skills like reflection, asking for and receiving forgiveness, and then extending that forgiveness to others are great life skills generally, and Christianity centers these practices as incredibly important.

Lent is also a time to empower parents to the primary agents of faith formation by giving them the tools to help their children develop a Lenten discipline. Maybe it is journaling, reading the Bible, writing notes and cards, or prayer daily. Whatever the practice, helping parents instill these values in their children will go a lot further in developing their spirituality than almost any other program the church can offer.

Lent is a time for forgiveness: looking at the things we have done that are wrong, asking God's and other people's forgiveness, and making a promise not to do them again. It is a time for giving up the things that keep us from being loving people; a time for doing extra things that will help us grow closer to God; a time to be more aware of what it means to love as God loves us; a time to ask God to help us to be more loving, remembering that God is always ready to strengthen us; and a time to think about our baptism and what it means to be a child of God. Encourage parents to help their child read the Bible every day. Invite them to reflect on the stories, particularly inviting reflection on the life of Jesus as he approaches the cross.

Through the Eyes of Youth

Communicating passion during the passion, the church is called to recognize Christ in the poor, the stranger at the gate; follow the Creed as rule of life; faithfully follow daily practices that imitate Christ for the sake of others; and explore the Penitential Order and how we can be reconciled within our families, our schools, our communities, our church. Demonstrating an outward and visible sign of Lenten participation, invite youth to lead a Lenten ingathering that serves the poor either in the church community or local areas. Invite the youth to serve at soup kitchens, at shelters, at the Salvation Army, or any other program or institution that serves the poor and hungry and homeless. Invite the youth to define evil and reflect upon the ways they see evil in the world and how the mission and ministry of the church responds. Offer overnight or day "retreats" for youth that include contemplation, reflection, and action.

Through the Eyes of Daily Life

Lent is a great time to encourage and stress the importance of the development of a spiritual life that goes beyond the outwardness of religion (hear Jesus' injunction from Ash Wednesday with new ears). Tools and resources should be created and distributed that help our faith communities understand how to develop a more vibrant spiritual life. The *Way of Love* materials from the Episcopal Church Evangelism Office and Church Publishing Incorporated are a great place to start.

The Season of Lent is marked by self-examination and repentance, culminating in the Rite of Reconciliation; by prayer and meditating on Holy Scripture; by fasting (not eating between sunrise and sunset on Fridays to remind us what food we need most for life); and by acts of self-denial, best understood as acts or positive practices that enhance an ever-growing and loving relationship with God. However, the main emphasis during Lent is for each person to prepare for the renewal of baptismal vows and covenant at the Easter vigil.

Through the Eyes of Those Outside of the Church

If the Church can invite people to be among us when we celebrate the joyous mysteries of Christ, how much more meaning might it hold if we invite people to be a part of us when we walk through the hard parts of our story, particularly because of how they resonate with the lived reality of a great many. Many people experience suffering—emotional, physical, economic, social/political—and how the Church explores these complex experiences might help the message of the Church land on new ears.

Through the Eyes of Our Global Community

Ethical issues are raised in the Litany of Penitence (BCP 267–269) during the Ash Wednesday liturgy:

- ◆ Exploitation of other people;
- ◆ Dishonesty in daily life and work;
- ◆ Indifference to injustice, human need, suffering, and cruelty;
- ◆ Prejudice and contempt toward those who differ from us;
- ◆ Waste and pollution of God's creation.

As we explore more fully the Baptismal Covenant and the covenant of the Torah during Lent, we become increasingly aware of how far we have strayed from God's ways.

Lent

Seasonal Rites for Lent

Lenten Blessings[1]

In Lent, in place of a seasonal blessing, a solemn Prayer over the People is used, as follows:

The Deacon or, in the absence of a deacon, the Celebrant says:
    Bow down before the Lord.
The people kneel and the Celebrant says one of the following prayers:

Ash Wednesday

Grant, most merciful Lord, to your faithful people pardon and peace, that they may be cleansed from all their sins, and serve you with a quiet mind; through Christ our Lord. *Amen.*

Lent 1

Grant, Almighty God, that your people may recognize their weakness and put their whole trust in your strength, so that they may rejoice for ever in the protection of your loving providence; through Jesus Christ our Lord. *Amen.*

Lent 2

Keep this your family, Lord, with your never-failing mercy, that relying solely on the help of your heavenly grace, they may be upheld by your divine protection; through Christ our Lord. *Amen.*

Lent 3

Look mercifully on this your family, Almighty God, that by your great goodness they may be governed and preserved evermore; through Christ our Lord. *Amen.*

Lent 4

Look down in mercy, Lord, on your people who kneel before you; and grant that those whom you have nourished by your Word and Sacraments may bring forth fruit worthy of repentance; through Christ our Lord. *Amen.*

Lent 5

Look with compassion, O Lord, upon this your people; that, rightly observing this holy season, they may learn to know you more fully, and to serve you with a more perfect will; through Christ our Lord. *Amen.*

Ash Wednesday Prayer[2]

The Lord God formed the human from the topsoil of the fertile land and blew life's breath into his nostrils. The human came to life. — Genesis 2:7

Almighty God,
you created us out of the dust of the earth,
and breathed life into us:
may the ashes of Ash Wednesday
be a sign that we are human
and will someday return to dust;
and may we always remember
that even though we will die,
you have promised us the gift of everlasting life.
Amen.

Lent

---

1 *Book of Occasional Services 2003* (New York: Church Publishing, 2004), 23–24.2.

2 Jenifer Gamber and Timothy J.S. Seamans. *Common Prayer for Children and Families* (New York: Church Publishing, 2019), 59.

Jesus in the Wilderness[3]

A Tableau Vivant

> *This tableau incorporates Psalm 91 and the hymn "Breathe on me, breath of God," for which the music is quietly played throughout and verses are printed in the bulletin.*
>
> *The beauties of a tableau vivant are that they are easy and quick to prepare, they can use actors of all ages, and the group of actors can come up with its own choreography, although some suggestions follow. In a tableau, worshipers close their eyes and the reading begins. While the reader is reading, the actors are creating a scene. They freeze, a bell is rung, the worshipers open their eyes and view the scene, in silence, for about ten seconds. The bell is rung again, the worshipers close their eyes again, the reader continues, and the actors get into their next scene, and so on.*
>
> *The more variety there is in terms of age, gender, posture, height, facial expression, arm positions, and placement of bodies, the more interesting and "real" will be the scene. Even a ladder works well for adding height dimension. Big facial expressions and creative use of hands add interest; you can't overdo it! Quiet music may be played during the tableau.*

Ring the bell, have worshipers close their eyes. The reader begins while the actors arrange themselves in the scene.

Reader 1: When Jesus was baptized, he came up out of the river, dripping with water, bursting with Spirit, and knowing himself as "Beloved," "Chosen." The Holy Spirit led him away from the Jordan and out toward the desert.

The bell is rung, and worshipers view the scene. Jesus is strong, upright, exuberant, confident, etc. After a few seconds, the people sing verse one, while Jesus remains frozen in his pose.

Breathe on me, breath of God. Fill me with life anew, that I may love what thou dost love and do what thou wouldst do.

The bell is rung, worshipers close their eyes; the reader and actors proceed as before.

Reader 1: He entered the desert to pray and to fast. He ate nothing at all for forty days and was famished, weary, and dry. He must have been terribly lonely. The cool, wet river seemed a distant dream. He remembered the psalms, and said them over and over.

The bell is rung, and worshipers view the scene. Now Jesus is in a whole other posture, defeated, weak, prayerfully imploring God for help.

Reader 2: Whoever dwells in the shelter of the Most High abides under God's shadow, and will say, "You, God, are my refuge, my stronghold; only you."

The bell is rung, worshipers close their eyes; the reader and actors proceed as before.

Reader 1: When Jesus' heart was very low and his body very weak, the devil came to him and said, "You don't really think you're God's son, do you? 'Beloved'? 'Chosen'? C'mon! . . . Well, then, prove it! Take this stone and turn it into bread."

The bell is rung, and worshipers view the scene. Jesus might be upright again, trying to resist the devil who is behind him, reaching to hold a stone in front of Jesus. They remain frozen while the readers continue.

Reader 1: But Jesus answered the devil with words from the Bible.

Reader 2: No one can live on just bread, and only God can fill us with the soul-food that lasts.

The bell is rung, worshipers close their eyes; the reader and actors proceed as before.

Reader 1: Then the devil led Jesus up to a high place and showed him all the kingdoms of the world. "I have power over all this," he said. "And I can give that power to you, if you'll bow down to me, and worship me." Jesus remembered the words of a psalm.

Reader 2: Whoever is bound to me in love will call upon my name, and that one I will answer, and rescue, and bring to honor. Not the honor of power, but the honor of my love.

The bell is rung, and worshipers view the scene. Jesus may be "sinking," that is, in a lower posture, perhaps of prayer, while the devil is standing upright, triumphant, powerful.

The people sing verse two of the hymn.

Breathe on me, breath of God, until my heart is pure, until with thee, I will one will, to do or to endure.

---

3 Susan K. Bock. *Liturgy for the Whole World* (New York: Church Publishing, 2008), 76

The bell is rung, worshipers close their eyes; the reader and actors proceed as before.

Reader 1: Then the devil took Jesus to Jerusalem, up to the top of the Temple, and said, "If you are God's son, then throw yourself down from here, for it is written (the devil knew words of the psalms, too, you see): 'God will command his angels to protect you. On their hands they will bear you up, so that you will not even scrape your foot against a stone.'" But Jesus answered the devil with words from the very same psalm.

The bell is rung, and worshipers view the scene. This scene should be elevated where people can see, as Jesus is at his lowest, weakest, neediest, most vulnerable point so far and the devil would be even lower, trying to look into his face.

Reader 2: Nothing evil shall happen to you. No plague shall come close to you. Even when you are near poisonous snakes and young lions, you shall be safe.

The bell is rung, worshipers close their eyes; the reader and actors proceed as before.

Reader 1: Jesus finally shut the devil up with more words from the Bible: "You shouldn't test God. You should trust God's love to always help you." So the devil gave up and left him alone. Jesus was exhausted and weak, but peaceful, and angels and wild beasts came to care for him.

The bell is rung, and worshipers view the scene. Jesus may be reclining among a group of ministering angels and beasts.

The people sing a last verse of the hymn.

Breathe on me, breath of God, till I am wholly thine, and all this earthly part of me glows with thy fire divine.

The bell is rung; the people close their eyes. The people could hum one more verse while the tableau disappears. When the bell is rung again, they open their eyes to a cleared "stage."

Reader 1: The Word of the Lord.

People: Thanks be to God.

The Catechumenate

Enrollment of Candidates for Baptism[4]

The enrollment of candidates for Baptism at the Great Vigil of Easter normally takes place on the First Sunday in Lent. After the Creed, the catechumens to be enrolled are invited to come forward with their sponsors. A book for them (and their sponsors) should be available to sign at the conclusion of this enrollment.

Catechist: I present to you these catechumens who have been strengthened by God's grace and supported by the example and prayers of this congregation, and I ask that *they* be enrolled as *candidates* for Holy Baptism.

Celebrant: Have they been regular in attending the worship of God and in receiving instruction?

Sponsors: They have. (*He* has.)

Celebrant: Are they seeking by prayer, study, and example to pattern their lives in accordance with the Gospel?

Sponsors: They are. (*He* is.)

Celebrant: As God is your witness, do you approve the enrolling of *these catechumens* as *candidates* for Holy Baptism?

Sponsors and the Congregation: They have. (*He* has.)

Celebrant: Do you desire to be baptized?

Catechumens: I do.

Celebrant: In the Name of God, and with the consent of this congregation, I accept you as candidates for Holy Baptism, and direct that your names be written in this book. God grant that they may also be written in the Book of Life.

Lent

---
4 *Book of Occasional Services,* 122–123.

Lent

Welcoming Those Who Are Preparing for the Reaffirmation of the Baptismal Covenant[5]

This rite is used at the principle Sunday Eucharist for those baptized persons who have returned to the life of the Church after a time away, from those baptized in other traditions, or those seeking to reaffirm their baptism at the Rite of Confirmation. This takes place at the time of the Prayers of the People.

Member of the Community: N., We present to you these persons *(or N., N.),* who are baptized members of the Body of Christ and we welcome them to our community as they undertake a process of growth in the meaning of their baptism.

Celebrant: (to each baptized person) What do you seek?

Renewal of my life to Christ.

Celebrant: In baptism, you died with Christ Jesus to the forces of evil and rose to new life as members of his Body. Will you study the promises made at your baptism, and strive to keep them in the fellowship of this community and the rest of the Church?

I will, with God's help.

Celebrant: Will you attend the worship of God regularly with us, to hear God's word and to celebrate the mystery of Christ's dying and rising?

I will, with God's help.

Celebrant: Will you participate in a life of service to those who are poor, outcast, or powerless?

I will, with God's help.

Celebrant: Will you strive to recognize the gifts that God has given you and discern how they are to be used in the building up of God's reign of peace and justice?

I will, with God's help.

Celebrant: (to the sponsors/companions/friends) You have been chosen by this community to serve as companions to these persons. Will you support them by prayer and example and help them to grow in the knowledge and love of God?

We will, with God's help.

Celebrant: (to the congregation) Will you who witness this new beginning keep *(N., N.)* in your prayers and help them, share with them your ministry, bear their burdens, and forgive and encourage them?

We will, with God's help.

In full view of all, the baptized write their names in the church's register of baptized persons.

Celebrant: (extending both hands toward the baptized, with sponsors placing a hand on the candidates' shoulders) Blessed are you, our God, our Maker, for you form us in your image and restore us in Jesus Christ. In baptism, N., N., were buried with Christ and rose to new life in him. Renew them in your Holy Spirit, that they may grow as members of Christ. Strengthen their union with the rest of his Body as they join us in our life of praise and service; through our Savior, Jesus Christ, who lives and reigns with you and the Holy Spirit, now and for ever.

Amen.

Celebrant: Please welcome the new members of the community.

We recognize you as members of the household of God. Confess the faith of Christ crucified, proclaim his resurrection, and share with us in his eternal priesthood.

A Prayer for Trying to Quit Drinking (or Anything Else)[6]

This is a short prayer for anyone who might find it helpful. If you notice nothing else, pay attention to this: God is known in these prayers as loving and gracious and named as the power that is always faithful to deliver us from our pain into abundant life

Loving God, I arrive to you in a space of my heart that only you have known, that great space of trying, the hole where I harbor my utmost sense of failure. I ask for your deliverance from the pain I'm facing, the pain I have faced before, the pain I fear I will face again. My heart is willing; my flesh is weak. May you, who entered the world to know the trials of being in a body, be present to me, strengthening me in my weakness, securing me in my willingness, reminding me in my perceived failure that there is no failure in the love of Jesus Christ. Amen.

---

5 Ibid. 140–141.

6 This prayer was developed by Rev. Erin Jeane Warde of *Discerning Sobriety*, and can be found at www.erinjeanewarde.com.

From the shame of another drink,

> *Good Lord, deliver me.*

From the regret of things I have said,

> *Good Lord, deliver me.*

From the anxiety of what I have done and cannot remember,

> *Good Lord, deliver me.*

For the ways I have mistreated those I love,

> *Good Lord, forgive me.*

For the urgencies I have neglected,

> *Good Lord, forgive me.*

For the opportunities for compassion I missed,

> *Good Lord, forgive me.*

Of the ways I have treated my body,

> *Good Lord, heal me.*

Of the assaults on my mind,

> *Good Lord, heal me.*

Of the hopelessness I assume as a way of life,

> *Good Lord, heal me.*

Gracious God, You knit us into our lives, each breath a thread bound to an inseparable grace. In the thread of this day, fasten us to your hope, that we may, with awareness of your faithfulness to us, be delivered from our afflictions. *Amen.*

World Day of Prayer

Friday, March 3

Sponsored by Church Women United, a Christian group of women that strives to work for justice and peace, the origin of World Day of Prayer dates back to 1887, when Mary Ellen Fairchild James, a Methodist from Brooklyn, NY called for a day of prayer for home missions. Each year, Church Women United selects a women's group from different parts of the world, to write a prayer service for the day. Then, everyone, men and women alike, are encouraged to attend a prayer service using what the group wrote. The theme for 2023 is "I Have Heard about Your Faith" and will be written by the World Day of Prayer Committee of Zimbabwe based on Ephesians 1:15-19. The prayer service will be available here: http://worlddayofprayer.net/index.html

International Women's Day

Wednesday, March 8

Grant, O God, that all may recognize women as equal partners in creation and prophesy. By the grace of the Holy Spirit, empower women at home, at work, in government, and in the hierarchies of churches, temples, mosques, synagogues, and all other places of worship. Provide safety and protection, O Gracious Divinity, and inspire just laws against all forms of violence against women. We ask this through Christ our Savior. *Amen.*[7]

World Water Day

Wednesday, March 22

Held annually as a means of focusing attention on the importance of freshwater and advocating for the sustainable management of freshwater resources, the UN General Assembly proclaimed 2018-2028 as the International Decade for Action.[8]

Learn more: https://www.un.org/en/events/waterdecade/

We thank you, Almighty God, for the gift of water. Over it your Holy Spirit moved in the beginning of creation. Through it you led the children of Israel out of their bondage . . . In it your Son Jesus received the Baptism of John and was anointed by the Holy Spirit as the Messiah, the Christ, to lead us, through his death and resurrection, from the bondage of sin into everlasting life. (BCP, 306)

Lent

---

7 "Equal Partners" by Chris Knight. *Lifting Women's Voices: Prayers to Change the World* Margaret Rose, Jenny Te Paa, Jeanne Person, Abagail Nelson, editors. (New York: Morehouse Publishing, 2009), 101-102.

8 Learn more at www.unwater.org/what-we-do/inspire-action/ (accessed March 28, 2018).

Ash Wednesday

February 22, 2023

God hates nothing he has made and forgives us when we are truly repentant. We ask God to give us new and contrite hearts, asking for God's perfect forgiveness through Jesus Christ our Lord.

Color
Violet / Lenten Array

Preface
Of Lent

Collect

Almighty and everlasting God, you hate nothing you have made and forgive the sins of all who are penitent: Create and make in us new and contrite hearts, that we, worthily lamenting our sins and acknowledging our wretchedness, may obtain of you, the God of all mercy, perfect remission and forgiveness; through Jesus Christ our Lord, who lives and reigns with you and the Holy Spirit, one God, for ever and ever. *Amen.*

Readings and Psalm

Joel 2:1–2, 12–17

In our Hebrew Bible reading the prophet pictures the day of the Lord as a time of judgment and darkness, but he holds out the hope of mercy if the people will repent. Some looked to the day of the Lord's coming as an event of great triumph and joy in Israel. But because of sin the sky will become black with swarms of locusts. The trumpet must be blown, calling for a solemn fast, a time for weeping, rending of hearts, and turning back to a compassionate Lord.

or

Isaiah 58:1–12

The lesson from the Hebrew Bible is a denunciation of the injustices of those who only act at their religion. There is a promise of the Lord's favor for those who genuinely repent and care for the needy. Fasts and many prayers are of no purpose and may be misused if they do not involve the liberation of the oppressed and help for the weak and afflicted. When there is justice and sharing, then the light of the Lord will rise out of the darkness and all the ruins will be rebuilt.

Psalm 103 or 103:8–14

A juxtaposition of God's enduring faithfulness with the temporary nature of human life.

2 Corinthians 5:20b–6:10

In this lesson Paul urges the new disciples to be reconciled to God in this time of deliverance, and he reminds them of all the hardships he has patiently endured for their sake and for the gospel. The disciples' task is to respond to God's reconciling work in Christ who has taken upon himself their sinfulness so that they might have a right relationship with God. In order that he might offer his service without presenting any personal obstacles, Paul has accepted many of the paradoxes that were part of Jesus' own ministry. Although himself poor, he brings true riches to many.

Matthew 6:1–6, 16–21

In our gospel Jesus describes genuine charity, prayer, and fasting. For religious people the temptation is always strong to want to be recognized as full of piety more than to want honestly to be seeking God and the good of others. Praise and rewards for an outward show of religion all pass away. The real treasure is found in our relationship with God.

Images in the Readings

Although cited only in the reading from Isaiah 58, **ashes** are the primary image for the day. Since the eleventh century, the ashes, made by burning last year's palms, cycle around from the triumphant celebration of Jesus' entry into Jerusalem to the humiliation of sinners covering their heads with the burnt greens. Ashes also bring to mind the fire of the Easter Vigil. Honesty is always good, if sometimes painful: this day we are honest about sin and death. The ash cross marks one's forehead as if it is the brand of one's owner. We journey forward wearing the sign of the cross.

The gospel reading is the source for the three **disciplines of Lent** that have proved useful for many of Christ's disciples. To increase one's giving to the poor, to intensify one's rituals of prayer, and to decrease one's focus on the self: the idea is that such disciplines open up the self to God and to the neighbor.

The **acceptable time**, the day of salvation, are ways Paul describes the here and now of the life of the baptized. Ash Wednesday calls us each day into life in Christ.

Several beloved hymns call Christ our **treasure**. The treasure described in both Matthew and Paul—"poor, yet making many rich"—is the countercultural value of the baptized life.

Ideas for the Day

- In *Goodnight iPad* by Ann Droyd, a parody of the classic picture book *Goodnight Moon*, the grandmother says goodnight to all of her family's electronic devices in order that her family can sleep for an evening. The action of turning off (or turning from) that which distracts us is so simple and so hard. At times we need others to support such actions. Ash Wednesday invites us to reflect on our humanity ("You are dust and to dust you shall return") and wonder where in our lives we need to turn off or turn from distraction in order to turn back to God.

- The Isaiah reading calls the people to fast by outward acts of justice and mercy rather than in ritualistic fashion. It reminds us of the kind of life the covenant calls us to. We act out our commitment to God in a life leading toward justice and liberation for every person. Just as in the gospel, we practice piety as a means of sharing God's love, not as an outward sign of virtue.

- We are humbled in the act of kneeling and accepting the imposition of ashes. We can no longer take life for granted or assume that the world was created just for us. Only from this humble stance can we move to the next step in the Ash Wednesday liturgy and review the ways we have "strayed from thy ways like lost sheep."

Making Connections

Jesus is clear: don't disfigure your face when you fast! But we do it anyway, wearing smudges of ash on our foreheads for all to see. Yes or no? I say yes. People see it as they pass you on the sidewalk. Some of them need desperately to know they belong to Christ and to a community. Some haven't felt like they belonged to anything in years. They know all too well about their own weakness. "Oh, right," they think, "Ash Wednesday." They know all about dust. The smudge on your forehead tells them they are not the only ones.

Engaging All Ages

An Ash Wednesday experiment: Find some large marshmallows, a stick, and a safe (but open) flame—outdoor fire pits are good for this. Char that marshmallow until it is black. Once the marshmallow has cooled enough, peel off the charred outer skin, noticing how easy it slips away. What do you notice about the innards of the once solid puffy snack? That's right—it is now gooey. What choices can you make that will help you to peel away things in your life that make it hard to connect with Jesus or others in a loving manner this Lenten season?

Hymns for the Day

Note: There is no Entrance Hymn on this day (see BCP, 264).

The Hymnal 1982
Eternal Lord of love, behold your Church 149
O bless the Lord, my soul! 411
The glory of these forty days 143
Before thy throne, O God, we kneel 574, 575
Kind Maker of the world, O hear 152
Lord Jesus, Sun of Righteousness 144
Creator of the earth and skies 148
Lord, whose love through humble service 610
Now quit your care 145
O day of God, draw nigh 600, 601
Lead us, heavenly Father, lead us 559
God himself is with us 475
Jesus, all my gladness 701

Lift Every Voice and Sing II
Bless the Lord, O my soul 65
Come, ye disconsolate 147
Close to thee 122
Give me a clean heart 124
In God we trust 55
I've decided to make Jesus my choice 68

Wonder, Love, and Praise
Almighty Lord Most High draw near 888
Bless the Lord, my soul 825
Gracious Spirit, give your servants 782

Lent

The First Sunday in Lent

February 26, 2023

Saying "no" to evil so that the Christian can say "yes" to Christ.

Lent

Color Violet / Lenten Array

Preface Of Lent

Collect

Almighty God, whose blessed Son was led by the Spirit to be tempted by Satan: Come quickly to help us who are assaulted by many temptations; and, as you know the weaknesses of each of us, let each one find you mighty to save; through Jesus Christ your Son our Lord, who lives and reigns with you and the Holy Spirit, one God, now and for ever. *Amen.*

Readings and Psalm

Genesis 2:15–17; 3:1–7

God placed a prohibition on the tree "of the knowledge of good and evil" (2:17), which represents the wisdom of conscience that comes not intellectually but by experience. Adam and Eve sought independence, the freedom to define for themselves what was good and what was evil apart from God's wisdom. Chapter 3 recounts the rebellion against God's prohibition. The temptation progresses from doubt about what God has said, through suspicion of God's motive, to awareness of the possibility of independence. The primary sin here is disobedience, which leads to the disordering of all relationships—with one's own body, with God, with one another, with nature, within families, and within societies.

Psalm 32

Psalm 32 is a prayer of thanksgiving for God's forgiveness. It divides naturally into six sections tracing the pattern of reconciliation: verses 1–2 are an introduction; verses 3–4 express the weight of guilt; verse 5 is a confession of sin; verses 6–7 offer sound advice; in verses 8–9, God speaks; in verses 10–11, the psalmist rejoices in his changed status before God.

Romans 5:12–19

In this rather complicated passage, Paul deals with the universal human condition of sin and death and its relationship to the gift of grace. The free gift of righteousness, a right relationship, does not merely undo sin and death and return humanity to Eden, but offers incomparable grace and life. The role of the law was to point out the measureless mercy of God by measuring sinfulness.

Matthew 4:1–11

Matthew's account of Jesus' temptation works out the implications of the voice present at Jesus' baptism, declaring him to be the Son of God. For Matthew, sonship is manifested in perfect obedience to God's will. The mountain and the ministry of angels also point to Jesus as Messiah. Jesus has manifested the perfect obedience that he teaches his disciples and has shown the Church how to respond to temptations concerning the power entrusted to the Church.

Prayers of the People

We do not live by bread alone, but by every word that comes from the mouth of God. Let us pray to the source of our sustenance, saying, "God, our hiding place, *preserve us from trouble.*"

Great God, you have called your people to worship and serve you alone. Instill in us such a singleness of heart that we might perfectly trust you to meet our needs.

Invite the congregation to add their thanksgivings, followed by silence

God, our hiding place,

Preserve us from trouble.

Great God, we live among many temptations. Free the people of this nation, and this world, from all sinful desires that draw us from the love of God.

Silence

God, our hiding place,

Preserve us from trouble.

Great Creator, you have surrounded us with blessings; you provide enough to meet our needs. And yet, we strive and scheme for more, always more. Have mercy on us.

Silence

God, our hiding place,

Preserve us from trouble.

O Lord, we pray for those bound by addiction, those for whom temptation is a constant threat. Set the captive free. Satisfy their cravings with abundant grace.

Silence

God, our hiding place,

Preserve us from trouble.

Be with the sick and suffering, Great Healer. Be for them a hiding place; preserve them from trouble; surround them with shouts of deliverance.

Invite the congregation to add their petitions, followed by silence

God, our hiding place,

Preserve us from trouble.

Through the righteousness of Jesus our Christ, give new and abundant life to all. Justify the dying and the dead. Keep them in your strong hands for ever.

Silence

God, our hiding place,

Preserve us from trouble.

Images in the Readings

Matthew writes that Jesus fasted for **forty days and forty nights.** In the Bible, forty is always the time between, the necessary span before the gracious conclusion. It is forty, days or years, that numbers the rain of Noah's flood, Moses on Mount Sinai, Israel in the wilderness, the spies scouting out Canaan, Israel in the hands of the Philistines, the taunting by Goliath, the reign of Saul, David, and Solomon, Ezekiel lying on his right side, Nineveh's repentance, and Jesus' appearance after Easter. For us, it is forty days until the celebration of the resurrection.

The **Tree of Knowledge of Good and Evil**—a stark contrast with the wondrous Tree of Life that appears again in Revelation 22—is a fascinating, ambiguous symbol, perhaps signifying the human tendency to replace God's way with one's own way, God's word with human knowledge. It is a mystery tree that according to the story represents all that is wrong in human life.

Who initiated sin? In Genesis it is **the woman,** in Paul it is **Adam**—characters whom we recognize as being essentially ourselves. The storyteller of Genesis 3 joined with many others in antiquity by blaming the woman for all the troubles of humanity. In accord with a Christian theological interpretation of this story, all people are Adam, creatures of earth, and all people are Eve, bearers of life.

The gospel describes the **devil** as the tempter, the power that seeks to lure us away from God. It is this devil that much Christian tradition has used to explain the talking serpent of Genesis 3. The tradition of art has not given us profound enough depictions of this primordial evil, but in the usual image of a creature part human, part monster, we can see another picture of ourselves.

Lent

Lent

Ideas for the Day

- For many, the story of Adam and Eve is loaded with the baggage of "original sin," shame, and blame, which do more harm than good. What would it look like to instead ground today's sacred stories of temptation and sin in the knowledge that we are all beloved children of God? Sin, most simply defined, is that which separates us from the love of God. What would it feel like to turn away from shame and reflect on what separates you from the love of God?

- The gospel points up the contrast between Adam (representing humankind) and Jesus. Jesus is tempted in the wilderness, but he does not fall into sin. We need to realize that this account of the temptation of Jesus is symbolic and poetic. Jesus was undoubtedly tempted all his life. The painful reality of that temptation is expressed profoundly in the wilderness scene. But Jesus did not give in to temptation; he reversed the story and destiny of Adam and Eve in the garden.

- During Lent in Year A, the readings provide a primer in Christianity as outlined in Paul's letters to the Romans and Ephesians. These epistle readings pick up the theme from Hebrew scripture readings and the gospel.

Making Connections

Right after Jesus is baptized, the devil is waiting for him. Notice that the Spirit drives him into the wilderness, but it is the devil who tempts him there. So, should Jesus not have gone? Does the presence of temptations and obstacles mean you're on the wrong path? Is it a sign that you're in the wrong place? No. It just means you've got work to do. In the wilderness, we both encounter God and reveal ourselves. In the wilderness, there is nowhere to hide. In the wilderness, we can't avoid our holy and difficult work.

Engaging All Ages

Rough camping can be a good Lenten practice. If you can't get far away, camping for one night in the backyard or maybe camping out in your living room will work. Strip away some of the comforts and conveniences (often taken for granted) in order to connect and meditate on the story of the Israelites in the desert, Jesus in the wilderness, and those who find themselves displaced from home and shelter. Sleep on the ground. Eat bread and water, or rice and water. Use no electricity to heat or cool. Use no devices. What do you notice?

Hymns for the Day

The Hymnal 1982

Creator of the earth and skies 148
Wilt thou forgive that sin, where I begun 140, 141
Praise to the Holiest in the height 445, 446
Forty days and forty nights 150
From God Christ's deity came forth 443
Lord, who throughout these forty days 142
Now let us all with one accord 146, 147
O love, how deep, how broad, how high 448, 449
The glory of these forty days 143

Lift Every Voice and Sing II
It is well with my soul 188
Sweet hour of prayer 178

Wonder, Love, and Praise

Weekday Commemorations

Monday, February 27
George Herbert, Priest 1633

This is what he preached: "Nothing is little in God's service." Herbert penned prose and poetry, describing the latter as "a picture of the many spiritual conflicts that have passed betwixt God and my soul . . ." Born in 1593, Herbert studied divinity as a young man; in 1626, he took Holy Orders. He served as rector of parishes in Fugglestone and Bemerton. According to Izaak Walton, his biographer, Herbert was a model of the saintly parish priest. He wrote *A Priest in the Temple: Or, The Country Parson: His Character and Rule of Holy Life* and *The Temple*; two of his poems, "Teach me, my God and King" and "Let all the world in every corner sing," became well-known hymns.

Tuesday, February 28
Julia Haywood Cooper, Educator, 1964

In 1870, Cooper, daughter of a Black slave and a free white, attended St. Augustine's, founded by the Episcopal Church to educate African American teachers and clergy. She became an Episcopalian and married one of the first African American Episcopal priests in North Carolina. Widowed, she moved to Washington, D.C., where she taught mathematics, advocated for African American women, and organized the Colored Women's League and the first Colored Settlement House. She challenged the church to support its African American members struggling under segregation. She received her doctorate in 1925 at 67 and lived to 105.

Wednesday, March 1
David, Bishop of Menevia, Wales, c. 544

Although David is held in reverence as the patron of Wales, little is known about the boy or the man. He was born in Menevia and founded a monastery near there, becoming abbot and, later, bishop. He wanted most of all to study and meditate in his monastery, but he was nearly dragooned to an assembly of bishops contesting a heresy. There, David was so eloquent that Archbishop Dubricius chose the young man to be his successor as Primate of Wales. David founded eleven more Welsh monasteries and also made a pilgrimage to Jerusalem. He filled his office as bishop with distinction as a scholar, administrator, and clergyman of moderation and courage.

Thursday, March 2
Chad, Bishop of Lichfield, 672

Ordained to the bishopric irregularly, that is, not following Roman Catholic custom, Chad appeared before Theodore, the new archbishop of Canterbury. Chad tendered his resignation, saying, "Indeed, I never believed myself worthy of it." Such humility prompted Theodore to re-ordain Chad and to appoint him Bishop of Mercia and Northumbria. Chad traveled his diocese by foot until Theodore commanded that he ride when needed. Chad was a devout administrator, who built a monastery at Barrow, near his see in Lichfield. Not three years after his ordination, Chad fell victim to the plague that killed many in his diocese. Of his death, the Venerable Bede wrote: "He joyfully beheld . . . the day of the Lord. . . ."

Friday, March 3
John and Charles Wesley, Priests, 1791, 1788

Born four years apart (John, 1703; Charles, 1707), the Brothers Wesley entwined their lives until their deaths, three years apart (Charles, 1788; John, 1791). They were the fifteenth and eighteenth children of Samuel, a rector of Epworth, Lincolnshire. They preached sermons and wrote theology, but they are best known through their hymns (Charles wrote more than six thousand). They were educated at Christ Church, Oxford, where they convened friends to adhere strictly to the discipline and worship of the prayer book (thus, they were called "Methodists"). They adhered confidently to the doctrine of the Church of England, which they loved. The schism of Methodists from the Church of England occurred after the deaths of the Wesleys.

The Second Sunday in Lent

March 5, 2023

Saying "yes" to Jesus.

Color   Violet / Lenten Array

Preface   Of Lent

Collect

O God, whose glory it is always to have mercy: Be gracious to all who have gone astray from your ways, and bring them again with penitent hearts and steadfast faith to embrace and hold fast the unchangeable truth of your Word, Jesus Christ your Son; who with you and the Holy Spirit lives and reigns, one God, for ever and ever. *Amen.*

Readings and Psalm

Genesis 12:1–4a

Abraham and his descendants are chosen to inherit a land, become a great nation, and mediate blessing to all the world. The story of Abraham shows how God acts in history through the responses of individuals and peoples. Abraham's decision to yield to the will of God no matter the sacrifice demonstrates the nature of the friendship he had with God.

Psalm 121

This psalm is in dialogue form, possibly between a group of worshippers and a priest, perhaps as a blessing at their arrival at or departure from the temple. The Lord, the Creator, will watch over the people day and night.

Romans 4:1–5, 13–17

Paul cites the example of Abraham to show that the concept of justification by faith is not contrary to the Hebrew Bible, but rather supported by it. In first-century Judaism, Abraham was held up as the ideal model of righteousness through works. Paul argues that Abraham's faith, his readiness to believe and act upon God's promise, was "reckoned to him as righteousness." It put him in a right relationship to God apart from works. The promised inheritance comes through faith to Abraham's true descendants, those who follow his example of faith.

John 3:1–17

Today's reading is taken from the first of John's lengthy expositions of Jesus' teachings. Two characteristic techniques are employed: the use of a question asked on the physical level and answered on the spiritual level, and the use of the questioner's misunderstanding. Nicodemus, a member of the Sanhedrin, comes to Jesus because of his interest in Jesus' works. Jesus seeks to draw him past these outward manifestations to a recognition of their inward significance. Jesus contrasts the realm of the Spirit, which is eternal and heavenly, with the realm of the flesh, which is earthly, weak and mortal (but not necessarily sinful). Both flesh and spirit make up human life, but the Spirit is life itself. The Greek and Hebrew words for wind also mean "spirit."

Prayers of the People

Behold, children of God, it is the Lord who watches over you. As people sent forth into the world, let us pray, saying, "Lord, bless us, *so that we may bless others.*"

Lord, preserve your Church from all evil. May we, who have been born of water and the Spirit, proclaim the kingdom of God in all the world.

Lent

Invite the congregation to add their thanksgiving, followed by silence

Lord, bless us,

So that we may bless others.

O God, may the leaders of the nations ever seek the truth. Open their hearts to true conversion and divine guidance.

Silence

Lord, bless us,

So that we may bless others.

Maker of heaven and earth, you have blessed us with a wondrous and dynamic creation. Protect us from its rage; comfort us by its tranquility. Give us eyes to see your handiwork in the world around us.

Silence

Lord, bless us,

So that we may bless others.

Lord, your eyes never close on your people. We thank you for your mindfulness of us and our community. Be our help and our safety.

Silence

Lord, bless us,

So that we may bless others.

You did not send your Son into the world to condemn the world, but in order that the world may see and experience your salvation. Bring wholeness to those who look to your Son for their help.

Invite the congregation to add their petitions, followed by silence

Lord, bless us,

So that we may bless others.

O God, who gives life to the dead and calls into existence the things that do not exist, keep the dying and the dead from this time forth and for evermore. Give eternal life to all those who trust in you.

Silence

Lord, bless us,

So that we may bless others.

Images in the Readings

John's language of being born again suggests the image of the **mother**. Historically, the church described itself as this mother and the font as the womb from which birth in God arises. Recently, also God is described as the mother who births a new creation. But birth is not easy, and Lent allows us forty days to reenvision that birth.

Abram's immigration to the land of promise offers the image of the **journey**. Lent provides forty days for the annual journey back to the mystery of the resurrection and the new life to which we are called. Paul's language of justification assumes that God is a **judge** who requires of us a life of righteousness.

That justification comes via faith does not eliminate the necessity for such a radical reorientation of the self before God. It is instructive to hold the image of judge next to that of the mother: each image is a nuance of the other.

Ideas for the Day

- Birth is messy, painful, loud, disruptive, and miraculous. Every episode of the BBC show *Call the Midwife* centers around a birth and the midwives who accompany the mother as she pushes her baby into the world. Not one of the babies is born of their own choosing, nor are they born alone. Their life is bestowed as a gift. When Jesus speaks of being born of the Spirit, what does that look like and feel like? Messy? Painful? Loud? Disruptive? Miraculous? How do we receive this gift? Who are the midwives accompanying birth of the Spirit?

- Abram had the faith to move to a strange, alien land. He could face the unknown. All ages know about fear in facing the unknown—how do we deal with our fears and anxieties? What does faith mean in our movement into new situations and new life?

- Faith leads us into relationship with God: "For God so loved the world that he gave his only Son, that whoever believes in him should not perish but have eternal life."

Making Connections

Most scriptural images of God are expressed in masculine terms, but not all of them. Here, Jesus images himself as a mother hen, gathering her chicks under her wings. Hmmm . . . now, when does a mother hen do that? All the time? No, only when danger is present. Usually, she is content to let them hop around the barnyard on their own, pecking at bugs and seeds. But her protection of them when they need it is fierce. You don't want to get in her way. She will endanger herself to save them. Her love is anything but soft.

Engaging All Ages

Look outside your window. What is happening with the weather, the trees or grasses, the sky, the animals? Is it bare or are things beginning to bud and turn green? Is there snow or a heat wave? The earth moves and shifts in seasons. So do our lives. Some seasons follow the expected schedule, but others take too long or pass too quickly. Lent is a season of turning, reorienting and centering our lives back on Jesus.

Sometimes this turning is easy, sometimes it is difficult and requires many tries. What action or attitude of Jesus do you need to turn back to?

Hymns for the Day

The Hymnal 1982
I to the hills will lift mine eyes 668
Now let us all with one accord 146, 147
Praise our great and gracious Lord 393
The God of Abraham praise 401
How firm a foundation, ye saints of the Lord 636, 637
I call on thee, Lord Jesus Christ 634
And now, O Father, mindful of the love 337
Lift high the cross 473
O love, how deep, how broad, how high 448, 449
The great Creator of the worlds 489
When Christ was lifted from the earth 603, 604

Lift Every Voice and Sing II
We've come this far by faith 208

Wonder, Love, and Praise

Weekday Commemorations

Tuesday, March 7
Perpetua and Felicity, Martyrs at Carthage, 202
Vibia Perpetua and her companions—Felicitas, Revocatus, Secundulus, and Saturninus—were martyred for their faith as Christians. Early in the third century, Emperor Septimius Severus decreed that everyone must sacrifice to his divinity. Perpetua could not and would not; she and her companions were arrested. In prison, Perpetua had visions. At her public hearing before the proconsul, she declared, "I am a Christian," even refusing entreaties of her father. On March 7, the troop was sent to the arena for mangling by a boar, bear, leopard, and a vicious cow. Perpetua exhorted the companions "to stand fast in the faith." Eventually, she guided the hand of the executioner sent to drive a sword through her throat.

Thursday, March 9
Gregory of Nyssa, Bishop and Theologian, c. 394
Born about 334 in Caesarea, a brother to Basil the Great, Gregory became besotted by Christ and his Passion. His faith was heartened when he was twenty by the transfer of relics of the Forty Martyrs of Sebaste, but he dismissed ministry to become a rhetorician like his father. Nevertheless, Basil convinced Gregory to become Bishop of Nyssa; ordination made Gregory miserable because he felt unworthy, knowing little of tact or budgets. Basil and Macrina, their sister, died in 379; his siblings' deaths opened the way for Gregory to develop as a philosopher and theologian (his *Great Catechism* is one of his most respected treatises). In 381, Gregory was honored as a "pillar of the church."

The Third Sunday in Lent

March 12, 2023

The baptismal waters become for the Christian "a spring of water gushing up to eternal life." (John 4:14)

Color   Violet / Lenten Array

Preface   Of Lent

Collect

Almighty God, you know that we have no power in ourselves to help ourselves: Keep us both outwardly in our bodies and inwardly in our souls, that we may be defended from all adversities which may happen to the body, and from all evil thoughts which may assault and hurt the soul; through Jesus Christ our Lord, who lives and reigns with you and the Holy Spirit, one God, for ever and ever. *Amen.*

Readings and Psalm

Exodus 17:1–7

This is the second story about thirst and water in Exodus (see also 15:22–27). For people living in an arid land, thirst was a powerful metaphor for a human's need for God. Moses now uses the staff that made the Nile foul to bring forth clean water. Israel's murmuring is a constant feature of the Exodus narratives. This incident at Massah (meaning "test") and Meribah (meaning "quarrel") became a byword for Israel's faithlessness.

Psalm 95

This psalm, like Psalm 81, outlines a liturgy celebrating God's kingship. It was probably used at the great autumnal New Year's festival. The first section (vv. 1–7a) is a processional hymn in two parts. One part is sung in the temple court, praising God as Creator (vv. 1–5), and the other marks the entry into the sanctuary, praising God as Lord of the covenant people. In the second section of the psalm (vv. 7b–11), the people are cautioned against repeating the disobedience and faithlessness of their ancestors.

Romans 5:1–11

Paul uses two metaphors to describe God's redeeming act in Christ: justification, the ending of a legal dispute, and reconciliation, the termination of a state of enmity. Christ's sacrifice demonstrates God's justifying, reconciling love for us. The work of salvation was begun in Christ's ministry, death, and resurrection and is now operative through the Holy Spirit. Whereas justification marks the beginning of this process, salvation marks its future completion. We enter more fully into salvation by participating in Christ's risen life and by anticipating a share in God's glory.

John 4:5–42

This is the second discourse in John on the meaning of Jesus as the revelation of God. The Samaritans were descendants of the peoples settled by the Assyrians in the northern area after the fall of Israel (721 BCE). These early settlers worshiped other gods as well as Yahweh. After the Jews returned from exile, enmity with the Samaritans developed and persisted. Though later the Samaritans worshiped Yahweh alone, they had their own center of worship on Mount Gerizim. The woman first recognizes Jesus as the prophet-like-Moses, the figure in whom the Samaritans centered their messianic expectations. She brings up the dispute over the proper place of worship, but Jesus' answer focuses on the important issue—on the response to God's gift of life. Jesus' reply finally invites the woman to acknowledge him as the Messiah.

Lent

Prayers of the People

Come, let us bow down, and bend the knee, and kneel before the Lord our Maker. With thankful hearts, let us pray to the Lord saying, "Great God and King, *hear our prayer.*"

Lord, give us eyes to see that the fields are ripe for harvesting. May the Church reap what has been sown by our forebears and sow the seeds that will bring forth the fruit of the future.

Silence

Great God and King,

Hear our prayer.

Lord, reveal the strength of your love to those around the world who are asking, "Is the Lord among us or not?" We pray for comfort and peace for all people.

Silence

Great God and King,

Hear our prayer.

Lord, you hold the caverns of the earth and the heights of the hills; your hands have formed the seas and the dry land. Bless and keep your creation.

Silence

Great God and King,

Hear our prayer.

Lord, where there is suffering in our city, produce endurance; where there is endurance, produce character; where there is character, produce hope. And where we place our hope in you, let us not be disappointed.

Silence

Great God and King,

Hear our prayer.

Lord, we pray for those who are sick or suffering. Give them that living water that comes only through your Son Jesus Christ, that their needs may be met and all their thirsts quenched.

Invite the congregation to add their petitions and thanksgivings, followed by silence

Great God and King,

Hear our prayer.

Lord, we pray for the dying and the dead. We pray in the assurance that all have been reconciled to you through the death of your Son and saved by his new life.

Silence

Great God and King,

Hear our prayer.

Images in the Readings

The primary image for this Sunday is **water**. Water: that life as we know it on earth requires water is perhaps the reason that water figures in countless stories in all cultures, stories of rivers and seas, wells and rain. The Bible is overflowing with water stories, some of which we will hear at the Easter Vigil. In our time, daily showers, public fountains, swimming pools, and water parks provide society with the refreshment of water. Yet we are told that the next world wars will be over water, and current Christian ecologists urge care for the waters of the earth. In medieval Christian art, a picture of Moses striking the rock so that water can flow was set next to a depiction of Christ on the cross being pierced with the sword, as the water of life flowed from his side.

Another image for the day is the **rock**. In the Psalms, God is called Rock twenty-two times. That water can flow from rock provides us with a double image for God.

Ideas for the Day

♦ Knowing someone's reputation is different from knowing that person. The conversation between Jesus and the Samaritan woman, whom society at the time did not believe should interact, is challenging, honest, and breaks through facades. It is Jesus' longest conversation in the Bible. Jesus truly sees the Samaritan woman beyond her reputation and offers her living water—both are holy gifts. Afterward the Samaritan woman shares with her people her experience with Jesus. We all need to be truly seen. We all need living water. What assumptions get in our way?

♦ The concept that lies behind the Old Testament readings during Lent is the idea of a quest or journey. God is always calling us into a new land and into new adventures. We resist, yet we long to move on. There is tension and tragedy in our response. Our own individual lives are filled with stories of being in the wilderness and the decisions that have come out of them. What have the signs been? Where are we moving now?

♦ Today's gospel could be centered on water, refreshment, faith, and the meaning of baptism. In baptism we recognize that water is still a sign of God's power and presence with us. Can we recognize ourselves with the Israelites in their demand for signs? How are the Eucharist and other sacraments signs of God's presence?

Making Connections

Jesus talks about a terrible accident at the Tower of Siloam as if we knew about it. It must have been something everyone knew about, that local headline lost to us. The same goes for the Galileans massacred in or near the temple—everyone knew about it. We have headlines of our own. Why didn't he stop off for a coffee and miss the moment when the planes hit? Why did she reschedule the meeting in the south tower for that morning? Did they deserve to die? No. But they did die unprepared. Take stock now. We may not have tomorrow.

Engaging All Ages

Frequently this time of year is when gardeners begin to work in earnest to prepare for their spring and summer gardens. They begin to clean out the greenhouse, repair tools, and brush cobwebs off their mucking boots and wheelbarrows. They order mulch and turn the compost pile. They also begin "starting seeds" in tiny paper pots with no more than three tablespoons of soil, often setting them under heat lamps to begin their germination process. Consider starting some seeds of your own or think about what spiritual tools might need cleaning.

Hymns for the Day

The Hymnal 1982
To God with gladness sing 399
Come, thou fount of every blessing 686
Glorious things of thee are spoken 522, 523
Guide me, O thou great Jehovah 690
O Food to pilgrims given 308, 309
O God, unseen yet ever near 332
Rock of ages, cleft for me 685
Shepherd of souls, refresh and bless 343
Surely it is God who saves me 678, 679
Hail, thou once despised Jesus 495
O Love of God, how strong and true 455, 456
There is a balm in Gilead (vs. 1–2) 676
You, Lord, we praise in songs of celebration 319
As longs the deer for cooling streams 658
Draw nigh and take the Body of the Lord 327, 328
I heard the voice of Jesus say 692
In your mercy, Lord, you called me 706
Jesus, Lover of my soul 699
O Jesus, joy of loving hearts 649, 650
O love that casts out fear 700
The first one ever, oh, ever to know 673

Lift Every Voice and Sing II
Come, thou fount of every blessing 111
There is a balm in Gilead (vs. 1–2) 203
Jesus, Lover of my soul 79
Grant me a blessing 166

Wonder, Love, and Praise
Camina, pueblo de Dios /
    Walk on, O people of God 739
As panting deer desire the waterbrooks 727

Lent

Lent

Weekday Commemorations

Monday, March 13
James Theodore Holly, Bishop of Haiti and of the Dominican Republic, 1911
Born a free Black, Holly was ordained a deacon in Detroit in 1855 and a priest in Connecticut in 1856. That year, he founded an antecedent to the Union of Black Episcopalians. He and Frederick Douglass worked together to promote the "extension of the church among colored people." Holly took his ministry to Haiti, where his wife, mother, and two children died. Holly continued to speak of God's love to Haitians. To build the church in Haiti, Holly was consecrated a missionary bishop in 1874, becoming the first African American bishop in the Episcopal Church.

Wednesday, March 15
Vincent de Paul, Priest, 1660, and
Louise de Marillac, Vowed Religious, 1660
In 1633, Vincent and Louise founded The Sisters of Charity of Saint Joseph (later the Company of the Daughters of Charity of Saint Vincent De Paul), the first non-cloistered religious order dedicated to acts of charity. Its charism is to found hospitals, orphanages, and schools. The Daughters of Charity influenced the nineteenth-century revival of religious orders within Anglicanism. Vincent came from peasant farmers in Gascony, was kidnapped and enslaved. He preached the Gospel to a master's wife, thus beginning his ministry. As it grew, Vincent depended on the widow Louise de Marillac to superintend the ministry to the poor and hungry and to lead the sisterhood.

Friday, March 17
Patrick of Ireland, Bishop and Missionary, 461
Patrick was born in a Christian family on the northwest coast of Britain about 390. As a teen, Patrick was kidnapped to Ireland and forced to serve as a shepherd; as a young man, he escaped back to Britain, where he was educated as a Christian and took holy orders. A vision returned him to Ireland about 432. Patrick's missions of conversion throughout Ireland continued until his death. He adapted pagan traditions to Christian: he had Christian churches built on sites considered sacred; he had crosses carved on druidic pillars; and he reassigned sacred wells to Christian status.
"St. Patrick's Breastplate," while attributed to him, is probably not his except as it expresses his zeal.

Saturday, March 18
Cyril of Jerusalem, Bishop and Theologian, 386
Holy Week: brought to you by Cyril. Also, Lent and inquirers' classes. Born in Jerusalem about 315, he became a bishop there around 349. He was banished and restored to this post three times due to disputes in church and state. Early in his episcopate, Cyril wrote *Catechetical Lectures*, comprising an introduction and eighteen catecheses based on the articles of the creed of the Church of Jerusalem. Likely, Cyril instituted observances of Palm Sunday and Holy Week as a practical way to organize devotions for locals and pilgrims around Jerusalem's sacred sites. Most likely, pilgrims took the practices home with them, exploiting the liturgies' development throughout the Church, as still seen in the 1979 Book of Common Prayer.

The Fourth Sunday in Lent

March 19, 2023

The Christian is given the gift of enlightenment through the Holy Spirit.

Color   Violet / Lenten Array or Rose

Preface   Of Lent

Collect

Gracious Father, whose blessed Son Jesus Christ came down from heaven to be the true bread which gives life to the world: Evermore give us this bread, that he may live in us, and we in him; who lives and reigns with you and the Holy Spirit, one God, now and for ever. *Amen.*

Readings and Psalm

1 Samuel 16:1–13

Prior to today's reading, God had already rejected Saul as king because of his disobedience and had indicated that another had been chosen. In grief and fear, Samuel refuses to see Saul again. Unlike Saul, Samuel waits for God's instructions and follows them precisely. These instructions seem to run contrary even to what Samuel might have expected. God teaches him that human wisdom does not penetrate the depths that God's wisdom does. David, unlike his predecessor, Saul, had found the secret of life: doing God's will.

Psalm 23

This psalm is probably the most familiar and popular psalm of all. It celebrates God's loving care for us under the guise of a good shepherd who provides food, security, and protection from all dangers. God guides us on our journey through life so that we might "dwell in the house of the Lord."

Ephesians 5:8–14

Today's reading comes from a section urging members of the Christian community to live out the reality of their new baptismal life, imitating God as known to them through Christ—forgiving, loving, and offering themselves. Gentile converts may have believed that physical actions were irrelevant to spiritual existence. Paul affirms that both words and deeds give evidence of new life.

John 9:1–41

The belief in a causal relationship between sin and suffering was widespread, but Jesus turns the attention from cause to purpose—the manifestation of God's works through Jesus' ministry. The interrogations that the healed man and his parents undergo become in effect a trial of Jesus. The increasing insight of the man is contrasted with the hardening blindness of the Pharisees. The man, who is not afraid to confess his ignorance, progresses from seeing Jesus as a man to seeing him as a prophet, then asserting that Jesus must be from God, and finally worshiping him as the Son of Man, through whom God would usher in the final era of judgment and salvation (v. 39). For the man born blind, his healing is more than sight regained. It is a new creation, a gift enabling him to see Jesus and believe in him.

Lent

Prayers of the People

Brothers and sisters, live as children of the light—for the fruit of the light is found in all that is good and right and true. Let us pray to the Lord, saying, "Light of the world, *open our eyes.*"

Lord our Shepherd, you have given your Church all that we need. Rain down on us mightily with your Spirit, that we may testify to the astonishing things you have done in our lives.

Invite the congregation to offer their thanksgivings, followed by silence

Light of the world,

Open our eyes.

God, you are present in the valley of the shadow of death. Comfort all those around the world who know danger or violence or war. By your love, cast out all evil and fear.

Silence

Light of the world,

Open our eyes.

Lord, you make us to lie down in green pastures; you lead us by still waters. You have blessed us with a beautiful planet. May we work to preserve the holy gift of nature.

Silence

Light of the world,

Open our eyes.

Lord, spread a table for those who are hungry; where there is scarcity and need in our neighborhoods, fill empty hearts, lives, and cups with your abundance. By your light expose all the unfruitful works of darkness.

Silence

Light of the world,

Open our eyes.

God of life, pursue the sick and sorrowful with your goodness and mercy. Reveal your works in those who are suffering. Make yourself known as Healer.

Invite the congregation to add their petitions, followed by silence

Light of the world,

Open our eyes.

Reviver of Souls, give to the dying and the dead your promise of new and unending life. May we one day live with them forever in the light of Christ.

Silence

Light of the world,

Open our eyes.

Images in the Readings

The primary image for the day is **light**. According to Genesis 1, light is the first creation of God. In John, Christ not only brings light, he is the very light of God. And so the synoptics describe the crucifixion as effecting an eclipse, and when Judas leaves the company for the betrayal, the author of John writes, "And it was night" (13:30). The Ephesians reading emphasizes that the light that is Christ is now the light within each believer.

Another image for the day is the **anointing**. In ancient times, and still today in the British monarchy, consecrated oil is poured on the head of the one chosen to lead. In some Christian churches, an anointing is a necessary part of the baptismal ritual.

What was dry and brittle is now limber with life.

David was a **shepherd**. According to Israelite memory, the people were nomadic herders before becoming urban dwellers. So David embodies the good old tradition, a more innocent time. Other ancient Near Eastern cultures also used the metaphor of the shepherd to describe their king. The sheep are the source of the people's life, and the shepherd ensures that livelihood.

Ideas for the Day

- So many questions! What happened? Whose fault is it? How is that possible? The man who was born blind can now see. Those who hold societal position cannot see. (Or can they?) Many of us have been taught, "There are no bad questions." Even if there are no bad questions, we sometimes do not hear the answers to the questions we are asking because they are not the answers we want to hear. We want answers that fit neatly within the way we know the world. Jesus and the formerly blind man answer each question in ways that point to God's action in the world.

- Through the anointing of the Holy Spirit at baptism, the Christian can see to follow Jesus. The early Church saw the healing of the man born blind as a metaphor of enlightenment: the Christian is called to see things differently.

- How do our goals for life stack up against the strange words of Jesus in today's gospel that were acted out in his own life and in the lives of the apostles? This is not a time for answering questions or resolving doubts. Rather, it is a time to raise questions. Everyone must find their own understanding of what the gospel proclaims, but we can do so only as our own views of life are challenged and confronted.

Making Connections

Notice that the elder son, angry at his father for welcoming his irresponsible brother back into the family, refers to him as "This son of yours." When the father explains, he takes aim at that: "This brother of yours was dead and has come to life." This son of yours. This brother of yours. One seeks to distance, while the other reminds us that—like it or not—we can't pretend those who have angered us don't exist. Someone may say, "He is dead to me." Not so. Our refusal to acknowledge another doesn't kill them. It only diminishes us.

Engaging All Ages

Lent is a season of simplicity—a season when we remind each other to depend on God and not on our "stuff" or accomplishments to bring us love or joy. In our churches we mark this season with a particular color and by changes around our altars and our buildings.

What changes have you noticed? Is there anything different about the cross(es), the altar, or the robes that people wear? What could you change in your home to reflect the simplicity of Lent? Are there material items that you are ready to part with?

Hymns for the Day

The Hymnal 1982
My Shepherd will supply my need 664
The King of love my shepherd is 645, 646
The Lord my God my shepherd is 663
God moves in a mysterious way 677
Seek the Lord while he wills to be found S217ff
Awake, O sleeper, rise from death 547
I want to walk as a child of the light 490
Lord Jesus, Sun of Righteousness 144
O splendor of God's glory bright 5
Christ, whose glory fills the skies 6, 7
Deck thyself, my soul, with gladness 339
Eternal light, shine in my heart 465, 466
God of mercy, God of grace 538
How wondrous and great thy works, God of praise! 532, 533
I'll praise my Maker while I've breath 429
I heard the voice of Jesus say 692
Lord God, you now have set your servant free 499
O for a thousand tongues to sing 493

Lift Every Voice and Sing II
The Lord is my shepherd 104
The Lord is my light 58

Wonder, Love, and Praise
So the day dawn for me 750
When from bondage we are summoned 753, 754
Lord, you have fulfilled your word 891

Lent

Lent

Weekday Commemorations

Monday, March 20
Cuthbert, Bishop, 687

Cuthbert, born about 625, entered a monastery after having a vision of angelic light and learning that Aidan of Lindisfarne had died at the time of this vision. Cuthbert was prior of Melrose Abbey from 651 to 664 and of Lindisfarne for a dozen years. He made it his habit to visit far-flung villages and to preach to the poor people who needed his discipline as a model to withstand the pull of the pagan. He became Bishop of Hexham in 684 but kept his see at Lindisfarne. Cuthbert was the most popular saint of the pre-conquest Anglo-Saxon church. Today, his relics and tomb remain at Durham.

Tuesday, March 21
Thomas Ken, Bishop, 1711

Born in 1637, Ken became known as a man of integrity during royal upheavals. He publicly rebuked the Prince of Orange's dastardly treatment of his wife and denied hospitality to the mistress of Charles II in 1683. In 1688, under James II, Ken refused to read the king's Declaration of Indulgence; he and his six cohorts were sent to the Tower, acquitted in court, then considered heroes. After the revolution of 1688, Ken refused to swear allegiance to William of Orange and so was deprived of his see. The accession of Queen Anne saw Ken in line again with the Church of England. He wrote the doxology that begins "Praise God from whom all blessings flow."

Thursday, March 23
Gregory the Illuminator,
Bishop and Missionary, c.332

Gregory, Apostle of the Armenians, was born about 257. Following his father's assassination of the Persian king, baby Gregory was removed to Caesarea in Cappadocia and raised as a Christian. He married and fathered two sons. About 280, he returned to Armenia and, after much effort, converted the king to Christianity, thereby ending paganism in his native land. About 300, Gregory was ordained a bishop at Caesarea; his cathedral at Valarshapat remains the center of Armenian Christianity. As the first nation-state to become officially Christian, Armenia set a precedent for adoption of Christianity by Emperor Constantine; as a buffer between empires in Rome and Persia, Armenia suffered through the vicissitudes of power and protection.

Friday, Tuesday, March 24
Óscar Romero, Archbishop and Martyr, 1980,
and the Martyrs of El Salvador

In and out of seminaries due to poverty, Romero (born in 1917 in San Salvador) was eventually sent to Rome to study theology. After ordination, he returned home to work among the poor. Appointed archbishop in 1977, Romero contended with radicals, who distrusted his conservative sympathies. He protested—even unto Pope John Paul II—the government's torturous injustice to the poor; he pled with America to stop military aid. Assassinated while celebrating Mass in 1980, Romero was canonized by the Roman Catholic Church in 2018. His fellow martyrs include Maryknoll and Ursuline sisters, Jesuit priests, and lay missioners and staff.

Saturday, March 25
The Annunciation of Our Lord Jesus Christ to
the Blessed Virgin Mary

Mary's willingness to assent to God's call paved the path for God to accomplish the salvation of the world. March 25 is the day to commemorate the story of how God made known to a young Jew that she was to be the mother of his son. Her acceptance is the reason generations have called her "blessèd." The Annunciation serves as a significant theme in the arts of the East and the West, a theme running through countless sermons and poems. The General Council of Ephesus in 451 affirmed the term, coined by Cyril of Jerusalem, for the Blessed Virgin: Theotokos ("the God-bearer"). Mary serves as God's human agent within the mystery of the Incarnation.

The Fifth Sunday in Lent

March 26, 2023

In baptism the Christian is freed from the tomb of sinfulness. Dry bones take on flesh and those who were dead are filled with the breath of God. The raising of Lazarus points ahead to the Resurrection.

Color Violet / Lenten Array

Preface Of Lent

Collect

Almighty God, you alone can bring into order the unruly wills and affections of sinners: Grant your people grace to love what you command and desire what you promise; that, among the swift and varied changes of the world, our hearts may surely there be fixed where true joys are to be found; through Jesus Christ our Lord, who lives and reigns with you and the Holy Spirit, one God, now and for ever. *Amen.*

Readings and Psalm

Ezekiel 37:1–14

Ezekiel's message of hope, addressed to the despairing exiles in Babylon, is founded on his vision of the valley of dry bones (vv. 1–11). Even as God shows Ezekiel the bones of those long dead lying dry and stripped of flesh, God promises renewal to Israel. In a radical act of new creation, not dependent on historical probability or on their moral or religious worthiness, the Lord will bring them out of the grave of Babylon to their home in Israel and put the Spirit in them. The vision is not of individual or even corporate resurrection, but of the community's restoration.

Psalm 130

This psalm is a lament, a plea for deliverance from unspecified trouble. The psalmist makes an implicit confession of sin (vv. 1–3), puts his trust in the Lord, and exhorts the community to do likewise.

Romans 8:6–11

In today's reading, Paul contrasts life in the flesh with life in the Spirit. Paul uses the "Spirit of God" (v. 9), the "Spirit of Christ" (v. 9) and "Christ in you" (v. 10) interchangeably. He emphasizes that the source of the Spirit is God, the full manifestation of the Spirit is in Christ, and that Christians experience the Spirit communally in the Body of Christ, the Church. The resurrection of Christ marked the beginning of the age to come. At the culmination of that age, death itself will be destroyed. Until then, through the Spirit, God brings that future into the present and Christians begin to live in their new life.

John 11:1–45

John here combines a miracle narrative and a teaching dialogue. The result makes clear the meaning of this last and greatest of Jesus' signs revealing "the glory of God" (v. 40), God's presence in the person and acts of Jesus. The note that Lazarus had been dead for four days (burial customarily took place within twenty-four hours) establishes that he was truly dead, for popular belief held that the soul of a person remained near the body for three days. Jesus reacts with intense emotion, mingling grief, compassion, and anger at the horror of death. He prays for the bystanders, that they may perceive the truth of this sign. As God's word gave life and light in creation, so now the incarnate Word gives light and life as signs of the eternal life he gives.

Lent

Prayers of the People

Brothers and sisters, the Spirit of God dwells in you. Let us appeal to our God, saying, "We call to you, O Lord; *Lord, hear our voice.*"

Breathe new life into your Church, O Lord. Where our bones are dried up, where our hope is lost, cause your life-giving breath to enter. Give us confidence in the truth that the same Spirit that raised Jesus from the dead dwells in us.

Invite the congregation to add their thanksgivings, followed by silence

We call to you, O Lord;

Lord, hear our voice.

Many are they who wait for you, O Lord. Speak into the souls of those suffering throughout the world, a word of hope.

Silence

We call to you, O Lord;

Lord, hear our voice.

Creating God, it is the wind of your Spirit that sweeps across this planet. Renew and refresh your creation; bring forth newness in dead places.

Silence

We call to you, O Lord;

Lord, hear our voice.

With you, O Lord, there is plenteous redemption. Restore the hope of this city. Renew our trust that you have a life-giving future in mind for us.

Silence

We call to you, O Lord;

Lord, hear our voice.

With you, O Lord, there is mercy. Consider well the voice of those who call out from their depths. As they wait for you in their pain and sorrow, give life to their mortal bodies by your healing Spirit.

Invite the congregation to add their petitions, followed by silence

We call to you, O Lord;

Lord, hear our voice.

God, we trust your Son Jesus to be for us resurrection and life. Give to the dead your life. Assure the living with the promise of resurrection.

Silence

We call to you, O Lord;

Lord, hear our voice.

Images in the Readings

Many medieval churches housed burials and contain even glass-cased skeletons, but most contemporary churches avoid picturing those bones that are left after the flesh has rotted away. Our culture avoids dealing directly and honestly with death: many people are even replacing the verb "died" with the term "passed," as if with everyone going off to heaven, there really is no death. In contrast, this Sunday presents us with the images of the **grave**, the **stink** of bodily decomposition, and the pile of **bones**. Furthermore, Paul's use of the term **flesh** as a metaphor for the misused human life intensifies this Sunday's honesty about human mortality. These texts represent the Bible's stark attention to the reality of death, both the "death" that is sin and the finality of death when our bodies die. For this Sunday, you might borrow a skeleton from a science classroom to hang prominently in the sanctuary. When we fully acknowledge the natural fact of death, we are ready to praise God's life as gift.

Ideas for the Day

- Jesus weeps with his followers before miraculously resuscitating Lazarus. In his tears, we see that Jesus knows what it feels like to mourn the death of a loved one. Jesus knows that Lazarus' regained life does not fully erase four days of mourning beforehand. Even though we believe in resurrection, when a loved one dies, first we grieve. We feel the raw human emotion of sadness. In our grief we know, and draw comfort from knowing, that God is with us. Even though we believe God can transform the direst of situations, when our hope is lying in tatters, we need to know that God is with us.

- In baptism the Christian is freed from the tomb of sinfulness. Dry bones take on flesh and those who are dead are filled with the breath of God. The raising of Lazarus points ahead to the resurrection.

- Even physical death does not end our growing relationship with the Creator. This covenant is a far deeper one than was understood by Abram as he struggled in the land of Canaan. The relationship is eternal.

Making Connections

Mary of Bethany anoints Jesus for burial before he has died. That's strange—they are at a dinner party, not at a grave. This happens in the gospel of John, immediately following the story of Lazarus raised from the dead. In her sorrow, Mary had rebuked Jesus, "Master, if you had been here, my brother would not have died." Looks like she's learned something since then about what Jesus' life will mean: his death is part of his life. Part of his mission among us. And so, a party: a feast to which life and death are both invited.

Engaging All Ages

Have you ever tried something new—like playing an instrument or ice skating? Were you perfect at it from the beginning? No! Part of learning something new is the willingness to be awkward and imperfect while you practice. Silence and stillness are two spiritual disciplines that anyone can practice—if they are willing to practice badly at first. It is hard to be still and silent—especially at the same time, but it can be done. This week see if you can practice stillness and silence in five-minute increments twice a day, each day. What did you notice? Did it get easier? How did you feel afterwards?

Hymns for the Day

The Hymnal 1982

From deepest woe I cry to thee 151
Out of the depths I call 666
Breathe on me, breath of God 508
Go forth for God; go to the world in peace 347
Put forth, O God, thy Spirit's might 521
Come down, O Love divine 516
Come, gracious Spirit, heavenly Dove 512
Come, Holy Spirit, heavenly Dove 510
Holy Spirit, ever living 511
O splendor of God's glory bright 5
Spirit divine, attend our prayers 509
Awake, O sleeper, rise from death 547
Eternal light, shine in my heart 465, 466
I am the bread of life (vs. 4, 5) 335
Lord, whose love through humble service 610
O bless the Lord, my soul 411
O for a thousand tongues to sing 493
O Love of God, how strong and true 455, 456
Thine arm, O Lord, in days of old 567
Thou art the Way, to thee alone 457
When Jesus wept 715

Lift Every Voice and Sing II

Let it breathe on me 116
Spirit of the living God 115
Come, Holy Ghost 112
Spirit of God, descend upon my heart 119
Take my hand, precious Lord 106

Wonder, Love, and Praise

Filled with the Spirit's power 741

Lent

Weekday Commemorations

Monday, March 27
Charles Henry Brent, Bishop, 1929

Brent served as a senior chaplain to the American Expeditionary Forces in World War I; at war's end, he accepted election as bishop of Western New York. He had turned down three prior elections so he could remain in the Philippines. Elected missionary bishop, Brent had been posted there in 1901. He crusaded against the opium trade in the islands as well as Asia. For twenty years, Brent stood tall in the Episcopal Church, focusing on Christian unity. In 1927, he led the church in the movement that resulted in the first World Conference on Faith and Order, over which he presided. One of his prayers is included in the Book of Common Prayer.

Tuesday, March 28
James Solomon Russell, Priest, 1935

Russell, born a slave in 1857 in Virginia, was the first student in what became Bishop Payne Divinity School, also in Virginia. In 1888, a year after his ordination in the Episcopal Church, he and his wife opened a school for academic and industrial education; religion was a mandatory subject. During his fifty-two years of ordained ministry, Russell worked tirelessly to encourage Black candidates to stand for ordination in order to care for the growing number of Black Episcopalians. Russell, elected the first African American bishop in the Episcopal Church (1927), fought adamantly against the idea of subordinate racial bishops.

Friday, March 31
John Donne, Priest and Poet, 1631

John Donne is one of the greatest of the English poets. Most famous for "Any man's death diminishes me, because I am involved in mankind. And therefore never send to know for whom the bell tolls: It tolls for thee." Born into a wealthy and pious Roman Catholic family in 1573, he was educated at Oxford and Cambridge and studied law at Lincoln's Inn. His sermons reflect the wide learning of the scholar, the passionate intensity of the poet, and the profound devotion of one struggling in his own life to relate the freedom and demands of the Gospel to the concerns of a common humanity, on every level, and in all its complexities.

Friday, April 1
Frederick Denison Maurice, Priest, 1872

Maurice's journey of faith did not describe a straight line: he dissented (refusing to agree to the Thirty-nine Articles of Religion) as often as he assented (working toward unity in the Church). Born in 1805, he studied civil law at Cambridge. He became an Anglican and was ordained in 1834. In 1838, he wrote *The Kingdom of Christ*, which delved into divisions within the Anglican Church and which served as a source for ecumenism within the wider Church. He taught English literature and history at King's College, London, in the 1840s but was dismissed because he led the Christian Socialist Movement. In his lifetime, Maurice encouraged Anglicans' concerns with society's problems.

Holy Week

Preparing for Holy Week

Theological Themes that Might Shape Liturgy, Catechesis, and Education

Holy Week, as its name might suggest, is the holiest week in the Christian calendar. It begins on Palm Sunday (or the Sunday of the Passion) and concludes on the Eve of Easter. It is a week of high drama that invites the faithful to walk with Jesus through the final moments of his pre-Resurrected life in ways that create new containers of meaning for our own lives.

While there are liturgies that might be observed through Holy Week, there are three proper liturgies which should be observed by every faith community (even if it means partnering with another faith community to do so). These liturgies, when observed according to the rubrics of the *Book of Common Prayer,* highlight important, often uncomfortable truths of the Christian faith. The proper liturgies comprise the Triduum—Maundy Thursday, Good Friday, and the Easter Vigil.

It can be incredibly tempting to either distill the events of this week into carefully crafted equations that somehow sort out our salvation or to ignore the disturbing bits altogether. Either extreme would be an incredible miscalculation and a missed opportunity. The events of Holy Week and how God uses these events to bring out the salvation of humanity and the restoration of Creation are concepts with which the biblical witness is deeply interested in engaging without having to settle on anything neat and polished. Holy Week doesn't explain salvation so much as it allows us to experience it by walking it.

The Incarnation, the mystery we celebrated in Christmas, is brought into starker focus during Holy Week. Jesus' ministry of healing, gathering, reconciliation, and social disruption is seemingly brought to a close by the executionary power of an insecure empire. The response of the temporally powerful to the divine power of Christ was to attempt to kill it by putting Jesus Christ to death. We walk through these moments, bringing into focus the ways we as individuals and as a society continue to reject the divine power of Christ that seeks to reshape us and our world.

While these liturgies can be hard to engage, it is appropriate for all generations to experience them in their fullness. The truths we experience as we walk with Jesus through the triumphal entry, the scene in the temple, the Upper Room, the Garden of Gethsemane, and then his final steps to Calvary are important to the development of a robust faith.

Liturgical Possibilities

Rites

As we explore the rites of this week, it should be noted that it would be appropriate to hold some sort of liturgy or even to celebrate the Eucharist on the Monday, Tuesday, and Wednesday of Holy Week while observing the other highlights of the week: Palm Sunday, Maundy Thursday, Good Friday, and the Easter Vigil.

The week begins on Palm Sunday, which is itself a long, dramatic liturgy. Whereas some faith communities have chosen to iron out the wrinkles of this service (choosing to read the Passion Gospel at the end of the service), this service is meant to be jarring. The jubilant "Hosannas" of the Liturgy of the Palms is almost immediately followed by the roughness of the "Crucify him!" in the gospel. Let it be.

Maundy Thursday should be observed using the proper liturgy in the prayer book, which is surprisingly light on "must dos." This presents the planner with options as to how to celebrate this night. There is something to be said about the standard, liturgical celebration of the evening, which aligns with the typical Sunday celebration of the Eucharist, but with options to observe foot washing and the ritual stripping of the altar as well as the observance of an Agape Feast beforehand; why not avail oneself to all of these options to make this service a distinct way of marking this moment in the week? Some congregations may choose to observe the Maundy Thursday Vigil, which puts us in the shoes of the disciples who are asked by Jesus to "stay awake" while he goes away to pray.

The Good Friday liturgy marks a moment of great importance for the Christian witness—the death of Christ. Everything about this service is a paradox, from the observance of the Veneration of the Cross (an instrument of death that becomes a tool and symbol of life) to the Solemn Collects, with loving pray for the world even as the world responded to Love (and continues to respond to love) with death.

The Holy Saturday liturgy is extremely brief and will likely not draw a huge crowd, but its emphasis on uncertainty, waiting, and expectation continue to pick up on themes that were explored during Advent and continue to resonate with the human experience—the eager longing for the revelation of the fullness of the Christ.

The Easter Vigil marks the culmination of the Triduum and Holy Week. It is a resounding response to the human cruelty exposed on Good Friday—neither death nor the tomb have any power over Christ, and the love of God cannot be extinguished even by the most cruel machinations of humanity. As it retells the story of salvation, each community has a wealth of options regarding how this important liturgy is observed.

Space

Holy Week intentionally takes us on a journey, so it would be appropriate to use space to indicate this. For example, beginning the Palm Sunday liturgy in one spot for the Liturgy of the Palms and then processing to another for the Liturgy of the Word would be something to consider. Additionally, given that the liturgies through the week are likely not going to be attended by the normal Sunday (or certainly not the Easter Sunday) crowds, what might it mean to engage space in a more dynamic way? Innovation aside, there are a lot of space-related questions to consider for Holy Week, and proper planning and rehearsal are key to ensure sufficient ritual effect without becoming a distraction.

Other Rituals and Resources

In addition to the Proper Liturgies and the celebration of the Holy Eucharist, a faith community might decide to observe a communal commemoration of the Stations of the Cross or Tenebrae service during the course of the week. There are resources in the *Book of Occasional Services* for these and other services.

Through the Eyes of a Child

Talking about death and grief with children is critical to their faith; however, even though it is Holy Week and not yet Easter it is necessary to give the proclamation, "Christ has died and Christ has risen from the dead." Children will be thinking bunny rabbits, Easter eggs and baskets, and time home from school; this is the time to instill in them through prayer and practice the importance of Holy Week in their faith. For example, you might want to do a "foot washing" at home in a special way after sharing the story of Jesus and the last supper. You might encourage the children to participate in a "Good Friday" service. Talk about how sad the disciples and Mary the Mother of Jesus must have been to see Jesus die, but there was a promise Jesus needed to complete. Attend an Easter Vigil service and remind them of the story of our salvation, from Old Testament times to the present. The children will want to act out the Good Friday/Easter story in much the same way they enjoy the Christmas story.

Through the Eyes of Youth

The Church is called to proclaim that Christ before his death invited us to remember how much God loves us, so much so that bread and wine mysteriously become what we share at Eucharist when we eat and drink of his flesh and blood, and that through his death new life would be offered for all humanity.

- ♦ The idea of an omniscient deity sending his only son to earth to die for the sins of humankind, only to be resurrected from the dead, can be difficult to grasp.
- ♦ Fear that we will lose our awareness of a connection with God, or even that we have "lost" God or our connection with him is invalid. We must be willing to let go of former experiences, no matter how powerful, and continually redefine what it means to be a follower of God at every stage, to be in new life.
- ♦ It is not easy to speak about God with friends; many of them see the Church as a reality that judges youth, that opposes their desire for happiness and love. It is a constant Good Friday struggle.

Holy Week is the time to stay current and connected to the youth. Consider with the youth ways in which twenty-first century discipleship calls us to go to the cross. What are the crosses youth will need to bear in the twenty-first century? Practice noticing all kinds of people and responding to them as Christ is in them.

Through the Eyes of Daily Life

During Holy Week some communities gather each day to meditate on Jesus' final days before his death on the cross. Begin the journey with Jesus, following his path to Jerusalem through prayer with others or in solitude. At the heart of the Maundy Thursday liturgy is Jesus' commandment to love one another. As Jesus washing the feet of his disciples, we are called to follow his example as we humbly care for one another, especially the poor and unloved. At the Lord's table, we remember Jesus' sacrifice of his life, even as we are called to offer ourselves in love for the life of the world. Plant the cross on your heart, so that in its power and love you can continue to be Christ's representative in the world at work, school, and play.

Through the Eyes of the Global Community

Two collects heard during Holy Week set the focus for social justice:

- ♦ Palm Sunday: Mercifully grant that we may walk in the way of his suffering. (BCP 272)
- ♦ Monday in Holy Week: Almighty God, whose most dear Son went not up to joy but first he suffered pain, and entered not into glory before he was crucified: Mercifully grant that we, walking in the way of the cross, may find it none other than the way of life and peace. (BCP 220)

These collects remind us that we are called:

- ♦ To identify with the suffering peoples of the nation and the world and not to remain aloof;
- ♦ To have compassion for "all sorts and conditions" of people (BCP 814).

Through the Eyes of Those Outside of the Church

If there were any season for the Church to play up its distinctiveness, Holy Week is one of them. Our faith is not one that is incapable of handling the hard parts of life. Not only can our faith hold them with care, but Christianity teaches us to interpret our own experiences through the saving lens of Jesus Christ. Holy Week is simply a weird week and as such presents opportunities for the Church to celebrate the love of Christ in ways that invite others to inquire more deeply about the message of the gospel.

Holy Week

Seasonal Rites for Holy Week

Holy Week Blessing[1]

The following blessing may be used by a bishop or priest whenever a blessing is appropriate from Palm Sunday through Maundy Thursday.

Almighty God, we pray you graciously to behold this your family, for whom our Lord Jesus Christ was willing to be betrayed, and given into the hands of sinners, and to suffer death upon the cross; who lives and reigns for ever and ever. *Amen.*

Tenebrae[2]

The name Tenebrae (the Latin word for "darkness" or "shadows") has, for centuries, been applied to the ancient monastic night and early morning services (Matins and Lauds) of the last three days of Holy Week, which in medieval times came to be celebrated on the preceding evening.

Apart from the chant of the Lamentations (in which each verse is introduced by a letter of the Hebrew alphabet), the most conspicuous feature of the service is the gradual extinguishing of candles and other lights in the church until only a single candle, considered a symbol of our Lord, remains. Toward the end of the service this candle is hidden, typifying the apparent victory of the forces of evil. At the very end, a loud noise is made, symbolizing the earthquake at the time of the Resurrection (Matthew 28:2), the hidden candle is restored to its place, and by its light all depart in silence.

This service is most appropriate for Wednesday of Holy Week.

Prayers for All Ages in Holy Week[3]

Palm Sunday

The one who enters in the Lord's name is blessed; we bless all of you from the Lord's house.
— Psalm 118:26

Praise God, praise God, praise God we say,
welcoming Jesus along the way.
Waving our branches of palms we say,
hosanna, hosanna along the way.
Welcome to Jesus, our blessed king.
Praise God, praise God, praise God we sing. Amen.

Monday of Holy Week

Jesus said, "Put on my yoke, and learn from me. I'm gentle and humble. And you will find rest for yourselves." — Matthew 11:29

Walk with me, Jesus, walk with me.
The way isn't always easy, you see.
But your love, it reaches up to the sky,
and carried me, so that I can try.
The way isn't always easy, you see.
Walk with me, Jesus, walk with me. Amen.

Tuesday of Holy Week

Jesus said, "Whoever serves me must follow me. Wherever I am, there my servant will also be." — John 12:26

I will follow you, Jesus, by following love,
and earth will grow closer to heaven above.
When we serve others and do good deeds,
when we show people kindness and care for their needs,
earth will grow closer to heaven above
when we follow you, Jesus, when we follow love.
Amen.

---

1 *Book of Occasional Services 2003* (New York: Church Publishing, 2004), 26.
2 The actual service of Tenebrae can be found in Ibid, 75–92.

3 Jenifer Gamber and Timothy J. S. Seamans, *Common Prayer for Children and Families* (New York: Church Publishing, Inc., 2019), 60–63.

Wednesday of Holy Week

Jesus said to the crowd, "The light is with you for a little longer . . . While you have the light, believe in the light, that you may become children of light."
— John 12:35–36, RSV, adapted

The light of Christ glows in me and in others,
and in the family of God all are sisters and brothers.
It's a light you must see with your heart to believe.
It's a light you can share, you can give and receive.
In the family of God we are sisters and brothers,
and the light of Christ shines in me and
in others. *Amen.*

Maundy Thursday

Jesus said to his disciples, "I give you a new commandment: Love each other. Just as I have loved you, so you also must love each other. This is how everyone will know that you are my disciples, when you love each other." — John 13:34–35

A new commandment, you gave at the table,
to love one another as you made us able.
When we love one another, all will know it is true
that we and our friends, indeed, follow you.
So let us remember the commandment to love
so the world becomes more like heaven above. *Amen.*

Good Friday

Jesus said, "It is completed." Bowing his head, he gave up his life. — John 19:30

When Jesus died that day on the cross
all creation together sighed, "This is a great loss."
Time grew empty and the afternoon dark
as the light of the world had not even a spark.
The women stood by at a distance in tears
wondering what would become of their fears.
Fear not, the angels soon will say.
Jesus' death has given us the way. *Amen.*

Holy Saturday

There was a garden in the place where Jesus died and in the garden was a new tomb in which no one had ever been laid. They laid Jesus in the tomb. — John 19:41–42, adapted

We speak few words this day that is hollow,
this day that signs with one great sorrow.
We sit in the garden next to the tomb
knowing that soon it will be a womb. *Amen.*

Easter Vigil

Sing, heavens! Rejoice, earth! Break out, mountains, with a song. — Isaiah 49:13

Alleluia! Alleluia! We sing this night,
joining heaven and earth that rejoice with delight.
Jesus, our Lord, is risen today.
God's love and light is here to stay.
Joining heaven and earth that rejoice with delight,
Alleluia! Alleluia! We sing this night. *Amen.*

Maundy Thursday

Thursday, April 6

Activity and Prayer[4]

Leader: Today we are going to think about the story of the washing of the feet. The washing of the feet took place at the last meal Jesus ate with his close friends, the meal where they celebrated the Passover together. Today we are going to remember that meal where Jesus washed the feet of his friends, teaching them how the leader has to be the one who is the servant of the others.

The Passover celebration was a time when the Jewish people looked back at their history, at the good times, and at the difficult times. They remembered how God was always there for them and helped them through their difficulties. So now, let's look back over our last year. What happened in our group over the past year?

---

4 Hazel Bradley and Jim Cargin, *Creative Ideas for Worship with All Abilities* (New York: Church Publishing, Inc., 2019), 149..

Ask some leading questions and encourage responses, for example:

- ◆ Who have we welcomed into our group?
- ◆ Can anyone remember any difficult moments?
- ◆ What funny stories can people remember?
- ◆ Do you remember when *(Name)* forgave *(Name)*?
- ◆ Who always helped with tea?
- ◆ Remember how *(Name)* was sad because his dog died and everyone comforted him.
- ◆ Remember *(Name)*'s birthday celebration.
- ◆ Remember when *(Name)* spoke in the group for the first time.

Leader: What have we learned from one another this year?

Allow time for responses. If necessary give some prompts, for example:

Leader: How to serve each other, how to make people welcome, how to take care of ourselves, and of each other, that we are each welcomed, accepted and loved as we are, that to love someone is not to do things for them but to waste time with them.

OR invite someone to talk about what the washing of the feet means to them (this person would need to be asked in advance so they have time to prepare what they want to say).

Good Friday

Friday, April 7

Litany[5]

You faced the crowd who shouted for blood;
we dared not object.
Lord have mercy,

Lord have mercy.

You stood before the ruler who washed his hands;
we accepted his decision.
Christ have mercy,

Christ have mercy.

You were mocked by the faithful who feared
for their power; we denied we ever knew you.
Lord have mercy,

Lord have mercy.

---

5 Steven Shakespeare, *Prayers for an Inclusive Church* (New York: Church Publishing, Inc., 2009), 155.

The Sunday of the Passion: Palm Sunday

April 2, 2023

We enter into Jesus' death through baptism so that "just as Christ was raised from the dead by the glory of the Father, so we too might walk in newness of life." (Romans 6:4b)

Color   Red / Oxblood

Preface   Of Holy Week

Collect

Almighty and everliving God, in your tender love for the human race you sent your Son our Savior Jesus Christ to take upon him our nature, and to suffer death upon the cross, giving us the example of his great humility: Mercifully grant that we may walk in the way of his suffering, and also share in his resurrection; through Jesus Christ our Lord, who lives and reigns with you and the Holy Spirit, one God, for ever and ever. *Amen.*

Readings and Psalm

The Liturgy of the Palms

Psalm 118:1–2, 19–29

A festival hymn sung in procession in praise of the Lord's salvation.

Matthew 21:1–11

In this gospel lesson Jesus comes to the holy city of Jerusalem and is hailed as the promised Son of David. He has a young donkey brought to him, and as did the kings of old in royal celebrations, Jesus rides on it, while the crowds spread their garments and branches in the way and shout in his honor. The evangelist perceives this as a fulfillment of the prophet Zechariah's words concerning the coming king. Here is both great drama and irony as Jesus enters the city he would save, while the people who will soon call for his blood rumor it about that the prophet from Galilee has arrived.

The Liturgy of the Passion

Isaiah 50:4–9a

Today's passage is the third of the four servant songs found in Isaiah (see also 42:1–4, 49:1–6 and 52:13–53:12). The servant probably represents Israel in its ideal form, which some thought would be fulfilled only in the unique person of the Messiah. The servant was considered a corporate personality, a single individual who would represent and incorporate in himself all the features of Israel's election and mission. The servant songs first provided a way for Israel to understand the significance of the suffering and humiliation of the exile and later helped the Church understand and proclaim the meaning of Jesus' suffering and resurrection.

Psalm 31:9–16

Psalm 31 is a lament by one surrounded by evil people. Trust in God encourages the psalmist to entrust himself to God's care. In anticipation of God's deliverance, the psalmist prays with thanksgiving and joy.

Philippians 2:5–11

Verses 6–11 are generally considered to be a pre-Pauline hymn to Christ that Paul adopts to make his own point. The hymn contains a summary of the Christian proclamation that includes divine preexistence (v. 6), incarnation (v. 7), death (v. 8), celestial exaltation (v. 9), heavenly adoration (v. 10), and Jesus' new title (v. 11). The first stanza (vv. 6–8) recounts Jesus' own action. His equality with God is not a prize to be exploited for his own advantage. The second stanza (vv. 9–11) stresses the response by God to bestow on Jesus the name Lord (Greek *kyrios*; Hebrew *adonai*) and our response to honor him as God is honored.

Matthew 26:14–27:66

or

Matthew 27:11–54

The power of the gospel accounts of Jesus' suffering lies not in an appeal to emotion but the stark witness to the presence of God and to the working out of God's purpose. The hearer is called not to pity, sorrow or even penitence, but to faith.

Each of the gospels presents a distinctive focus on Jesus in his suffering. Matthew adds more explicit references to material from the Hebrew Bible, thereby enhancing his theme of Jesus' goal to carry out God's plan for salvation. Matthew also stressed that Jesus was the royal Messiah who was completely willing to suffer in order to inaugurate God's plan for a new world. Though Matthew based his account closely on Mark, he tightened up the narrative and introduced new material about the betrayal and suicide of Judas, the dream of Pilate's wife, Pilate washing his hands, the crowd's responsibility for Jesus' death, the cosmic events when Jesus dies, and the guards at the tomb.

Prayers of the People

The spirit indeed is willing, but the flesh is weak. So, let us cry out to our Lord, saying, "Crucified King, *have mercy on us."*

Have mercy on your Church, O Lord, for the times we have denied you. We have not been humble as you are humble. We have been unwilling to share the gospel with our friends and families.

Silence

Crucified King,

Have mercy on us.

Have mercy on those who hold authority in the nations of the world, O Lord—especially those who are threatened by your message of love and justice. Have mercy on us for our silence and complicity.

Silence

Crucified King,

Have mercy on us.

Have mercy on those of us who are called to be stewards of your creation, O Lord. We have exploited and mistreated your masterpiece. Have mercy on us and teach us to love what you have called good.

Silence

Crucified King,

Have mercy on us.

Have mercy on us, O Lord. Teach us to value what you value. Increase in us love for our neighbors.

Silence

Crucified King,

Have mercy on us.

Have mercy on all who are sick and suffering, O Lord. Strengthen those whose strength fails them. Comfort and care for those wasted with grief. Make your face to shine upon your servants.

Invite the congregation to add their petitions and thanksgivings, followed by silence

Crucified King,

Have mercy on us.

Merciful Lord, you know the pain of death—even death on a cross. Have mercy on the dying and the dead. Bring them to the joy of everlasting life in you.

Silence

Crucified King,

Have mercy on us.

Images in the Readings

Two opposite images of Christ come in the readings. First, Christ is **king**. In Matthew's passion narrative, he is acclaimed as the Son of David; he is the apocalyptic Son of Man, who will judge the world at the end of time; he is accused of falsely presenting himself as Messiah, yet is affirmed by believers as the Christ; he is mocked as the "king of the Jews"; and ironically, even when dead, his body is attended by Roman guards. Much in American culture resists "king" as a positive image. Yet the hope that someone has ultimate power, absolute justice, and endless mercy persists in human imagination.

In an image that derives from the first and second readings. Christ is **servant**. God will vindicate the servant, even though he is now suffering. We are to adopt the mind of Christ Jesus, who became a servant, indeed a slave, for us. Once again, much in American culture resists "servant" as a positive image. Martin Luther's essay "The Freedom of the Christian" can help us here: through our baptism, we are both free, slaves to none, and simultaneously servants to all.

Making Connections

Some Pharisees tell Jesus "Order your disciples to stop." They are afraid the motley procession of Jesus' followers might attract the wrong kind of attention. But it's too late. The chain of events that will ultimately lead to the destruction of the temple and the dispersal of the Jews throughout the ancient world is already underway. It began before Jesus was born and continued after his death. To historians, Jesus' life and death are but one moment in a long train of fateful events. To us, though, they are the beginning of a resurrection in which the whole world shares.

Engaging All Ages

Our country today embodies W. B. Yeats', "The best lack all conviction, while the worst are full of passionate intensity." America needs courage. The NT readings this week instruct us. Pay attention.

Today's reading shows us the crowd's bravado as they applaud Jesus' approach. They even strew the filthy streets with their clothes.

An intoxicating scene indeed. But as some of us know, intoxication makes hangovers – or worse. There were lots of people that Sunday. Where would they be Friday? What would they be shouting? When would they stay dumb?

The Bible shows us that durable courage is a gift of God's Spirit. As we proceed through Holy Week— this year so pivotal for our democracy—pay attention to the presence or absence of courage.

Ask our Lord to make you braver.

Hymns for the Day

The Hymnal 1982
Palm Sunday Anthems 153
All glory, laud, and honor 154, 155
Ride on! ride on in majesty 156
Alone, thou goest forth, O Lord 164
Hail, thou once despised Jesus! (vs. 1–2) 495
To mock your reign, O dearest Lord 170
Cross of Jesus, cross of sorrow 160
Morning glory, starlit sky (vs. 4–6) 585
The flaming banners of our King 161
The royal banners forward go 162
What wondrous love is this 439
Ah, holy Jesus, how hast thou offended 158
And now, O Father, mindful of the love (vs. 1–2) 337
Let thy Blood in mercy poured 313
My song is love unknown 458
Nature with open volume stands 434
O sacred head, sore wounded 168, 169
When I survey the wondrous cross 474

Lift Every Voice and Sing II
Ride on, King Jesus 97
Simon of Cyrene 49
O sacred head, sore wounded 36

Wonder, Love, and Praise
Mantos y palmas esparciendo /
    Filled with excitement 728
O sacred head, sore wounded 735

Holy Week

Monday in Holy Week

April 3, 2023

We pray that we may find the way of the Cross to be the way of life and peace.

Color   Red / Oxblood

Preface   Of Holy Week

Collect

Almighty God, whose most dear Son went not up to joy but first he suffered pain, and entered not into glory before he was crucified: Mercifully grant that we, walking in the way of the cross, may find it none other than the way of life and peace; through Jesus Christ your Son our Lord, who lives and reigns with you and the Holy Spirit, one God, for ever and ever. *Amen.*

Readings and Psalm

Isaiah 42:1–9

In our reading from the Hebrew scriptures we hear of the mission of the Lord's servant, the one whom God has chosen to bring forth justice and salvation. This is the first of the "servant songs" that form a portion of the Book of Isaiah written at the time when the exile in Babylon was ending and the city of Jerusalem had begun to be restored. The servant is sometimes thought to be an historical individual, or is understood as an idealization of Israel. Christians see in the servant a prefigurement of the ministry of Jesus, who will become a light to the nations of the world.

Psalm 36:5–11

The psalmist celebrates the expansive love of God expressed in faithfulness and justice. God is a river of delight in whose light we see light.

Hebrews 9:11–15

Christ has inaugurated a new covenant, accomplishing all that was anticipated by the rites and rituals of the first covenant, that is, redemption from sin and transgression and the purification of conscience for the right worship of the living God.

John 12:1–11

Six days before the Passover, Jesus gathers with his friends in Bethany at the home of Lazarus, whom he had raised from the dead. Mary, the sister of Martha and Lazarus, anoints Jesus' feet with costly perfume, wiping his feet with her hair. This extravagant devotion is criticized by Judas Iscariot, but Jesus defends the action in ways that seem to prefigure his fast-approaching death.

Ideas for the Day

♦ The smell of Grandma's cookies, of your beloved's perfume, or lilacs on the first spring day—all of us have scents that bring back a flood of memories and emotions. Mary fills her home with the scent of the perfume with which she anointed Jesus' feet. The smell of oil used to anoint a corpse, not a king, indicates that Mary, as a close follower of Jesus, understands what is next to come. How did that sweet scent linger after the death of Jesus? What scents remind of our sacred stories?

♦ In the Old Testament, anointing commonly signified a transmittal of power and blessing. In the New Testament, it came to be a sign of love, of identity as a Christian, and of the reception of the Holy Spirit. These flowed from the Church's understanding of Jesus as the "Messiah" or "Christ," which means "the anointed one."

Making Connections

Lazarus was an embarrassment to those in power: living proof of Jesus' lordship over death. So the chief priests laid plans to kill him. We don't know if they succeeded. There are legends about Lazarus' ongoing life after the resurrection of Jesus—that he became a priest, that he fed Mary his sister the eucharistic bread every day, bringing it to the cave in the south of France where she lived with two other women, also named Mary. That this bread was all she ever ate. My goodness. Truth and legend, side by side in the vivid imaginations of the faithful.

Engaging All Ages

Today's gospel reading contrasts the unnamed woman with the onlookers who pretend concern to disapprove of Jesus. German speakers have a word we need: *scheinheilig*: persons wearing a façade of virtue masking harm. We might use it to describe Christians who reproach others, implicating God in their disapproval.

Luke 7 offers a similar story where the woman is a prostitute—and scorned for it. Jesus uses her as a good example, different from his scheinheilig host.

Putting a religious mask on criticizing others is not brave. It's a violation of the Second Commandment: "Do not invoke with malice the Name of the Lord your God."

Reflect on the people you criticize. Ask forgiveness for using God as a fig leaf.

Does anything in your heart change? Especially as you watch the news . . . .

Hymns for the Day

We sing the praise of him who died 471
Ancient of Days, who sittest throned in glory 363
Jesus shall reign where'er the sun 544
Thy strong word did cleave the darkness 381
Weary of all trumpeting 572
Come, thou fount of every blessing 686
Cross of Jesus, cross of sorrow 160
Draw nigh and take the Body of the Lord 327, 328
Glory be to Jesus 479
Holy Father, great Creator 368
Let thy Blood in mercy poured 313
God himself is with us 475
Jesus, all my gladness 701
Jesus, the very thought of thee 642
Just as I am, without one plea 693
There's a wideness in God's mercy 469, 470

Lift Every Voice and Sing II
Come, thou fount of every blessing 111
Just as I am 137

Wonder, Love, and Praise

Holy Week

Tuesday in Holy Week

April 4, 2023

Through God, Jesus' shameful death on the Cross has become the means of life for us.

Color   Red / Oxblood

Preface   Of Holy Week

Collect

O God, by the passion of your blessed Son you made an instrument of shameful death to be for us the means of life: Grant us so to glory in the cross of Christ, that we may gladly suffer shame and loss for the sake of your Son our Savior Jesus Christ; who lives and reigns with you and the Holy Spirit, one God, for ever and ever. *Amen.*

Readings and Psalm

Isaiah 49:1–7

The servant of the Lord reflects movingly on his mission—its sorrows and frustrations—and God's high calling and promise to be with him. The servant is sometimes thought to be an historical individual, or is understood as an idealization of Israel. This song was probably composed as the exiles from Jerusalem were preparing to return to their devastated city. Despite appearances, the Lord will make this servant a light to the nations.

Psalm 71:1–14

The psalmist prays that God will continue to be his refuge and stronghold.

1 Corinthians 1:18–31

In this lesson Paul directs the attention of the Corinthians to God's way of using what is weak and lowly—even what the world regards as foolish—to accomplish the divine purposes. Paul emphasizes this understanding because a number of these new Christians had come to think of themselves as especially gifted, powerful, and wise. As the cross has shown, however, God's ideas about what is wise and noble are often quite different from ours. Our only boast can be in the Lord.

John 12:20–36

In this gospel passage Jesus presents teaching concerning the meaning of his death. After his prayer to God a voice from heaven is heard. Greeks wish to see Jesus, but he will not draw all others to himself until after he has died and risen. Then, like a seed which falls into the earth, he will bear much fruit. Now is the hour for the Son of Man to be glorified—glorified both by his willingness to be lifted up on the cross to die for others, and afterward to be lifted up to heaven. Disciples must learn to follow Jesus in his way—not walking in darkness but in the light.

Making Connections

Nobody understands Jesus when he talks about his impending death. Those who love him won't hear of it. Those who think he may be the Messiah can't fit a humiliating execution into their expectation of what a messiah should be about. Those who don't know him just don't know what he's talking about. Eventually he departs from them and hides. Even the Son of God longs to be understood. I imagine Jesus especially wanted those he loved most to embrace his mission. But human love is limited, as his love is not. We do the best we can.

Engaging All Ages

Today Jesus meets official incredulity. Their positions meant more to them than their functions.

Consider the question, "What should I really be scared of?" It's likely that deep down you know what God wants of you. Now it's a question of courage: your courage. Will you face it?

Courage is only visible from the outside. Nobody being brave feels brave.

That's the point of contact between the Spirit and your courage. Being embraced with God's love makes it possible to stand fast.

Recent holidays were often tense instead of joyous. The media pelted us with articles about dealing with cranky relatives. Few told us what we need to know: God's truth (including God's love for the cranky) alone matters.

Scary. But it's what our country needs today more than ever.

Hymns for the Day

The Hymnal 1982

My song is love unknown (vs. 1–2, 7) 458
Christ, whose glory fills the skies 6, 7
God of mercy, God of grace 538
How wondrous and great thy works,
   God of praise! 532, 533
Beneath the cross of Jesus 498
Cross of Jesus, cross of sorrow 160
In the cross of Christ I glory 441, 442
Nature with open volume stands 434
We sing the praise of him who died 471
When I survey the wondrous cross 474
I heard the voice of Jesus say 692
I want to walk as a child of the Light 490
O Jesus, I have promised 655
The great Creator of the worlds 489
When Christ was lifted from the earth 603, 604

Lift Every Voice and Sing II

Near the cross 29
The old rugged cross 38

Wonder, Love, and Praise

Holy Week

Wednesday in Holy Week

April 5, 2023

We ask God for the grace to accept our present sufferings joyfully, secure in the glory that will be revealed.

Holy Week

Color   Red / Oxblood

Preface   Of Holy Week

Collect

Lord God, whose blessed Son our Savior gave his body to be whipped and his face to be spit upon: Give us grace to accept joyfully the sufferings of the present time, confident of the glory that shall be revealed; through Jesus Christ your Son our Lord, who lives and reigns with you and the Holy Spirit, one God, for ever and ever. *Amen.*

Readings and Psalm

Isaiah 50:4–9a

Our first reading tells of the servant who speaks for the Lord and suffers persecution, but still trusts in God's help and vindication. This is the third of the "servant songs" that come from a period late in Israel's exile. The servant might be thought to be the faithful of Israel, the prophet himself, or another historical or idealized figure. The people are weary and tired of the Lord's calling, but the servant steadfastly continues. Christians have long perceived in these words a foretelling of Jesus' mission.

Psalm 70

A prayer for help and vindication.

Hebrews 12:1–3

The author of the Book of Hebrews exhorts hearers to persevere in the face of adversity, looking to the example of Jesus and encouraged by all those through the generations who have sought to be faithful to God in difficult circumstances.

John 13:21–32

At his final supper with his disciples Jesus is troubled by the knowledge of Judas' impending betrayal but tells his disciples that God is at work in the glorification of the Son of Man. Judas Iscariot departs into the night to do what he has determined to do.

Ideas for the Day

- Betrayal in books creates an exciting who-done-it page-turning energy. The reader hopes that the betrayer will get what they deserve by the end of the book. In our own lives, betrayal can break our hearts, causing us to sever relationships or put up armor so that no one else can hurt us. Although troubled in spirit, Jesus responds to betrayal in another way. He knew who would betray him when he washed all of his disciples' feet. Although it troubled his spirit, Jesus shared bread with the one he knew would betray him. Jesus chose to love his betrayer.

- Jesus foretells his betrayal by Judas and Peter's denial of him before the last cock-crow. How have we denied Jesus by our words and actions in our daily life?

Making Connections

It seems Judas and Jesus understand each other. Jesus knows what Judas is going to do, and Judas knows he knows. He doesn't protest his innocence, nor is he puzzled. John tells us that Satan enters into him in this moment. Other writers insist that Judas was always a bad apple. But note that Jesus views this whole terrible sequence of events as part of his being glorified. Everyone at the table wonders who the traitor might be—in Matthew, each wonders if he might be the one. As we have potential for good, we also have potential for evil.

Engaging All Ages

This reading John (13:21–35) won't make sense until we understand Jesus' warning about "temptation"/ "the time of trial."

In this reading, Jesus is brought to the first of several times of trial that show who he really is.

Jesus knew Judas' intention. Yet he clenched his jaw and let it happen.

Then there's a lengthy discussion of "glory." Why? Consider what John's gospel means by glory. John doesn't mean an effulgence of light. It's more like an x-ray—something that "displays" what you are. The word John uses refers to showing. The "time of trial" shows what Peter and the others are; Jesus' "time of trial" shows us what he is.

American public life is filled with glory-seeking. When we catch whiffs of genuine courage it's . . . glorious.

Hymns for the Day

The Hymnal 1982

Alone thou goest forth, O Lord 164
Bread of heaven, on thee we feed 323
Let thy Blood in mercy poured 313
To mock your reign, O dearest Lord 170
Hail, thou once despised Jesus 495
Lo! what a cloud of witnesses 545
The head that once was crowned with thorns 483
Ah, holy Jesus, how hast thou offended 158
Bread of the world, in mercy broken 301
O love, how deep, how broad, how high 448, 449

Lift Every Voice and Sing II

Wonder, Love, and Praise

Holy Week

Maundy Thursday

April 6, 2023

We pray that Jesus will give us grace to receive the Sacrament of his Body and Blood thankfully, remembering that in these holy mysteries we have been given a promise of eternal life.

Color   Red, Oxblood, or White

Preface   Of Holy Week

Collect

Almighty Father, whose dear Son, on the night before he suffered, instituted the Sacrament of his Body and Blood: Mercifully grant that we may receive it thankfully in remembrance of Jesus Christ our Lord, who in these holy mysteries gives us a pledge of eternal life; and who now lives and reigns with you and the Holy Spirit, one God, for ever and ever. *Amen.*

Readings and Psalm

Exodus 12:1–4 (5–10), 11–14

In our first reading instructions are given, and the meaning of the Passover meal is told: it is a remembrance and reenactment of Israel's beginnings as a people when they were saved out of slavery in Egypt. The details indicate that several different traditions stand behind the Passover memorial. Perhaps it was the Israelites' attempts to keep ancient spring rites, derived from their shepherding and agricultural backgrounds, that caused the Egyptians to persecute them. With these traditions the story of God's judgment on Egypt and victory for God's people has become richly entwined.

Psalm 116:1, 10–17

An offering of thanksgiving and praise by one who has been rescued from death.

1 Corinthians 11:23–26

In this lection Paul recalls the tradition he received concerning the supper of the Lord on the night he was betrayed. The apostle reminds the Corinthians, who have shown an alarming tendency to divide up into factions, of the message he first delivered to them. This meal is a remembrance and reenactment of the Lord's offering of himself and forming of the new covenant. It proclaims the Lord's saving death and looks forward to his coming.

John 13:1–17, 31b–35

Our gospel tells how Jesus washes his disciples' feet during his last meal with them. This action symbolizes the love and humility of Christ in stooping down to wash those whom he loves from their sins. He has set for them an example, for he must soon depart. His disciples are to be characterized by servant love for one another.

Prayers of the People

In the company of Jesus and in unity with his faithful followers in years past and in our present day, let us offer our prayers responding, "Kyrie eleison."

For the gift of humility, that we may mirror the servanthood of Jesus, bending the knee of our hearts to all whose feet have journeyed a long distance, and whose hands have washed away the burdens of others; let us pray.

Kyrie eleison.

For peace throughout the world, especially in _____ and all places where the lust for power fosters tyranny and war; let us pray.

Kyrie eleison.

For the courage to face our own unfaithfulness: the kisses of deception, the subtle betrayals, our spiritual sleepiness; that in turning to Christ we may receive the grace that changes lives; let us pray.

Kyrie eleison.

For those who keep watch this night, that in watching they may be found, in seeking they may be filled with the Spirit, and in waiting they may find peace; let us pray.

Kyrie eleison.

For those who keep watch every night: the hungry, the homeless, the fearful, that Christ may find them in their own gardens of Gethsemane and not leave them in despair; let us pray.

Kyrie eleison.

In thanksgiving for this eucharistic meal, which gathers us into the fellowship of all the beloved, uniting us with Jesus, whose Divine Presence we now share; let us pray.

Kyrie eleison.

In companionship with Peter, John, and all the apostles, let us continue our prayers.

(Special intentions of the congregation, the diocese, and the Anglican Communion may be added here or before the formal intercessions.)

The Celebrant adds a concluding Collect.

Images in the Readings

A primary image for Maundy Thursday is the **servant**. We recall from Passion Sunday's Servant Song that the image of servant is not a readily accessible symbol in today's society. Even the wait staff in many restaurants now present themselves not as servants but as personal friends. John's gospel offers us a lowly, even dirty, task as appropriate for a true servant.

The readings are filled with **body**: the body of the dead lamb, cooked and eaten; the body of Christ, shared in the bread; the body of the neighbor's actual feet. For people who like to keep their individual space, it is countercultural to share in one another's body in this public way.

The first reading says that it is the lamb's **blood** that reminds God not to punish the Israelites, and Paul says that the wine is a new covenant in Jesus' blood. In the ancient world, life was seen as residing in the blood. Thus pouring out of blood is giving up of life. Isn't it interesting that small children lick a bleeding wound, in hopes of keeping their blood inside their body?

In all three readings, the people of God experience themselves as a **meal** community. Humans must eat to live, and humans eat together to become and maintain community. The Israelites are to keep the Passover meal "as a perpetual ordinance"; Paul assumes and corrects the meal practice of the Corinthians; John describes the last loving meal Jesus had with his disciples before his arrest. So it is over the centuries most Christian assemblies have shared a meal at their weekly meeting. The liturgy of the three days begins with this meal.

Ideas for the Day

♦ When we are babies and children, we are fully dependent on the help of others. As adults, many of us have lost the ability to receive something so intimate as having our feet washed. To receive can be very uncomfortable. To receive means we are dependent and we are not in control. Jesus teaches that we must learn to receive and are dependent upon God's love. k. d. lang's "Wash Me Clean" embraces the humility and grace of receiving. How do we pray these words or others in order that we may also embrace the spiritual discipline of receiving?

♦ Commemorate this day with an Agapé Meal, or love feast, as a community event. The setting should be plain and food simple, in keeping with the solemnity of the Lenten fast that continues through this week. A meal of soup, cheese, olives, dried fruit, bread, and wine is appropriate. Eat the meal in silence while someone reads passages from scripture or poetry that allows for introspection while eating, or have soft music playing in the background.

Making Connections

Jesus washing his disciples' feet can be seen in two ways. One is as the inversion of power—the master behaving as a slave. Peter articulates this: "You will never wash my feet!" We see it also in the practice of the pope washing the feet of beggars on this day—the Holy Father stooping to serve the lowly. But maybe it's not so much a reversal of power as a universal expression of love. Whether you're mighty or not, wash one another's feet. It's no more holy when the pope does it than it is when you do.

Engaging All Ages

We associate this day with Holy Communion.

How does the Eucharist connect to courage?

Controversy has raged about what "This is my Body," and "This is my Blood" mean. Those quarrels are beside the point.

When Jesus said, "This is my Body," he didn't point to the bread—he gave it. It was when he gave the cup to another he said, "This is my Blood." The "this" in both instances meant the giving. He then said, "When you do this, you'll be back together with me."

We miss Jesus' point thinking he meant what we do in church where only the clergy do it. Are you brave enough to know that Jesus wants to be with you? That you can be in his presence when you make gifts to other people?

That would be courageous.

Hymns for the Day

The Hymnal 1982
Go to dark Gethsemane 171
Praise to the Holiest in the height 445, 446
What wondrous love is this 439
Now, my tongue, the mystery telling 329, 330, 331
When Jesus died to save us 322
Zion, praise thy Savior singing 320
Thou, who at thy first Eucharist didst pray 315

Lift Every Voice and Sing II
In remembrance of me, eat this bread 149
This is my body given for you 155

Wonder, Love, and Praise
O wheat whose crushing was for bread 760
As in that upper room you left your seat 729, 730
Three holy days enfold us now 731, 732, 733
You laid aside your rightful reputation 734

At the footwashing:

The Hymnal 1982
God is love, and where true love is 576, 577
Jesu, Jesu, fill us with your love 602
Where charity and love prevail 581
Where true charity and love dwell 606

Lift Every Voice and Sing II
Jesu, Jesu, fill us with your love 74

Wonder, Love, and Praise
Ubi caritas et amor 831

At the stripping of the altar:

Wonder, Love, and Praise
Stay with me 826

Good Friday

April 7, 2023

We ask God to look with kindness at us his family, for whom our Lord Jesus Christ died on the Cross and lives and reigns forever with God and the Holy Spirit.

Color Red / Oxblood

Preface Of Holy Week

Collect

Almighty God, we pray you graciously to behold this your family, for whom our Lord Jesus Christ was willing to be betrayed, and given into the hands of sinners, and to suffer death upon the cross; who now lives and reigns with you and the Holy Spirit, one God, for ever and ever. *Amen.*

Readings and Psalm

Isaiah 52:13–53:12

Our opening lesson is the poem of the Lord's servant who suffers and bears the sins of many. The passage is the fourth and last of the "servant songs" that form a portion of the Book of Isaiah written when the exile was coming to an end. The servant is sometimes thought to be an historical individual, or is understood as an idealization of the faithful of Israel. This "man of sorrows," who was "despised and rejected," "wounded for our transgressions," and one whom the Lord at last vindicates, is perceived by Christians to be a prefigurement of Jesus.

Psalm 22

A psalm of lamentation and a plea for deliverance by one who feels deserted and pressed in on every side, expressing final confidence in God and God's goodness.

Hebrews 10:16–25

In this reading we hear that God has established the promised new covenant through which our sins are forgiven and God's laws are written on our hearts. Given such confidence, we are to be unswerving in our hope and strong in our encouragement of one another.

or

Hebrews 4:14–16; 5:7–9

In our New Testament reading we are encouraged to have full confidence in drawing near to God because Jesus, our great high priest, knows our every weakness and temptation and makes intercession for us. Having learned obedience through suffering, he has become the source of salvation for all who obey him.

John 18:1–19:42

Our gospel is the story of Jesus' trials before the Jewish council and Pilate, followed by his final sufferings and death.

Prayers of the People

Washed in the waters of Christ's death and resurrection, that we might enter the community of faith, let us praise our Lord by offering our prayers and thanksgivings as we respond, "Hear us, O risen Christ."

Risen Lord, mold us into your new creation, that we may seek the radiance of your light as found in the lives of the saints, and as revealed through the generosity of our sisters and brothers; let us pray.

Hear us, O risen Christ.

Eternal Christ, help us journey through this life with compassion and vision, entering into the sufferings of the world, that we might know the depth of your truth and the dwelling place of your love; let us pray.

Hear us, O risen Christ.

Saving Lord, stretch out the strong arms of your grace and lift up those who are hungry and downtrodden, lonely and forgotten, so that all of humanity may be reconciled to you and to one another; let us pray.

Hear us, O risen Christ.

Christ our Passover, may the nations of the world seek after peace and thirst anew for the freedom of men and women everywhere; may we pass from domination to mutual trust, from economic intimidation to a responsible use of the world's resources, from thoughts of destruction to a respect for all life; let us pray.

Hear us, O risen Christ.

Jesus, Bread of Heaven, nourish us in this Holy Sacrament of your unending Presence, that we may become for one another your bread of hope and your cup of joy; let us pray.

Hear us, O risen Christ.

Jesus, Savior, Risen Lord, we thank you for all the blessings of this life: for family and friends who reveal your love, for those who have died in the faith, for those who have entered our communities through baptism, for all things which enliven our spirits, and especially for the Paschal Flame that outshines every darkness; let us pray.

Hear us, O risen Christ.

Rejoicing in the garments of new life, let us continue our prayers.

(Special intentions of the congregation, the diocese, and the Anglican Communion may be added here or before the formal intercessions.)

The Celebrant adds a concluding Collect.

Images in the Readings

The **cross** was the electric chair of the Roman Empire, the means of execution for low-class criminals. Some cultures have used the shape of the cross as a sign of the four corners of the earth. Christians mark the newly baptized with this sign, God coming through suffering and death, aligned with all who are rejected, and surprisingly in this way bringing life to the whole earth. In the suggested sixth-century hymn "Sing, My Tongue," the cross is paradoxically likened to the archetypal Tree of Life.

In John's passion narrative, Jesus of Nazareth is called King of the Jews, the Son of God, and most significantly, I AM, the very **name** of God. Christians see in the man dying on the cross the mystery of God's self-giving love. Along with the witnesses in John's passion, we can sing with the hymn writer Caroline Noel, "At the name of Jesus every knee shall bow, every tongue confess him king of glory now."

In the Israelite sacrificial system, the **lamb** represented the life of the nomadic herders, and killing the lamb symbolized a plea that God would receive the animal's death as a gift that would prompt divine mercy. The New Testament often uses the image of the lamb as one way to understand the meaning of Jesus' death. The book of Revelation recalls Good Friday and Easter in its paradoxical vision of a lamb seated on a throne and standing as if slaughtered. But any single image—such as the lamb—is not sufficient. Thus we are given the opposite image, Christ as the **high priest** who does the slaughtering.

According to Israelite religion, the people needed an intermediary to approach God. Christ then is the mediator who prays to God for us. Yet for John, Christ is the God whom our prayers address.

Good Friday lays each image next to another one, for no single metaphor can fully explain the mystery of Christ.

Ideas for the Day

◆ Good Friday is our companion when darkness has set in and transformation has yet to break in. God has lived it. Good Friday is our story when we hear a life-limiting diagnosis; when we stand with our loved ones looking at the ashes of their home; when we feel so empty we cannot get out of bed; when we do not know what to feel or do or think when tragedy occurs; and when the last embers of our dreams have died. Good Friday entreats us to bring our brokenness to the cross that Jesus carried, not for a quick fix, but to know that we are never alone. We are in holy company.

◆ The vigil at the foot of the cross can be shared in various ways, but the congregation should experience it, whether it be in a three-hour vigil or in a briefer liturgy of reading, prayer, meditation, and discussing the feelings of the participants.

Making Connections

We have heard this story (John 18:1–19:42) many times. We are accustomed to it. We also know its joyous ending. We experience it as liturgy, pointing toward a resurrection we know is coming. The people who experienced it first had no such knowledge. It wasn't liturgy to them: it was a terrible now, unfolding before their horrified eyes. The undoing of everything for which they had hoped and upon which they had staked their lives. Reading it together today, as if it were a play, helps us feel it all more: the unjustness, the despair, the raw sorrow of new bereavement.

Engaging All Ages

First, dare to face the damage this passage (John 18:1–40, 19:1–37) has wrought. The drumming repetition of "the Jews" has funded violent anti-Semitism for centuries. We owe Jewish friends a constant apology and protection against Christians who think they enjoy God's permission to be bigots.

Second, use the bad examples of the crowds to scrutinize when we have sold out justice to keep our own peace. We'll grieve. Grieving takes courage. God's Spirit will assist us.

Third, admire the open courage of the women at the Cross and the sneakier courage of Joseph of Arimathea and Nicodemus. Admiring the admirable releases their characteristics in ourselves.

We owe it to our country to release civic courage into our public life. G. K. Chesterton defined mobs as crowds that contain no citizen.

Beg the Spirit to make us citizens.

Hymns for the Day

Note: There is no Entrance Hymn on this day (see BCP, 276).

The Hymnal 1982
Ah, holy Jesus, how hast thou offended 158
O sacred head, sore wounded 168, 169
To mock your reign, O dearest Lord 170
Alone thou goest forth, O Lord 164
Cross of Jesus, cross of sorrow 160
From God Christ's deity came forth 443
There is a green hill far away 167
At the cross her vigil keeping 159
Go to dark Gethsemane 171
In the cross of Christ I glory 441, 442
Lord Christ, when first thou cam'st to earth 598
Morning glory, starlit sky 585
Sing, my tongue, the glorious battle 165, 166
Sunset to sunrise changes now 163
Were you there when they crucified
     my Lord? (vs. 1–3) 172
When I survey the wondrous cross 474

Lift Every Voice and Sing II
O sacred head, sore wounded 36
Calvary 32
Near the cross 29
Lead me to Calvary 31
O how he loves you and me 35
The old rugged cross 38
There is a fountain 39
He never said a mumbalin' word 33
Were you there? (vv. 1–3) 37
He will remember me 34

Wonder, Love, and Praise
O sacred head, sore wounded 735
Faithful cross, above all other 737
When Jesus came to Golgotha 736

Holy Saturday

April 8, 2023

We ask God that we may wait with Christ for the coming of the third day and rise with him to newness of life.

Color Red / Oxblood

Preface Of Holy Week

Collect

O God, Creator of heaven and earth: Grant that, as the crucified body of your dear Son was laid in the tomb and rested on this holy Sabbath, so we may await with him the coming of the third day, and rise with him to newness of life; who now lives and reigns with you and the Holy Spirit, one God, for ever and ever. *Amen.*

Readings and Psalm

Job 14:1–14
Job reflects on the brevity of human life. Nature may renew itself but not mortals who have but an impossible hope that they might meet God after the grave.

or

Lamentations 3:1–9, 19–24
Our first reading is a poem of lamentation and complaint from one who feels besieged by God and circumstance yet chooses to affirm the steadfast love of the Lord and a belief that confidence in God is ultimately well placed.

Psalm 31:1–4, 15–16
A song of trust by one who looks to the Lord for mercy and protection.

1 Peter 4:1–8
Believers are encouraged to live lives devoted to the will of God, steering clear of all forms of dissipation. Because Christ has suffered in the flesh, his followers must be willing to do likewise, disciplining themselves for the goal of life in the spirit. Of primary importance is the practice of love for one another.

Matthew 27:57–66
A man of privilege and a disciple, Joseph of Arimathea, wraps the body of Jesus in clean linen and places the corpse in his own newly hewn tomb. Other disciples of Jesus witness the burial. Jesus' religious opponents appeal to Pilate to place a guard at the tomb lest Jesus' disciples steal his body, and Pilate gives them permission to seal the tomb.

or

John 19:38–42
Nicodemus and Joseph of Arimathea prepare Jesus' body for burial according to custom, interring Jesus' corpse in a new tomb in a garden where nobody had previously been laid.

Prayers of the People

Washed in the waters of Christ's death and resurrection, that we might enter the community of faith, let us praise our Lord by offering our prayers and thanksgivings as we respond, "Hear us, O risen Christ."

Risen Lord, mold us into your new creation, that we may seek the radiance of your light as found in the lives of the saints, and as revealed through the generosity of our sisters and brothers; let us pray.

Hear us, O risen Christ.

Eternal Christ, help us journey through this life with compassion and vision, entering into the sufferings of the world, that we might know the depth of your truth and the dwelling place of your love; let us pray.

Hear us, O risen Christ.

Saving Lord, stretch out the strong arms of your grace and lift up those who are hungry and downtrodden, lonely and forgotten, so that all of humanity may be reconciled to you and to one another; let us pray.

Hear us, O risen Christ.

Christ our Passover, may the nations of the world seek after peace and thirst anew for the freedom of men and women everywhere; may we pass from domination to mutual trust, from economic intimidation to a responsible use of the world's resources, from thoughts of destruction to a respect for all life; let us pray.

Hear us, O risen Christ.

Jesus, Bread of Heaven, nourish us in this Holy Sacrament of your unending Presence, that we may become for one another your bread of hope and your cup of joy; let us pray.

Hear us, O risen Christ.

Jesus, Savior, Risen Lord, we thank you for all the blessings of this life: for family and friends who reveal your love, for those who have died in the faith, for those who have entered our communities through baptism, for all things which enliven our spirits, and especially for the Paschal Flame that outshines every darkness; let us pray.

Hear us, O risen Christ.

Rejoicing in the garments of new life, let us continue our prayers.

(Special intentions of the congregation, the diocese, and the Anglican Communion may be added here or before the formal intercessions.)

The Celebrant adds a concluding Collect.

Ideas for the Day

- Jesus is dead. His followers are lamenting. Joseph of Arimathea, a disciple, follows the proper burial rituals for Jesus' body. He lays Jesus in a tomb, a sign of respect. This ritual is intimate and personal, like when we bury our own loved ones. The ritual is a known next step after a tragedy that has fully thwarted Jesus' followers' understanding of Jesus and the world. On Holy Saturday, we are invited to lament our beloved Jesus' death. We are invited into the rituals of grief and mourning. We are invited to imagine a word in which Jesus is dead.

- The church remains darkened. The bare altar and sanctuary is stark. A quiet liturgy of Morning Prayer can be offered.

Making Connections

Silence in the stone tomb. Silence and darkness—the mutilated one who lies there has no further need of light. Sometime in the night, though, something stirs. The flutter of a heartbeat? The twitch of a finger? What happens there, as the long night yields to the morning of the third day? You know that many modern people don't believe anything happened. But if nothing happened, would we still be talking about it two thousand years later? Would lives still be transformed by it? Maybe—a delusion can have great staying power. Or maybe something did happen, still happens. In us.

Engaging All Ages

Everybody thinks it's over.

For Joseph of Arimathea and Nicodemus it's over for five years, when they'll sweep the tomb for Joseph's own occupancy.

The chief priests and Pilate think it's over—with relief. The affair dishonored them and they know it.

The women who'll come tomorrow morning think it's over, as clearly as morticians do.

Nobody had hope. The admirable people are able to face into tragedy. Raw pain and, for the disciples, shame. Bravely faced.

God will insert the miracle that defines human history into their lives tomorrow morning. Not today.

That's the account they bequeathed to us. Our task is to be brave and trust it. In the face of danger, risk, and embarrassment, whisper, "Come, Holy Spirit; release in me the glory of Jesus. I'll try to be brave."

Hymns for the Day

The Hymnal 1982

From deepest woe I cry to thee 151
Immortal, invisible, God only wise 423
Out of the depths I call 666
O love, how deep, how broad, how high
    (vs. 1–4, 6) 448, 449
O Love of God, how strong and true
    (vs. 1–3) 455, 456
My song is love unknown (vs. 1–2, 6–7) 458
O sorrow deep! 173
Were you there when they crucified
    my Lord? (vs. 1–3) 172

Lift Every Voice and Sing II

Lead me to the calvary 31
Were you there? (vs. 1–3) 37

Wonder, Love, and Praise

The steadfast love of the Lord never ceases 755

Easter

Preparing for Easter

Theological Themes that Might Shape Liturgy, Catechesis, and Education

Eastertide is God's ultimate rejection of violence and clear declaration of the core values of the kingdom of God—abundant life, reconciliation, joy, peace. These themes are explored throughout the Easter season. Like Christmas, the religious celebration of Easter is often shrouded by a broader, albeit less clear, celebration of Easter in the wider culture. This is seen in the marked uptick in attendance on Easter. How we choose to celebrate this holy season can draw a distinction between broader celebrations of springtime and a more meaningful celebration of the resurrection of Jesus Christ.

Easter is a season that lasts fifty days through Ascension Day and up to and including Pentecost. The length of the season underscores the importance of the event we are celebrating. It also presents us with many opportunities for celebration in our faith communities, including long after the neighborhood Easter egg rolls are over and the discount store has begun putting up red, white, and blue decor for the impending celebration of Independence Day.

Liturgical Possibilities

Rites

Easter begins on Easter Sunday, the first of seven Sundays of Easter. In stark contrast to the liturgies that occurred during Lent, and especially Holy Week, Easter should be filled with celebratory music and plenty of opportunities for the congregation to respond to liturgical actions with joy. Eucharistic Prayer D, though the longest of those in the prayer book, might be a suitable choice here (chanted if possible, Mozarabic if you're daring). The next week, the Octave of Easter, is suitable for daily eucharistic celebration, another nod towards the sheer importance of this event.

There are some liturgical variations that might occur during this season too, including the omission of the Confession and Absolution. Whatever the decision is here, a note in the bulletin (if printed bulletins are present) or some other form of communication might be a helpful form of catechesis, emphasizing grace, love, and reconciliation as themes of the season.

In addition to Easter Sunday, there are at least two other Major Feasts during Eastertide—Ascension Day and Pentecost. Ascension Day, which occurs mid-week, forty days into the Easter season, is another opportunity to observe Eucharist as a community. Pentecost, which falls on the "eighth" Sunday of Easter, or fifty days after the Resurrection, celebrates the coming of the Holy Spirit on the community of disciples and the continued presence of the Holy Spirit as the animating force of the Church. It is a perfect day for baptisms and for worshipers to renew their own baptismal vows.

Space

The Paschal Candle is one of the central foci of the Easter season. Having it lit and prominently placed is important to convey a central theme of Easter—the unconquered Light of Christ.

Other Rituals and Resources

Easter is a suitable season to welcome new people who have circled into the faith community in the past year. As Easter celebrates the new life that is possible in Christ, newcomers to our faith communities represent the new life that comes when we encounter and are transformed by the presence of another.

Easter

Through the Eyes of a Child

Jesus is risen from the dead! Easter has brought us everlasting life because of Jesus' resurrection. The alleluias are said and sung. God's love is stronger than anything, even death. Because of God's love, we do not have to be afraid of death. Easter is about new life, coming from what we thought was death and bringing unexpected possibilities and surprises. Easter eggs, Easter chicks, Easter flowers all remind us of the new life in Christ. We received new life at our baptism, and during Easter we think about what that baptism means in our lives. Reflect with the children on the ways we keep our baptismal promises:

+ How do we keep the promises we make?

+ How do we show our love for God?

+ How do we show love for each other?

Make an alleluia banner for the table, and talk about why Jesus' resurrection would make us so happy. Take a walk and look at all the new life you begin to spot during the walk. Read stories of transformation and new life, such as *The Very Hungry Caterpillar*[1] by Eric Carle. Name the baptismal promises and reflect on them with pictures of how you live each of them out with your family and friends, at home and at school.

As with Christmas, though to a lesser extent, Easter occupies a privileged place in our social memory. Children will hear messages of Easter that may conflict with or complicate the message the Church teaches. A robust celebration of Easter that includes children where possible or that empowers the parents and guardians of children to become evangelists for the Resurrection is of utmost importance. Liturgical ritual is filled with opportunities to draw children into the mystery. Therefore, planning the liturgy with a mind towards the inclusion of younger people might be key. How can we use the liturgy to teach children about the cultivation of joy? The power of hope? The unstoppable love of God?

Through the Eyes of Youth

This is the time to encourage youth to Easter reflection and action. Reflect upon the individual baptismal promises found in the Easter Vigil service, and invite the youth to respond to new ways that they can serve within the congregation:

+ Take Easter flowers to shut-ins.

+ Become part of a lay eucharistic visiting team.

+ Color Easter eggs for the young children and engage them in an Easter egg hunt.

+ Invite someone to church who does not have a "home" church.

+ Through the Sundays of Easter put closure on their Lenten project.

Above all, give youth an opportunity to witness to the fact that they believe Jesus has risen from the dead.

+ Go: "Where does God need us to go—in school, in our neighborhood, town, and beyond?"

+ Visit: "Who are the friendless, lonely, outcast people in our lives and how do we connect with them?"

+ Listen: "Who are the people that no one pays attention to?"

+ Care: "Why, God, are your people suffering?"

+ Ask: "What can we do for needy people near and far?"

+ Pray: "God, open our eyes and ears and hearts. Who will help us to live for others?"

+ Invite: "Who will go with us? Which adults and teens can we invite to follow, to encounter, and to become Christ today?"

---

1 New York: World Publishing Co., 1969.

Through the Eyes of Daily Life

On this day the Lord has acted! On the first day of the week God began creation, transforming darkness into light. On this, the "eighth day" of the week, Jesus Christ was raised from the dead. We celebrate this new creation in the waters of baptism and in the feast of victory. Reflect on your baptism and how you live out the promises in every facet of your life. Throughout this season, we hear stories of the men and women who recognized who Jesus really is, after failing to do so during his earthly life. We are enlightened by their visions and their visits with the Risen Christ as they proclaim that our Lord is alive and is life for the world. As we begin the Great Fifty Days of Easter filled with hope and joy, be prepared to go forth to share the news that Christ is risen!

While a fifty-day party might sound like a lot of fun, sustaining the energy for that long might prove more daunting than originally thought. However, the rich themes of Easter can have direct bearing on the lives of the faithful. Structuring liturgy, formation, and fellowship in ways that allow people to get the themes of Easter into their bones might be extremely helpful here. While Lenten calendars might help us structure our fast and devotion, what might an Easter calendar that helps us structure our celebration and gratitude look like?

Through the Eyes of Those Outside of the Church

As with Christmas, how the Church chooses to mark Easter can either distinguish the Church as an alternative community centered around a different set of values or just another repository of prevailing culture. Not only should our liturgical celebration be joyous and meaningful, but we might think seriously about what it means to turn our worshipers into evangelists of the Resurrection, empowering them with tools to be a blessing to those they meet outside of church. Expecting people to come to church to experience the fullness of the Resurrection is a wasted opportunity. Instead, it might be helpful to turn what might be a rote celebration of a religious ritual into an opportunity to serve the world in the name of him who died and rose again.

Through the Eyes of the Global Community

The collects for Easter petition the living power of Jesus to open up new life to all. Our prayers and action can reflect God's desire of reconciliation for all. During the Easter season, direct attention is placed in prayer to alleviate the extreme poverty of the world. The Christ-centeredness of the Sustainable Development Goals (SDGs) is an example of how making a commitment to others is a commitment to Jesus (John 10:10). For the sake of the poor and suffering of the world, our conversion (turning our lives around) at the individual, congregational, diocesan, church-wide, and global level, a difference can be made (Luke 18:18–23). Focus on one SDG for the whole liturgical cycle so that during the Easter season, a particular geographic area can be chosen to learn about the people, worship, and need in that area of the world or domestically. The Easter season can be a time to build direct relationships with another location in the Anglican Communion. Enter into mission with another, to help alleviate extreme poverty.

Easter

Seasonal Rites for Easter

Easter Season Blessings²

The following blessing may be used by a bishop or priest whenever a blessing is appropriate. It is a three-fold form, with an Amen at the end of each sentence, leading into a Trinitarian blessing.

May Almighty God, who has redeemed us and made us his children through the resurrection of his Son our Lord, bestow upon you the riches of his blessing. *Amen.*

May God, who through the water of baptism has raised us from sin into newness of life, make you holy and worthy to be united with Christ for ever. *Amen.*

May God, who has brought us out of bondage to sin into true lasting freedom in the Redeemer, bring you to your eternal inheritance. *Amen.*

And the blessing of God Almighty, the Father, the Son, and the Holy Spirit, be upon you and remain with you for ever. *Amen.*

Blessings Over Food at Easter³

These blessings are appropriate for a parish meal following the Easter Vigil or over foods brought to the church for blessing.

Over Wine

Blessed are you, O Lord our God, creator of the fruit of the vine: Grant that we who share this wine, which gladdens our hearts, may share for ever the new life of the true Vine, your Son Jesus Christ our Lord. *Amen.*

Over Bread

Blessed are you, O Lord our God: you bring forth bread from the earth and make the risen Lord to be for us the Bread of life: Grant that we who daily seek the bread which sustains our bodies may also hunger for the food of everlasting life, Jesus Christ our Lord. *Amen.*

Over Lamb

Stir up our memory, O Lord, as we eat this Easter lamb, remembering Israel of old, who in obedience to your command ate the Pascal lamb and was delivered from the bondage of slavery, that we, your new Israel, may rejoice in the resurrection of Jesus Christ, the true Lamb who has delivered us from the bondage of sin and death, and who lives and reigns for ever and ever. *Amen.*

Over Eggs

O Lord our God, in celebration of the Pascal feast we have prepared these eggs from your creation: Grant that they may be to us a sign of the new life and immortality promised to those who follow your Son, Jesus Christ our Lord. *Amen.*

Over Other Foods

Blessed are you, O Lord our God; you have given us the risen Savior to be the Shepherd of your people: Lead us, by him, to springs of living waters, and feed us with the food that endures to eternal life; where with you, O Father, and with the Holy Spirit, he lives and reigns, One God, for ever and ever. *Amen.*

---

2 *Book of Occasional Services 2003* (New York: Church Publishing, 2004), 26.
3 Ibid, 97–98.

Earth Day Litany[4]

Wednesday, April 22
We have forgotten who we are.
We have become separate from the movements
    of the earth.
We have turned our backs on the cycles of life.
We have forgotten who we are.

We have sought only our own security.
We have exploited simply for our own ends.
We have distorted our knowledge.
We have abused our power.
We have forgotten who we are.

Now the land is barren
And the waters are poisoned
And the air is polluted.
We have forgotten who we are.

Now the forests are dying
And the creatures are disappearing
And the humans are despairing.
We have forgotten who we are.

We ask forgiveness.
We ask for the gift of remembering.
**We ask for the strength to change,
all for the love of our Creator. *Amen.***

Rogation Days[5]

*The Rogation Days are traditionally observed on the
Monday, Tuesday, and Wednesday before Ascension
Day. They may, however, be observed on other days,
depending on local conditions and the convenience of the
congregation.*

*In ancient times, the observance consisted of an outdoor
procession that culminated in a special celebration of the
Eucharist. In more recent centuries, the procession has
frequently taken place on a Sunday afternoon, apart from
the Eucharist.*

*Hymns, psalms, canticles, and anthems are sung during the
procession. The following are appropriate:*

Canticle 1 or 12 (Benedicite)
Psalm 102 (Refrain: "Bless the Lord, O my soul")
Psalm 104 (Refrain: "Hallelujah")

*At suitable places the procession may halt for appropriate
Bible readings and prayers. Some examples include:*

Station: At a place of work

Ecclesiasticus 38:27–32a

Presider: Let us pray.
Almighty God, whose Son Jesus Christ in his earthly
life shared our toil and hallowed our labor: Be present
with your people where they work. Make those
who carry on the industries and commerce of this
land responsive to your will, and bring all workers
satisfaction in what they do and a just return for their
labor; through Jesus Christ our Redeemer. *Amen.*

Station: For scientists and explorers

Genesis 1:1–5 or Ecclesiasticus 17:1–11

Presider: Let us pray.
God of Mystery, you made the universe with its
marvelous order and chaos, its atoms, worlds,
and galaxies, and the infinite complexity of living
creatures. We give you thanks for all who study the
mysteries of creation and ask that their work may
increase our curiosity, wonder, and joy, that we may
come to know you more truly and serve you more
humbly; in the name of Jesus Christ, your Wisdom and
your Word. *Amen.*

4 United Nations Environment Programme. "Only One Earth," a United
Nations Environment Programme publication for Environmental Sabbath/
Earth Rest Day, June 1990. UN Environment Programme, DC2-803,
United Nations, New York, NY 10017. Used by permission.

5 *Book of Occasional Services*, 2003, 90–94, 103–104.

Station: For a place of healing

Matthew 8:14–16

Presider: Let us pray.

Merciful God, whose Son Jesus healed many who were sick: We commend to your care all who suffer, and those who care for them. By your grace lend compassion and skill to health and veterinary workers here and everywhere, and bring healing and comfort to those in need, that all may know your power and goodness and rise up to serve you, in the strength of your Holy Spirit. *Amen.*

Station: At a place where trash, compost, or recycling is handled

Luke 13:6–9

Presider: Let us pray.

Renewing God: Bless all whose labor here supports the well-being of our community. Strengthen and encourage them in their service, and make us mindful of their contribution to the stewardship of the earth, that all may be ministers of your new creation; in the name of Jesus our Redeemer. *Amen.*

> *In addition to the readings listed on page 930 of the Book of Common Prayer, any of the following passages are appropriate:*

Genesis 8:13–23
Leviticus 26:1–13 (14–20)
Deuteronomy 8:1–19 (11–20)
Hosea 2:18–23
Ezekiel 34:25–31
James 4:7–11
Matthew 6:25–34
John 12:23–26

> *In addition to the prayers in the Book of Common Prayer, the following can be used:*

Almighty and everlasting God, Creator of all things and giver of all life, let your blessing be upon this (see, livestock, plow, forest, _____) and grant that *it* may serve to your glory and the welfare of your people; through Jesus Christ our Lord. *Amen.*

A Prayer for Stewardship of Creation Harvest[6]

Demanding God,
you call us to account
for the use of your gifts:
pull down the storehouses
of accumulated greed
which impoverish people
and despoil the earth;
put our hands to work
sowing the seeds
and reaping the growth
of justice, thanksgiving and praise;
through Jesus Christ, the Lord of the harvest. Amen.

A Mother's Day Prayer[7]

Sunday, May 10

On this Mother's Day, we give thanks to God for the divine gift of motherhood in all its diverse forms. Let us pray for all the mothers among us today; for our own mothers, those living and those who have passed away; for the mothers who loved us and for those who fell short of loving us fully; for all who hope to be mothers someday and for those whose hope to have children has been frustrated; for all the mothers who have lost children; for all women and men who have mothered others in any way—those who have been our substitute mothers and we who have done so for those in need; and for the earth that bore us and provides us with our sustenance. We pray this all in the name of God, our great and loving Mother. *Amen.*

6 Steven Shakespeare, *Prayers for an Inclusive Church* (New York: Church Publishing, Inc., 2009), 128.

7 Leslie Nipps, "For Mother's Day" in *Women's Uncommon Prayers* (Harrisburg, PA: Morehouse Publishing, 2000), 364.

Ascensiontide Prayer[8]

Thursday, May 21

Jesus lifted his hands and blessed his disciples. As he blessed them, he left them and was taken up to heaven. They worshipped him and returned to Jerusalem overwhelmed with joy. — Luke 24:50–52

God of all times and all places,
when you arrived in Christ Jesus
you began to bring heaven down to earth,
and when you departed
you began to draw earth up to heaven:
bless us so that we may continue
to worship you joyfully in the power of the Holy Spirit,
inviting all the people of earth
to become part of your heavenly kingdom. Amen.

A Prayer for Memorial Day[9]

Monday, May 25

Lord God, in whom there is life and light: Accept our thanks for those who died for us, our prayers for those who mourn, our praise for the hope you have given us. Refresh our hearts with dedication to heroic ideas, with appreciation for the honesty of the just, with obedience to upright laws. Forgive us when our patriotism is hollow, when our nationalism is arrogant, when our allegiance is halfhearted. Stir within us thanksgiving for all we have inherited, vigilance for the freedoms of all people, willingness to sacrifice for fellow citizens. Comfort us with the joy that Christ died for all those who died for us, bringing life and immortality to light for all who believe in him. *Amen.*

---

8 Jenifer Gamber and Timothy J. S. Seamans, *Common Prayer for Children and Families* (New York: Church Publishing, Inc., 2019), 64.

9 "The Last Monday in May," in *An American Prayer Book*, ed. Christopher L. Webber (Harrisburg, PA: Morehouse Publishing, 2008), 141–142.

The Great Vigil of Easter

April 8, 2023

Celebrating Christ's glorious resurrection, we pray that we may be renewed in body and mind, being raised from the dead of sin by God's life-giving Spirit.

Color White

Preface Of Easter

Collect

Almighty God, who for our redemption gave your only-begotten Son to the death of the cross, and by his glorious resurrection delivered us from the power of the enemy: Grant us so to die daily to sin, that we may evermore live with him in the joy of his resurrection; through Jesus Christ your Son our Lord, who lives and reigns with you and the Holy Spirit, one God, now and for ever. *Amen.*

or

O God, who made this most holy night to shine with the glory of the Lord's resurrection: Stir up in your Church that Spirit of adoption which is given to us in Baptism, that we, being renewed both in body and mind, may worship you in sincerity and truth; through Jesus Christ our Lord, who lives and reigns with you, in the unity of the Holy Spirit, one God, now and for ever. *Amen.*

Readings and Psalm

Genesis 1:1–2:4a

Our lesson is the story of creation. As this ancient narrative opens, the Spirit of the Lord hovers like a great mother bird over the shapeless world. God then forms the heaven and the earth and all its creatures in six days. The seventh day is set aside as a day of rest. God's ultimate creative act is human life, made in God's own image, to whom rulership and responsibility over all other life are given.

Psalm 136:1–9, 23–26

A psalm in praise of a good Creator, a God of enduring mercy.

Genesis 7:1–5, 11–18; 8:6–18; 9:8–13

Noah and his household are commanded by the Lord to enter the ark, together with pairs of all animals. Forty days and nights of rain and flood cover the earth in water. Finally the waters subside, and the Lord makes a covenant with Noah, promising never again to destroy the earth by flood. As a sign of this covenant, God hangs God's own warrior's bow in the clouds, the rainbow which stretches in the sky's vast expanse.

Psalm 46

The earth may be moved and kingdoms shaken, but God is our refuge.

Genesis 22:1–18

This reading is the story of Abraham's willingness in obedience to the Lord's command to sacrifice his only son, Isaac, and the Lord's blessing of him. The narrative illustrates Abraham's readiness to abandon all to serve the Lord. Originally it probably also was used as a model story encouraging the substitution of animal for human sacrifices. Ancient Israel was given a better understanding of God's will, and because of his obedience, Abraham received God's promise to him and his descendants.

Psalm 16

Contentment, refuge, and joy are found in the presence of the Lord, who does not abandon God's faithful servant at death.

Exodus 14:10–31; 15:20–21

This reading is the story of the deliverance of Israel from bondage in Egypt. The people are terrified when they see the pursuing army and complain that it would have been better to live in slavery than to die in the wilderness. Moses urges them to courage, for they will see the salvation of the Lord, who has called them to freedom to serve the one true God. The Lord then brings them safely through the sea and destroys the army of the Egyptians.

Canticle 8 (The Song of Moses, Exodus 15:1b–13, 17–18)

A song of praise to God for deliverance from captivity in Egypt and from the peril of pursuing armies.

Isaiah 55:1–11

In this lesson we hear how the return from exile will be a time of prosperity and abundance when God's covenant will be renewed. The prophet pictures the great day: for a people who have been near death there will be food and drink without cost. God's covenant with David is to be extended to all Israel, and other nations will come to see her glory. The life-giving word of the Lord will not fail to produce its fruit and, together with Israel, the natural world will rejoice and reflect God's power.

Canticle 9 (The First Song of Isaiah, Isaiah 12:2–6)

A song of praise and thanksgiving to God, the Holy One of Israel.

Baruch 3:9–15, 3:32–4:4

The lesson is a poem of praise to Wisdom, God's companion in the process of creation and God's precious gift to humankind. All who find her will be blessed, and she is embodied most especially in the Torah, the book of God's commandments.

or

Proverbs 8:1–8, 19–21; 9:4b–6

In this lesson Wisdom calls to all who will hear, offering understanding, direction, and insight into the way of righteousness and justice. She is God's gift to the wise and simple alike, and those who learn her ways will prosper.

Psalm 19

A hymn that glorifies the Creator God, with special praise for God's law and a prayer for avoidance of sin.

Ezekiel 36:24–28

A time is coming when God will place a new heart and spirit within the people, who will cleave to God and walk in righteousness. Ezekiel prophesies the restoration of the dispersed and humiliated people of Israel.

Psalm 42

The psalmist laments his inability to come to the house of God and thirsts for the presence of the Lord.

and

Psalm 43

A plea to God by one who is persecuted and in distress, to be able to come and worship in the Lord's temple.

Ezekiel 37:1–14

The prophet has a vision of the bones of a dead and hopeless people being restored to new life in their homeland. The Lord calls upon Ezekiel as son of man to prophesy that the people who have experienced exile and many hardships will live again. The Spirit of the Lord restores their spirit and breath, and they rise from death. Although this passage can be understood to anticipate the hope of individual resurrection, Israel did not yet have this belief.

Psalm 143

The psalmist prays earnestly for the help of God's presence.

Zephaniah 3:14–20

In this lesson the prophet foretells a time when the judgment of Israel will be ended and the mighty Lord will bring victory and renewal to the people. The city of Jerusalem and its holy Mount Zion may rejoice and sing. All enemies will be defeated and the crippled healed. The fortunes of Israel will be restored, and the nation will be praised by all peoples.

Psalm 98

A song of thanksgiving and praise to the victorious Lord, who has made righteousness known and shown faithfulness to God's people.

Romans 6:3–11

In this reading we hear that, as Christian disciples have been joined with Christ in his death through baptism, so they are to know a resurrection life like his. In union with Christ we have died to our sinful selves and have begun to experience a new way of life. In one sense our freedom from death still awaits us in the future, but, in another sense, we already know what it means to be alive to God in Christ Jesus and to realize the true meaning of life.

Psalm 114

A song of praise to the Lord, who has brought the people safely out of Egypt and through the wilderness to the Promised Land.

Matthew 28:1–10

Our gospel tells of Jesus' resurrection. It is about daybreak as the women come to the grave. No human eye sees Jesus rise, but there is an earthquake and an angel of the Lord rolls away the stone covering the tomb. He tells the two Marys that Jesus is going before his disciples to Galilee. With both fear and joy in their hearts, they run to tell the disciples and, on the way, are met by their risen Lord.

Images in the Readings

At the beginning of the Vigil, Christ is symbolized by the candle, which gives **light** to our darkness and remains bright even when we all share in its flame. The early church called baptism enlightenment. Sharing this light outdoors in darkness makes the image emotionally effective.

Each reading offers an image with which to picture salvation: the earth is God's perfect creation; we are saved in the ark during the flood; we are granted a reprieve from sacrifice; we escape the enemy army; we are enlivened by spring rains; we are instructed by Woman Wisdom; we are given a new heart; our bones are brought back to life; we enjoy a homeland; swallowed by the fish, we do not drown but are coughed up on dry ground; we wear party clothes; when thrown into a furnace, we emerge untouched by the fire; we are risen with Christ; and although we do mistake Christ for the gardener, he appears to us and enlivens our faith.

Ideas for the Day

- The tradition on Easter Vigil is to read at least two of the Lessons for the day; the only Lesson that is required to be read is the Exodus text (the Parting of the Red Sea). Many hymns and songs have been written about this Bible story, including "Go Down Moses" (LEVS II #228), "Wade in the Water" (LEVS II #143), and the children's camp song "Pharoah, Pharoah" (to the tune of "Louie Louie"). What about this story makes it so important? How is God freeing God's people today?

- In Romans 6, we hear that we are baptized into Jesus' death as well as his resurrection. Our "old self" is put to death through baptism, and we are then able to "walk in newness of life." In baptism, we not only become part of God's family in the Church, God also puts to death our old selves and gifts us with new life. Historically, Easter Vigil is often when people are baptized and those gathered who are already baptized give thanks for their own baptisms. Because we are brought to new life through baptism, Easter Vigil is a perfect time to literally connect our baptismal new life with the celebration of Jesus' resurrection.

- In Matthew's resurrection story, it is the two Marys who first hear of Jesus' resurrection and witness the risen Christ. They are the ones Jesus sends to tell the rest of the disciples about Jesus' resurrection, and that he will meet them all in Galilee. Though women have been silenced in the Church throughout history, here we see Jesus empowering the women to be the first to proclaim the good news of the resurrection. Jesus continues to call women to share the good news; we are invited by God to empower women and lift up the voices of those who aren't always listened to.

Easter

Making Connections

The Easter Vigil has been compared to a campfire where we gather to tell our story. Some also say this is the finest liturgy in Christianity. We relive God's saving work in history: the creation of the world and humankind, God's intervention in the lives of the children of Israel, and the assurance of new life in the Resurrection of Jesus. This is our story. This is our song. The Vigil tells who we are as a people redeemed by our God and as a people of the Resurrection; death does not have the final word. Alleluia!

Engaging All Ages

Don't be hard on the soldiers guarding the tomb. Standing still at the actual Resurrection was above their paygrade.

More instructive is the sad courage of the women who came to anoint Jesus' carcass. They'd have to face down bored soldiers only, if successful, to address a nauseating task.

Instead, their courage is rewarded by two breathtaking encounters. First by an angel who, as always with angels, has to begin by saying, "Fear not!"

And the second encounter is with Jesus himself. He has chosen to reward their courage by making them the first real apostles, witnesses to our Lord's Resurrection.

As we've noted, courage is the Spirit's gift.

Jesus' embrace is courage's reward.

People of God: be brave!

Hymns for the Day

The Hymnal 1982

I sing the almighty power of God 398
Let us, with a gladsome mind [P] 389
Many and great, O God, are thy works 385
Most High, omnipotent, good Lord 406, 407
Most Holy God, the Lord of heaven 31, 32
O blest Creator, source of light (vs. 1–4) 27, 28
A mighty fortress is our God [P] 687, 688
Eternal Father, strong to save 608
Lord Jesus, think on me 641
O sorrow deep! 173
The God of Abraham praise 401
Sing now with joy unto the Lord [Canticle] 425
God moves in a mysterious way 677
Surely it is God who saves me [Canticle] 678, 679
The stars declare his glory 431
God, you have given us power to sound 584
The stars declare his glory [P] 431
As longs the deer for cooling streams 658
Before thy throne, O God, we kneel 574, 575
Breathe on me, Breath of God 508
Go forth for God; go to the world in peace 347
Put forth, O God, thy Spirit's might 521
New songs of celebration render 413
Surely it is God who saves me 678, 679

Lift Every Voice and Sing II

Go down, Moses 228
Let it breathe on me 116
Spirit of the living God 115

Wonder, Love, and Praise

Camina, pueblo de Dios /
    Walk on, O people of God 739
Wisdom freed a holy people 905
Even when young, I prayed for wisdom's grace 906
As panting deer desire the waterbrooks 727

The Sunday of the Resurrection: Easter Day

April 9, 2023

Celebrating Christ's glorious resurrection, we pray that we may be renewed in body and mind, being raised from the death of sin by God's life-giving Spirit.

Color White

Preface Easter

Collect

O God, who for our redemption gave your only-begotten Son to the death of the cross, and by his glorious resurrection delivered us from the power of our enemy: Grant us so to die daily to sin, that we may evermore live with him in the joy of his resurrection; through Jesus Christ your Son our Lord, who lives and reigns with you and the Holy Spirit, one God, now and for ever. *Amen.*

Readings and Psalm

Acts 10:34–43

The conversion of Cornelius marks an important turning point in the understanding of God as impartial and consequently the outreach of the Church to Gentiles. Many "circumcised believers" (11:2) rejected and feared the possible inclusion of Gentiles in the Church, but Luke makes clear that Peter himself (even before Paul) began the mission to the Gentiles under the direction of the Holy Spirit (1:8) because his idea of God had changed. Cornelius was a "God-fearing man" (10:2, 22); that is, a Gentile who worshiped Israel's God but had not adopted all of the Jewish religious practices. Peter's sermon summarizes the basic preaching of the early Church. God anointed Jesus as Messiah "with the Holy Spirit and power" for a ministry of "doing good and healing" (10:38). God's saving action in Jesus is supported by apostolic witness (10:39, 41) and scriptural proof (10:43), issuing in a call to conversion. Along with the apostles, all those who celebrate the eucharist on Easter Day are witnesses to Jesus' resurrection.

or

Isaiah 65:17–25

In chapter 65, God responds to the psalm of intercession in 63:7–64:12. Today's reading, the last three stanzas of God's reply, builds on the historical act of redemption proclaimed in 40:1–11 and expands it into a promise of a new creation. The Hebrew Bible descriptions of the age to come reveal the new world as a restoration of God's original purpose in creation. The reference to life expectancy (v. 20) designates more than a promise of longevity. The elimination of sorrow, impossible when death remains, and the earlier promise that God "will swallow up death forever" (25:7) seem to suggest a return to the Eden-like conditions before the fall. Then the tree of life was accessible and granted immortality. Adam's experience of futility in labor, also a result of the fall, will vanish.

Psalm 118:1–2, 14–24

This psalm is the final psalm of the "Egyptian Hallel" (Psalms 113–118), a cycle of psalms used during the Passover festival. Its original use before the exile was probably as a liturgy of thanksgiving said at the temple gates.

1 Corinthians 15:19–26

In this lesson Paul describes the plan of the resurrection age: it has begun with Christ's rising, and this event gives us confidence that God will defeat death, the last enemy. Some of the Corinthians either doubted Christ's resurrection or held that Christians could already live a fully resurrected life of the spirit without any regard for the body. Paul insists on the reality of Christ's rising, which has made possible the hope of a new life in a world where all presently die.

or

Easter

Acts 10:34–43

In preparation for the next topic of discussion, the resurrection of the dead (15:12), Paul reminds the Corinthians of their common ground of belief. By quoting a traditional formulation of the essential proclamation about Christ (15:3–5), he recalls the basic credal statements he taught them. What particular verses of the "scriptures" (that is, the Old Testament) Paul means in verses 3 and 4 is not explicit. In general, the statement "in accordance with the scriptures" expresses the conviction that these events took place according to God's purpose. It was, however, the lived experience of the early Christians, not merely the evidence of the Old Testament, that shaped their belief.

John 20:1–18

Today's reading describes the experience of the discovery of the empty tomb, and the different responses of the disciples and the appearance of the Risen Jesus to Mary Magdalene. Early on the first day after the Sabbath, Mary Magdalene discovers that Jesus' tomb lies open. Her first instinct is to tell Peter and the others. After hearing her breathless message that Jesus's body has been taken, Peter and the beloved disciple run to visit the tomb. They find only the burial cloths but not the body of Jesus. The simple fact of the empty tomb does not produce faith for Mary or for Peter. Mary experiences the Risen Lord, whom she mistakes for a gardener. Until she hears his voice, Mary does not recognize the Risen Jesus as the earthly Jesus whom she knew. The process of recognizing the Risen Jesus highlights both the continuity and the difference between his earthly and his risen forms. The focus of the disciples' relationship to Jesus must now shift from his physical presence to his spiritual presence within the community and in the believer. Jesus' permanent presence in the community will not be through appearances but through the Spirit, who will be the presence of the absent Jesus just as Jesus was the presence of the invisible Father. Jesus must "go away" for that to be accomplished (John 16:7).

or

Luke 24:1–12

For the disciples, the empty tomb was not a "proof" that Jesus had risen from the dead. Rather, it presented the disciples with perplexing information that led in many directions and demanded an interpretation of its meaning. Only when some divine help was provided (here by the angelic messenger and later by the risen Jesus who appeared to the disciples in Jerusalem and on the way to Emmaus) did the true meaning emerge. Like us, the women are told that in order to discover the meaning of his resurrection, they must remember everything that Jesus said and did. Only by seeing this event in continuity with his birth, life, ministry, and death can they recognize that the resurrection is the culmination of all that Jesus was trying to accomplish. Today's reading gives a selection from Peter's missionary speech to Cornelius, a Gentile centurion, and his household. The conversion of Cornelius marks an important turning point in the understanding of God as impartial and consequently the outreach of the Church to Gentiles. Cornelius was a "God-fearing man" (10:2, 22); that is, a Gentile who worshiped Israel's God but had not adopted all of the Jewish religious practices. Peter's sermon summarizes the basic preaching of the early Church. God anointed Jesus as Messiah "with the Holy Spirit and power" for a ministry of "doing good and healing" (10:38). God's saving action in Jesus is supported by apostolic witness (10:39, 41) and scriptural proof (10:43), issuing in a call to conversion. Along with the apostles, all those who celebrate the Eucharist on Easter Day are witnesses to Jesus' resurrection.

or

Jeremiah 31:1–6

Today's reading comes from a section (chaps. 30–33) consisting of promises of restoration (30:1–4). In it are gathered Jeremiah's oracles of hope for an eventual renewal for Israel. Jeremiah envisions the restoration of Judah by imagining God's fashioning a new exodus through which God will once again deliver the covenant people.

Psalm 118:1–2, 14–24

This psalm is the final psalm of the "Egyptian Hallel" (Psalms 113–118), a cycle of psalms used during the Passover festival. Its original use before the exile was probably as a liturgy of thanksgiving said at the temple gates.

Colossians 3:1–4

This reading points toward the implications of Christ's resurrection for himself and for the believer. Jesus is now "seated at the right hand of God," that is, he has been vindicated, returned to his heavenly glory, and enthroned as King. The believer now shares in his risen life.

or

Acts 10:34–43

(See above)

John 20:1–18

Today's reading describes the experience of the discovery of the empty tomb and the different responses of the disciples and the appearance of the risen Jesus to Mary Magdalene. Early on the first day after the Sabbath, Mary Magdalene discovers that Jesus' tomb lies open. Her first instinct is to tell Peter and the others. Mary experiences the risen Lord, whom she mistakes for a gardener. Until she hears his voice, Mary does not recognize the risen Jesus as the earthly Jesus whom she knew. The process of recognizing the risen Jesus highlights both the continuity and the difference between his earthly and his risen forms.

or

Matthew 28:1–10

Matthew's resurrection narrative describes the discovery of the empty tomb by Mary Magdalene and the other Mary and the drama of an earthquake and an angel who rolls back the stone and sits upon it—a sign that the tomb is permanently open so they can enter and discover that Jesus is not there. The angel allays their fear and then sends them to announce the good news of the resurrection to the disciples. The risen Jesus himself surprises them on their way back and personally gives them the same commission that the angel did to go to the disciples with the easter message.

Prayers of the People

Jesus Christ is risen today, our triumphant holy day. Alleluia! So let us pray to our Lord, saying, "Risen Christ, *to you we give undying praise.*"

Heavenly King, for us you endured the cross and the grave. When we were yet sinners, you redeemed and saved us. May we sing your eternal praises everywhere we go.

Silence

Risen Christ,

> *To you we give undying praise.*

Incarnate Love, where hearts are wintry, grieving or in pain, call forth new life by your touch. Bring forth life in the barren places of your world.

Silence

Risen Christ,

> *To you we give undying praise.*

Author of Life, you are the ruler of creation. All things created on earth sing to your glory. From the death of the winter, raise the fair beauty of earth.

Silence

Risen Christ,

> *To you we give undying praise.*

Resurrected One, bring our neighbors from sadness into joy. Where they live in darkness, brighten their lives with a day of splendor and give to all that peace that passes human knowing.

Invite the congregation to add their thanksgivings, followed by silence

Risen Christ,

> *To you we give undying praise.*

Triumphant Lord, gladden the faces of all who are sad and fearful-hearted. May they rejoice in your victory over sin and pain—even as they share in your glorious triumph.

Invite the congregation to add their petitions, followed by silence

Risen Christ,

> *To you we give undying praise.*

Easter

Risen Christ, you have opened heaven's gate. You have freed us from the power of sin and death. Through your resurrection, you give us the promise of resurrection to a holier state. Bless the dying and the dead.

Silence

Risen Christ,

To you we give undying praise.

Images in the Readings

Matthew's accounts of the crucifixion (27:51) and the resurrection (28:2) include **earthquakes**. The eastern Mediterranean area is prone to earthquakes. Although we explain earthquakes in geological terms, often at theophanies or in apocalyptic material in the Hebrew scriptures earthquakes are interpreted as manifestations of the power of God. Matthew means to say that the entire world was shaken by the actions of God at the tomb.

In biblical symbolism, **angels** are messengers of God, extensions of the power of God. The description of angels attending God suggests that heaven resembles an ancient royal court, in which the monarch has servants who carry out the sovereign's will. Like the Elohist source of the Old Testament, Matthew has people seeing an angel, rather than seeing the being of God. Luther's morning and evening prayers ask for God's presence in the form of "your holy angel."

The language of being **raised** from death relies on the commonplace human idea, evident in speech and story, that up is good and down is bad. The ancient three-tier universe placed divine powers on the top level, humans in the middle—between life and death—and the dead below the earth. In today's readings, God raised Jesus (Acts), we go up to Zion (Jeremiah), Christ is above at the right hand of God (Colossians), and the angel descends like lightning. Current scientific understandings of the universe teach us that there is no "up." Thus this language must function for us symbolically: up is life, down is death.

Ideas for the Day

- In Psalm 118, the Psalmist says, "The stone that the builders rejected has become the chief cornerstone" (v. 22). We are invited to think about how Jesus is that rejected stone on Good Friday—and, through resurrection on Easter Day, Jesus becomes our strong foundation. History is littered with people who were first rejected and then were later able to share their gifts with the world: Fred Astaire's first screen test prompted this assessment: "Can't act, can't sing, can dance a little"; Michael Jordan didn't make the high school varsity basketball team and was relegated to junior varsity for two years; J. K. Rowling's Harry Potter series was turned down by twelve publishing houses. Rejection is not the end of the story—for Jesus, or for us. God makes a way.

- In Matthew's resurrection, an earthquake marks the rolling away of the stone from the empty tomb. Often when big things happen, there is a "shaking up" that occurs; things that seemed impossible are now possible, and we become more aware of God's actions. This "shaking up" can even start a new chapter or era—in our lives, in our communities, in our world. What are some ways Jesus' resurrection power "shakes us up" today? How can we partner in this new life together?

- Peter's speech in Acts 10 mentions "witnesses" to Jesus' resurrection and our call to "testify" about Jesus. In many Christian circles today, there is a tradition of asking for a witness, or for someone to testify—to share their faith story. Personal stories are powerful. One of the main ways we can share Jesus' love with others is to share our own faith stories. Incorporating people's faith stories into worship, Bible studies, and other activities in the church can help us get comfortable with telling our own faith stories and sharing them with others.

Making Connections

We can imagine Mary Magdalene's heart was bursting with joy when she recognized Jesus. All of the texts for this day convey a sense of celebration, victory, urgency, exclamation points! One can almost hear the brass section as you read. For us followers of Jesus, this is our big day, and our sanctuaries, our special music and enthusiastic "Alleluias" reflect that. How might we bring this joy to the liturgy on all the other days? Imagine a worship service that inspires people to move and sway because they feel so much joy in their hearts, like in many Black churches. Our liturgy is consistent, which is often comforting. Let's look for the joy, too. May we find ways to infuse it with joy and exclamation points! Imagine a world where we would be recognized as Christians by our joy.

Engaging All Ages

Would that this reading (John 20:1–10) were longer. Past the (self-referential) note about the Beloved Disciple's faith, there's Magdalene weeping—and getting rewarded by a delightful encounter with Christ himself.

Through centuries the pattern has been the same. In the face of evil, saints get infused with courage welling up from the very universe itself. In hidden ways they enjoy Jesus' own embrace.

God blesses us today with opportunities to test this pattern. Over the shouts of bullies, we face occasions to speak truth into lies, authentic citizenship in the face of ersatz patriotism.

Pray that the Spirit embolden us to move our country from the old "might makes right" curse of history. That God would use us to continue the American story so imperfectly yet wonderfully begun.

Hymns for the Day

The Hymnal 1982

At the Lamb's high feast we sing 174
Christ is arisen 713
Christ Jesus lay in death's strong bands 185, 186
Come, ye faithful, raise the strain 199, 200
Good Christians all, rejoice and sing 205
Jesus Christ is risen today 207
Look there! the Christ, our brother, comes 196, 197
The Lamb's high banquet called to share 202
The strife is o'er, the battle done 208
Hail thee, festival day 175
In Christ there is no East or West 529
Sing, ye faithful, sing with gladness 492
"Welcome, happy morning!" age to age shall say 179
Awake and sing the song 181
Come away to the skies 213
O Zion, tune thy voice 543
Thou hallowed chosen morn of praise 198
Alleluia, alleluia! Hearts and voices
    heavenward raise 191
Love's redeeming work is done 188, 189
The day of resurrection 210
We know that Christ is raised and dies no more 296
Christ the Lord is risen again 184
Christians, to the Paschal victim 183
Lift your voice rejoicing, Mary 190
O sons and daughters, let us sing (vs. 1–3, 5) 203
On earth has dawned this day of days 201

Lift Every Voice and Sing II

Amen 233
Christ has arisen 41
This is the day 219
In Christ there is no East or West 62
Great is thy faithfulness 189
In the garden 69
He 'rose 40

Wonder, Love, and Praise

Christ is risen from the dead 816, 817
Day of delight and beauty unbounded 738
God's Paschal Lamb is sacrificed for us 880

Easter

The Second Sunday of Easter

April 16, 2023

We pray that all the people who have been reborn into Christ's Body the Church may live their faith.

Easter

Color   White

Preface   Easter

Collect

Almighty and everlasting God, who in the Paschal mystery established the new covenant of reconciliation: Grant that all who have been reborn into the fellowship of Christ's Body may show forth in their lives what they profess by their faith; through Jesus Christ our Lord, who lives and reigns with you and the Holy Spirit, one God, for ever and ever. *Amen.*

Readings and Psalm

Acts 2:14a, 22–32

In the Easter season, following an ancient tradition, a reading from the Acts of the Apostles is used as the first reading. The book of the Acts recounts the early growth of the Church. One of the major features of Acts is Luke's use of speeches by the principal figures, providing reflection on and analysis of events. Today's reading is taken from the first of these discourses, in which Peter addresses the crowd on the Day of Pentecost. The account stresses the providence of God in the disposition of these events. In the paradoxical fate of the Messiah, human freedom and divine necessity are intertwined. Humanity's act of rejection is reversed by God's act of affirmation.

Psalm 16

This song of trust in God seems to be set in a context where some Israelites worship other gods (v. 4). Though the psalm is one of supplication, the petition itself takes only one half of a verse (v. 1). The remainder of the prayer is a meditation on the reasons the psalmist can turn to God in this time of need. Some scholars believe this psalm to be written by a foreigner in Israel, who has put his faith in Israel's God.

1 Peter 1:3–9

Today's reading is a prayer of thanksgiving for God's opening to believers a rebirth and new life through the resurrection of Jesus. This life is lived in the hope of an inheritance kept in heaven (v. 4). The Christian is guarded now even in trial, sustained by the faith of those who have not seen.

John 20:19–31

The first appearance of the risen Lord to the disciples stresses Jesus' fulfillment of the promises that he made in the long farewell address at the Last Supper in chapters 14–17. Thomas will not accept the Easter proclamation on the word of others but wishes to experience the risen Christ directly. Yet he can still penetrate the meaning behind the marvel and make a full affirmation of Christian faith. He consummates the sequence of titles given to Jesus by giving him the ultimate title, God. Verses 30–31 serve as a conclusion to the gospel. They evaluate the content of the gospel, inviting all to understand the meaning of Jesus' life, death, and resurrection and, through belief, to share in a saving relationship with him.

Prayers of the People

Brothers and sisters, peace be with you. Let us pray to our merciful Lord, saying, "Our Lord and our God, *have mercy on us.*"

Lord Jesus Christ, you have given your Church the gift of your Holy Spirit. May that same Spirit comfort and strengthen us as we proclaim your resurrection to the world.

Silence

Our Lord and our God,

Have mercy on us.

God of wisdom, teach and counsel the leaders of the nations. May this world be filled with justice and peace.

Silence

Our Lord and our God,

Have mercy on us.

God our provider, you have given us this pleasant earth as a goodly heritage. May we use its resources wisely and always according to your purpose.

Invite the congregation to add their thanksgivings, followed by silence

Our Lord and our God,

Have mercy on us.

All-knowing God, raise up for this community people who will stand and voice your truth. May we be led by you on good paths of life.

Silence

Our Lord and our God,

Have mercy on us.

Merciful God, you are a strong refuge for those in trouble. Protect all those who suffer various trials. Reveal yourself to those who struggle to believe in you. Make all your people glad by the living hope that is found in you.

Invite the congregation to add their petitions, followed by silence

Our Lord and our God,

Have mercy on us.

God of Life, may the dying and the dead rest in hope. Give us faith that you do not abandon anyone—even to the grave. And preserve us for the great inheritance you give us through the resurrection of your Son from the dead.

Silence

Our Lord and our God,

Have mercy on us.

Images in the Readings

Usually depictions of the crucified Christ include the marks on his **hands and side**. Our archeological knowledge that for crucifixions nails were driven through the wrist ought not negate the symbolism of the palm, which is central to a person's hand. Neither need we get fascinated by the accounts of the stigmata, for we all carry the mark of the crucified and risen Christ on our palm each time we receive the body of Christ at communion. In John 19:34, blood and water flow from the wound on Jesus' side, and church tradition has seen in this detail not an erroneous description of human anatomy, but rather the proclamation that baptism and Eucharist flow from the death of Christ.

Each year on the second Sunday of Easter we meet **"Doubting Thomas."** He is all of us, and we doubters are glad to share with all other doubters the peace of the risen Christ.

That Christ is **king** is an image behind the reading from Acts: King David testifies to this power; Jesus is now on David's throne; Christ is the anointed one, the Messiah.

God is the Father of our Lord Jesus Christ, and in baptism we have been given a new **birth**, to live as children of this heavenly father. The imagery continues: only children receive the full inheritance.

Ideas for the Day

♦ The Gospel Lesson from John for today is one of the most famous Bible passages of all time; Thomas has been forever known as "Doubting Thomas" because he wished to see Jesus' injuries from the cross before believing Jesus was resurrection. But Thomas only wanted to see that which his fellow disciples had already seen, since he was "not with them" when the resurrected Jesus first appeared. In fact, Thomas gives a most definitive answer of who Jesus is: "My Lord and my God!" Thomas could be nicknamed "Proclaiming Thomas" rather than "Doubting Thomas!"

Easter

Easter

◆ Peter's speech in Acts follows the amazing outpouring of the Holy Spirit at Pentecost. The people gathered have just heard the mighty acts of God proclaimed in their own languages, from the mouths of the disciples (who did not know all of these languages of their own accord, and were clearly given the ability by the Spirit). Amazed by God, the people listen to Peter's retelling of the resurrection through the lens of scripture. Imagine what it may have been like in that moment, to have experienced the Holy Spirit's powerful presence and then heard the good news about Jesus' resurrection from Peter.

◆ In the Gospel Lesson, the resurrected Jesus says "Peace be with you" to the disciples twice. Jesus then tells the disciples he is sending them just as the Father sent him, and invites them to receive the Holy Spirit. For Jesus in this passage, God's peace accompanies being sent and receiving the Spirit. Before fulfilling a calling from God, we often feel a sense of peace. This peace can be a sign that we are on the right track. We can notice the peace Jesus offers us as we continue to serve the resurrected Christ.

Making Connections

Jesus' followers must have been devasted. They left their homes, families, jobs to walk with Jesus. Now he's been crucified and they're hiding in an upper room—in fear, confusion, shame—or some combination of all. Then Jesus shows up and says one thing, "Peace be with you." It's a phrase that acknowledges the weight of the human experience and reminds us to let our hearts be still knowing that God loves us enough to become human and tell us so. The phrase induces a big exhale, every time. We commemorate this moment every Sunday when we "pass the peace" to one another. We take this peace into our bodies when we step up to the communion rail, hungering and thirsting for solace. God's peace is the foundation to our lives, older even than Jesus. "Shalom," in the Hebrew Bible. In this peace we find respite and strength to walk in the ways of God.

Engaging All Ages

Jesus' appearance cloaks the second miracle: Thomas remained with his friends.

"Doubting Thomas"? No, "pouting." Others enjoyed experiences he'd missed. He was awash with resentment.

Yet there he remains when Jesus returns. How?

Look no further than Jesus' first gift to the disciples: "Receive the Holy Spirit!" Being now filled with the Spirit that animated Jesus, their bearing toward Thomas made his remaining possible.

They would have continued to report the truth: Jesus had in fact visited them. No, they didn't know why Thomas was not given a similar assurance. Yes, they were clear that Thomas was equally precious to God as any of them.

So Thomas, likely sulking, stayed—and received his own visitation.

Has Jesus given you his Spirit? Has it transformed your dealings with wounded or difficult people?

Hymns for the Day

The Hymnal 1982
Christ the Lord is risen again 184
Good Christians all, rejoice and sing 205
Jesus is Lord of all the earth 178
Jesus lives! thy terrors now 194, 195
Sing, ye faithful, sing with gladness 492
This joyful Eastertide 192
Glorious the day when Christ was born 452
Hope of the world, thou Christ of great compassion 472
Awake, arise, lift up your voice 212
By all your saints still striving (2: St. Thomas) 231, 232
How oft, O Lord, thy face hath shone 242
O sons and daughters, let us sing 206
We walk by faith and not by sight 209

Lift Every Voice and Sing II
We walk by faith 206

Wonder, Love, and Praise

Weekday Commemorations

Monday, April 17
Kateri Tekakwitha, Lay Contemplative, 1680

Known as the Lily of the Mohawks, Kateri was the first Native American canonized in the Roman Catholic Church. She was born in Upstate New York around 1656, and then orphaned and scarred by smallpox. Baptized at age nineteen, she adapted Catherine of Siena's name. As the bride of Christ and the daughter of the Virgin Mary, she chose to live chaste. Not only was she mocked, but local priests dissuaded her from forming a monastic community of indigenous women, so she modeled simply a life of good works. Leonard Cohen enfolded her story into his novel, *Beautiful Losers*.

Tuesday, April 18
Juana Inés de la Cruz, Monastic and Theologian, 1695

Born illegitimate in 1648 near Mexico City, Juana proved herself a child prodigy, reading and writing by three and composing religious poetry by eight. Prevented from formal schooling by her sex, she studied privately while serving as a lady-in-waiting. She defended her knowledge before a tribunal of theologians and justices when she was seventeen. In 1669, Juana entered the Order of St. Jerome, where her writing career blossomed. Admirers praised her concision and elegance, especially in indigenous Mexican literature; loud condemners declared that a nun should not be writing philosophy or science, stopping her from publishing by 1693.

Wednesday, April 19
Alphege, Archbishop of Canterbury, and Martyr, 1012

"And his holy blood fell on the earth, whist his sacred soul was sent to the realm of God." Thus, the *Anglo-Saxon Chronicle* recorded the death of Alphege (or Aelfheah) at the hands of the Danes, who "smote him with an axe-iron . . . " Alphege, born in 954, served the Church during the second series of Scandinavian invasions and settlement in England. Following a time as a monk at Deerhurst and an abbot at Bath, Alphege became bishop of Winchester. He helped bring Norse king Olaf Tryggvason to King Aethelred in 994 to make peace and be confirmed. Captured by the Danes in 1011, Alphege refused to satisfy the ransom and was killed seven months later.

Friday, April 21
Anselm, Archbishop of Canterbury and Theologian, 1109

Anselm, born in Italy about 1033, took monastic vows in 1060 in Normandy and became archbishop of Canterbury in 1093. Although his greatest gifts lay in theology and spiritual direction, he served in a time of conflict between church and state. Anselm exploited the so-called "ontological argument" for God's existence: God is "that than which nothing greater can be thought." Anselm is also the most famous exponent of the "satisfaction theory" of the atonement, explaining Christ's work in terms of the contemporary feudal society. Supporting his thinking and arguing was profound piety, captured in the words, "unless I first believe, I shall not understand."

Saturday, April 22
Hadewijch of Brabant, Poet and Mystic, 13th century

Hadewijch produced an influential body of spiritual writings. She was probably a Beguine. Her learned writings in her native Dutch as well as theological work in both Latin and French suggest she benefited from wealth. Credited as a creator of Dutch lyrical poetry to extol love between the poet and God, she also wrote couplets on religious themes. In *Book of Visions*, she dialogues with Christ. Hadewijch was widely known in the fourteenth and fifteenth centuries. Today, she, who defined Love as female, is recognized for influencing male mystics such as Meister Eckhart and John of Ruusbroec.

Easter

The Third Sunday of Easter

April 23, 2023

We pray that God will open the eyes of our faith so that we may recognize Christ in all his redemptive work.

Easter

Color White

Preface Easter

Collect

O God, whose blessed Son made himself known to his disciples in the breaking of bread: Open the eyes of our faith, that we may behold him in all his redeeming work; who lives and reigns with you, in the unity of the Holy Spirit, one God, now and for ever. *Amen.*

Readings and Psalm

Acts 2:14a, 36–41

Today's reading is the first of the major summaries to link together the specific events and teachings of Luke's narrative. These verses give an overview of the Church's life and growth. Verse 42 mentions four aspects of that life. The "apostles' teaching" was carried on both in public and within the community. Likewise, the community continued to offer "the prayers" both at the temple and in the community. The "fellowship" (Greek, *koinonia*) was apparent especially in the sharing of resources. This probably meant not an automatic divestiture of all possessions, but the placing of one's assets at the disposal of the community to be used as needed. The "breaking of the bread" probably indicates a common meal that included the Lord's Supper at which the table-fellowship of the apostles with the risen Lord was extended to the community.

Psalm 116:1, 10-17

This psalm of thanksgiving recounts the vindication of a righteous sufferer. Such a psalm was recited as a testimony to other worshipers.

1 Peter 1:17–23

In today's reading, believers are exhorted to a standard of life that reflects what God has done for them. The appropriate response to God's greatness and goodness is behavior pleasing to God.

The image of ransoming, or redemption, is taken from the Hebrew Bible where it has both a secular and a theological use. In Hebrew society an enslaved person or alienated land was bought back by the next of kin, and the first-born was bought back by the family. In the New Testament, the metaphor of the legal transaction of redemption is of great significance. Jesus applies the term to his death, and Paul also speaks of the price of Jesus' blood. The term *redemption* is used most often, however, in the general sense of paying the price.

Luke 24:13–35

The two disciples on the way to Emmaus share the popular view of Jesus as a prophet and point to the hope that Jesus was in fact the expected prophet-like-Moses. Comprehension begins with the interpretation of the scriptures, which pointed toward the suffering and glory of the Messiah. The power of the word of God prepared them to receive the broken bread in full recognition of Jesus. The post-resurrection table fellowship with Jesus links the feeding during his early ministry and the pledge at the Last Supper with the eucharistic experiences of the early Church. Although Jesus' physical presence is withdrawn, his self-revelation in scripture and his manifestation in the Eucharist remain. The pattern of word and sacrament in the story becomes that of the Christian liturgy and life.

Prayers of the People

How shall we repay the Lord for all the good God has done? Let us offers the prayers of our hearts, saying, "Stay with us, Lord Jesus; *and set our hearts on fire.*"

Lord Jesus Christ, you have ransomed us by your own precious blood. Once again, as a holy community, we place our faith and hope in you.

Silence

Stay with us, Lord Jesus;

And set our hearts on fire.

Save us, O Lord, from corruption. Deliver the nations and peoples from greed and hatred. Place in your children hearts of repentance.

Silence

Stay with us, Lord Jesus;

And set our hearts on fire.

O Lord, you are the giver of good things. We thank you for this planet; we thank you for its gifts. We pray a blessing on the seeds that were sown this spring that the harvest might be bountiful.

Invite the congregation to add their thanksgivings, followed by silence

Stay with us, Lord Jesus;

And set our hearts on fire.

O Lord, you are made known in the breaking of bread and so we pray for all those who lack bread. We pray for the hungry. You feed us generously at your table. Help us to generously feed the world.

Silence

Stay with us, Lord Jesus;

And set our hearts on fire.

Whenever we call upon you, gracious Lord, you incline your ear to us. We raise our voices for those for whom we care: those who are ill, those who are struggling, those who are in need of your mercy.

Invite the congregation to add their petitions, followed by silence

Stay with us, Lord Jesus;

And set our hearts on fire.

Precious in your sight, O Lord, is the death of your servants. We trust you with our dead and with our dying. Jesus, be gracious with them, we pray.

Silence

Stay with us, Lord Jesus;

And set our hearts on fire.

Images in the Readings

The **meal** of Emmaus is one of the many Lukan accounts of eating with Jesus, and Luke's accounts follow the biblical theme that God feeds the people. To be true to the biblical image of the life shared with Christ, the bread that we break, the wine that we share, and our methods of distribution ought to make clear that holy communion is a meal. A loaf of bread or a large circular flat bread, home baked or purchased from a local store and broken for all to see, presents a quite different image of salvation than do medieval quarter-sized tasteless hosts bought from an ecclesiastical supply company. Think about the image presented by your eating and drinking.

The **preaching** of Peter and the teaching of Christ along the road are images of our receiving the "living and enduring" saving word.

The passage from 1 Peter presents an array of images, one rushing along after another. A significant image for the book of 1 Peter is **exile**: the baptized are living in an alien land. When Christians become too comfortable in what Acts calls "this corrupt generation," we are called to be ransomed out of it and purified by obedience to the truth.

Easter

Ideas for the Day

♦ We hear Luke's account of the Road to Emmaus today, when two disciples talking about the crucifixion and the resurrection meet Jesus on the road—but don't recognize him until he breaks bread with them. As we go about our everyday lives Jesus is with us, yet we often don't notice him until something "opens our eyes." The disciples acknowledge that "their hearts were burning within them," while talking with Jesus on the road, yet they didn't fully see that it was Jesus himself until they were at the table together. How can we trust our own "spiritual radar," so that we can fully see what the resurrected Christ is up to in our lives and in the lives of others?

♦ In Acts 2, Peter finishes his speech after the amazing events at Pentecost, and the people listening want to know what to do next. Peter tells them to repent and be baptized, and they do get baptized—about 3,000 people were brought into God's family that day! Remember that Peter was a fisherman before following Jesus; he was not educated or considered a man people would expect to listen to. Yet, the Holy Spirit gives him the words to say, and thousands of people were baptized. We can think that we don't have authority to speak about God because we don't know enough, or we aren't someone who is "important," but we see through Peter's speech and the subsequent baptisms that God can use anyone to share the good news of Jesus.

♦ The disciples who meet Jesus on the road are on a journey from Jerusalem to Emmaus. There are many well-known stories that remind us of the importance of journeys, including Homer's *Odyssey* (and the modern retellings, *Gulliver's Travels* by Jonathan Swift, and the film by the Coen Brothers *O Brother, Where Art Thou?*) Journeys and traveling tend to be where we learn new things about ourselves and about God. It is while we are away from home and everything we are used to that we tend to be more open to God's actions and new adventures.

Making Connections

It's easy to recognize Jesus, when we are practicing baptism, or focused on our faith and wondering how we can offer praise to the Lord. The letter to Peter reminds us we are born anew. But when we least expect it, like the disciples on the road to Emmaus, will we recognize Jesus? We expect to meet him in our sanctuaries, hope to meet him in our Sunday school rooms and Bible studies. Where are the places and who are the people in whom we do not see Jesus? Our Baptismal Covenant asks us to ". . . seek and serve Christ in all persons, loving [our] neighbor as [ourselves]. . . . " The neighbor whose trash is constantly blowing on our lawn, the person with opposing political views, the rude store clerk—it's a lot harder to see Christ in those persons. And still, Christ is there.

Engaging All Ages

"Eucharistic" accounts include the feeding stories of 4000/5000 and so on and the lakeside fish breakfast. Bread appears in each, wine only in the Last Supper.

Each account is somehow "eucharistic." Should we be cautious, insisting that it's only "valid" if wine is present? Only priests "do it"?

The essential in each is bread. Even that precise stuff is not the point. The point in each account is sharing.

Cleopus and his friend only recognize Jesus at dinner when he says, "Friends, dinner is on me," breaks the bread, and shares it.

The Church's care with host and cup has kept the sacrament alive for two thousand years. But it must not veil the Lord's purpose.

Jesus is among us again when we share with others.

That's how they recognized him.

Hymns for the Day

The Hymnal 1982

All who believe and are baptized 298
Baptized in water 294
Over the chaos of the empty waters 176, 177
The head that once was crowned with thorns 483
We know that Christ is raised and dies no more 296
Hail, thou once despised Jesus! 495
Lord, enthroned in heavenly splendor 307
Now the green blade riseth 204
This is the feast of victory for our God 417, 418
Come, risen Lord, and deign to be our guest 305, 306
He is risen, he is risen! 180
Shepherd of souls, refresh and bless 343

Lift Every Voice and Sing II

Baptized in water 121

Wonder, Love, and Praise

Baptized in water 767
As we gather at your Table 763

Weekday Commemorations

Tuesday, April 25
Saint Mark the Evangelist

All New Testament references to a man named Mark may not be to the same man, but if they are, he was the son of a woman householder in Jerusalem—perhaps the house in which Jesus ate his Last Supper. Mark may have been the naked young man who fled when Jesus was arrested in the Garden of Gethsemane. Paul referred to Mark in a letter to the Colossians as the cousin of Barnabas, with whom he was imprisoned; Paul was not satisfied by the reasons Mark gave for not accompanying Paul and Barnabas, so Paul refused Mark's company on a second journey. Early tradition names Mark as the author of the Gospel of Mark.

Thursday, April 27
Zita of Tuscany, Worker of Charity, 1271

Zita, a Christian, never forgot that she was born in poverty (in Tuscany, 1271). As an adult, she gave away most of her income. At twelve, she went to work for the Fatinelli family in Lucca, but she continued to practice her faith, embodying Paul's advice to work "for the Lord, not for your masters." Although her diligence met with scorn, she was not dissuaded and eventually earned the household's respect. As keeper of the keys of the household staff, she came to be venerated throughout Lucca. In popular piety, Zita is entreated to find lost keys.

Saturday, April 29
Catherine of Siena, Mystic, 1380

Catherine Benincasa was the youngest of twenty-five children of a wealthy dyer of Siena. At six years of age, she had a remarkable vision that probably decided her life's vocation. Walking home from a visit, she stopped on the road and gazed upward, oblivious to everything around her. "I beheld our Lord seated in glory with St. Peter, St. Paul, and St. John." She went on to say, later, that the Savior smiled on her and blessed her. From then on, Catherine spent most of her time in prayer and meditation, despite her mother's attempts to force her to be like other girls. Eventually, she was accepted as a Dominican postulant.

Easter

The Fourth Sunday of Easter

April 30, 2023

Ministry as a way of revealing the risen Christ through word, action, and prayer.

Color   White

Preface   Easter

Collect

O God, whose Son Jesus is the good shepherd of your people: Grant that when we hear his voice we may know him who calls us each by name, and follow where he leads; who, with you and the Holy Spirit, lives and reigns, one God, for ever and ever. *Amen.*

Readings and Psalm

Acts 2:42–47

Peter concludes his sermon with the proclamation that the crucified Jesus has been exalted as Lord and Messiah. Now the saving name is Jesus Christ. In response to the plea of the crowd, Peter outlines the way of salvation. The first step is repentance (Greek *metanoia*, meaning "change of heart, conversion"). The second step is baptism "in the name" (v. 38) that brings salvation. Those who submit to repentance and baptism receive forgiveness and the gift of the Holy Spirit, who provides the fundamental principle of life in the Christian community.

Psalm 23

This psalm is probably the most familiar and popular psalm of all. It celebrates God's loving care for us under the guise of a good shepherd who provides food, security, and protection from all dangers. God guides us on our journey through life so that we might "dwell in the house of the Lord."

1 Peter 2:19–25

The author recognizes that living our faith is often difficult since we continue to live in a world that does not acknowledge God's sovereignty. We are called to the patient endurance of unjust suffering, for that is the example given by Christ. But Christ's endurance of suffering is not only exemplary, it is redemptive. The fact and consequence of atonement are stated but not explained.

John 10:1–10

John's identification of Jesus as shepherd and gate is similar to the synoptic gospels' portrayal of Jesus' ministry in terms of shepherding. In Luke 15:3–7, the parable of the lost sheep is told in response to the Pharisees' lack of care for the outcast. The Pharisees' inability to accept Jesus' challenge provokes further teaching. Jesus is "the gate" (v. 7), the way the true shepherd approaches the sheep and the way the sheep go in and out. Jesus provides freedom, refuge from sin, true sustenance, and life itself.

Prayers of the People

Brothers and Sisters, Jesus bore our sins on the cross so that we, free from sins, might live in righteousness. Let us pray to our Lord, saying, "Revive our souls, *and guide us along right pathways.*"

Guardian of our souls, call your Church to greater righteousness. Help us to live by your example and follow in your steps.

Silence

Revive our souls,

And guide us along right pathways.

Guardian of our souls, spread out your table in the presence of those who are troubled. Feed their souls and bodies with your good and generous gifts.

Silence

Revive our souls,

> ***And guide us along right pathways.***

Guardian of our souls, you have blessed us with a beautiful planet full of places where we can find rest and peace. May we care for it, as you care deeply for all you have made.

Invite the congregation to add thanksgivings, followed by silence

Revive our souls,

> ***And guide us along right pathways.***

Guardian of our souls, you desire the goodwill of all the people. Give us generous hearts and open hands.

Silence

Revive our souls,

> ***And guide us along right pathways.***

Guardian of our souls, it is your presence that comforts us. Make your presence known to the sick and the sorrowful, to the fearful and the weak.

Invite the congregation to add their petitions, followed by silence

Revive our souls,

> ***And guide us along right pathways.***

Guardian of our souls, you came that we may have life, and have it abundantly. Bring the dying and the dead into your eternal home.

Silence

Revive our souls,

> ***And guide us along right pathways.***

Images in the Readings

To deepen our contemplation of the metaphor of Christ as **shepherd**, it is good to review the positive use that the Bible makes of the image of **sheep**. The Jewish scriptures remembered their people as having been sheep and goat herders. Sheep signified the communal life of the people, constituted a source of food and clothing, and functioned as the primary sacrificial gifts to God. The single wandering lamb from the parable of the lost sheep is not the image in John 10. Nor is a barefooted, white-robed man a realistic depiction of the shepherd, who by the first century was thought of as lower-class and religiously unclean. In Genesis 29, Rachel is a shepherd.

Still today some herders in Iran, after gathering the sheep into an enclosure at night, lay themselves down to sleep at the opening of the pen. The wolf cannot enter through the opening, because the body of the herder has become the **gate**. In some medieval churches, the main doorway was elaborately decorated with biblical scenes, sometimes also surrounded with the signs of the zodiac, as if the door was a symbol of Christ, proclaimed in the Bible and encompassing the universe. The body of our Lord, taken in holy communion, is a gate to eternal life.

The image in Acts 2 of the Christian **commune** connects with the Church's actual history and present situation, in that the baptized, living with generous hearts, contribute to all who have need. It is appropriate that at every meeting of Christians for worship there be a collection of money, goods, or services for the needy.

Easter

Easter

Ideas for the Day

- Jesus tells us in John 10:10 "I came that they may have life, and have it abundantly." Consumer culture tells us that an abundant life is one filled with material possessions, wealth, fame, and social status. Jesus, however, reminds us in this Gospel Lesson that our lives are filled with abundance because we follow Jesus and serve others in his name. Jesus invites us to listen and follow his voice, rather than the voice of consumer culture and the message that we must constantly buy and consume.

- We read in Acts 2 about the early Jesus followers; they held things in common, sold all of their possessions and gave to those in need, shared food with one another, devoted themselves to learning about Jesus, being with one another, and praying. It sounds like a hippie Christian commune, and not an ideal that we could achieve today. Yet we can hear an invitation in this Lesson to find ways to live in community that make sense in our own context. We are invited to share with one another and those in need, eat and spend time with one another, and pray and learn about Jesus together. This is what Church looks like.

- Psalm 23 is often a funeral text, as it tells us that "we will dwell in the house of the Lord forever." But this psalm is so much more than an eternal life reminder; we hear in Psalm 23 that God is our shepherd, who leads us and takes care of us. Even when we struggle and deal with the pain of life, God is with us. In just a few short verses, the Psalmist offers us hope when we think all hope is lost. God is with us, always.

Making Connections

The shepherd stories are often quoted in difficult times, as a means of offering comfort to those who struggle. Indeed, they are comforting words. The passage from Acts helps us to focus on the flock. Who are we, the sheep, and how do we live our lives? John tells us "the sheep hear his voice, and he calls his own sheep by name and leads them out." God knows each of us, and calls us by name! This is good news for us in the flock. As we see in Acts, being the flock is an active commitment. Communal living is a stretch for most of us in 2023, but we can strive to live in community, taking care that no one is in need. The flock must care for one another.

Engaging All Ages

We may not understand this teaching: Is Jesus the shepherd or is he the gate to the pen?

What both share is the door.

The first part, describing the shepherd, is a warm description of the affection between sheep and their protector. That intimacy lets the sheep spot counterfeits.

The second part shows Jesus opens us to safety, indeed to abundant life, safe from harm.

Don't puzzle over the metaphors; go for the point. Do you know Jesus personally? If that question spurs your interest, try three things.

First, read and reread the Gospels. Second, hang around the church to discuss other people's experience of him. Third, when by yourself, talk to him. When a gracious thought occurs to you that doesn't feel like yours, that's likely him.

Hymns for the Day

The Hymnal 1982

Good Christians all, rejoice and sing! (vs. 1, 3–5) 205
My Shepherd will supply my need 664
The King of love my shepherd is 645, 646
The Lord my God my shepherd is 663
I come with joy to meet my Lord 304
Christ the Lord is risen again 184
Shepherd of souls, refresh and bless 343
Sing, ye faithful, sing with gladness 492
The strife is o'er, the battle done 208
Jesus, our mighty Lord 478
Praise the Lord, rise up rejoicing 334
Savior, like a shepherd lead us 708

Lift Every Voice and Sing II

The Lord is my Shepherd 104

Wonder, Love, and Praise

Come now, O Prince of Peace, make us one body 795

Weekday Commemorations

Monday, May 1

The Apostles Saint Philip and Saint James

Philip and James are known but a little—and that through the gospels. James has been called "the Less" to distinguish him from James the son of Zebedee and from Jesus' brother James—or maybe he was young, or short. He was listed among the Twelve as James the son of Alpheus, and he may also be the person labeled in Mark's gospel as "James the younger," who witnessed the crucifixion. In John's gospel, Philip has a greater presence: Jesus called Philip as a disciple right after naming Andrew and Peter; in turn, Philip convinced his friend Nathaniel to see the Messiah. Philip, at the Last Supper, declared, "Lord, show us the Father, and we shall be satisfied."

Tuesday, May 2

Athanasius of Alexandria, Bishop and Theologian, 373

Athanasius significantly determined the direction of the Church in the fourth century. Born about 295 in Alexandria, he was ordained a deacon in 319. He attended the first council at Nicaea in 325 as secretary and adviser to Alexander, the bishop of Alexandria. Athanasius won approval for the phrase in the Nicene Creed that expresses the godhead of Christ, "one Being with the Father." Athanasius succeeded Alexander in 328. He defended the Nicene Christology against powers political and clerical, and he was exiled five times. He wrote volumes, from treatises to theology, sermons, and letters. His *On the Incarnation of the Word of God* is a classic.

Thursday, May 4

Monnica, Mother of Augustine of Hippo, 387

Tucked into *The Confessions of Saint Augustine* is the story of his mother, Monnica, who was born in North Africa around 331. Within her deepening life of prayer, she converted her husband Patricius to Christianity, and she longed to bring her son to Christ as well. He was baptized in Milan in 387. Monnica became sick as she and her two sons awaited a ship in the port of Rome to return them home to Africa. As she lay dying, she asked that her sons remember her "at the altar of the Lord." Her mortal remains were buried in 1430 at the Church of St. Augustine in Rome.

Friday, May 5

Martyrs of the Reformation Era

On this date, the Church of England commemorates all of the English saints and martyrs of the Reformation Era—not just Anglican martyrs like Thomas Cranmer, Hugh Latimer, and Nicholas Ridley but also those Roman Catholics who were killed by Anglicans as well as other Christians who were persecuted by fellow Christians, most notably the Anabaptists and the Quakers. Baptized Christians are incorporated into God's one Church and, thus, heirs of both martyrs and their executioners. Such a double heritage encourages efforts to heal divisions for a future in Christ in which all are one.

Easter

The Fifth Sunday of Easter

May 7, 2023

One cannot be Christian alone; apart from the Body, we can do nothing.

Color   White

Preface   Easter

Collect

Almighty God, whom truly to know is everlasting life: Grant us so perfectly to know your Son Jesus Christ to be the way, the truth, and the life, that we may steadfastly follow his steps in the way that leads to eternal life; through Jesus Christ your Son our Lord, who lives and reigns with you, in the unity of the Holy Spirit, one God, for ever and ever. *Amen.*

Readings and Psalm

Acts 7:55–60

Luke records in detail the death of the first Christian martyr, Stephen. Those who resisted the growing Christian community latched on to its unique teachings and used them as weapons against Stephen. Stephen understood that faith in Jesus would eventually change the traditional forms of worship. This forceful teaching stirred up the anger and jealousy of his opponents. The final straw came when Stephen declared that he saw Jesus standing at God's right hand. Stephen's audience understood the enormous significance of this claim and resisted it, fulfilling Stephen's description of their nature (7:51–53).

Psalm 31:1–5, 15–16

A lament by one surrounded by evil people. Trust in God encourages the psalmist to entrust himself to God's care. In anticipation of God's deliverance, the psalmist prays with thanksgiving and joy.

1 Peter 2:2–10

In today's reading, the Christian community is described in several interwoven images. It is a spiritual house. The symbol of Jesus as the cornerstone was frequently used in the early preaching, especially as a touchstone for response to him. To some he is precious, but to others he is a stumbling-block. The community is also a holy priesthood appointed to offer the spiritual sacrifice of obedience. Finally, the titles given to Israel are extended to Christians. Their duty is to declare the Lord's deeds. They are now a family, a nation, a people transcending all ethnic barriers, for they are God's own who have received mercy.

John 14:1–14

The gospel reading is taken from the farewell discourse of Jesus, explaining the significance and implications of Jesus' glorification (13:31–17:26). As God's glory is revealed in Jesus' obedient suffering, so Jesus' glory will be seen in his exaltation by God. Thus, his glorification means his departure from the disciples and return to Abba God; it brings not separation but deeper fellowship. They will be able to abide with him always, in the body of Christ, the Christian community. Philip's request to see the Father and so be satisfied expresses the human longing for a real and intimate knowledge of God. This desire is answered in the present. Jesus is the revelation of God in words and works.

Prayers of the People

Brothers and Sisters, once we were not a people, but now we are God's people. Let us pray to our good God, saying, "Make your face to shine upon us, *and in your loving-kindness save us.*"

In you, O Lord, does your Church take refuge. Strengthen us by your Holy Spirit to do great works in Jesus' name. May your Church glorify you in all our doings.

Silence

Make your face to shine upon us,

> *And in your loving-kindness save us.*

Ancient of Days, rescue the innocent from the hands of those who persecute them. Hold in your strong hands the oppressed and the abused.

Silence

Make your face to shine upon us,

> *And in your loving-kindness save us.*

God, our strong rock, give us eyes to see your hand at work in our world. Lead us and guide us that we may be good stewards of your creation.

Silence

Make your face to shine upon us,

> *And in your loving-kindness save us.*

Tower of Strength, assure those who are unemployed or living in poverty that they are precious in your sight.

Silence

Make your face to shine upon us,

> *And in your loving-kindness save us.*

Merciful God, incline your ear to those in need of deliverance. Calm the troubled hearts of the suffering and the sorrowful, of the sick and the anxiety-plagued.

Invite the congregation to add their petitions and thanksgivings, followed by silence

Make your face to shine upon us,

> *And in your loving-kindness save us.*

God of truth, we commend the dying and the dead into your hands. We rejoice in Jesus' promise that he has prepared for us a place in your eternal home.

Silence

Make your face to shine upon us,

> *And in your loving-kindness save us.*

Images in the Readings

For some Christians and pieties, the image of Christ as the **Way** has been used to condemn most other people. John's community did indeed think of itself as enjoying the greatest **truth** and **life** eternal. However, we are called to recognize the Way as the good news that God loves the whole world, as the wideness of God's mercy.

John's metaphor of the Father's **house** and its many dwelling places has been literalized for many Christians, as if heaven were a king's mansion with outbuildings provided for the lesser inhabitants. In a different application of this image, the house is the room in which we weekly gather: here God dwells. Here God serves up our meals. 1 Peter uses the image of house to be a metaphor for the believing community.

1 Peter is filled with images. Several medieval mystics used the image of the Eucharist being **milk**. The central image of this passage is Christ as the **cornerstone**, the living stone, of the house that is the Church. Many cornerstones are engraved with the date of construction. For Christians, this date is the year of our baptism. Perhaps those congregations that publish members' birthdays could replace these dates with their baptismal anniversary.

Ideas for the Day

- In Acts 7 we read about the martyrdom of Stephen. He is willing to give up everything to follow Jesus, including his life. Very quickly, almost as an afterthought, we hear about a young man named Saul who was at Stephen's execution—this is the same Saul who becomes Saint Paul later, after he has his famous conversion experience on the Damascus road (Acts 9). Imagine overseeing the executions of Jesus' followers, and then becoming one yourself! This is the amazing work of Jesus; an experience of Jesus is life-changing and can completely change the trajectory of one's life.

Easter

Easter

♦ In 1 Peter 2 Jesus is described as the cornerstone that we are all built upon (as we heard on Easter Day in Psalm 118). Jesus is the foundation of the Church; we then build up from him. We learned as children that when we build something out of blocks or Legos, we have to have a strong foundation—or the whole structure will come tumbling down! Unlike children playing with blocks, we can rest in the assurance that Jesus is a never-failing foundation. We can rely on Jesus to keep us solid.

♦ Jesus promises in John 14 that he goes ahead of us to prepare a place for us in his Father's house. We often read this Lesson at funerals, because it reminds us that death is not the end for us. We know that Jesus has saved a place for us in eternal life; we share in Jesus' resurrection. We find out in this Lesson that we don't necessarily have to understand all the details about how eternal life works—we only need to know that Jesus has everything covered.

Making Connections

The disciples are very confused about who is Jesus and what is Jesus' relationship with God. Thomas wants to know how they will get to where Jesus is going. We can hear Jesus' exasperation at the end of the passage. "If you had known me, you would have known my Father; henceforth you know him and have seen him." In Matthew 25:40 Jesus says " . . . as you did it to one of the least of these, you did it to me." When we apply logical principals, we get: God is in Jesus; Jesus is in us, therefore God is in us. Two thousand years later we're still struggling with this. Like the disciples, we try to make it a lot more complicated than it is. We are each and every one of us children of God, called to love one another as we love God. God is love.

Engaging All Ages

Another reading insisting that we must know Jesus personally. The reason for that insistence is not so elementary as Jesus simply preferring his own devotees. It's that personal knowledge of Jesus releases in us a new quality of humanity. It allows us to discern God's presence and purpose all around us. It lets us sense Jesus' will so clearly that we can confidently shape our prayers to fit it.

As important as that is, it's not a license for religious bigotry. That's "taking God's Name in vain." Knowing Jesus intimately instructs our prayers for people who are not yet as far along as God's wish for them.

Hymns for the Day

The Hymnal 1982

Come away to the skies 213
When Stephen full of power and grace 243
By all your saints still striving (St. Stephen) 231, 232
Christ is made the sure foundation 518
Open your ears, O faithful people 536
God of the prophets 359
The Church's one foundation 525
We the Lord's people, heart and voice uniting 51
Come, my Way, my Truth, my Life 487
Father, we praise thee, now the night is over 1, 2
He is the Way 463, 464
Praise the Lord through every nation 484, 485
Thou art the Way, to thee alone 457

Lift Every Voice and Sing II

Wonder, Love, and Praise

When from bondage we are summoned 753, 754
Here, O Lord, your servants gather 793

Weekday Commemorations

Monday, May 8
Julian of Norwich, Mystic and Theologian, c.1417

Little is known of Julian's life. Born about 1342, the only writing of hers we have is *Revelations of Divine Love*, the description of her "showings," or visions, which she experienced after an illness when she was thirty. Prior to her illness, Julian had desired three gifts from God: "the mind of his passion, bodily sickness in youth, and three wounds—of contrition, of compassion, of willful longing toward God." Although she forgot about the first two until after her illness, the third was always with her. After recovering, she became an anchorite at Norwich, living alone in a hut attached to the Church of St. Julian (hence, her name) and gaining fame as a mystic.

Tuesday, May 9
Gregory of Nazianzus, Bishop and Theologian, 389

This Cappadocian Father loved God, *belle lettres*, and humankind. Born about 330, he studied rhetoric in Athens; with his friend Basil of Caesarea he compiled the works of Origen. He was ordained a presbyter against his will in 361 and attempted a life of austerity; however, the times were against living peacefully. He became bishop of Sasima ("a detestable little place," he wrote) before moving to Constantinople in 379 with hope renewed. There, he preached five sermons on the doctrine of the Trinity: therein rests his reputation. Among the Fathers of the Church, he is known as "The Theologian."

Thursday, May 11
Johann Arndt and Jacob Boehme, Mystics, 1621 and 1624

Arndt (b. 1555) and Boehme (b. 1575), prominent Lutheran mystical writers, influenced contemporaries as well as descendants. A peacemaker, Arndt devoted his life to serving God as a diligent pastor. *True Christianity*, his major work, seeks to deemphasize the legal aspect of salvation and highlight abiding in Christ through praying and reading scripture. Boehme had mystical visions in his youth, one of which led him to write *The Rising of the Dawn* in 1600; later, he produced many more works on mystical theology and cosmology. He influenced radical pietists, including the Quakers, and English Romantics, notably William Blake.

Saturday, May 13
Frances Perkins, Social Reformer, 1965

Perkins, born in 1880 and confirmed an Episcopalian in 1905, served President Franklin Roosevelt, also an Episcopalian, as Secretary of Labor—the first woman in a Cabinet and the only member throughout Roosevelt's twelve years in office. With Roosevelt, Perkins shaped New Deal legislation, including banning child labor and establishing the Social Security program. They outlined lofty goals in 1933 for American society and accomplished all but universal healthcare. An eloquent laywoman, she attended church as well as monthly retreats at an Episcopal convent. In creating a just world order, she served as the face of Christ to this nation.

Easter

The Sixth Sunday of Easter

May 14, 2023

One cannot be Christian alone; apart from the Body we can do nothing.

Color White

Preface Easter

Collect

O God, you have prepared for those who love you such good things as surpass our understanding: Pour into our hearts such love towards you, that we, loving you in all things and above all things, may obtain your promises, which exceed all that we can desire; through Jesus Christ our Lord, who lives and reigns with you and the Holy Spirit, one God, for ever and ever. *Amen.*

Readings and Psalm

Acts 17:22–31

Rather than drawing upon the fulfillment of Hebrew texts about the Messiah, Paul presents to learned Greeks the one God as Creator. The Creator of the world is not dependent upon human shrines or offerings. Humans "search for God" (v. 27), who is indeed "not far from each one of us" (v. 27). Paul supports this point by alluding to Greek literature. Paul then advances an argument against popular polytheism. In the last two verses, his listeners are called to repent before judgment by "a man" (v. 31) whose authority was validated by resurrection.

Psalm 66:7–18

This psalm of praise and thanksgiving is divided into several parts. Verses 4–11 give thanks for the deliverance of people through God's saving power. In verses 12–18, one who has experienced rescue helps others understand what God has done.

1 Peter 3:13–22

Peter recognizes that those who follow Christ often encounter painful trials, just as Christ did. The Christian's call in Christ is both the reason and the source of strength to answer evil with good. Christians are to give an explanation, possibly before formal tribunals but more likely in day-to-day interactions with hostile neighbors, for the hope that characterizes their attitude both in the present and toward the future. The Christian attitude is grounded in Christ's example.

John 14:15–21

Today's reading contains Jesus' repeated assurances that his death will not leave his disciples "orphaned." Jesus promises an indwelling presence to those who keep his commandments. That presence is described in three ways. First, God will send "another Advocate" (v. 15), who will remain with believers. The word "Advocate" (Greek *paracletos*) may also be translated Counselor or Helper. Second, Jesus himself will come, visibly after the resurrection, invisibly in the Christian community, and finally at the second coming. Third, Jesus and the Father are in union and they will dwell with those who love Jesus and obey him (v. 23). John does not particularly distinguish among these three kinds of presence.

Prayers of the People

Bless our God, you peoples; make the voice of God's praise to be heard, saying, "We call out to you with our mouths; *your praise is on our tongues.*"

Lord Christ, you have not left us orphaned, but have given your Church an Advocate. May that same Holy Spirit teach us to keep your commandments and comfort us with divine love.

Silence

We call out to you with our mouths;

Your praise is on our tongues.

Loving God, bless the suffering. May those who suffer for doing good find a friend in Christ Jesus. May those who suffer from disasters beyond their control find you attentive to the voice of their prayers.

Silence

We call out to you with our mouths;

Your praise is on our tongues.

Lord of heaven and earth, you made the world and everything in it. You give to all mortals life and breath and all things. May we be faithful stewards of all you have created.

Invite the congregation to add thanksgivings, followed by silence

We call out to you with our mouths;

Your praise is on our tongues.

Merciful Lord, bless the people of this city with a spirit of gentleness and reverence. May we be set free from fear to live, instead, in hope.

Silence

We call out to you with our mouths;

Your praise is on our tongues.

God, you are not far from each one of us. You love us as your children. Reveal your love, especially this day, to the sick and sorrowful.

Invite the congregation to add their petitions, followed by silence

We call out to you with our mouths;

Your praise is on our tongues.

Heavenly Father, you hold our souls in life. You have saved us in baptism. Because your Son Jesus lives so do we rejoice in the hope of unending life in you.

Silence

We call out to you with our mouths;

Your praise is on our tongues.

Images in the Readings

John calls the Spirit of truth our **Advocate**. This image implies a trial and the probability of judgment. Standing before God, we need someone to speak on our behalf. The reading from 1 Peter also includes the image of a trial in which we must defend our stance. In John 14, Jesus uses adoption imagery for those who receive the Spirit of truth. Yet Paul's sermon at the Areopagus calls all his pagan hearers God's **offspring**. For centuries, Jewish and Christian theologians have discussed how humans are both like and unlike God, how we enact our relationship to the Divine. A dominant teaching has been that, just as God cares for creation, so as God's offspring we are to be dedicated to that care.

The church is the **ark**, floating above the chaos of the seas, brought in safety to the harbor. One early Christian bishop directed his clergy to hold the baptismal candidates down under the water three times until they rose up gasping for air. The water of baptism not only gently washes the infant; it also joins the candidate to the death and resurrection of Christ. The eighteenth-century Welsh Methodist poet Ann Griffiths wrote, "We'll yet escape the drowning / Because God is our ark."

Ideas for the Day

♦ In John 14, Jesus promises the disciples that he "will not leave them orphaned." Life as an orphan is difficult; orphans are left without anyone to love or guide them. Modern stories are littered with orphans: Little Orphan Annie, Harry Potter, Oliver Twist, Bruce Wayne, Clark Kent, Pollyanna, Heidi, Pippi Longstocking, and Frodo Baggins are just a few. In all of these stories, the main orphan character finds their way through the help of friends and loved ones, and often through something greater than themselves. Jesus promises us that, like our favorite stories about orphans, he will continue to love us and guide us—including through our loved ones.

Easter

Easter

- The Lesson from 1 Peter is a good reminder that following Jesus is not always smooth sailing. Often when we do what's right, we are met not with happiness from others but with ridicule and rejection. Following Jesus is a counter-cultural endeavor; it was counter-cultural to follow Jesus when Jesus walked the earth, and it continues to be today. We hear in this Lesson that Jesus doesn't leave us to deal with living counter-culturally on our own, though. Jesus understands our suffering because of the cross and is with us in our own suffering, and through baptism we are further sustained to follow Jesus.

- The Lesson from Psalm 66 ends with this exaltation: "Blessed be God, because he has not rejected my prayer or removed his steadfast love from me." Sometimes we have a difficult time because it's hard for us to see God's actions in our lives. We may even feel like our prayers have been rejected or that God doesn't love us anymore. But the Psalmist reminds us that no matter what has happened or what we've done, God never rejects our prayers or keeps love from us. God loves us unconditionally.

Making Connections

Jesus is trying to explain to his disciples how he will be with them, after he has left this earthly place. After Paul finds an altar "To an unknown god," he tells the people of Athens that the God who made heaven and earth does not live in shrines made by man. The Holy Spirit is in and among us, lives in us! The words "keep my commandments" sometimes feel like a checklist, intentional, goal-oriented. When it's not obvious to us what is the goal of our endeavors, we often resist, and perhaps miss the places where the Holy Spirit might surprise us. Moving from judgment to curiosity and wondering about possibilities when we see them is a helpful way to invite the Holy Spirit into our lives. The Holy Spirit is hard to define, sometimes harder to recognize, but the warmth in our hearts when we feel it is unmistakable.

Engaging All Ages

The New Testament offers several metaphors for the Church: the Body of Christ, the Bride of Christ, Living Stones, and so on.

This one is the most organic:

Visit a vineyard in late winter: the branches are pruned back to stubs. Within months they will climb their frames and produce grapes so plentifully that harvesting buckets can scarcely be lifted. Again the organic closeness to Jesus brings our wills so into conformity with his that we can pray with confidence.

This way of thinking helps us reflect on "pruning" events in our lives and search for fruitful outcomes that may not have been apparent to us.

Mostly it helps us live with a confident sense of Jesus' personal attachment to us in all circumstances.

Try living with it and see.

Hymns for the Day

The Hymnal 1982
Alleluia, alleluia! Hearts and voices heavenward raise 191
As those of old their first fruits brought [Rogation] 705
Now the green blade riseth 204
O Jesus, crowned with all renown [Rogation] 292
All things bright and beautiful 405
Creating God, your fingers trace 394, 395
Many and great, O God, are thy works 385
This is my Father's world 651
We plow the fields, and scatter 291
We sing of God, the mighty source 386, 387
O Love of God, how strong and true 455, 456
Sing, ye faithful, sing with gladness 492
Come down, O Love divine 516
Come, gracious Spirit, heavenly Dove 512
Creator Spirit, by whose aid 500
O thou who camest from above 704
To thee, O Comforter divine 514

Lift Every Voice and Sing II
He lives 42
More love to thee, O Christ 87

Wonder, Love, and Praise
God the sculptor of the mountains 746, 747

Weekday Commemorations

Monday, May 15
Pachomius of Tabenissi, Monastic, 348

The founder of monastic life wherein members live in community rather than as hermits, Pachomius had encountered caring, loving Christians while imprisoned. He was baptized upon release, after which he led an ascetic life of manual labor and prayer while caring for the poor. Followers—especially the young, very old, or ill—were drawn to his definition of a monasticism not so strict and hard. He and his disciples wrote the first rubric for that monastic life, quite controversial then. Within a generation of Pachomius' death, his monastic federation included several thousand monks and nuns, spreading from Europe to Palestine.

Wednesday, May 17
Thurgood Marshall, Public Servant, 1993

A distinguished American jurist and the first African American to become an associate justice of the United States Supreme Court, Marshall was born on July 2, 1908, in Baltimore, Maryland. As a lawyer, his crowning achievement was arguing successfully for the plaintiffs in *Brown v. Board of Education of Topeka* in 1954. Appointed to the Supreme Court in 1967, Marshall compiled a long and impressive record of decisions on civil rights, not only for African Americans, but also for women, Native Americans, and the incarcerated. A strong advocate for individual freedoms and human rights, he adamantly believed that capital punishment was unconstitutional and should be abolished.

Thursday, May 18
Ascension Day

Friday, May 19
Dunstan, Archbishop of Canterbury, 988

Although the phrase "contemplatives in action" sounds like a contradiction in terms, the work of Bishops Dunstan, Aethelwold of Winchester, and Oswald of Worcester (his former pupils), manifested just that. After King Edgar named Dunstan archbishop of Canterbury in 960 (at about age fifty), Dunstan exploited the vigorous currents of the Benedictine monastic revival by raising the monastic prayer life to the attention of the English Church. The three men sought better education and discipline among clergy, the end of landed family influence in the Church, restoration and establishment of monasteries, revival of the monastic life for women, and closer ordering of the liturgy. Effects of the "Monastic Agreement" lasted long.

Saturday, May 20
Alcuin of York, Deacon, 804

Born in York about 730 into a noble family related to Willibrord, first missionary to the Netherlands, Alcuin inherited a strong tradition and zeal for learning from the early English Church. At the cathedral in York, Alcuin was schooled under Archbishop Egbert, a pupil of Bede's. As a deacon (770), Alcuin headed the school. In 796, he became abbot of Tours, where he remained until he died. He was a man of learning, charm, and integrity. As director of Charlemagne's Palace School at Aachen and under Charlemagne's authority, Alcuin oversaw reform of the liturgy as well as the adaptation and editing of service books from Rome, thus preserving many Collects, including the Collect for Purity, which opens the Eucharist.

Easter

Ascension Day

May 18, 2023

The risen Jesus is lifted up into heaven and no longer seen by the disciples.

Color   White

Preface   Ascension

Collect

Almighty God, whose blessed Son our Savior Jesus
Christ ascended far above all heavens that he might
fill all things: Mercifully give us faith to perceive that,
according to his promise, he abides with his Church
on earth, even to the end of the ages; through Jesus
Christ our Lord, who lives and reigns with you and
the Holy Spirit, one God, in glory everlasting. *Amen.*

or this

Grant, we pray, Almighty God, that as we believe
your only-begotten Son our Lord Jesus Christ to have
ascended into heaven, so we may also in heart and
mind there ascend, and with him continually dwell;
who lives and reigns with you and the Holy Spirit, one
God, for ever and ever. *Amen.*

Readings and Psalm

Acts 1:1–11

In the opening passage of the Acts of the Apostles the
author summarizes the last events and instructions
of Jesus' earthly ministry before he is lifted up into
heaven. The book is formally dedicated to Theophilus,
who may have been an early convert to Christianity.
Jesus tells his followers to wait for their baptism in
the Holy Spirit, after which their missionary work
will spread from Jerusalem out to all the world. Jesus
will one day come again, but his disciples now have a
message to bring to all peoples.

Psalm 47

A hymn of praise to the mighty king who is raised up
and enthroned on high.

or

Psalm 93

God reigns, the Lord of all creation, and has
established the earth and subdued the great waters.

Ephesians 1:15–23

In this lesson Paul gives thanks for the faith and love
of the Ephesians and prays that they may see with
their inward eyes the power of God, who has raised
and enthroned Jesus far above all earthly and heavenly
dominions. How vast is the treasure that God offers to
those who trust in God! The Lord Christ now reigns
as head of the Church, which is his body and which
experiences the fullness of his love.

Luke 24:44–53

In our gospel Jesus leaves his followers with the
promise of the Holy Spirit and is carried up into
heaven. The disciples are to await their empowerment
from on high before beginning their mission to the
world. Joyfully they return from Bethany, the town
where Jesus had stayed before his passion. They enter
the temple and praise God.

Prayers of the People

Come, let us pray with thanksgiving to him who ascended with great triumph to God's heavenly kingdom, responding to each petition by saying, "Hear us, Ascended Lord."

Open our minds to understand the truth of holy scripture, fashioning our lives to proclaim its saving message, and bearing witness to the power of forgiveness and mercy; for this we pray.

Hear us, ascended Lord.

Send us into places of poverty and despair, that we may feed the hungry, comfort those who are ill, be present to the lonely, offer hope to the downtrodden, and reveal the healing power of the Risen and Ascended Christ; for this we pray.

Hear us, ascended Lord.

Turn our hearts toward your will, that we may choose new life, receive the grace of your forgiveness, and bear witness to your loving and sacrificial hope; for this we pray.

Hear us, ascended Lord.

Move the leaders of Church and government to guide us into a simplicity of living, discovering our worth through virtuous living, and leaving behind the false promises of the world's wealth; for this we pray.

Hear us, ascended Lord.

Give us faith to perceive that Christ dwells with his Church on earth and prepares for us a heavenly mansion, especially remembering today _____ and all who have died; for this we pray.

Hear us, ascended Lord.

In thanksgiving for the faith of the apostles, whose devotion to Jesus inspires our holy and life-giving commitment to proclaim his message today; for this we pray.

Hear us, ascended Lord.

With the freedom of an enlightened heart, we join in the inheritance of the saints as we continue our prayers and thanksgivings.

(Special intentions of the congregation, the diocese, and the Anglican Communion may be added here or before the formal intercessions.)

The Celebrant adds a concluding Collect.

Images in the Readings

Ascension Day plays with the ancient cosmological picture of the three-tier universe, the highest level of which is **heaven**, or "the heavens." Over the centuries, Christians have speculated in quite different ways about what this heaven is. By the nineteenth century, heaven came to be described as a kind of family summer camp, perfection in populist human terms.

However, in the Bible, heaven is often a synonym for God, a way to speak about divine majesty and mercy. In Acts, the ascending Jesus is covered with a cloud, which in the Hebrew scriptures usually refers to the elusive presence yet cosmic power of God. It is important that today's references to heaven not suggest that it is a place that is far away. The risen Christ is here in the assembly of believers.

Luke has two men in **white robes** speaking with the disciples. The Christian church has regularized the wearing of white robes as the sign of baptism. We all can speak of the power of the ascended Christ.

In Ephesians, the **body of Christ** is the Church imagined like Atlas, a giant standing on earth holding up the skies, the head being Christ, and the body being the church that fills the world. Today we blend this understanding of "body of Christ" with the bread we eat and the assembly gathered to worship.

Ideas for the Day

- ◆ Ascension Day celebrates Jesus' ascension into heaven, as read in the Acts passage for the day. The resurrected Jesus appeared to his followers after his death and resurrection multiple times, and then the disciples watched him ascend into heaven (Acts 11:9; Luke 24:51). Though Jesus is not often with us as he was when he walked the earth (both before and after resurrection), the ascended and resurrected Christ continued to be active in our world and in our lives today. Share some stories about Jesus' presence in your own life, or how you've seen Jesus present in the lives of others.

Easter

- In Acts 1:1–11, Jesus promises the disciples twice that the Holy Spirit will be coming (vv. 5 and 8). It's not an accident that Jesus continually tells the disciples that the Holy Spirit is on the way. Jesus is about to leave them as God's immediate and visual presence on earth—and the Holy Spirit will be God present with them on earth after Jesus leaves. Jesus and the Holy Spirit are basically "ships passing in the night" as one Person of the Trinity leaves earth in the way he was before, and another arrives on earth in a powerful way. "Missed Connections" is a section on Craig's List where people can post, looking for people or things that they briefly passed and would like to reconnect. What are some local examples of "missed connections"?

- In the Gospel passage for the day (Luke 24:44–53) Jesus blessing the disciples accompanies his ascension into heaven. Blessings/being blessed have taken on new meaning in pop culture; saying one is blessed or #blessed is used as a way to "humble brag," or brag about an accomplishment or good thing in one's life while feigning humility. The Church still uses blessings in the way Jesus blesses his disciples: to pray for God's protection, favor, and peace, or to set apart for holy service. Find a way to liturgically bless those in worship today.

Making Connections

In the Catechism we say that what we believe about ascension is this: "that Jesus took our human nature into heaven where he now reigns with the Father and intercedes for us" (BCP, 850). It is through this that we can believe that God truly knows our experience on earth, as humans. Our passion and sorrow. Our feelings of isolation and joy. This is where the incarnation still works for us, if you will, in the revelation not only as God on earth, but as us in heaven. When Luke was written most people believed the world was divided into three parts—heaven, the earth, and the underworld. What do you believe? Why?

Engaging All Ages

Rogation Days are the three days before Ascension Day. In some cultures farmers have their crops blessed by a priest during these days, in other cultures congregations process around the perimeters of their village or their church grounds, asking for God's blessing and protection over them in the coming year. (This is often called "beating the boundaries.") Consider walking the perimeters of your church grounds, your neighborhood, your apartment building or property. Stop at each corner and ask God to bless and protect the land and all those who live, work, rest, and worship within that space.

Hymns for the Day

The Hymnal 1982
And have the bright immensities 459
Hail thee, festival day! 216
A hymn of glory let us sing 217, 218
Alleluia! sing to Jesus! 460, 461
Hail the day that sees him rise 214
See the Conqueror mounts in triumph 215
The Lord ascendeth up on high 219
Crown him with many crowns 494
Hail, thou once despised Jesus 495
It was poor little Jesus, yes, yes 468
Lord, enthroned in heavenly splendor 307
O Lord most high, eternal King 220, 221
Rejoice, the Lord is King 481
Rejoice, the Lord of life ascends 222

Lift Every Voice and Sing II
Go preach my gospel 161
He is king of kings 96

Wonder, Love, and Praise
God the sculptor of the mountains 746, 747

The Seventh Sunday of Easter: The Sunday after Ascension Day

May 21, 2023

The church consecrated as the Body of Christ.

Color White

Preface Easter

Collect

O God, the King of glory, you have exalted your only Son Jesus Christ with great triumph to your kingdom in heaven: Do not leave us comfortless, but send us your Holy Spirit to strengthen us, and exalt us to that place where our Savior Christ has gone before; who lives and reigns with you and the Holy Spirit, one God, in glory everlasting. *Amen.*

Readings and Psalm

Acts 1:6–14

In this reading we hear of Jesus' promise of empowerment for mission by the Holy Spirit, after which he is envisioned being lifted up into heaven. The author of Acts pictures the missionary work of the church spreading outward from Jerusalem. In obedience to Jesus' command, the disciples return to the city and, with others of Jesus' followers and relatives, prayerfully await the coming of the Spirit. Although Jesus will one day appear again, his community now has a ministry to bring the good news to the world.

Psalm 68:1–10, 33–36

A psalm of praise to the mighty God who has brought the people out of Egypt and saved Israel from her enemies. God reigns on high.

1 Peter 4:12–14; 5:6–11

In this lesson we learn that when Christians find it necessary to suffer for their faith, they are to know that they are sharing in Christ's sufferings. They can even find cause for rejoicing, recognizing that this may well be a sign that God's Spirit is with them. The advice was given during an outbreak of persecution of Christians in Asia Minor. The disciples are urged to make sure that they only suffer in a right cause and are then unashamed to confess Christ's name.

John 17:1–11

In our gospel Jesus asks the Father that his glory may be made fully known in his Son, and he prays for his disciples, through whom this glory now shines. These words are part of what is called Jesus' high-priestly prayer offered before his death. God's glory has been shown forth in Jesus' ministry and will be radiant in his crucifixion and resurrection. Now and afterward Jesus' followers will realize that all which Jesus has given to them has come from the Father.

Prayers of the People

To our God be the power forever and ever. Amen. Let us appeal to the Lord, saying, "We are yours; *be glorified in us.*"

Holy Father, protect your Church for your name's sake, so that we may be one even as you are one with your Son Jesus and the Holy Spirit. Restore, support, strengthen, and establish us and always for your glory.

Silence

We are yours;

Be glorified in us.

Loving God, raise up witnesses to your love in all the world, even to the ends of the earth. Be a parent to orphans, a defender of widows and a provider to the poor.

Silence

We are yours;

> ### Be glorified in us.

Great God of heaven and earth, you graciously send rain to dry places. Give to the people of the earth enough to meet their needs; and yet protect us from dangerous excess. May we acknowledge that all good gifts come from your hand.

Invite the congregation to add thanksgivings, followed by silence

We are yours;

> ### Be glorified in us.

Mighty God, in our own community, exalt the humble in due time. May those who have known suffering and struggle have their dignity renewed. Bless them with gladness. Make their voices heard in shouts of joy.
Silence

We are yours;

> ### Be glorified in us.

God of all grace, we pray for the lonely and for prisoners, for the sick and the suffering. As they cast their anxieties upon you, may they experience your freedom and care.

Invite the congregation to add their petitions, followed by silence

We are yours;

> ### Be glorified in us.

Heavenly Father, we have been granted eternal life in knowing you through your Son Jesus. Prepare a home for all of the dying and the dead, that they may continue forever in your goodness.

Silence

We are yours;

> ### Be glorified in us.

Images in the Readings

John writes about the **name** of God. When we say, "Stop in the name of the law," we mean that our very invoking of "the law" brings with it the powerful authority behind the law. So the name of God conveys divine mercy and might. Jews still today, careful not to misuse God's name, invoke *Hashem*, "the Name," as a circumlocution for God. Christians can call upon the name of the Lord by invoking Jesus Christ.

    Eternal life, John writes in this chapter, is knowing God now. As did the Gospel of the first Sunday of Lent, 1 Peter speaks in a literal way about the **devil**. One of the primary questions raised by the world's religions is why there is evil in the world and within the human heart. Borrowed from dualistic religions, the image of the devil personifies the power of evil into a kind of perpetually troublesome anti-God. Christians trust in the mighty hand of God to protect them against this adversary.

Ideas for the Day

+ After Jesus ascends to heaven in Acts 1, the disciples stay and look to heaven for a while until two men show up and let them know that they don't have to stand there looking for Jesus forever—Jesus will return again. It's easy to want to focus all our attention on what happens in eternal life or when Jesus returns, but these two men remind us that we aren't called to just stand still waiting. We have been given the Holy Spirit, just like those first disciples, so that we can serve God and others while living here on earth.

+ In John 17, Jesus prays before his crucifixion that the disciples "may be one" as they continue serving Jesus in the world. The disciples are brought together in unity of mission—though they are all very different as individuals, Jesus brings them together. We as modern disciples are the same; though we are all different people individually, given different gifts and skills by God, we are all called to serve Jesus and others in his name together. How can we work together for this common purpose?

♦ We read in 1 Peter 4 that we can "cast all our anxiety on [Jesus], because he cares for us." There is much to be anxious about in our world, and it can sometimes feel overwhelming. Jesus invites us to bring our struggles and anxiety to him. In the hymn "What a Friend We Have in Jesus" (LEVS II #109) we sing about how we are able to bring all our difficulties to God in prayer. We are reminded as we sing this song that we will find solace in Jesus.

Making Connections

The readings for today foretell that it will be a rocky road ahead, as followers of Jesus. Peter writes to the exiles, to "not be surprised at the fiery ordeal which comes upon you." The Psalmist recalls the hardships of Israel and reminds the people to "ascribe power to God" (v. 34). Always with reassurance that in the end, God will "restore, establish and strengthen" us. In the Gospel story, Jesus prays for the disciples, acknowledging he's done all he can do, and now it's up to them. Jesus' prayer is imploring God to be with these humans as they go forward on their own. Over and over we hear that God's got our backs. The two men in white robes that appear after Jesus ascended ask, "Why do you stand looking into heaven?"—as if to say, "Get going! You have work to do!" The travails and the urgency of doing God's work on earth have not changed and it's us who needs to go and do.

Engaging All Ages

In this Gospel, "glorify" means to reveal someone's true nature. Jesus has displayed God's true nature by all the things he has done. Simply put, God is not your critic. God is your loving rescuer both from disorders like illness and from your own folly.

Jesus asks God to glorify him. Why? In order that his reality would attract all people so his real nature would transform and complete us.

The last verse shows the final "glory": if we can be one with each other, that unity will glorify the communal relatedness of the very Trinity. God is community. When fully realized, so shall we be.

Think about that when you're next tempted to allow a disagreement to decay into a quarrel.

And pray for help.

Hymns for the Day

The Hymnal 1982
All hail the power of Jesus' name 450, 451
Crown him with many crowns 494
Praise the Lord through every nation 484, 485
Rejoice, the Lord is King 481
Alleluia! sing to Jesus! 460, 461
Hail, thou once despised Jesus 495
Lord, enthroned in heavenly splendor 307
Christ is alive! Let Christians sing 182
If thou but trust in God to guide thee 635
Rejoice, the Lord of life ascends 222
The head that once was crowned with thorns 483
Thou, who at thy first Eucharist didst pray 315

Lift Every Voice and Sing II
Go preach my gospel 161

Wonder, Love, and Praise
Come now, O Prince of peace 795
No saint on earth lives life to self alone 776
The church of Christ in every age 779
Unidos, unidos / Together, together 796
We are all one in mission 778

Easter

Easter

Weekday Commemorations

Monday, May 22
Helena of Constantinople,
Protector of the Holy Places, 330

Helena was mother of Emperor Constantine of Rome and a devout Christian who cared for the poor. About 325, when she was granted the title of Empress of the Western Empire, she traveled to the Holy Land to seek places cited in the Gospels. Her most important finds were the Cross of the Crucifixion and the site of the Resurrection. Legend has it that she had the latter area excavated, and three crosses imprinted with "Jesus, King of the Jews" were discovered. The church Helena built there became the Church of the Holy Sepulcher.

Thursday, May 25
Bede, Priest and Historian, 735

Of his life's work, Bede wrote, "I always took delight in learning, teaching, and writing." He was ordained a deacon at nineteen, a presbyter at thirty. Bede, the greatest scholar of his time in the Western Church, also boasted of exemplary character as a model monk, a devout Christian, and a man of manners. The title "Venerable," added a century after his death, was unusual but deserved. Bede commented on the scriptures based on patristic interpretations, and his treatise on chronology was a standard. His most famous work, *The Ecclesiastical History of England*, remains the primary source for Anglo-Saxon culture of the period 597–731.

Friday, May 26
Augustine of Canterbury,
First Archbishop of Canterbury, 605

Pope Gregory the Great sent a mission to the pagan Anglo-Saxons in 596, led by Augustine, the prior of Gregory's own monastery in Rome. They carried a silver cross and an iconic image of the Christ. About 601, King Ethelbert was converted and became the first Christian king in England; around the same time, Augustine was ordained bishop somewhere in France and named "Archbishop of the English Nation" (the chair of Saint Augustine in Canterbury Cathedral dates from the thirteenth century). A remnant of Gregory and Augustine's correspondence from this time deals with "unity in diversity" in the young English Church, foundational to the modern ecumenical movement.

The Day of Pentecost

May 28, 2023

The gift of the Holy Spirit empowers Christians for ministry in the world.

Color   Red

Preface   Pentecost

Collect

Almighty God, on this day you opened the way of eternal life to every race and nation by the promised gift of your Holy Spirit: Shed abroad this gift throughout the world by the preaching of the Gospel, that it may reach to the ends of the earth; through Jesus Christ our Lord, who lives and reigns with you, in the unity of the Holy Spirit, one God, for ever and ever. *Amen.*

or this

O God, who on this day taught the hearts of your faithful people by sending to them the light of your Holy Spirit: Grant us by the same Spirit to have a right judgment in all things, and evermore to rejoice in his holy comfort; through Jesus Christ your Son our Lord, who lives and reigns with you, in the unity of the Holy Spirit, one God, for ever and ever. *Amen.*

Readings and Psalm

Acts 2:1–21

Luke sees the gift of the Spirit as a reversal of Babel (see Genesis 11:1–9) and the fulfillment of the promise of a new covenant (see Jeremiah 31:33). The law will indwell each individual believer. The words given by the Spirit are not babbling but proclamation. The variety of languages in which the message about God's powerful works was communicated represent the potential spread of the gospel to all nations. Peter interprets the experience for the crowd. While some could only explain the peculiar events as the result of

human dissipation, Peter calls the events supernatural generosity and the marvelous fulfillment of an ancient promise found in Joel 2:28–32.

or

Numbers 11:24–30

God speaks to Moses, who is the pattern for later Jewish prophets. God shares Moses' gift of the Spirit with seventy elders. But Eldad and Medad, who were not with these elders, also receive God's Spirit and prophesy. When told of this, instead of thinking he is in control of prophetic gifts, Moses recognizes that such a gift from God ought to be bestowed on everyone. Moses sees that prophecy is a gift, given freely to whomever God wants. He refuses to limit God's Spirit and is willing to acknowledge God's gifts in people who are not part of the "in" group.

Psalm 104:25–35, 37

This hymn to God as Creator shares the imagery of many near-Eastern nature poems and myths but changes their emphasis. Leviathan, the primeval water monster of chaos, is God's plaything. The created world is under God's sway and owes God praise. Sin disrupts the harmony of creation, and the psalmist prays for a restoration of the original wholeness.

1 Corinthians 12:3b–13

The Corinthian community was torn by dissension over the characteristics, distribution, and use of "spiritual gifts" (12:1). Paul emphasizes that these are gifts of grace to all, not just the private possession of certain people. He points out the triune operation of God in these gifts: the Holy Spirit as the giver, Jesus as the One to whom service is given, and God the Father as the One at work in the gift. The gifts are complementary and meant for the common good. Every gift has an important place in the life of the community.

Easter

or

Acts 2:1–21

Luke sees the gift of the Spirit as a reversal of Babel (see Genesis 11:1–9) and the fulfillment of the promise of a new covenant (see Jeremiah 31:33). The law will indwell each individual believer. The words given by the Spirit are not babbling but proclamation. The variety of languages in which the message about God's powerful works was communicated represent the potential spread of the gospel to all nations. Peter interprets the experience for the crowd. While some could only explain the peculiar events as the result of human dissipation, Peter calls the events supernatural generosity and the marvelous fulfillment of an ancient promise found in Joel 2:28–32.

John 20:19-23

This post-resurrection appearance of Jesus is shared with the other gospels. Jesus shows his wounds to establish that the crucified Jesus and the risen Christ are one and the same. John's account stresses the fulfillment of the promises made in the Farewell Discourse: Christ's return and the gift of the Holy Spirit. For John, the coming of the Holy Spirit is intimately linked to the resurrection. Jesus breathes the Holy Spirit upon the disciples, creating humanity anew for eternal life. To this new creation, the Church, he then bestows the power to mediate forgiveness. Its mission will divide people by their response.

or

John 7:37–39

Jesus shows his wounds to establish that the crucified Jesus and the risen Christ are one and the same. John's account stresses the fulfillment of the promises made in the Farewell Discourse: Christ's return and the gift of the Holy Spirit. For John, the coming of the Holy Spirit is intimately linked to the resurrection. Jesus breathes the Holy Spirit upon the disciples, creating humanity anew for eternal life. To this new creation, the Church, he then bestows the power to mediate forgiveness.

Prayers of the People

Peace be with you, brothers and sisters. In wonder and gratitude, let us pray, saying, "You send forth your Spirit: *Come, Holy Spirit.*"

Holy God, by your Spirit you gave birth to your Church: may our many members be the one Body of Christ in this world. Give to each member of your Church the manifestation of the Spirit for the common good.

Silence

You send forth your Spirit:

> ### Come, Holy Spirit.

Holy God, you gave your disciples the ability to speak in the languages of the people: may we also speak about your deeds of power throughout the world, that all may know of your salvation.

Silence

You send forth your Spirit:

> ### Come, Holy Spirit.

Holy God, the earth is full of your creatures: may all who look to you be given food in due season. Open your hand in desolate places and fill the hungry with good things.

Invite the congregation to add thanksgivings, followed by silence

You send forth your Spirit:

> ### Come, Holy Spirit.

Holy God, you poured out your Holy Spirit in your Holy City Jerusalem: pour out your Spirit in our own city. Raise up prophets and dreamers; give us vision.

Silence

You send forth your Spirit:

> ### Come, Holy Spirit.

Holy God, you give the gift of healing by your Spirit: bring healing and wholeness to all those on our hearts and minds this day. You renew the face of the earth; bring renewal to those in need.

Invite the congregation to add their petitions, followed by silence

You send forth your Spirit:

Come, Holy Spirit.

Holy God, we pray for our sisters and brothers who were baptized into the one body, who were made to drink of the one Spirit, and who now have died in Christ. May those who have called upon your name, O Lord, be saved forever.

Silence

You send forth your Spirit:

Come, Holy Spirit.

Images in the Readings

Anthropologists describe **fire** as one of the markers of the human species. For tens of thousands of years, humans gathered around fire for light, warmth, protection, community, and better food. Many passages in the Bible liken God to fire. The Holy Spirit of God appeared on Sinai in flames of fire, which on Pentecost appeared on the forehead of each believer. Moses experienced God in fire; through fire the Israelites presented offerings to God; God led the people through the wilderness with a pillar of fire. Seraphim are fire spirits, extensions of the divine. Yet fire is also a sign of divine judgment: the angel in Eden hides the tree of life from humanity with a sword of fire, and John the Baptist predicts that fire will consume the chaff. Fire both occasions human life and has the power to destroy. Think fire, think God.

The Hebrew noun *ruah* can be translated into English as **spirit**, breath, or wind. Spirit is the most amorphous of these words. In Christian theology, the Spirit that we experience is the Spirit of the risen Christ, a spirit of service, a spirit of love, a spirit of resurrection beyond death.

In the narrative in Numbers, **seventy** elders receive the Spirit. In the Bible, seventy is a number that connotes totality, seven times ten. In Genesis 10, there are seventy nations in Israel's world, Jacob moves to Egypt with seventy family members, and there are many more seventies. Luke says that seventy were sent out to preach the word.

Ideas for the Day

- When the disciples receive the power of the Holy Spirit and speak in languages they couldn't previously speak (Acts 2:1–21), many are amazed. Others sneer and chalk it up to the disciples being drunk (they were not). Often when God acts powerfully, there will be a tendency to try to "explain it away" or think it's fake. Yet, God continues to surprise us and act in ways we don't expect. How can we be more open to the Holy Spirit moving powerfully in our midst, rather than immediately explaining things away or assuming falsity?

- A Christian symbol for the Holy Spirit is fire, because of the tongues of fire that rested on each of the disciples on the Day of Pentecost (Acts 2:3). Fire is especially known for keeping humans alive because it can help sanitize water (when boiled) so that it's safe to drink, cooks food that would be harmful if eaten raw, and keeps us warm. When in the wilderness, one of the first things survivalists do is make a fire so that they can safely drink water, cook food, and stay warm. Similarly, the Holy Spirit keeps us spiritually alive by sustaining us with spiritual food, satisfying our spiritual thirst, and sparking our passion to be on fire for Jesus.

- Another Christian symbol for the Holy Spirit is wind or breath, illustrated by the "rush of a violent wind" that happens during the Pentecost story (Acts 2:2). The Greek word for "spirit" is pneuma, which can also mean wind or breath. In Hebrew, the word for "spirit" is *ruach*, which, just like the Greek *pneuma*, also means wind or breath. Both in the Hebrew scriptures and in the New Testament these two spirit words are used to describe the action or movement of God's Spirit.

Easter

Making Connections

We the Church have a lot of work to do on earth, more even than the disciples who were charged to go around the earth to spread the word. We have more people with infinitely diverse gifts and amazing tools to enhance our ability to do the work. Tongues of fire are no match for an iPhone. Every person, every age, has a place in ministry, if only we can empower them: Youth who show up to shovel snow so everyone can safely get inside for worship. Techie adult who volunteers time to keep the church computers safe from bad actors. Children who help set up and clean up coffee hour. These are ministries to be celebrated and lifted up alongside ordained or paid staff ministry. Every person contributes to our life together in Christ.

Engaging All Ages

The Gospels offer different accounts of the Church's birth. Matthew implies it happened as Jesus breathed his last from the Cross. When Jesus releases his Spirit, the dead are raised and the temple veil separating us from God tears open.

Luke puts it in the Upper Room fifty days after Easter. The gathered disciples discover what Jesus loved about each with a force making their rushing pulses feel like an earthquake and tornado combined.

John places it on Easter evening. A delighted community is born consisting of candid loving truth that, as we saw, was able to enfold a wounded Thomas.

Accept no substitute. All those describe communities that result from concentrating on Jesus today.

Even Episcopalians.

Hymns for the Day

The Hymnal 1982

Come down, O Love divine 516
Come, Holy Ghost, our souls inspire 503, 504
Come, thou Holy Spirit bright 226, 227
Creator Spirit, by whose aid 500
Holy Spirit, font of light 228
O day of radiant gladness 48
O Holy Spirit, by whose breath 501, 502
O Spirit of the living God 531
Praise the Spirit in creation 506, 507
Spirit of mercy, truth, and love 229
This day at thy creating word 52
To thee, O Comforter divine 514
We the Lord's people, heart and voice uniting 51
Praise to the living God! 372
Go forth for God; go to the world in peace 347
Gracious Spirit, Holy Ghost 612
Holy Spirit, Lord of love 349
Lord, you give the great commission 528
O thou who camest from above 704
On this day, the first of days 47
Sing praise to our Creator 295
'Tis the gift to be simple 554
Breathe on me, Breath of God 508
Holy Spirit, ever living 511
I heard the voice of Jesus say 692
All who believe and are baptized 298
Baptized in water 294
Descend, O Spirit, purging flame 297
Over the chaos of the empty waters 176, 177
Spirit of God, unleashed on earth 299

Lift Every Voice and Sing II

Come, Holy Ghost 112
I'm goin'-a sing when the Spirit says sing 117
Sprit of God, descend upon my heart 119
There's a sweet, sweet Spirit in this place 120
Let it breathe on me 116
Baptized in water 121

Wonder, Love, and Praise

If you believe and I believe 806
Loving Spirit, loving Spirit 742
Veni Sancte Spiritus 832
Lord, you give the great commission 780
O God of gentle strength 770, 771
We all are one in mission 778
Baptized in water 767

Weekday Commemorations

Monday, May 29
The First Book of Common Prayer

In 1549, the second year of the reign of King Edward VI, the first Book of Common Prayer began its service to Anglicans. Through subsequent editions and revisions, the BCP continues to serve the Anglican Communion. The book was prepared by a commission, comprising learned priests and bishops, but Thomas Cranmer, archbishop of Canterbury (1533–1556), stamped the book in style, substance, and format. Bishops and priests compiled the book from, among other sources, medieval Latin service books, Greek liturgies, ancient Gallican rites, and vernacular German forms. The English "Great Bible" (authorized by King Henry VII in 1539) supplied the Psalter, and the Litany came from the English form going back to 1544.

Wednesday, May 31
The Visitation of the Blessed Virgin Mary

The Feast commemorates the visit of the Virgin Mary to her cousin Elizabeth (Luke 1:39–56). The pregnant Elizabeth greeted Mary, "Blessed are you among women, and blessed is the fruit of your womb." Mary responded with a song of praise, a thanksgiving known as the Magnificat: "My soul proclaims the greatness of the Lord." The dramatic scene places the unborn John the Baptist, who was to prepare the way of the Lord to all Israel, in proximity with the Lord himself. The gospel weaves in the story that when Mary heard her cousin's greeting, John leapt for joy in his mother's womb.

Friday, June 2
The Martyrs of Lyons, 177

Sanctus. Attalus. Maturus. Blandina. Pothinus. A deacon, a recent convert, a slave, a bishop—these are the some of the martyrs of Lyons, who refused to deny their faith. "I am a Christian," Blandina declared before the mob. Before persecution began in 177, Christians had lived under the guidance of Pothinus, Bishop of Lyons, in parts of Gaul, which had drawn them from Asia and Greece. After public torments, the Christians were subjected to public spectacle. Blandina, the last one living, was finally beaten, torn, burned with irons; having been wrapped in a net, she was thrown to a wild bull. Her endurance impressed the mob.

Saturday, June 3
The Martyrs of Uganda, 1886

Mwanga, king of Buganda, grew angry that some of his people put fealty to the Christ ahead of loyalty to him. He ordered thirty-two young men to burn on this day at Namugongo because they refused to renounce their faith. Martyrdoms, including those of Bishop Hannington and his companions, had begun in 1885, and many Christians were put to death in days to come as Mwanga determined to end Christianity in his land. However, the killings produced the opposite. Martyrs went to their deaths singing hymns and praying for their enemies. Their example encouraged new missions and also served as righteous history when persecutions were renewed in the 1970s by a Muslim dictatorship.

Easter

Pentecost

Preparing for Pentecost

Theological Themes that Might Shape Liturgy, Catechesis, and Education

In both the Incarnation (Advent, Christmastide, and Epiphanytide) and the Paschal (Lent, Holy Week, and Eastertide) the Church walks through and celebrates the defining moments of the life of Christ, mining these events for meaning and spiritual nourishment. In the long season that follows Pentecost (often referred to as Ordinary Time), we apply these teachings to our presence in the world, living the values of the kingdom of God in light of what we've experienced in the months prior.

Jerome Berryman's Godly Play curriculum refers to Ordinary Time as the "great, green, growing season." Inasmuch as this half of the Christian year invites us to continue to plumb the depths of the teachings of Jesus, this is an apt description. This is also a wonderful time of year to emphasize the teachings of Jesus as practical ways that we live out the mysteries we've celebrated in the major events of his life.

Liturgical Possibilities

Rites

While the weekly celebration of the Holy Eucharist in the six months that follow Pentecost can come across as repetitive, there is something to be said about the sanctifying rhythm of this pattern. Unlike Christmas and Easter, those who attend worship during this part of the year represent those who are most disposed towards the further development of their spirituality. Celebrating the Eucharist in ways that speak to that depth might include varying the ways the congregation experiences the Psalms (chanted or not, choir with congregation, and so on) as well as the way they hear the Eucharistic Prayer.

There are also a whole slew of major feasts during this season that cannot rubricly be transferred to Sundays (except in the instance of a patronal/matronal feast day) and therefore present more opportunities to explore mysteries of the church.

There are many ways that different congregations will choose to break up what might be seen as the monotony of Ordinary Time. A word of caution might be to be intentional both in restraining innovation and preserving a pattern. Finding a balance is important during this season.

Space

Depending on the flexibility of space and the occasion of the day, periodically mixing up the space during this season might be a helpful way to assist people in seeing similar liturgies through a different light (literally). If your congregation is one that travels heavily during the summer, that might be a time of greater innovation and liturgical variation.

Other Rituals and Resources

The *Book of Occasional Services* and *Enriching Our Worship* (where permitted) are filled with resources that might be helpful in providing some additional liturgical resources.

Pentecost

Through the Eyes of a Child

Indwelling inspiration: breathing in and out reminds us that our very life is dependent upon the gift of the Holy Spirit. Words and thoughts for young children include: mighty wind, teacher that leads into all truth, New Covenant proclaiming renewal, tongues of fire, witnesses all gathered with new awareness of God and each other. God promises to be with us always, and we are strengthened from within by the Holy Spirit, whose power, like a strong wind, we can feel even though we cannot see it. Now the church will continue to grow and learn more about Jesus, even after his death and resurrection. Mission, building and rebuilding the church (what some call "congregational development") with and for children is critical during the Season of Pentecost. This is the time the children will wonder: What are the adventures of building the early church? How was the early church built? The travels of Saint Paul with maps and cities where Paul founded churches, as well as the travels of Saints Peter, James, and John can be inspiring for children as they enjoy the concept of building something new.

With the noticeable absence of large, culturally observed religious holidays, some may find it difficult to convey Christian truths to younger members of our communities. There is something to be said about instilling simple, Christian values and practices such as prayer, generosity, and service throughout this season. Christianity is not just about the big events that punctuate the life and ministry of Jesus Christ. Christianity is also that body of teaching that helps us understand how to live compassionately and justly in the world. This is an important lesson to teach younger generations.

Through the Eyes of Youth

Developing an authentic faith in the understanding of "God as Three" (Creator, Redeemer, Sustainer) is a vital part of youth spirituality. Youth are developing their identity and part of that identity is formed through the gifts God has given them, including gifts of the spirit. Questions to consider with youth:

- What will be and what will we leave to the next generation?
- Are we building our lives on firm foundations, building something that will endure?
- Are we living our lives in a way that opens up space for the Spirit in the midst of a world that wants to forget God, or even rejects him in the name of a falsely conceived freedom?

Pentecost is a perfect time to invite the youth to reflect upon the gifts that God has given them. Not only the gifts they see in themselves, but the gifts they see in each other. Retreats can be most helpful to give the young people some time to remember the gifts the Spirit gave to the disciples, and the gifts that the Spirit gives to them.

Through the Eyes of Daily Life

On the fiftieth day of Easter we celebrate the Holy Spirit as the power of God among us that heals, forgives, inspires, and unites. Images of wind and fire describe the Spirit poured out on disciples of all nations. In John's gospel, the risen Christ breathes the Spirit on his followers on Easter evening. In the one Spirit we were baptized into one body, and at the Lord's table, the Spirit unites us for witness in the world. The Spirit calls us to follow in the way and in the pattern and in the shape of the life of Jesus.

The slow, steady growth of faith is a central focus of Ordinary Time. Liturgy, particularly in places where there is no formal Christian formation, should strive not only to create a worshipful encounter with God, but also to teach spiritual practices. The Way of Love materials from the Church Center (and Church Publishing Incorporated) might be helpful to apply here.

Through the Eyes of Those Outside of the Church

Without any major reason to look at the church, many beyond the church simply will not. That doesn't mean that we should deemphasize evangelism and services in ways that speak to the reality of the kingdom of God. Again, Ordinary Time is a fine time to live out the values of the kingdom of God; therefore, empowering the faithful to be agents and bearers of Good News in practical, tangible ways is a helpful practice.

Through the Eyes of Our Global Community

The Day of Pentecost opened the way of eternal life to every race and nation. On this day it is appropriate to study racism, sexism, and all other attitudes and actions that deny God's love for all people. It is common to see in the gift of the Spirit at Pentecost a sign that reveals God's purposes to heal and restore creation, including overcoming the disorder and confusion of languages that was told to have happen at Babel. The Spirit of God crosses over the boundaries of language and culture to create a new people of God, a human family renewed and made whole. Consider the global perspective of how the Church has made its journey from the time of Paul to today and how the message of Christ has spread throughout the world in its many forms and traditions.

Pentecost

Seasonal Blessings[1]

The following blessings may be used by a bishop or priest whenever a blessing is appropriate for the following season and noted Sundays.

The Day of Pentecost

May the Spirit of truth lead you into all truth, giving you grace to confess that Jesus Christ is Lord, and to proclaim the wonderful works of God; and the blessing of God Almighty, the Father, the Son, and the Holy Spirit, be among you, and remain with you always. *Amen.*

Trinity Sunday

May God the Holy Trinity make you strong in faith and love, defend you on every side, and guide you in truth and peace; and the blessing of God Almighty, the Father, the Son, and the Holy Spirit, be among you, and remain with you always. *Amen.*

All Saints

May God give you grace to follow his saints in faith and hope and love; and the blessing of God Almighty, the Father, the Son, and the Holy Spirit, be among you, and remain with you always. *Amen.*

Pentecost Hymn

Spirit, moving over chaos,
Bringing light where there was none,
Be to us a light, revealing
Where the work is to be done.
Praise to God, among us dwelling:
Praise the Spirit giving light.

Breath, instilling animation,
Giving life, informing soul,
Breathe into this congregation
Life that makes the Body whole.
Praise to God, among us dwelling:
Praise the Spirit giving life.

Easter Wind, inflaming fear-filled bodies,
Sending them to tell the News,
Fire anew your church's spirit,
Show the path we ought to choose.
Praise to God, among us dwelling:
Praise the Spirit giving fire.

Power, Life-force, Inspiration,
Blowing, breathing, brooding here,
Call, enliven, and empower
For your work, both far and near.
Praise to God, among us dwelling:
Praise the Spirit giving strength.

This hymn can be sung to the tune Regent Square, *Hymn 93 in* The Hymnal 1982.

Graduation Prayers

A Graduation Collect[2]

Precious Father, *I* especially pray for our teenagers and young adults at this time of school graduations; where they are lost, find them; when they are afraid, bring them comfort and love; and where they are confused, show them your will. Protect them, Father, and be with parents as they ride the roller coaster of these years with their children. May they have the courage, the strength, the wisdom through your Holy Spirit to help guide them and in many cases just to hold on, and to be there as their children take on adult responsibilities in a chaotic, sinful world. *I* now place them under your loving wings. *Amen.*

---

1 *The Book of Occasional Services 2003* (New York: Church Publishing, 2004), 27–28.

2 Stephanie Douglas, "Protect Them and Lead Them," in *Women's Uncommon Prayers* (Harrisburg, PA: Morehouse Publishing, 2000), 155.

Graduating from High School[3]

In every beginning is an ending, O Lord, and in every end something new begins. These young people will soon/have graduate/d from high school, and are ready now for new learning and experiences. Grant that childhood's innocence and hope may remain alive in them, bringing joy as they mature. Grant that they may hear your still small voice in their heart saying, "This is the way; walk in it." Help them preserve old friendships while creating new ones. Grant that we who love them may help them to find their own voice, their own words, and their own work in Christ's true way, who knows the persons they were created to be; we pray this in Jesus' name. *Amen.*

Go in Peace: For a Young Adult Leaving Home[4]

Departure from home for college, work, or military service can give rise to complex feelings of anxiety and loss. This rite is designed to equip the young adult/s with the assurances and well wishes of those who have supported them through childhood and/or their youth. A quilt, blanket, or afghan may be presented by the family or congregation during the rite.

Leader: The Lord be with you

And also with you.

Reader #1:   A reading from Isaiah 43:1–3a:

Do not fear, for I have redeemed you;
 I have called you by name, you are mine.
When you pass through the waters, I will be with you;
 and through the rivers, they shall not overwhelm you;
when you walk through fire you shall not be burned,
 and the flame shall not consume you.
For I am the Lord your God,
 the Holy One of Israel, your Savior.

The Word of the Lord.

Thanks be to God.

Leader: (addressing the community) A young adult's departure from home is a significant event in their life and in the lives of their families. As _____ prepares to leave home for _____, we gather to mark the significance of their leaving.

(addressing young adult/s) Are you prepared to leave the familiarity of family and friends in order to begin this important new chapter in your journey to adulthood?

Young Adult/s: Yes, with God's help.

Leader: We know that you will face opportunities and challenges and that you will experience joys and disappointments. We know that you will encounter new ways, new images, and new models that you will test and learn from. We ask that, in your learning and growing, you will be mindful of the people and experiences that brought you to this crossroads and of the God whose love will journey with you wherever you go.

Leader: (addressing the community) What symbol will accompany _____ on their journey into new experiences?

Parent/s or Community: This gift represents our assurance that you will be surrounded by our love wherever you go. *(The parent/s or community place the quilt, blanket, or afghan around the young adults' shoulders.)*

Leader: Let us pray. Almighty God, be with _____ at this important crossroads in their journey into a future of wondrous possibility. Bless their efforts, guide their choices, confirm their gifts, and support their growth that they may faithfully discern your will for their life. Be with us that we may appropriately share in their joys, support them in their disappointments, and confidently commend them to your loving care. In the name of Jesus, your Son and our Savior, who journeys with _____ wherever they go.

Amen! May it be so!

---

3 Adapted from *Changes: Prayers and Services Honoring Rites of Passage* (New York: Church Publishing, Inc., 2007), 22.

4 Adapted from Linda Witte Henke, *Marking Time: Christian Rituals for All Our Days* (Harrisburg, PA: Morehouse, 2001), 74–76.

Gun Violence Prevention Day

Friday, June 2

Prayer for People Harmed by Gun Violence[5]

Wisdom is better than weapons of war.
— Ecclesiastes 9:18

Loving Lord, Source of all healing,
you weep when love gives way to hatred,
and our souls, once again, weep
for those who have been harmed by gun violence;
where peace is overcome with anger,
may our hearts grow bold,
and may our communities be transformed
by our actions and voices,
working through the power of your Holy Spirit. Amen.

An Independence Day Litany[6]

Saturday, July 4

This litany is designed for use on days of national celebration (like Independence Day) or in times of national crisis.

Mighty God: the earth is yours and nations are your people. Take away our pride and bring to mind your goodness, so that, living together in this land, we may enjoy your gifts and be thankful.

Amen.

For clouded mountains, fields, and woodland; for shoreline and running streams; for all that makes our nation good and lovely;

We thank you, God.

For farms and villages where food is gathered to feed our people;

We thank you, God.

For cities where people talk and work together in factories, shops, or schools to shape those things we need for living;

We thank you, God.

For explorers, planners, diplomats; for prophets who speak out, and for silent faithful people; for all who love our land and guard our freedom;

We thank you, God.

For vision to see your purpose hidden in our nation's history, and courage to seek it in human love exchanged;

We thank you, God.

O God, your justice is like a rock, and your mercy like pure flowing water. Judge and forgive us. If we have turned from you, return us to your way; for without you we are lost people. From brassy patriotism and a blind trust in power;

Deliver us, O God.

From public deceptions that weaken trust; from self-seeking high political places;

Deliver us, O God.

From divisions among us of class or race; from wealth that will not share, and poverty that feeds on food of bitterness;

Deliver us, O God.

From neglecting rights; from overlooking the hurt, the imprisoned, and the needy among us;

Deliver us, O God.

From a lack of concern for other lands and peoples; from narrowness of national purpose; from failure to welcome the peace you promise on earth;

Deliver us, O God.

Eternal God: before you nations rise and fall; they grow strong or wither by your design. Help us to repent our country's wrong, and to choose your right in reunion and renewal.

Amen.

Give us a glimpse of the Holy City you are bringing to earth, where death and pain and crying will be gone away; and nations gather in the light of your presence.

Great God, renew this nation.

Teach us peace, so that we may plow up battlefields and pound weapons into building tools, and learn to talk across old boundaries as brothers and sisters in your love.

Great God, renew this nation.

5 Jenifer Gamber and Timothy J. S. Seamans, *Common Prayer for Children and Families* (New York: Church Publishing, Inc., 2019), 112.

6 "Litany for the Nation," in *An American Prayer Book*, ed. Christopher L. Webber (Harrisburg, PA: Morehouse Publishing, 2008), 39–41.

Pentecost

Pentecost

Talk sense to us, so that we may wisely end all prejudice, and may put a stop to cruelty, which divides or wounds the human family.

> *Great God, renew this nation.*

Draw us together as one people who do your will, so that our land may be a light to the nations, leading the way to your promised kingdom, which is coming among us.

> *Great God, renew this nation.*

Great God, eternal Lord: long years ago you gave our fathers this land as a home for the free. Show us there is no law or liberty apart from you; and let us serve you modestly, as devoted people; through Jesus Christ our Lord.

> *Amen.*

A Prayer for Digital Ministry[7]

Prayers for the Renewal of the Mind

We pray and ask for God's heart of promoting life and justice for and with all the people and leaders creating and using digital technology.

We pray for a digital space that is rooted and grounded in the sacred human identity of being made in the image of God. We pray that God would renew the minds of all engaged in digital communications to be led by the Spirit which promotes life and peace and to have a good spirit of wisdom and revelation in their decision-making that impacts billions of people.

Labor Day[8]

September 7

Lord God, our Creator. We deserve to labor among thorns and thistles, to eat by the sweat of our brow, to work without reward. For we confess we have spoiled you creation by our sin, we have marred your work by our neglect, we have hurt your work by our rebellion. We pray you, bless our labor by him who was once a carpenter, by him who came to be our servant, by him who saved us to serve. For his sake keep us and all who labor from false dealing and unfair practice, from excessive profit and unjust gain, from slovenly service and irrational demands. Help us to labor with love, to labor with joy, to labor with faithfulness. Teach us that the best labor we give you is loving service to others. In Christ's name we ask it. *Amen.*

Back to School

Marking the Beginning of a School Year[9]

God of all wisdom, we praise you for wisely gifting us with sons and daughters. Give to each one a clear sense of your love, that they may feel your presence supporting them throughout this school year. Guide their choices, direct their quest for knowledge, bless their relationships, and use their successes and failures as opportunities to grow in understanding of who you would have them be. Continue, we pray, to shape them as branches of the one true vine, that they may ever walk in the way of Christ, grow strong in your Spirit's love for all people, and know the complete joy of life in you. In the name of Christ, we pray. *Amen.*

---

7 From *A Closing Prayer Reflection of the International Symposium on Communication for Social Justice in a Digital Age* https://www.oikoumene.org/resources/prayers/speaking-life-and-justice-in-the-digital-space, accessed February 10, 2022.

8 "The First Monday in September," in *An American Prayer Book*, ed. Christopher L. Webber (Harrisburg, PA: Morehouse Publishing, 2008), 148–149..

9 Linda Witte Henke, "From the Vine," in *Marking Time: Christian Rituals for All Our Days* (Harrisburg, PA: Morehouse Publishing, 2001), 63.

The Blessing of Backpacks[10]

(Children are invited to gather in the chancel with their backpacks. Following the blessing, small wooden crosses may be given out for the children to place inside the backpacks.)

God of Wisdom, we give you thanks for schools and classrooms and for the teachers and students who fill them each day. We thank you for this new beginning, for new books and new ideas. We thank you for sharpened pencils, pointy crayons, and crisp blank pages waiting to be filled. We thank you for the gift of making mistakes and trying again. Help us to remember that asking the right questions is often as important as giving the right answers. Today we give you thanks for these your children, and we ask you to bless them with curiosity, understanding, and respect. May their backpacks be a sign to them that they have everything they need to learn and grow this year in school and in Sunday school. May they be guided by your love. All this we ask in the name of Jesus, who as a child in the temple showed his longing to learn about you, and as an adult taught by story and example your great love for us. *Amen.*

Remembering September 11, 2001[11]

A prayer to be used in observances of the anniversary of September 11, 2001.

God the compassionate one, whose loving care extends to all the world, we remember this day your children of many nations and many faiths whose lives were cut short by the fierce flames of anger and hatred. Console those who continue to suffer and grieve, and give them comfort and hope as they look to the future. Out of what we have endured, give us the grace to examine our relationships with those who perceive us as the enemy, and show our leaders the way to use our power to serve the good of all for the healing of the nations. This we ask through Jesus Christ our Lord who, in reconciling love, was lifted up from the earth that he might draw all things to himself. *Amen.*

The Feast of St. Francis

October 4

A Litany for St. Francis Day[12]

With all our heart and with all our mind, we pray to you, O God:

> *Lord, make us instruments of your peace.*

For our President and for all who are in authority, and for the people and leaders of every nation, that we may truly respect each other and learn to live together peacefully, we pray to you, O God:

> *Where there is hatred, let us sow love.*

For this community gathered, for our families and friends, our neighbors and co-workers, especially for those whom we have hurt, we pray to you, O God:

> *Where there is injury, let us sow pardon.*

For all those who seek you, God, and for those who shut you out, that they may be touched by your presence, power and grace, we pray to you, O God:

> *Where there is doubt, let us sow faith.*

For the poor, for prisoners, for refugees, for those who are oppressed and persecuted, that they may be delivered from danger and fear, we pray to you, O God:

> *Where there is despair, let us sow hope.*

For the people of God throughout the world, that the good news of God's redeeming love may be known in all places, we pray to you, O God:

> *Where there is darkness, let us sow light.*

For those who are sick, unhappy, lonely or bereft, that they may be healed and comforted, we pray to you, O God:

> *Where there is sadness, let us sow joy.*

For those who have died, especially those we now name, we pray to you, O God. *(People may add their own petitions.)*

For what is in our hearts today, we ask you to hear us, O God. *(People may add their own petitions.)*

10 Wendy Claire Barrie, *Skiturgies: Pageants, Plays, Rites, and Rituals* (New York: Church Publishing, Inc., 2011). www.skiturgies.com.

11 Frank W. Griswold, "Remembering September 11, 2001," in *An American Prayer Book*, ed. Christopher L. Webber (Harrisburg, PA: Morehouse Publishing, 2008), 113.

12 The Intercessions from "Liturgy for the Feast of St. Francis" by Wendy Claire Barrie, *Skiturgies: Pageants, Plays, Rites, and Rituals* (New York: Church Publishing, Inc., 2011). www.skiturgies.com

For all the gifts of your creation, and for the trust and joy you have given us in these our pets, we thank you and praise you, O God. *(People may add their own thanksgivings.)*

> *Grant that we may not so much seek*
> *to be consoled as to console,*
> *to be understood as to understand,*
> *to be loved as to love,*
> *for it is in giving that we receive,*
> *it is in pardoning that we are pardoned,*
> *and it is in dying that we are born to eternal life.*
> *Amen.*

A Blessing of Pets[13]

The Lord be with you.

> *And also with you.*

O Lord, how manifold are your works!

> *You stretch out the heavens like a tent.*
> *You set the earth on its foundations.*
> *You make springs gush forth in the valleys*
> *and give drink to every animal.*

You plant trees where birds may build their nests.

> *You cause the grass to grow for the cattle*
> *and plants for people to use.*
> *You open your hand and give all creatures*
> *their food in good season. (Psalm 104)*

We have come together to acknowledge with gratitude the goodness of God in all creatures, great and small, and to seek God's blessing on the pets that are our companions in life. Let us pray:

On this day, O God, we offer thanks for these, our pets, who are your daily instruments of joy and comfort in our lives. Even as you demonstrate care for us, so also move us to demonstrate care for these and all your creatures, knowing that, in so doing, we are privileged to share in your love of creation. We pray in the name of Jesus, in whose power we are made a new creation.

> ***Amen! May it be so!***

[As the leader approaches each pet, the pet's owner speaks the pet's name aloud so that all those gathered may hear. The leader then raises his/her hand above the pet and speaks a word of blessing.]

May God the Creator bless you and keep you through all the days of your life.

> ***Thanks be to God!***

[If some participants have brought mementos of former pets, the leader may touch each memento, while speaking these or similar words.]

May God bless the memory of this pet's presence in your life!

> ***Thanks be to God!***

[If children have brought stuffed animals to receive a blessing, the leader may touch each toy, while speaking these or similar words.]

May this animal's presence be a source of joy and comfort in this child's life.

> ***Thanks be to God!***

May God Almighty, Father, Son, and Holy Spirit, use us as instruments of blessing for all creatures, great and small.

> ***Amen! Thanks be to God!***

---

13 Linda Witte Henke, "All Creatures Great and Small," in *Marking Time: Christian Rituals for All Our Days* (Harrisburg, PA: Morehouse Publishing, 2001), 80–82.

A Native American Thanksgiving for the Americas and Their People[14]

Columbus Day: October 14

For our ancestors who built nations and cultures; who thrived and prospered long before the coming of strangers; for the forfeit of their lives, their homes, their lands, and their freedoms sacrificed to the rise of new nations and new worlds.

We offer a song of honor and thanks.

For the wealth of our lands; for minerals in the earth; for the plants and waters and animals on the earth; for the birds, the clouds, and rain; for the sun and moon in the sky and the gifts they gave to our people that enabled the rise of new world economics.

We offer a song of honor and thanks.

For the many foods coaxed from the heart of Mother Earth; for the skills we were given to develop foods that now belong to the world: potatoes, corn, beans, squash, peanuts, tomatoes, peppers, coffee, cocoa, sugar, and many, many more.

We offer a song of honor and thanks.

For the medicines first discovered by our ancestors and now known to the world: quinine, ipecac, iodine, curare, petroleum jelly, witch hazel, and others; for the healing skills of our people and those who now care for us. For tobacco, sage, sweet grass, and cedar that give spiritual healing by the power of their meaning.

We offer a song of honor and thanks.

For oceans, streams, rivers, lakes, and other waters of our lands that provide bountifully for us; for clams, lobsters, salmon, trout, shrimp, and abalone; for the pathways the waters provide.

We offer a song of honor and thanks.

For the friendship that first welcomed all to our shores; for the courage of those who watched their worlds change and disappear and for those who led in the search for new lives; for our leaders today who fight with courage and great heart for us.

We offer a song of honor and praise.

For the friends who suffered with us and stand with us today to help bring the promise and the hope that the New World meant to their ancestors.

We offer a song of honor and thanks.

For the strength and beauty of our diverse Native cultures; for the traditions that give structure to our lives, that define who we are; for the skills of our artists and craftspeople and the gifts of their hands.

We offer a song of honor and thanks.

For the spirituality and vision that gave our people the courage and faith to endure; that brought many to an understanding and acceptance of the love of Christ, our Brother and Savior.

We offer a song of honor and thanks.

Accept, O God, Creator, our honor song, and make our hearts thankful for what we have been given. Make us humble for what we have taken. Make us glad as we return some measure of what we have been given. Strengthen our faith and make us strong in the service of our people, in the name of our Brother and Savior, Jesus Christ, your Son, in the power of the Holy Spirit. *Amen.*

---

14 "1492–1992: A Celebration of Native American Survival. Earth and All the Stars," in *The Wideness in God's Mercy: Litanies to Enlarge Our Prayer*, ed. Jeffrey W. Rowthorn (New York: Church Publishing, Inc., 2007), 298–299. This litany was prepared for use at a service commemorating the quincentenary of the landing of Christopher Columbus in 1492 with its fateful impact on the Native American peoples, who despite all have survived to this day. The service was held on October 12, 1992, in the National Cathedral in Washington, DC.

Pentecost

A Litany for Children's Sabbath[15]

October 18

Grant, O God, that all who gather in Christ's name will throw wide our doors and our hearts and lift our hands and voices to proclaim your promise of love and will for justice, especially for those who are young, poor, vulnerable, and oppressed.

Silence

Mighty God, Lover of Justice,

Hear our prayer.

Guide our nation and all of our leaders, that they will champion the cause of the children and families most oppressed and govern with truth, compassion, and justice.

Silence

Mighty God, Lover of Justice,

Hear our prayer.

Bless the families of our world, especially the billions who lack the income, clean water, health care, or education needed to live into the fullness of life.

Silence

Mighty God, Lover of Justice,

Hear our prayer.

Strengthen us to create a nation and world of justice so that every child may live with plenty and not poverty, with peace and not threatened by violence, surrounded by family, not separated, so that all children have lives of hope, not despair.

Silence

Mighty God, Lover of Justice,

Hear our prayer.

Comfort all who suffer, especially those who are hungry, are victims of violence, or struggle without a job or enough income to meet their needs.

Silence

Mighty God, Lover of Justice,

Hear our prayer.

Gather to yourself all who have died, especially those who died from poverty, violence, and other causes we could have prevented.

Silence

Mighty God, Lover of Justice,

Hear our prayer.

Almighty God, Lover of Justice, hear these the prayers of your children and grant them for the sake of your beloved child Jesus Christ our Lord. *Amen.*

Election Day[16]

Tuesday, November 10

Holy God, throughout the ages you have called men and women to serve you in various ways, giving them gifts for the task to which they were called and strengthening and guiding them in the fulfillment of their calling; in this free land you share with us that great responsibility and enable us to choose those who will serve you in positions of leadership in various offices of government.

Help us in so choosing to seek those who have an understanding of your will for us, a commitment to justice, a concern for those in greatest need, a love of truth, and a deep humility before you; Send your Spirit among us that we may be guided in the choices we make so your will may be done on earth as it is in heaven. *Amen.*

---

15 Children's Defense Fund, *Christian Worship Resources for the Children's Sabbath*, 13. https://www.childrensdefense.org/wp-content/uploads/2018/09/Sabbath-2018_CHRISTIAN-FINAL.pdf (accessed February 11, 2019).

16 Christopher L. Webber, "Before an Election," in *An American Prayer Book,* ed. Christopher L. Webber (Harrisburg, PA: Morehouse Publishing, 2008), 150.

A Stewardship Litany[17]

God of life and love: We are quick to accept bounteous gifts from you, but slow to give thanks and to express our gratitude.

We hold too tightly the things of this life,
giving them the allegiance we owe only to you.

Take my life and let it be consecrated,
Lord, to thee.
Take my moments and my days;
let them flow in ceaseless praise,
let them flow in ceaseless praise.

Gracious God, we admit that our lives are too often out of balance; we are more willing to receive than to share, more ready to take than to give.

Create in us grateful and generous hearts,
we pray, and restore us the joy of our salvation.

Take my hands and let them move
at the impulse of thy love.
Take my feet, and let them be swift and
beautiful to thee, swift and beautiful to thee.

Merciful God, from whom comes every good and perfect gift, we praise you for your mercies:

your goodness that has created us,
your grace that has sustained us,

Your discipline that has corrected us, your patience that has borne with us,

and your love that has redeemed us.

Take my will, and make it thine;
it shall be no longer mine.
Take my heart, it is thine own; it shall be
thy royal throne, it shall be thy royal throne.

Help us to love you, and to be thankful for all your gifts by serving you and delighting to do your will.

Accept now, Gracious God, our offerings,
these our pledges of resources and talents for
your service, and the commitment of our lives,
through Jesus Christ, who gave his all for us.

Take my silver and my gold,
not a mite would I withhold;
take my intellect, and use every power
as thou shalt choose, every power
as thou shalt choose.

Take my love; my Lord,
I pour at thy feet its treasure store,
Take myself, and I will be ever, only,
all for thee, ever, only, all for thee. Amen.

Pentecost

---

17 W. Alfred Tisdale Jr., "A Stewardship Litany," hymn stanzas by Frances Ridley Havergal, in *The Wideness of God's Mercy: Litanies to Enlarge Our Prayer,* ed. Jeffery W. Rowthorn (New York: Church Publishing, Inc., 2007), 124–125.

The First Sunday after Pentecost: Trinity Sunday

June 4, 2023

The God who creates, redeems, and sanctifies is revealed to us in three persons.

Color   White

Preface   Trinity Sunday

Collect

Almighty and everlasting God, you have given to us your servants grace, by the confession of a true faith, to acknowledge the glory of the eternal Trinity, and in the power of your divine Majesty to worship the Unity: Keep us steadfast in this faith and worship, and bring us at last to see you in your one and eternal glory, O Father; who with the Son and the Holy Spirit live and reign, one God, for ever and ever. *Amen.*

Readings and Psalm

Genesis 1:1–2:4a

Today's reading is the first of the two creation accounts. In contrast to the strongly dualistic interpretation of this world view in other traditions, where chaos always threatens to overwhelm the world again, God's sovereignty over creation is affirmed. God says, "Let us make humankind" (v. 26). The "us" was taken by early Christian writers to be an allusion to the Trinity. The writer, however, may be referring to a heavenly court. "Humankind," a collective singular noun without indication of number or gender, is created in God's image and likeness, to enter into relationship with God and to be God's representative on earth, especially to share in God's dominion.

Psalm 8 or Canticle 2 or 13

This psalm is a hymn to God's glory and the God-given dignity of humans. The psalmist marvels at God's sovereignty, is awestruck at God's handiwork and humbled by humanity's place within God's creation. As humanity fulfills this unexpected gift and privilege, God's glory is revealed.

2 Corinthians 13:11–13

Paul concludes his second letter to the church in Corinth with an exhortation to be reconciled to one another. The exchange of the "holy kiss" (v. 12), the customary Eastern embrace, became a regular feature of the early liturgy, signaling the reconciliation of the community members. The closing triadic formula expresses a three-fold understanding of Christian experience: grace received through Jesus leads one to the Father's love, which is expressed through the Spirit.

Matthew 28:16–20

This Great Commission gathers up the themes that Matthew has woven throughout his work. Jesus' ministry begins and ends on a mountain in Galilee, the place of revelation. There he inaugurates the mission of the Church. Jesus makes a declaration, delivers a command, and gives a promise. To the disciples, Jesus now extends the full range of his ministry to them. Before they had been commissioned only to preach and heal, now they are to teach all that Jesus commanded them. Finally Jesus promises to the disciples his ongoing presence. The pledge of his name, Emmanuel, "God-with-us," is now fulfilled for his gathered people.

Pentecost

Prayers of the People

Brothers and sisters, live in peace. With gracious hearts appeal to the Lord, saying, "Glory to you, Holy Trinity; *we will praise you and highly exalt you forever."*

Holy Trinity, you separated the light from the darkness: may your Church ever dwell in your radiance and walk in the light of your love.

Silence

Glory to you, Holy Trinity;

> *We will praise you and highly exalt you forever.*

Holy Trinity, you placed the same sky above all people: may people all over the world live in peace with one another.

Silence

Glory to you, Holy Trinity;

> *We will praise you and highly exalt you forever.*

Holy Trinity, you created all things good: give us the will to respect and preserve your creation, that future generations may experience the goodness of all you have made.

Invite the congregation to add thanksgivings, followed by silence

Glory to you, Holy Trinity;

> *We will praise you and highly exalt you forever.*

Holy Trinity, you created the sun to give us light: shine your light on our city, that the shadow places may be exposed. May your justice and peace reign in our neighborhoods.

Silence

Glory to you, Holy Trinity;

> *We will praise you and highly exalt you forever.*

Holy Trinity, from your hand comes forth creatures great and small: as you care for even the smallest creature, show your loving-kindness to all who call out to you for help. Grace the lives of your children with healing and strength.

Invite the congregation to add their petitions, followed by silence

Glory to you, Holy Trinity;

> *We will praise you and highly exalt you forever.*

Holy Trinity, you created humankind in your image and you promised to be with us always: may those who have died take comfort in your eternal presence.

Silence

Glory to you, Holy Trinity;

> *We will praise you and highly exalt you forever.*

Images in the Readings

If by Matthew's language of **Father, Son, and Holy Spirit** we imagine two males and a mist, the biblical imagery is failing us. God is beyond all things, dead and alive in Jesus Christ, and experienced in the assembly. Many contemporary hymns add to the doctrinal language other imagery in hopes of opening up the mystery of God. In Genesis 1, God is creator, word, and breath. In Paul, God is love, grace, and communion.

The rhetorically magnificent story of **creation** in Genesis 1 poetically describes the entire universe as originally perfect and formed by God to focus on human need. According to biblical scholars, Genesis 1 was written as praise of the God of Israel, rather than as revealed science, and according to Christian theology, God's creating continues throughout time, rather than being a single prehistoric event. Creation by God through the Word in the Spirit happens today. The post-exilic authors sought also to ground the Jewish Sabbath in God's resting on the seventh day. Christians have moved their holy day from Saturday rest to Sunday assembly so as to meet the Risen Christ on the day of the resurrection.

Ideas for the Day

♦ The doctrine of the Trinity is decisive; one of the critical common denominators between Christian churches. However, it is also a sacred mystery that we experience and celebrate, but may never be able to contain with the exact right words. This is more frustrating for some than for others, yet we still all belong to God and are welcomed with our questions and doubts. The Trinity offers us a loving relationship instead of fractured arguments; a good example for us to follow. A delighted and powerful intimacy of the Holy Trinity sails through today's lessons. Can this experience of God's dynamism buoy our discipleship with an evermoving and cooperative example of how to live together faithfully?

♦ Why didn't we learn this in Sunday school? With a little digging into the Hebrew we find that the sixth word in Genesis might just turn our world upside-down. The word we read as "created" comes from a word in Hebrew that can easily mean "the plural of compassion" or "compassions." This word means womb! So a good translation could be "In the beginning God 'wombed' the heavens and the earth." Last I knew, guys don't have wombs! Perhaps this gives us a different insight on the verse, "So God created humankind in God's image, in the image of God, [God] created them, male and female, [God] created them."

♦ The relationship of love among the three persons of the Trinity serves as a model for communities of baptized Christians living together in unity. One way this is exemplified is in Rublev's Icon of the Trinity (www.wellsprings.org/uk/rublevs_icon/rublev.htm).

Making Connections

God-in-Three-Persons is a mystery, but God's commandment to proclaim the reign of God is clear. Patience, gentleness, and self-control, listed in Galatians as fruits of the Spirit, can be thought of as characteristics of God shaped in each of us. These three characteristics have self-sacrifice in common—of putting the needs of others before self-indulgence. When public discourse on social justice becomes divisive, patience, gentleness, and self-control help us see each other as beloved children of God, created in God's image. True freedom and joy come from dwelling in God's love, following Jesus before addressing other life demands and duties.

Engaging All Ages

For most people, this is the time of an unofficial "end of the year." School is ending. Work is slowing down. Graduations and weddings mark a sense of transition and hope for the future. Today's Old Testament reading is especially appropriate for this season, as it reminds us of the intention and beauty of creation—something we can step outside our doors and see, feel, sometimes even taste for ourselves. Encourage families who are able to get outside, to bask in the sacramentality of creation. For those who are not mobile, or if the weather isn't cooperating, something as simple as opening a window, going for a drive with the intention of simply seeing and being in God's creation can be a wonderful experience.

Hymns for the Day

The Hymnal 1982

All glory be to God on high 421
Ancient of Days, who sittest throned in glory 363
Come, thou almighty King 365
Holy Father, great Creator 368
Holy God, we praise thy Name 366
Holy, holy, holy! Lord God Almighty! 362
How wondrous great, how glorious bright 369
I bind unto myself today 370
O God, we praise thee, and confess 364
O Trinity of blessed light 29, 30
Round the Lord in glory seated 367
Sing praise to our Creator 295
All creatures of our God and King 400
All things bright and beautiful 405
I sing the almighty power of God 398
Immortal, invisible, God only wise 423
Many and great, O God, are thy works 385
Most High, omnipotent, good Lord 406, 407
Most Holy God, the Lord of heaven 31, 32
O all ye works of God now come 428
O blest Creator, source of light (vs. 1–4) 27, 28
The spacious firmament on high 409
The stars declare his glory 431
Thou, whose almighty word 371
Alleluia! sing to Jesus! 460, 461
Lord, you give the great commission 528

Pentecost

Lift Every Voice and Sing II
Oh Lord, how perfect is your name 57
He's got the whole world in his hand 217

Wonder, Love, and Praise
You are the Holy One 745
God the sculptor of the mountains 746, 747
O Trinity of blessed light 744
O threefold God of tender unity 743
O all ye works of God now come 884
Gracious Spirit, give your servants 782
Lord, you give the great commission 780
We all are one in mission 778

Weekday Commemorations

Monday, June 5
Boniface, Bishop and Missionary, 754
He was born Winfred in Devonshire, England, about 675 and decided to be a missionary after being professed a monk then ordained to the presbyterate. He traveled to Frisia (Netherlands) but met little success; before traveling next in 719, he first went to Rome for approval from Pope Gregory, who named him Boniface. Thereafter, Boniface dedicated his life to reforming, planting, and organizing churches, monasteries, and dioceses in Hesse, Thuringia, and Bavaria. In 722, Gregory ordained Boniface a bishop and, in 732, an archbishop; he was given a fixed see at Mainz in 743. After resigning his see, Boniface and his fellow missionaries were murdered by pagans.

Thursday, June 8
Melania the Elder, Monastic, 410
Melania (b. 341) was a first-generation Roman aristocrat, who embraced Christianity; she lived to see it become the official religion of the Empire. As a twenty-two-year-old widow, she moved to Alexandria from Rome to spread her wealth among monastics, teachers, and pilgrims. She studied asceticism with the desert mothers and fathers. She arrived in Jerusalem after 372 and founded two monasteries; she underwrote their hospitality for pilgrims seeking holy sites. Despite social mores for rich widows to remain reserved, Melania spoke out for asceticism and learning. She studied, taught, and served as a spiritual director, most notably for Evagrius.

Friday, June 9
Columba of Iona, Monastic, 567
Almost immediately upon being ordained a monk, Columba, born in Ireland in 521, set forth on his mission; before being ordained a presbyter in 551, he had founded monasteries at Derry and Durrow. Twelve years later, Columba and a dozen companions journeyed to northern Britain to evangelize among the Picts. Columba was encouraged to preach, convert, and baptize; he was also given the island of Iona, where, according to legend, his small boat had washed ashore. There, he founded the famous monastery. From Iona, for thirty years, Columba founded other monasteries and traveled through the Highlands, thereby establishing Iona as a link between Irish and Pictish Christians. He died while copying the Psalter.

Saturday, June 10
Ephrem of Nisibis, Deacon and Poet, 373
Ephrem, born in Nisibis in Mesopotamia, spoke Aramaic, the language of Jesus. Edessa, a Syrian city, was the hub of the wheel of Christianity careering throughout the East, long before conversion of the western Roman Empire. His people called him "the Harp of the Holy Spirit" for his words, which influenced development of church doctrine; his women-sung hymns, composed to oppose Gnostic hymns, still enrich liturgies of the Syrian Church. After Christians were driven out of Nisibis in 363 by Persians, Ephrem lived abstemiously in a cave above Edessa, where he preached occasionally. During a famine in 372–73, Ephrem fed the hungry and cared for the sick until his own death from exhaustion.

The Second Sunday after Pentecost, Proper 5

June 11, 2023

God calls a people into intimate covenant relationship.

Color   Green

Preface   Of the Lord's Day

Collect

O God, from whom all good proceeds: Grant that by your inspiration we may think those things that are right, and by your merciful guiding may do them; through Jesus Christ our Lord, who lives and reigns with you and the Holy Spirit, one God, for ever and ever. *Amen.*

Readings and Psalm

Genesis 12:1–9

At this point in the book of Genesis, the focus changes from the story of all humanity to the story of one man, Abram, and through him to the story of a chosen people. The Lord takes the initiative and calls Abram (Abraham) out of his family structure and the social and cultural security of his present location in Haran to go to the unknown land God will show him. His response is the first of the trustful acts that define him as preeminently the Old Testament man of faith. Abraham and his descendants are chosen to inherit a land, become a great nation and mediate blessing to all the world. The story of Abraham shows how God acts in history through the responses of individuals and peoples.

Psalm 33:1–12

This psalm was probably recited at the great autumn festival of Tabernacles, which celebrated both the creation and the history of Israel. The psalmist knows that God's word and works are unchanging (v. 4) and that God delivers the chosen people (v. 12) because of the covenant promises.

or

Hosea 5:15–6:6

Today's reading most likely comes from about 733 BCE, after Israel (often called by the tribal name, Ephraim) had allied itself with Syria and attacked Judah. In retaliation, Judah called upon the Assyrian empire, which willingly invaded and annexed most of Israel, leaving only a small area to continue briefly as a vassal state. In this time of upheaval the absence of the Lord is sensed; God has withdrawn in order to invite repentance from the people.

Psalm 50:7–15

Psalm 50 focuses on the meaning of sacrifice. God's people have abandoned the covenant and forgotten the real significance of sacrifice. Their offerings do not feed a hungry God nor assure God's favor; they should rather be an expression of the people's reliance upon and thankfulness to God.

Romans 4:13–25

In his proclamation that salvation comes through Christ and not the Mosaic Law, Paul calls upon the example of Abraham's faith to show that a right relationship with God (justification) was available through faith long before Moses codified the covenant law. Paul argues that Abraham's readiness to believe and act upon God's promise (the foundation of the covenant) put him in right relationship to God. This covenant relationship is now available to all—Jew or Gentile—who trust in God, regardless of whether they keep the Mosaic Law. The promised inheritance comes through faith to Abraham's true descendants who are those who follow his example of faith.

Matthew 9:9–13, 18–26

Today's reading narrates the calling of Matthew, a controversy with the Pharisees, and a double healing story. In this section, Matthew follows Mark very closely, except for a few specific changes. The first of these is giving the name of the tax collector as Matthew rather than Levi, as in Mark and Luke (Mark 3:18; Luke 6:15).

Prayers of the People

Offer to God a sacrifice of thanksgiving, and pay your vows to the Most High. Call on the Lord, saying, "O God, we long to see your face; *show us your favor.*"

Forgive us, O God. You desire steadfast love and yet too often our hearts are fickle. You long for us to be people of mercy and yet it is much easier to simply go through the motions. Help your Church, O God.

Silence

O God, we long to see your face;

> **Show us your favor.**

God of Abraham, you have made of one blood all the peoples of the earth. Restore us to unity. Help your people, O God.

Silence

O God, we long to see your face;

> **Show us your favor.**

Most High, every wild animal of the forest is yours; all that moves in the field is yours. The world and all that is in it is yours. Make us good stewards of your creation. Help us, O God.

Silence

O God, we long to see your face;

> **Show us your favor.**

Mighty God, come to us like the spring rains that water the earth. Restore this community; refresh its people. Help our city, O God.

Silence

O God, we long to see your face;

> **Show us your favor.**

Holy Jesus, you have come to heal the sick. Heal us. Bind us up. Help those who are suffering, O God.

Invite the congregation to add their petitions and thanksgivings, followed by silence

O God, we long to see your face;

> **Show us your favor.**

Living God, your Holy Child was raised for our justification. We pray for the dead. Raise them up on the last day, that they may live before you in eternity. Help the dying and the dead, O God.

Silence

O God, we long to see your face;

> **Show us your favor.**

Images in the Readings

Each of the scripture passages focus on relationships, both God's relationship to us and our relationships to one another. Genesis 12 details how Abram's relationship with God changes everything about his life. He moves to a new place following the promise that God will create a whole new people—a whole new web of relationships.

Hosea speaks to the power of broken relationships. Paul talks about how we are reconciled to God. Matthew recounts being called by Jesus. All of them together offer a kaleidescope of what it means to belong to God and to one another.

Ideas for the Day

- Every age and place has its distractions and demands but like the Desert Fathers and Mothers, following the path of God's steadfast love calls us to "strike out fearlessly into the unknown, even if that unknown is right around the corner. If someone is comfortable in the country, they may be dismayed by the lifestyle of the city; and the reverse is also true. These lessons move from the negotiations of a nomadic life into the challenges of ancient urban settings: all of which are full of both rebuke and successes. The commission of Jesus is not one of easy relaxation, but of a daring love for all in response to the love of God. Is the Spirit leading your community to "strike out fearlessly" in some new way?

- When we read or hear the Ten Commandments, they are not usually offered in the context of where they are found in scripture. What we hear today *is* the context. "I bore you on eagles' wings" and "you are my treasured people" and "you shall be for me a priestly kingdom," is the context of what the famous commandments are about. It is right after this loving declaration that the people are consecrated and then that the Ten Commandments are offered. Here the commandments are not rules handed down, but a gift given to God's people. In an interesting way, there are some parallels to what happens when we baptize someone. We declare they are treasured and holy. They are blessed. And then the community affirms to continually offer them the gift of love.

- The time we have entered into on the Christian calendar is called the "Season after Pentecost." Traditionally it has been called "Ordinary Time." We recognize God in the ordinary moments of our lives as well as in the times of intense revelation and celebration.

Making Connections

To be a disciple of Christ (a Christian) is to realize our call, as the disciples realized their call. Moreover, to be a disciple of Christ is to accept the New Covenant. We open ourselves to the power of the Holy Spirit and live as servants of the Lord. As we do this, we go forth into the world with new authority and a new power. Look over the liturgy of baptism in the prayer book and talk about the kind of commitment that is made in baptism. The Baptismal Covenant is found on pages 304–305 of the Book of Common Prayer.

Engaging All Ages

When was the last time you got lost? It probably isn't something you remember fondly, especially if it involved any amount of anxiety. However, getting lost is increasingly becoming more and more difficult in our modern world. You might be thinking: good! However, what if our carefully planned excursions—lives?—help in stunting the Holy Spirit? What if getting lost means finding something unexpected? This week, encourage families to "get lost" (perhaps not at the beginning of a service!) with the intent of being surprised by something in their general vicinity. What can they find? How can they report back to the parish?

Hymns for the Day

The Hymnal 1982
O God of Bethel, by whose hand 709
  (semi-continuous)
The God of Abraham praise 401 (SC)
Praise our great and gracious Lord 393
By all your saints still striving 231, 232
He sat to watch o'er customs paid 281
Hope of the world, thou Christ
  of great compassion 472
In your mercy, Lord, you called me 706
O for a thousand tongues to sing 493
O Jesus Christ, may grateful hymns be rising 590
There is a balm in Gilead 676
Thine arm, O Lord, in days of old 567
What does it mean to follow Jesus? 89

Lift Every Voice and Sing II
There is a balm in Gilead 203

Wonder, Love, and Praise
From miles around the sick ones came 774
Heal me, hands of Jesus 773
O Christ, the healer, we have come 772
Will you come and follow me 757
You laid aside your rightful reputation 734

Pentecost

Weekday Commemorations

Monday, June 12 (transferred)
Saint Barnabas the Apostle

Barnabas, born Joseph, was called an apostle, along with the Twelve, for his missions. Like Paul, Barnabas was a Jew of the Dispersion; Barnabas presented Paul to the apostles with the story of Saul's conversion to Paul. Later, Barnabas, having settled in Antioch, sent for Paul to help lead the Christian church there. The two men, sent by the disciples, carried food and relief to the church during a famine in Jerusalem. Afterwards, the church sent out the pair, starting from Cyprus. Their friendship split over Mark, who had left the mission to return to Jerusalem. Barnabas and Mark traveled to Cyprus, where tradition honors Barnabas as the founder of the church and places his martyrdom.

Wednesday, June 14
Basil the Great, Bishop of Caesarea, 379

Born a Christian about 329 in Caesarea, Basil knew wealth and education. He was baptized in 357, then ordained a deacon. His sister Macrina's faith fired his own to study the anchorites in Egypt and beyond. Following his sister, who had founded the first monastic order for women at Annesi, he founded the first monastery for men at Ibora. The *Rules* he wrote with Gregory Nazianzus lay the foundation for all Eastern monastics. Basil was ordained presbyter in 364. The road to bishop of Caesarea was not so smooth, but he persevered in his effort to restore discipline to the clergy, defend the Nicene faith, adore God, and care for the poor.

Thursday, June 15
Evelyn Underhill

Born December 6, 1875, Underhill was a fine writer whose essays and books appealed to many also drawn by her definitive mysticism. She grew up in London and was confirmed in the Church of England. In the 1890s, she began journeying to Europe, especially Italy, enticed by art and religion. Despite 15 years' wrestling with profound interest in the Roman Catholic Church, she stayed true to her Anglican roots. Although she had little formal religious education, she was curious about religion and spirituality from childhood, when she met Hubert Moore. They married in 1907 and are buried together in London. She believed mysticism belongs not just to a few saints but to any nurturing soul.

Friday, June 16
Joseph Butler, Bishop of Durham, 1752

Butler, born in 1692, became an Anglican despite having been raised a Presbyterian and educated at Dissenting schools. He was ordained in 1718. He rose to be called "the greatest of all the thinkers of the English Church." His sermons on human nature, preached during his eight years at Rolls Chapel, first brought him to prominence. After a series of rectorships, he was appointed bishop of Bristol. He declined the primacy of Canterbury and accepted the bishopric of Durham (1750). His fame resides in his profound support for orthodox Christianity against the Deist thinking in England; in 1736, he published *The Analogy of Religion, Natural and Revealed, to the Constitution and Course of Nature.*

Saturday, June 17
Marina the Monk, Monastic, 5th century

Marina rejected her widowed father's intent to marry her off then retreat to a monastery: "Why would you save your own soul at the cost of destroying mine?" She shaved her hair, donned men's clothes, sold her possessions with his. They proceeded to a monastic settlement in the Qadisha Valley, where he introduced her as his son, Marinos. She lived as a man unto death. When a young woman accused "Marinos" of fathering her child, Marina accepted the accusation and the responsibility of raising the boy in the monastery. She is venerated today in Lebanon, Cyprus, and Italy.

The Third Sunday after Pentecost: Proper 6

June 18, 2023

God calls a people into intimate covenant relationship.

Color   Green

Preface   Of the Lord's Day

Collect

Keep, O Lord, your household the Church in your steadfast faith and love, that through your grace we may proclaim your truth with boldness, and minister your justice with compassion; for the sake of our Savior Jesus Christ, who lives and reigns with you and the Holy Spirit, one God, now and for ever. *Amen.*

Readings and Psalm

Genesis 18:1–15 (21:1–7)

Today's reading is both an epiphany story—an account of the Lord's appearance to Abraham—and an annunciation story—a proclamation of the coming birth, contrary to all human expectation, of a significant person. The precise identity of the "three men" is not clear; that is, whether all three are angels representing the Lord in earthly manifestation (hence the shift from plural to singular in vv. 1, 13) or whether one is indeed the Lord and the other two are attendants (18:22, 19:1). Abraham's reception of these sudden guests illustrates the hospitality of a nomadic society. As Abraham has typified the natural virtue of hospitality, so he also typifies the theological virtue of trust in the Lord's promise. The meaning of Isaac's name is here explained by Sarah's incredulous laugh.

Psalm 116:1, 10–17

This psalm of thanksgiving recounts the vindication of a righteous sufferer. Such a psalm was recited as a testimony to other worshipers.

or

Exodus 19:2–8a

Today's reading brings the people of Israel to their goal in the wilderness, to the place of God's self-revelation. Here God offers to humankind a response to their sin (Genesis 2–3), a call to one particular people to enter into covenant with God. God proclaims the background of the covenant: mighty acts of deliverance, especially the exodus from Egypt when God bore the people "on eagles' wings" (an image of the female eagle's care of her young). Then God sets forth the conditions of the covenant. Israel is to obey God, especially in commandments to be set forth later.

Psalm 100

Psalm 100, a hymn of praise to God, is a joyous affirmation of the people's loyalty to and dependence upon God.

Romans 5:1–8

Paul uses two equivalent metaphors to describe God's redeeming act in Christ: justification, that is, the ending of a legal dispute (3:21–26), and reconciliation, that is, the termination of a state of enmity. Paul makes it clear that it is we who are estranged from God; there is no room here for a doctrine of the cross in which Christ's sacrifice pacified an angry God. Instead, in Christ's sacrifice God manifests God's justifying, reconciling love for us.

Matthew 9:35–10:8 (9–23)

Jesus' ministry is identified as teaching, preaching, and healing (4:23; 9:35). The people are "like sheep without a shepherd," a traditional description of the people of Israel when their leadership has failed (Ezekiel 34:1–6; Zechariah 10:2). He tells the disciples to ask God "to send out laborers." The harvest is often an image of the last judgment (13:39), already underway in Jesus' ministry. The twelve named disciples symbolize the fullness of the new covenant community. Jesus now gives them the authority to preach and heal (10:7–8) but reserves authority to teach until after the resurrection (28:20).

Prayers of the People

My sisters and brothers, worship the Lord with gladness. Let us pray, with joyful hearts, "We give you thanks! *We bless your name!*"

O Lord, you are good; while we were yet sinners Christ died for us. Send us out to share your love. Send your Church out to gather in a plentiful harvest.

Silence

We give you thanks!

We bless your name!

O Lord, you are good; your faithfulness endures to all generations. To those who suffer, give hope. And visit the lonely with your peace.

Silence

We give you thanks!

We bless your name!

O Lord, you are good; all the earth praises you with joyful noise. And we join the song of creation: you are worthy to be praised!

Invite the congregation to add their thanksgivings, followed by silence

We give you thanks!

We bless your name!

O Lord, you are good; you offer us your peace. We pray, Jesus, that you would go about our city— speak a word of good news and healing.

Silence

We give you thanks!

We bless your name!

O Lord, you are good; while we were still weak, Christ died for us. Touch us in our weakness even now. And heal those afflicted with disease or sickness.

Invite the congregation to add their petitions, followed by silence

We give you thanks!

We bless your name!

O Lord, you are good; hope placed in you does not disappoint. We hope for the resurrection of the body and the life everlasting.

Silence

We give you thanks!

We bless your name!

Images in the Readings

Once the Israelites were settled in Canaan, nomads became famers, and many biblical passages use the image of the **harvest** to connote fulfillment. Some of the Jewish religious festivals that commemorated their past memories were actually reinterpretations of more ancient harvest festivals, Passover at the barley harvest, and Pentecost at the end of the wheat harvest and beginning of the grape harvest. Because God is given credit for all growth of life, harvest is an occasion for thanksgiving. Yet God calls us to work the harvest, a task seen in our culture as far too much hard work for its meager pay, a job for other poor people to fill.

The **mother eagle** swoops under the fledglings, her wings outspread to catch them if they falter. The **twelve** is the number of completion, from the twelve sons of Jacob to the twelve gates in the city of Jerusalem at the end of time. The two lists of the twelve cited in the synoptics are not identical. The point is not historical accuracy, but rather the perfection of Jesus' ministry and the church's mission. The apostles replace the twelve tribes of Israel and begin the completion of all things.

Ideas for the Day

- Perhaps you have heard the Mexican proverb—they thought they buried us, but they didn't know we were seeds. Many congregations today may feel down but not out due to forces beyond their control. There is plenty of stumbling and struggle and angst to go around. Daydreams of perfection and easy bounty have eroded, and yet this new perspective is a call not to give up, but to dig deep into the resources of humility and creativity. Tilth can refer to preparing the soil for new growth, but it can also refer to spiritual preparation. How can the compost of our wounds and little deaths nurture the growth of fidelity to God's reign and abundant feasts for all?

- There was a woman named Helen. Helen radiated the love of God, and shared a sense of peace with whoever she was around. When asked if she knew what opened that door of abundant love and grace within her she said, "There is a lot of death underneath the love. I moved from the pain of death to the joy of love with the help of Jesus." There are many holy people who know this story and have lived it. Who could you name that exemplifies the peace and love of God?

- There have been Christian saints and martyrs who have suffered as a result of witnessing to their faith. One who is such an example is Dietrich Bonhoeffer, author of *The Cost of Discipleship*. Formerly a pacifist, he became persuaded of the need for violence against the Nazi regime and joined a group called the Abwehr, whose primary mission was to assassinate Hitler. Ultimately, Bonhoeffer was arrested for his involvement in helping Jews flee the country. Still, he continued to teach with the help of guards who smuggled out his writing, until he was transferred to a concentration camp. When his association with other Abwehr agents was discovered, Bonhoeffer was sentenced to death. He was hanged in April 1945, just one month before Germany surrendered. More than seventy years after his death, his life and writings serve as a touchstone for all of us who seek to understand a Christian's responsibility in the face of injustice—and as an encouragement to serve no matter how great the cost.

Making Connections

The sentence the bishop says at the time of confirmation speak of the cost of taking up the role of disciple in the world today: Strengthen, O Lord, your servant N. with your Holy Spirit; empower N. for your service; and sustain N. with your heavenly grace, that N. may continue as yours forever . . . (BCP, 309)

Engaging All Ages

Have you ever seen a butterfly being born? Find a video online. Egg. Caterpillar. Chrysalis. Butterfly. A chrysalis might look like nothing interesting but on the inside a miracle is happening. See the butterfly wriggle its way out of its old self and into its new self. If baptism is like a dove descending, perhaps this is what dying, being buried, and rising again with Christ, being alive to God looks like. Being a chrysalis trying to shed your old self isn't the pretty or easy part of life and faith, but it can produce something new and beautiful.

Hymns for the Day

The Hymnal 1982
Lord, whose love through humble service 610
The God of Abraham praise 401 [semi-continuous]
All people that on earth do dwell 377, 378 [gospel-related]
Before the Lord's eternal throne 391 [GR]
Come down, O Love divine 516
Come, thou fount of every blessing 686
Hail, thou once despised Jesus! 495
O love of God, how strong and true 455, 456
Awake, thou Spirit of the watchmen 540
Come, labor on 541
For the fruit of all creation 424
Hope of the word, thou Christ of great compassion 472
Lord, you give the great commission 528
My God, thy table now is spread 321
Ye servants of God, your Master proclaim 535

Lift Every Voice and Sing II
Here am I, send me 126

Wonder, Love, and Praise
You who dwell in the shelter of the Lord 810 [GR]
Lord, you give the great commission 780

Pentecost

Pentecost

Weekday Commemorations

Monday, June 19
Adelaide Teague Case, Educator, 1948

After Case (b. 1887) earned her doctorate from Columbia University, she accepted a custom-created faculty position at Columbia's Teachers College. As head of the Department of Religious Education, Case advocated a child-centered versus teacher-centered approach: her book *Liberal Christianity and Religious Education* supported children's inquiry into their faith. She was a pacifist who identified with the liberal Catholic tradition in Anglicanism. At the height of her career at Columbia, she was convinced to accept appointment by the Episcopal Theological School in Cambridge as professor of Christian education. Case believed that practicing one's Christian faith means making a difference in the world.

Thursday, June 22
Alban, First Martyr of Britain, c. 304

According to tradition, Alban is the first British martyr. He was a Roman soldier, stationed in a city now called St. Alban's, twenty miles northeast of London. He sheltered a Christian priest fleeing from persecution and then dressed as the priest to be tortured and martyred in his place. The site became a shrine soon after the incident: a monastery was established there in 793 and was ranked in the Middle Ages as the premier abbey in England. The Cathedral of St. Alban's, begun in 1077, stands on the site of Alban's martyrdom; it is the second longest church in England. Alban's remains lie in a chapel east of the choir.

Saturday, June 24
The Nativity of Saint John the Baptist

John was born the son of Elizabeth and Zachariah, who were aged. His birth is celebrated six months before that of Jesus since Elizabeth, Mary's cousin, had become pregnant six months before Mary. John has a role in all four gospels. His father lost speech when he disbelieved a vision foretelling John's birth, but when his speech was restored he sang a canticle of praise, the *Benedictus*, now part of the Daily Office. John lived in abstention in the desert, clothed with camel's hair and a belt; he ate locusts and honey. He preached repentance, importuning hearers to prepare for the kingdom and the Messiah and baptized them to signify new life. He baptized Jesus in the Jordan.

The Fourth Sunday after Pentecost: Proper 7

June 25, 2023

The cost of discipleship.

Color   Green

Preface   Of the Lord's Day

Collect

O Lord, make us have perpetual love and reverence for your holy Name, for you never fail to help and govern those whom you have set upon the sure foundation of your loving-kindness; through Jesus Christ our Lord, who lives and reigns with you and the Holy Spirit, one God, for ever and ever. *Amen.*

Readings and Psalm

Genesis 21:8–21

Hagar, Sarah's Egyptian servant, had borne Ishmael when it seemed impossible for Sarah to conceive. Her fertility was a sore point with Sarah, who remained childless. After Sarah gave birth to Isaac, the child of God's promise to Abraham and Sarah, Sarah's jealousy erupted. She demanded that Abraham get rid of Hagar and the child. When her provisions ran out, Hagar cried to God in her despair. God answered by sending an angel to ensure their survival. God continued to be with them as the child grew and prospered.

Psalm 69:8–11 (12–17), 18–20

This personal lament by one of God's devoted servants calls upon God's help in a time of distress.

or

Jeremiah 20:7–13

In a series of six laments or "confessions" (11:18–20, 12:1–4, 15:10–21, 17:14–18, 18:18–23, 20:7–18), Jeremiah reveals more of his personal struggle than any other Old Testament prophet. He is caught in the tension between his vocation as a speaker of God's word and his natural reaction to the hatred he aroused. Today's reading is a portion of the last of these laments. Jeremiah has been beaten and put in stocks for announcing the Lord's judgment (19:14–20:2). He then accuses the Lord of having deceived him. Though he preaches God's word of judgment, destruction has not come and Jeremiah is feeling like a fool. But he cannot keep silent.

Psalm 69:7–10 (11–15), 16–18

This psalm is a lament, a cry for God's help in a time of great distress. Even though suffering great pain, the psalmist never loses hope that God will be there to help and console.

Romans 6:1b–11

The Christian has put off, like old clothes, the old "body of sin"—not the physical body as opposed to the soul, but the sinful impulses of both body and mind. In rabbinical understanding, death freed one from the claims of the commandments, "death pays all debts." Thus the Christian is no longer enslaved to sin, for Paul asserts that death in baptism frees one from sin. The Christian has been justified, set right, by being united to Christ. Now he or she begins to grow into this reality, although full participation in the resurrection is a future event (6:8). The Christian lives between the already and the not yet, called to "become (in life) what you are (through baptism)."

Matthew 10:24–39

Today's reading is a part of Jesus' instructions to the twelve (10:1–42), whom he sends out to continue his ministry. Much of the material in the first section is found in Mark and Luke, not in their mission discourses, but in the eschatological discourses near the end of the gospels (Mark 13:9–13; Luke 21:12–19). The same kind of warnings are found also in the farewell discourse in John (chaps. 14–16). Matthew, however, indicates that he sees persecution as part of the normal life of the Church rather than as a special sign of the end.

Prayers of the People

Children of God, praise the Lord! Our God is faithful and hears our prayers, so let us pray, "In your great mercy, O God, *answer us with your unfailing help.*"

To the baptized, O God, grant newness of life. Strengthen us to follow in the footsteps of your Son.

Silence

In your great mercy, O God,

> **Answer us with your unfailing help.**

To the nations of earth, O God of hosts, grant freedom and peace. Deliver the lives of the needy from the hands of evildoers.

Silence

In your great mercy, O God,

> **Answer us with your unfailing help.**

To your created order, O God, grant your help. May the waters, soil, and air be made clean and healthy again.

Invite the congregation to add their thanksgivings, followed by silence

In your great mercy, O God,

> **Answer us with your unfailing help.**

To this city, O God, grant your deliverance. Set us free from violence and destruction. Make safe our streets.

Silence

In your great mercy, O God,

> **Answer us with your unfailing help.**

To those who feel the deep about to swallow them, O God, grant your salvation. In your great compassion, turn to all those in need.

Invite the congregation to add their petitions and thanksgivings, followed by silence

In your great mercy, O God,

> **Answer us with your unfailing help.**

To the dead, O God, grant life eternal with Christ. May all those who have been baptized into the death of Christ be united with him in his resurrection.

Silence

In your great mercy, O God,

> **Answer us with your unfailing help.**

Images in the Readings

God's care for **sparrows** calls us to trust in God, since Matthew states here and in chapter 7 (see Lectionary 8) that humans have more value than birds. Sparrows were among the cheapest birds sold in the markets of Matthew's time. Unfortunately, such biblical passages have been used to devalue God's creation, as if humans are the only creatures to receive divine blessing. Here Matthew states that God does indeed care for the sparrow.

Of course Matthew's description of the natural and married **family** experiencing hatred is disturbing. Matthew even assumes that discipleship will bring about such dissension. Pacifist Christians assert that Matthew's word about the **sword** is only metaphoric, but even as metaphor, it is a harsh word about the difficulties of the Christian life. In Paul's imagery, the Christian life requires our old self to be crucified, as if baptism aims the sword at oneself.

Probing biblical images helps us avoid taming the Bible into Precious Moments™. Matthew's words about a reversal of **slave and master** may sound benign to Americans who believe in equality, but such words would have sounded bizarre—like losing one's life to live—to citizens of a slave culture. Matthew is saying that cultural patterns may be totally inappropriate for those who follow Christ.

Ideas for the Day

♦ Perhaps you have heard the Mexican proverb—they thought they buried us, but they didn't know we were seeds. Many congregations today may feel down but not out due to forces beyond their control. There is plenty of stumbling and struggle and angst to go around. Daydreams of perfection and easy bounty have eroded, and yet this new perspective is a call not to give up, but to dig deep into the resources of humility and creativity. "Tilth" can refer to preparing the soil for new growth, but "tilth" can also refer to spiritual preparation. How can the compost of our wounds and little deaths nurture the growth of fidelity to God's reign and abundant feasts for all?

♦ There was a woman named Helen. Helen radiated the love of God, and shared a sense of peace with whoever she was around. When asked if she knew what opened that door of abundant love and grace within her she said, "There is a lot of death underneath the love. I moved from the pain of death to the joy of love with the help of Jesus." There are many holy people who know this story and have lived it. Who could you name that exemplifies the peace and love of God?

There have been Christian saints and martyrs who have suffered as a result of witnessing to their faith. One who is such an example is Dietrich Bonhoeffer, author of *The Cost of Discipleship*. Formerly a pacifist, he became persuaded of the need for violence against the Nazi regime and joined a group called the Abwehr, whose primary mission was to assassinate Hitler. Ultimately, Bonhoeffer was arrested for his involvement in helping Jews flee the country. Still, he continued to teach with the help of guards who smuggled out his writing, until he was transferred to a concentration camp. When his association with other Abwehr agents was discovered, Bonhoeffer was sentenced to death. He was hanged in April 1945, just one month before Germany surrendered. More than seventy years after his death, his life and writings serve as a touchstone for all of us who seek to understand a Christian's responsibility in the face of injustice—and as an encouragement to serve no matter how great the cost.

Making Connections

The sentence the bishop says at the time of confirmation speaks of the cost of taking up the role of disciple in the world today: "Strengthen, O Lord, your servant N. with your Holy Spirit; empower N. for your service; and sustain N. with your heavenly grace, that N. may continue as yours forever" . . . (BCP, 309).

Engaging All Ages

In advertising, certain brands can become so universal that their name comes to represent an entire category of products or actions. Think: Google, Band-Aids, Kleenex. This isn't necessarily a bad thing. It means you've done well. On the other hand, it also represents an opportunity to lose your trademark. What is the Church's trademark? Does the church have a proprietary eponym? This week, encourage parishioners of all ages to think about a buzz word of sorts in our churches: welcoming. How can we be welcoming? What does it mean? Consider group art projects to make door hangers for the community, or a banner that can hang outside the church. What would it say?

Hymns for the Day

The Hymnal 1982
Praise to the living God! 372
I love thy kingdom, Lord 524 [GR]
Surely it is God who saves me 678, 679 [GR]
All who believe and are baptized 298
Alleluia, alleluia! Give thanks to the risen Lord 178
We know that Christ is raised and dies no more 296
Christ for the world we sing! 537
Day by day 654
He who would valiant be 564, 565
O Jesus, I have promised 655
Praise the Lord through every nation 484, 485
Spread, O spread, thou mighty word 530
Take up your cross, the Savior said 675
They cast their nets in Galilee 661

Lift Every Voice and Sing II
Where He leads me 144
I have decided to follow Jesus 136
He'll understand, and say "well done" 190

Wonder, Love, and Praise
You shall cross the barren desert 811 [SC]
God's Paschal Lamb is sacrificed for us 880
Will you come and follow me 757

Weekday Commemorations

Monday, June 26
Isabel Florence Hapgood, Ecumenist, 1929

Around 1900, Hapgood encouraged ecumenical relations between her Episcopal Church and Russian Orthodoxy in the United States. She excelled as a student, especially with languages—from Latin and French to Church Slavonic and Russian (she translated Dostoyevsky, Tolstoy, Gorky, and Chekov into English). From 1887–1889 she traveled throughout Russia, solidifying her love of the language, the culture, and the Russian Orthodox Church. She sought permission of the church hierarchy to translate the rites into English, completing *Service Book of the Holy Orthodox-Catholic Church* in eleven years. Russian Orthodox bishops, particularly Archbishop Tikhon (April 7), supported Hapgood's work.

Wednesday, June 28
Irenaeus, Bishop of Lyons, c. 202

Recognized by Protestants and Catholics as the first great systematic theologian, Irenaeus learned Christianity in Ephesus from Polycarp, who had known John the Evangelist. In 177, when Irenaeus was probably still a teenager, a flood of heresy threatened to wash away the Church. Irenaeus, whose name means "the peaceable one," was sent to Rome as mediator. Upon his return to Lyons, he was elected bishop of Lyons to succeed Pothinus. Irenaeus' chief work, *Against Heresies*, brought him fame, addressed the major Gnostic systems (often with sharp wit), and stressed the resurrection of the body and the goodness of creation. He may have been martyred about 202.

Thursday, June 29
Saint Peter and Saint Paul, Apostles

Peter and Paul, each with his own commemoration as a renowned Church leader, are also remembered together because, by tradition, they were martyred together in Rome under Nero in 64. Paul was a well-educated, urbane Jew of the Dispersion; Peter was an untutored fisher from Galilee. The two disagreed on the issue of mission to the Gentiles in the early years of the Church, but they were committed to Christ and to proclaiming the gospel, which they bore to Rome. According to tradition, Paul was decapitated by sword swipe, as befitted a Roman citizen; Peter suffered death on the cross, it is said, with his head pointed downward.

Saturday, July 1
Pauli Murray, priest, 1985

Born in Baltimore in 1910, Murray was raised in Durham, North Carolina, and graduated from Hunter College in 1933. She was denied entry to graduate school at the University of North Carolina in 1938 due to her race; she went on to graduate from Howard University Law School in 1944. While a student at Howard, she participated in sit-in demonstrations that challenged racial segregation in drugstores and cafeterias in Washington, DC. Denied admission to Harvard University for an advanced law degree because of her gender, Murray received her Masters of Law from the University of California, Berkeley, in 1945. In later life, she discerned a call to ordained ministry and began studies at General Theological Seminary in 1973. She was ordained as a deacon in June 1976, and, on January 8, 1977, she was ordained as a priest at Washington National Cathedral, the first African American woman to receive the sacrament of priestly ordination in the Episcopal Church. Murray served at Church of the Atonement in Washington, DC, from 1979 to 1981 and at Holy Nativity Church in Baltimore until her death in 1985.

The Fifth Sunday after Pentecost: Proper 8

July 2, 2023

God has built the church on the foundation of the apostles and prophets with Jesus Christ as the cornerstone.

Color Green

Preface Of the Lord's Day

Collect

Almighty God, you have built your Church upon the foundation of the apostles and prophets, Jesus Christ himself being the chief cornerstone: Grant us so to be joined together in unity of spirit by their teaching, that we may be made a holy temple acceptable to you; through Jesus Christ our Lord, who lives and reigns with you and the Holy Spirit, one God, for ever and ever. *Amen.*

Readings and Psalm

Genesis 22:1–14

The account of Isaac's offering comes as the climax of the story of Abraham's relationship with God. At God's command, Abraham has already cut himself off from his past, from country and family, and retains only the promise of new status. Now God commands him to cut off his future, the heir of the promise, his beloved son Isaac—and no new promise is given.

Psalm 13

The psalmist feels abandoned by God and pleads for God's return. He concludes by making a decision to trust in God's steadfast love.

or

Jeremiah 28:5–9

In today's reading, dated approximately seven years after the exile has begun (c. 594 BCE, Jeremiah and his opponents who are still in Jerusalem offer alternative versions of what God is doing. Hananiah, perhaps to inspire a sense of revolt against Babylon, has prophesied that the exiles will return in two years and God will once again grant peace to the nation. Jeremiah represents the minority opinion that God is requiring the people to be conquered and go into exile and consequently revolt is futile. To resist the Babylonians as God's agent is to resist God—which only leads to one's own destruction.

Psalm 89:1–4, 15–18

Psalm 89 is a royal psalm comprised of a hymn praising God's power and faithfulness (vv. 1–18), a recapitulation of the covenant between God and David's descendants (vv. 19–37) and a lament praying for deliverance from enemies (vv. 38–52).

Romans 6:12–23

Paul defends himself against the charge (3:8; 6:1) that his emphasis upon grace as a free gift not dependent upon works was an encouragement to sin (5:20). He replies by pointing out the fact and nature of the Christian's new relationship to God: in baptism the Christian has died to sin. The waters of baptism identify the believer with Christ, indeed with the very act of redemption—his death and resurrection. By Jesus' act, the penalty for sin—death—has been paid; baptism credits us with that payment. The Christian has been justified, set right, by being united to Christ.

Matthew 10:40–42

As Jesus sends the disciples to continue his proclaiming and healing ministry, like every messenger they are invested with the power of the one who sent them. Christian disciples thus convey not only their message but the presence of Jesus and therefore of God. So people's response to these "prophets" and "little ones" is at the same time a response to Christ himself. While there are rewards for disciples and even for those who receive them, true "life" (Greek, *psyche*, self) is found only in losing it for Jesus' sake (John 12:25).

Prayers of the People

Brothers and sisters, present yourselves to God as those who have been brought from death to life. And with humble hearts, pray to the Lord, saying, "Look upon us; *answer us, O Lord our God.*"

Lord God, you have freed your Church from sin: sanctify us that we may be wholly dedicated to you and your purposes.

Silence

Look upon us;

Answer us, O Lord our God.

Incarnate God, help us to welcome Christ by welcoming the other. Give us eyes to seek and serve Christ in all persons, loving our neighbors as ourselves.

Silence

Look upon us;

Answer us, O Lord our God.

Righteous God, just as you provided a ram for Abraham, you have given us all we need. Encourage us to share what we have so that all may have their needs met.

Invite the congregation to add thanksgivings, followed by silence

Look upon us;

Answer us, O Lord our God.

O Lord, we put our trust in your mercy. We pray you make joyful the hearts of our neighbors—especially the displaced and sorrowful.

Silence

Look upon us;

Answer us, O Lord our God.

O Lord, answer those who cry out in their pain. Comfort those who feel forgotten. Give peace to those who are perplexed and grieving.

Invite the congregation to add their petitions, followed by silence

Look upon us;

Answer us, O Lord our God.

Gracious God, your free gift is eternal life in Christ Jesus our Lord: Bless and keep the dying and the dead.

Silence

Look upon us;

Answer us, O Lord our God.

Images in the Readings

Both of the two primary images in today's readings are somewhat alien to us. In the Bible, a true **prophet** is not a fortune teller or a court appointee, but rather the mouthpiece of God, proclaiming not what will be, but what is. For Christians, the preeminent prophet is Christ, whose words of God are spoken through the scriptures and in the bread and wine. The words are always double-sided, attending to both human sin and divine mercy—what Lutherans have called "law and gospel."

The idea in a **slave** economy is that everyone is born into a lifelong place in a hierarchy in which each obeys those who are above and cares for those who are below. Persons could not choose or alter their place in the hierarchy, and many Christians taught that God was responsible for who was placed where in this ordering of obedience. Despite our resistance to this idea, Paul writes that we are all born slaves of sin. The freedom of our will comes only through baptism, administered in many denominations even to infants, transferring our allegiance over to God and the neighbor. We are enslaved to God—in our culture, not an attractive suggestion.

Ideas for the Day

♦ In two out of the three Episcopal lectionary cycles we can potentially hear the near-sacrifice of Isaac three times a year (and at least two times every year). Again and again, the lesson fosters discomfort and outrage and even heavy doubts. It is an important scene in salvation history that we cannot turn away from, but as people in relationship with each other, God, and the texts, we are also given the freedom to protest. Yet for all our potential outrage, it begs a hard question of us: what altars of adult needs, vices, and priorities do we sacrifice the well-being of our children on? We don't have to have a rock and a knife to be complicit in the terribleness of reliving this scene in our communities.

◆ This is one of the few times when historical context doesn't really matter. We don't know what really caused Abraham to take his son Isaac up to Moriah. The story says that God told him to, but why? Our common experience of God and our common experience of love, mercy, grace, and forgiveness, makes it clear that God would never actually ask or expect that we would kill our child. So the story has to be about something different than the cause of a lot of family therapy. Perhaps we find the reason for the story in the words, "The Lord will provide." And yes God does!

◆ Liberation theology focuses on God's liberating action among the oppressed. From this theological perspective, God is always on the side of the exploited. God led the Israelites out of the oppression of Egypt into the promised land. God is acting through the persecuted in Central America, Africa, and our own land. The Magnificat or Song of Mary (BCP, 91) says, "… he has cast down the mighty from their thrones, and has lifted up the lowly" (Luke 1:52).

Making Connections

We continue to deal with the theme of discipleship in our readings this week. Continue the story, telling about those who have spoken God's word and suffered for their witness. Francis of Assisi rejected his parents' wealth and power to follow Christ. Martin Luther King, Jr. was controversial as he set about to bring liberation to people of color. It cost him his life. Who are some contemporary persons through whom God may be working in our nation and throughout the world? What is their word, and how is it received by the "proud" and by the "humble"? What is our role as disciples and prophets called to speak out in Jesus' name?

Engaging All Ages

In worship, is there someone playing a piano, an organ, or another instrument? Does it sound pretty? Does your church have a choir who use their voices to make a beautiful sound together? Have you ever heard bad music in church? God is like a composer who writes music. People are God's instruments and choir. Each person has a part to play. You can play your part however you want. God hopes you would be an instrument of righteousness doing good, loving people, and bringing harmony into the world. This week, how will you choose to be an instrument of righteousness?

Hymns for the Day

Christ is made the sure foundation 518
The Church's one foundation 525
O sorrow deep! (vs. 2–4) 173 [SC]
The God of Abraham praise 401 [SC]
Blessed be the God of Israel 444 [GR]
O day of God, draw nigh 600, 601 [GR]
O God of every nation 607 [GR]
Savior, again to thy dear Name we raise 345 [GR]
Creator of the stars of night (vs. 1–4, 6) 60
Crown him with many crowns 494
Here, O my Lord, I see thee face to face 318
Lord Jesus, think on me 641
Now that the daylight fills the sky 3, 4
Wilt thou forgive that sin, where I begun 140, 141
Where cross the crowded ways of life 609

Lift Every Voice and Sing II

Wonder, Love, and Praise
Blessed be the God of Israel 889 [GR]
Lord Jesus, think on me 798
No saint on earth lives life to self alone 776
We are all one in mission 778
Gracious Spirit, give your servants 782

Pentecost

Weekday Commemorations

Tuesday, July 4
Independence Day

Ten years after July 4, 1776, General Convention called for observance of Independence Day throughout "this Church, on the fourth of July, for ever." Proper psalms, lessons, and prayers were appointed for the national recognition of this day; however, they were rescinded in 1789 by General Convention with the intervention of Bishop William White. Although he supported the American Revolution, White revolted against observing the day, given that the majority of the Church's clericals remained loyal to the British government. Not until 1928 was provision made again for the liturgical notice of the day.

Thursday, July 6
Eva Lee Matthews, Monastic, 1928

Matthews (b. 1862) grew up in Ohio as an active member of her Episcopal church. Mathews and a coworker at Bethany Mission House, Beatrice Henderson, created a new religious order to assist Cincinnati's poor, especially the children. As Mother Eva Mary, Matthews led the group as superior until her death. In 1898, the Episcopal Church recognized the women's order, naming it the Community of the Transfiguration. The order relocated to Glendale, Matthews' childhood home, from Cincinnati. By the 1920s, the community had members ministering in two states and China; today it also serves the poor in the Dominican Republic.

Saturday, July 8
Priscilla and Aquila, Coworkers of the Apostle Paul

Around the year 50, the apostle Paul went to Corinth, where he met Priscilla and Aquila. The married couple, tentmakers, had just arrived from Rome, from which Emperor Claudius had expelled the Jews. The two may have been Christians before meeting Paul or were converted by his preaching. After eighteen months, the three traveled to Ephesus, where the couple remained while Paul continued to Antioch. The two were apparently in Rome when Paul wrote to that congregation and in Ephesus when Paul wrote his last letter to Timothy. Clearly dear to Paul, they earnestly and effectively spread the Gospel.

The Sixth Sunday after Pentecost: Proper 9

July 9, 2023

God's wisdom, which brings rest and peace, is personified in Jesus.

Color Green

Preface Of the Lord's Day

Collect

O God, you have taught us to keep all your commandments by loving you and our neighbor: Grant us the grace of your Holy Spirit, that we may be devoted to you with our whole heart, and united to one another with pure affection; through Jesus Christ our Lord, who lives and reigns with you and the Holy Spirit, one God, for ever and ever. *Amen.*

Readings and Psalm

Genesis 24:34–38, 42–49, 58–67

In today's reading, the story of the fulfillment of God's promises takes its next step with the marriage of Isaac. Abraham attempts to provide a wife for Isaac from his ancestral homeland, not from the Canaanites among whom he is now living. So he sends a servant with instructions about what to do. While pausing at a spring, the servant asks God for a sign about who the suitable wife might be. The woman who appears and fulfills the sign is Rebekah, who takes the servant back to her family. The family allows Rebekah to go back with the servant to the land of Canaan, where she meets and marries Isaac. Through them the fulfillment of God's promises will continue when their child Jacob is born.

Psalm 45:11–18

This psalm celebrates the royal wedding of the Davidic king with a princess from Tyre in Phoenicia. First the psalmist praises the king (verses 1–10), who has been chosen and anointed by God to establish justice and so receive the perks of kingship, including his new wife.

or

Song of Solomon 2:8–13

In this reading, amidst the vibrant springtime imagery, the woman anticipates the excitement of meeting with her beloved and pictures his approach until she can hear his voice inviting her to fly away with him.

or

Zechariah 9:9–12

The prophecies of Zechariah were made in the early period of reconstruction after the exile, about 520–518 BCE. Zechariah was especially concerned for the rebuilding of the temple, the reinstitution of the Levitical priesthood, and the purification of the disunited community. He looked for the restoration of the Davidic monarchy to bring about the messianic age.

Psalm 145:8–15

This is an acrostic psalm, each verse beginning with a successive letter of the Hebrew alphabet. It invites praise for God's greatness (vv. 2–3), love of the people (vv. 8–10), and God's kingship.

Romans 7:15–25a

Paul is struggling with the relationship of the law of Moses to human sin. Paul sees several laws at work in the human sphere. There is first the moral law, "the law of God," which is both natural law as known to the Gentiles and more specifically the Jewish law. This law is approved by the mind (2:14–16) but cannot grant the power to keep it; this law has right but not might. Opposed to this law is "the law of sin and of death," which has might but not right.

Matthew 11:16–19, 25–30

Chapters 11–12 mark a turning point in the Gospel of Matthew. Chapters 1–10 have established the authority of Jesus in word and deed and his gift of that authority to his disciples; chapters 11–28 will chronicle the rejection of Jesus' authority by the false Israel and his description and designation of the true Israel. Today's reading summarizes these themes.

Prayers of the People

Thanks be to God through Jesus Christ our Lord! With grateful hearts we pray to our Loving God, saying, "We thank you, Father; *you hear the voice of your beloved.*"

Loving God, you call your Church "my love" and "my beauty." Look upon your Church with eyes of great compassion and love. May we generously share the love with which we have been so greatly blessed.

Invite the congregation to add thanksgivings, followed by silence

We thank you, Father;

> ***You hear the voice of your beloved.***

Loving God, you have blessed our nation with great freedoms. Grant us, and all the people of this land, the grace to maintain our liberties in righteousness and peace.

Silence

We thank you, Father;

> ***You hear the voice of your beloved.***

Loving God, all that you have created tells of your love for us. May flowers and birds, but even more so our human relationships, remind us of your great care and presence.

Silence

We thank you, Father;

> ***You hear the voice of your beloved.***

Loving God, you promise to give rest to all those who carry heavy burdens. Lift up those who are weighed down by the burdens of violence, depression, and despair.

Silence

We thank you, Father;

> ***You hear the voice of your beloved.***

Loving God, your Son Jesus revealed your heart to be gentle and humble. We pray for those who have restless souls. We pray that all the sorrowful and the suffering may find their rest in you.

Invite the congregation to add their petitions, followed by silence

We thank you, Father;

> ***You hear the voice of your beloved.***

Loving God, you rescue us from death. We pray that all who have died, especially those who strived for freedom and peace, may come to know that heavenly comfort you have prepared us.

Silence

We thank you, Father;

> ***You hear the voice of your beloved.***

Images in the Readings

The **yoke** ties together two beasts of burden. According to this image, Christians do not walk alone, but are tied to Christ and to one another. In the several centuries before Christ, Jewish poetry developed the image of **wisdom**. Borrowing from neighboring polytheistic religions the picture of the divine consort, the great goddess who personified wisdom, Jews adapted this divine female figure into a way to speak of God's law, a beautiful and powerful aspect of the Almighty, who guided the people into truth. Christians altered the image once again, seeing Christ as this Wisdom, whose words sound like foolishness to the world.

Ideas for the Day

- Maybe you have had a bunkmate, sibling, child, neighbor, or coworker with whom there should have been peace, but there was often turmoil—a bit like living with Jacob. He seems to have never come home with a "plays well with others" report card; he is a bit of an anti-hero. Have you ever imagined this lesson from the perspective of Jacob, who probably doesn't see himself as much of a scoundrel as the holy author seems to? What were his motivations—was it just deceit and money-grabbing or was he well-intentioned in his own mind? Living together is what we are made for, yet it is also our constant trouble because we cannot always know the intentions of people we struggle to love wholeheartedly.

- A new person comes to church and then never returns. A new person comes to church and gets so excited they want to join everything. They stay for two months and then never return. A new person drives into the parking lot, pauses, and then decides to go get some coffee instead. And a new person comes to church and fully integrates and there is much joy in the community. It almost comes off like there is only one winner; one good end. But don't you think that God is actively working in all four of the new people? Don't you think that even for the person that drove into the parking lot, even in that ten-second stop, God might have done something wonderful?

- In the frustrations we feel in the "seeds" that seem to be dying all around us, the parable of the sower can give us the same encouragement as it did to the disciples who saw so many of Jesus' seeds seemingly fall by the wayside. What is happening in our time in the church? In the world? Where and how do we hear God's word being uttered? Where do the seeds of God's word seem to be falling on hard ground and dying?

Making Connections

The radical nature of the gospel is the theme carried over from previous weeks. Notice the sense of justice, healing, and love that Jesus offers to those who do come seeking the wholeness that the Lord offers. The proud and powerful miss that strength as they rely on their own power. The church is called to witness to the wisdom of God, which often contradicts the "wisdom" of the culture. The church is to proclaim the way of God's wisdom and peace in every action and word.

Engaging All Ages

Backpacks and bags can get heavy. Heavy from what is needed for day-to-day life. Heavy with things you might find useful in certain circumstances. Heavy with all the stuff picked up along the way. Life gets heavy too. You carry around the needed stuff and potentially useful stuff. There is also the burden of excess baggage that most likely should just be tossed out. Jesus says that he and God are there to help no matter how heavy life gets or the reason for its heaviness. Jesus and God support you as you carry all of your burdens.

Hymns for the Day

The Hymnal 1982

Love divine, all loves excelling 657
Come away to the skies 213 [SC]
God, my King, thy might confessing 414 [GR]
Hail to the Lord's Anointed 616 [GR]
Jesus shall reign where'er the sun 544 [GR]
We will extol you, ever-blessed Lord 404 [GR]
Awake, my soul, and with the sun 11
Hope of the world, thou Christ of great compassion 472
Just as I am, without one plea 693
Blest be the King whose coming 74
Can we by searching find out God 476
Christ the worker 611
Father, we thank thee who hast planted 302, 303
Go forth for God; go to the world in peace 347
How sweet the Name of Jesus sounds 644
I heard the voice of Jesus say 692
Lord of all hopefulness, Lord of all joy 482
O Bread of life, for sinners broken 342

Lift Every Voice and Sing II

Just as I am 137
Come to me 156
Softly and tenderly Jesus is calling 101

Wonder, Love, and Praise

Weekday Commemorations

Tuesday, July 11
Benedict of Nursia, Abbot of
Monte Cassino, c. 540

Benedict, "the father of Western monasticism," was born about 480 in Nursia in central Italy during a time rife with barbarism. Benedict secluded himself from the noise by removing to a cave above Lake Subiaco. He does not seem to have been ordained or to have considered founding an "order"; however, a community grew up around him. Between 525 and 530, he moved south with a few disciples to Mount Cassino to establish another monastery. There, about 540, he laid out his monastic *Rules*. In the Anglican Communion today, many religious orders' rules have been influenced by Benedict's. He is buried in the same grave with his sister, Scholastica.

Friday, July 14
Argula von Grumbach, Scholar and
Church Reformer, c. 1554

The brilliant Argula shone gemlike in Germany in her day. She was born in 1492 a noblewoman. Her father gave her a German Bible when she was ten to spur her studies. Her education continued as she served as a lady-in-waiting at the court when reform defined Germany. She married at eighteen and moved to be chatelaine of her household, mother of four, and a theology student. She provided succor for a condemned seminarian, accusing the clerics at the university of "foolish violence against the word of God." She spoke out vociferously, despite being lay and female.

The Seventh Sunday after Pentecost: Proper 10

July 16, 2023

God's word is power (The Parable of the Sower).

Color Green

Preface Of the Lord's Day

Collect

O Lord, mercifully receive the prayers of your people who call upon you, and grant that they may know and understand what things they ought to do, and also may have grace and power faithfully to accomplish them; through Jesus Christ our Lord, who lives and reigns with you and the Holy Spirit, one God, now and for ever. *Amen.*

Readings and Psalm

Genesis 25:19–34

Today's reading begins the story of Esau and Jacob, through whom the promise of God to Abraham for descendants is being fulfilled. It also highlights a favorite theme in the narratives about the prominence of younger sons who receive the coveted blessings that move the covenant story forward. The twin brothers Esau and Jacob are rivals even in Rebekah's womb. She struggles to understand the painful conflict and through an oracle learns that the two children will always be in conflict. They are unlike in appearance, interests, and behavior. The final section describes how a hungry Esau exchanges his inheritance—his birthright—to the wily Jacob in exchange for a warm meal.

Psalm 119:105–112

In this reading, the psalmist, despite his troubles, pledges to remain faithful to God's teachings to reap the rewards of faithful living.

or

Isaiah 55:10–13

Today's reading comes from a triumphant hymn exulting in Israel's ultimate restoration. With the cry of a street vendor, God calls to Israel and invites the people to a banquet that would foreshadow the final consummation (25:6). Isaiah declares that God's grace cannot be purchased; it is both priceless and free. The Lord offers not only the bread and water of the wilderness but the wine and milk of the Promised Land.

Psalm 65:(1–8) 9–13

This psalm of thanksgiving rejoices because of the blessings that occur when God's creative power is unleashed during the agricultural year.

Romans 8:1–11

Paul continues his discussion of the contrast between life in the flesh and life in the Spirit. Paul uses the "Spirit of God," the "Spirit of Christ," and "Christ in you" almost interchangeably, emphasizing that the source of the Spirit is God, that the full manifestation of the Spirit is in Christ, and that Christians experience the Spirit communally in the Body of Christ, the Church.

Matthew 13:1–9, 18–23

Today's reading begins this gospel's third great discourse, called the discourse of the kingdom, or the parable discourse, because it is built up from seven parables. In its original setting, the parable of the sower was probably one of contrast, pointing to the superabundant yield for the kingdom in the last days despite the past and present frustrations and the apparent lack of success of God's work in Israel's history and in Jesus' ministry. The allegorical interpretation of the parable shifts attention from the harvest to the varying conditions in the field, from the coming of judgment to the spiritual receptivity of the hearers of the gospel. It exhorts converts to assess the depth of their response.

Prayers of the People

Sisters and brothers, you are in the Spirit, since the Spirit of God dwells in you. By that same Spirit let us pray, saying, "Accept, O Lord, the willing tribute of our lips, *and teach us your judgments.*"

Great God, may the word of your kingdom find good soil in your Church. Cause your word to grow in our hearts and bear an abundance of fruit.

Silence

Accept, O Lord, the willing tribute of our lips,

And teach us your judgments.

God of our ancestors, we pray that divided nations be united and warring nations find peace. May we recognize that we are created by your will and are all members of one human family.

Silence

Accept, O Lord, the willing tribute of our lips,

And teach us your judgments.

God of the harvest, bless the seeds and the soil of the world. Give us the wisdom to bring forth its yield wisely and according to your will, that all people may have enough to eat.

Invite the congregation to add their thanksgivings, followed by silence

Accept, O Lord, the willing tribute of our lips,

And teach us your judgments.

Caring God, we are deeply troubled by the gun violence in our city. May all who set their minds on death, even now, be converted to the Spirit of life and peace.

Silence

Accept, O Lord, the willing tribute of our lips,

And teach us your judgments.

Healing God, preserve the lives of the suffering and sick, according to your word. Speak joy into the hearts of the sorrowful.

Invite the congregation to add their petitions, followed by silence

Accept, O Lord, the willing tribute of our lips,

And teach us your judgments.

Eternal God, you preserve all who are in Christ Jesus from condemnation. By the resurrection of your Son we trust, that in the fullness of time, you will give life to our mortal bodies through his Spirit that dwells in us.

Silence

Accept, O Lord, the willing tribute of our lips,

And teach us your judgments.

Images in the Readings

Although seed was valuable, the **sower** strewed the seed widely. In Christian imagination, the sower is Christ, and also the preacher, and also every Christian spreading the Good News to others. Those who live in the Spirit bear good **fruit**, says Matthew. The imagery of plentiful growth recurs throughout the Bible and can alert us to the beauteous variety of plants and trees we humans can enjoy. In the vision of the heavenly city in the Revelation to John, the Tree of Life can by itself produce twelve different fruits.

The **trees** are clapping their hands. The troublesome thorn is replaced by the medicinally useful evergreen cypress, identified as a tree used in the building of the temple. The briar has been replaced with myrtle, an aromatic evergreen used in the rituals of Sukkoth.

Ideas for the Day

- ◆ Maybe you have had a bunkmate, sibling, child, neighbor, or coworker with whom there should have been peace, but there was often turmoil—a bit like living with Jacob. He seems to have never come home with a "plays well with others" report card; he is a bit of an anti-hero. Have you ever imagined this lesson from the perspective of Jacob, who probably doesn't see himself as as much of a scoundrel as the holy author seems to? What were his motivations—was it just deceit and money-grabbing or was he well-intentioned in his own mind? Living together is what we are made for, yet it is also our constant trouble because we cannot always know the intentions of people we struggle to love wholeheartedly.

A new person comes to church and then never returns. A new person comes to church and gets so excited they want to join everything. They stay for two months and then never return. A new person drives into the parking lot, pauses, and then decides to go get some coffee instead. And a new person comes to church and fully integrates and there is much joy in the community. It almost comes off like there is only one winner; one good end. But don't you think that God is actively working in all four of the new people? Don't you think that even for the person that drove into the parking lot, even in that ten-second stop, God might have done something wonderful?

In the frustrations we feel in the "seeds" that seem to be dying all around us, the parable of the sower can give us the same encouragement as it did to the disciples who saw so many of Jesus' seeds seemingly fall by the wayside. What is happening in our time in the church? In the world? Where and how do we hear God's word being uttered? Where do the seeds of God's word seem to be falling on hard ground and dying?

Making Connections

Today's focus is the Word of God. Tie it in with John 1, "In the beginning was the Word." The Word of God is not just something we hear; it has a power. It is something we "see" in what is happening around us. The word is the wisdom that makes sense of creation and puts us in touch with the reality of that sense. Nothing can keep the Word of God from accomplishing its purpose. No matter how discouraged we may feel with the way our history is seemingly working out, God's word will be accomplished

Engaging All Ages

This week's Gospel passage feels tangible, something we can test out on our own in very literal ways. So let's do that! Gather some seed and make it available to church attendees. After the service, have them spread the seed across different areas surrounding the church. (Wildflowers are a great choice.) Over the rest of the summer, see what pops up and where. Perhaps even use the moment for a "walking sermon" or other sort of formation event. If your context doesn't allow for this sort of exploration and rogue seed planting, encourage families to take seeds home and experiment in their neighborhoods.

Hymns for the Day

The Hymnal 1982
Lamp of our feet, whereby we trace 627 [SC]
O Christ, the Word Incarnate 632 [SC]
Surely it is God who saves me 678, 679 [GR]
Eternal Spirit of the living Christ 698
O Spirit of Life, O Spirit of God 505
Almighty God, your word is cast 588, 589
Blessed Jesus, at thy word 440
Father, we thank thee who hast planted 302, 303
God is working his purpose out 534
Lord, make us servants of your peace 593
Spread, O spread, thou mighty word 530

Lift Every Voice and Sing II
Spirit of the living God 115
One bread, one body 151

Wonder, Love, and Praise

Weekday Commemorations

Monday, July 17
William White, Bishop, 1836
The founding of the American Episcopal Church and the United States of America followed many parallel lines, not least of which were drawn by the venerable White. The chief designer of the church's constitution was born (1747) and educated in Philadelphia. He was ordained a deacon in England in 1770, priest in 1772; returning home, he ministered at Christ and St. Peter's for seven years, whereupon he began a rectorship that continued unto his death. He served as chaplain to the Continental Congress (1777–1789) and of the Senate until 1800. He was presiding bishop at the church's organizing General Convention in 1789, then from 1795 until he died.

Thursday, July 20
Elizabeth Cady Stanton, Amelia Jenks Bloomer, Sojourner Truth, and Harriett Ross Tubman
Born on November 12, 1815, into an affluent, strict Calvinist family in Johnstown, New York, Elizabeth, as a young woman, took seriously the Presbyterian doctrines of predestination and human depravity. She became very depressed but resolved her mental crises through action. She dedicated her life to righting the wrongs perpetrated upon women by the Church and society. She and four other women organized the first Women's Rights Convention at Seneca Falls, New York, July 19–20, 1848.

Pentecost

Amelia Jenks Bloomer, the youngest of six children, was born in New York on May 27, 1818, to a pious Presbyterian family, and early on demonstrated a kindness of heart and strict regard for truth and right. As a young woman, she joined in the temperance, antislavery, and women's rights movements, but never intended to make dress reform a major platform in women's struggle for justice. But, women's fashion of the day prescribed waist-cinching corsets, even for pregnant women, resulting in severe health problems. Faith and fashion collided explosively when she published in her newspaper, *The Lily,* a picture of herself in loose-fitting Turkish trousers, and began wearing them publicly.

Isabella (Sojourner Truth) was the next-to-youngest child of several born to James and Elizabeth, slaves owned by a wealthy Dutchman in New York, in 1797 or 1798. For the first twenty-eight years of her life she was a slave, sold from household to household. During a women's rights convention in Ohio, Sojourner gave the speech for which she is best remembered: "Ain't I a Woman." She had listened for hours to clergy attack women's rights and abolition, using the Bible to support their oppressive logic: God had created women to be weak and Black people to be a subservient race. In her speech she retorted, "If the first woman God ever made was strong enough to turn the world upside down all alone, these women together ought to be able to turn it back, and get it right side up again! And now they is asking to do it, the men better let them."

Slave births were recorded under property, not as persons with names, but we know that Harriet Ross, born sometime during 1820 on a Maryland Chesapeake Bay plantation, was the sixth of eleven children born to Ben Ross and Harriet Green. When she was about twenty-four, Harriet escaped to Canada, but could not forget her parents and other slaves she left behind. Working with the Quakers, she made at least nineteen trips back to Maryland between 1851 and 1861, freeing over three hundred people by leading them into Canada. She was so successful, $40,000 was offered for her capture. Guided by God through omens, dreams, warnings, she claimed her struggle against slavery had been commanded by God. She foresaw the Civil War in a vision. When it began, she quickly joined the Union Army, serving as cook and nurse, caring for both Confederate and Union soldiers. She served as a spy and scout. She led 300 black troops on a raid that freed over 750 slaves, making her the first American woman to lead troops into military action.

Friday, July 21
Maria Skobtsova, Monastic and Martyr, 1945

Divorced from her first husband, suffering the death of a child, and separated from her second husband, Skobtsova (b. 1891) worked with the needy in Paris. In 1932, she became a nun. When Nazis took Paris in 1940, she provided a haven for Jews, who sought her help to prevent deportation through baptismal certificates provided by her chaplain. Nazis caught her and imprisoned her in Ravensbrück. Maria defined Christian asceticism as responses to the needs of others in creating a better society and defined her fellow inmates as "the very icon of God incarnate." She died in a Nazi gas chamber.

Saturday, July 22
Saint Mary Magdalene

Mary of Magdala, near Capernaum, followed Jesus and cared for Him-who-healed-her. She appears in all four gospels' stories of the crucifixion as witness to Christ's death. She exemplifies women's faithful ministry for Jesus, as she and her sisters-in-faith went to the tomb to mourn and attend Jesus' body. That Jesus revealed himself to her, calling her by name, makes her the first witness to the risen Lord. She told the disciples, "I have seen the Lord." According to the Gospel of Mary, Peter, for one, did not believe that Jesus would show himself first to a woman. Mary's reputation, although twisted for centuries, maintains that she was an apostle.

The Eighth Sunday after Pentecost: Proper 11

July 23, 2023

God's patience and mercy.

Color   Green

Preface   Of the Lord's Day

Collect

Almighty God, the fountain of all wisdom, you know our necessities before we ask and our ignorance in asking: Have compassion on our weakness, and mercifully give us those things which for our unworthiness we dare not, and for our blindness we cannot, ask; through the worthiness of your Son Jesus Christ our Lord, who lives and reigns with you and the Holy Spirit, one God, now and for ever. *Amen.*

Readings and Psalm

Genesis 28:10–19a

Today's reading describes a revelation of God (a theophany) in which the journeying Jacob dreams of a ladder (more literally a ramp) connecting heaven and earth on which messengers (angels) ascend and descend. This reinforces the notion that heaven and earth are in constant contact with one another. God then appears and speaks now to Jacob the promises that were made previously to Abraham for descendants and the land. Overcome by the awe-inspiring character of the place because of God's surprising presence, Jacob realizes that this sacred place is the "house of God (in Hebrew, Bethel) and gate of heaven."

Psalm 139:1–11, 22–23

This is a prayer for deliverance, uttered either in hopes of or in thanksgiving for God's verdict of innocence upon one accused of sin.

or

Isaiah 44:6–8

Today's reading comes from the second part of the book of the Prophet Isaiah (chaps. 40–66) that dates from the return of the Jews from exile and the time of restoration. It collects the words of comfort that encouraged the Jews in their task of rebuilding not only their nation but also their spirits.

Wisdom of Solomon 12:13, 16–19

God, who is sovereign over all things, is also a God of mercy and forbearance.

or

Psalm 86:11–17

This personal lament by one of God's devoted servants calls upon God's help in a time of distress.

Romans 8:12–25

In today's reading, Paul continues his discussion of the contrast between life in the flesh and life in the Spirit. The indwelling of Christ fills the Christian with a new quality of life that will triumph over death. Christ's resurrection marked the beginning of the "age to come." At the culmination of that age, death itself will be destroyed (1 Corinthians 15:26). Until then, through the Spirit, God brings that future into the present and Christians begin to live in their new life.

Matthew 13:24–30, 36–43

The parable of the weeds (13:24–30) and its interpretation (13:36–43) are found only in Matthew. The parable itself compares the kingdom of heaven to the harvest of a field of wheat mixed with weeds. The weeds are commonly identified as darnel, a poisonous weed with strong roots that looks like wheat (13:29). Because trees were scarce, weeds were usually gathered and burned for fuel (13:30). The central injunction of the parable is "let both of them grow together until the harvest."

Prayers of the People

Sisters and brothers, surely the Lord is in this place! So let us cry out to God, saying, "Abba! Father! *Hear our prayer.*"

O Great Parent, you have adopted us as your own children. You have made us joint heirs with Christ. You love us. Lead us by your Spirit and strengthen our hope.

Invite the congregation to add thanksgivings, followed by silence

Abba! Father!

Hear our prayer.

God our King, you have planted us in a complex and often confusing world. Give us patience to live with each other, not judging our neighbors but trusting in your wisdom.

Silence

Abba! Father!

Hear our prayer.

Present God, even creation groans as it waits on you for freedom. Forgive us for the times in which we have subjected it to futility. Give us eyes to see your presence in the heavens, on the earth, and in the seas.

Silence

Abba! Father!

Hear our prayer.

God of Light, darkness is not dark to you. Brighten the places in our city where darkness serves as a cover for crime and violence. Redeem all who are lost.

Silence

Abba! Father!

Hear our prayer.

God of Glory, we wait in hope for the day when we will be set free from the bondage of decay. Even now, free the suffering from pain and the sorrowful from heartache.

Invite the congregation to add their petitions, followed by silence

Abba! Father!

Hear our prayer.

Eternal God, may the righteous shine like the sun in your kingdom. We trust that, even in the grave, you are with us. In hope, save the dying and the dead.

Silence

Abba! Father!

Hear our prayer.

Images in the Readings

Contemporary English-language Bibles cleverly translate this parable with nouns that sound nearly identical: wheat and **weeds**. It is easy to think of the other as a weed. Christian theology reminds us that each one of us is both wheat and weed. In Martin Luther's language, we are always both saint and sinner.

Once again this Sunday's readings give us the images of the seed and the harvest. In explicating the allegory, Matthew writes about the furnace of **fire**, where there will be weeping and gnashing of teeth. Scholars suggest that the image of eternal separation from God as fire, Gehenna, recalled the perpetually burning refuse dump that was outside the city walls. Thus God's judgmental fire was about expulsion from the community and destruction of what is worthless. That this fire is an image is made clear in that people are gnashing their teeth; thus they still have bodies that are, however, not being burned up.

We are **children** of God: not natural offspring, but instead adopted, beloved, dependent, obedient. That the entire universe is **in labor** is a striking image of God's creation that rejects a commonplace Christian notion that God cares only for human beings. According to biblical theology, all God's creation is good; all creation has fallen; all is groaning in pain until God brings about new birth. As in the natural world, so in the human part of it: countless mothers die in childbirth, for new birth is a painful, even dangerous event. The image of all the earth in labor fits well with our scientific knowledge of the earth and its creatures, all of which must continually struggle for life. The natural world is not a benign zoo, but rather billions of life forms created by God that all are headed toward decay.

God is **the first and the last**. Revelation casts this as Alpha and Omega, A and Z. So Christian theology has taught that God was before all things, and when all things come to their end, what will remain is God.

Ideas for the Day

♦ Leaving the scene after "stealing" the birthright, Jacob has this revelatory experience of the borderland between the infinite and the finite. The psalm is an expression of awe and wonder and closeness with God, but perhaps also a hint of God's intentions being at times uncomfortable too. Together the two may recall the scene from the movie *Contact* where the rational Dr. Arroway is overwhelmed by a vision of deepest space and declares, "They should have sent a poet to report the beauty and intimacy of that moment." It is intriguing to imagine Psalm 139 as the inner narrative of Jacob during this revelation.

♦ Don't you love to have God dreams? It has been said that it is a good idea to set a piece of paper and pen next to your bed and try in the moments just before you fall asleep to ask God for a dream. And then the moment you realize your God dream has ended, tell yourself to wake up and write down your dream. After a couple of times doing this, you might actually have something new, something exciting. Jacob found himself in a holy place and was able to hear blessing. Hopefully, we don't need to use a rock as a pillow, but it is during our sleep that we are less likely to try to control God and hear what we actually need to hear.

♦ The Gospel reading is a response to the age-old question, "Why does God allow evil to exist?" The evil in the world seems to grow stronger. But God's time is not our time, we hear today. God's patience encompasses eternity, while we live but a moment. What do you think prompted Jesus to tell this parable? What kinds of questions do you think people were asking him?

Making Connections

The reading from Romans is often read at a burial service because it expresses with power the Christian hope. According to the Catechism, the Christian hope is to live with confidence in newness and fullness of life, and to await the coming of Christ in glory, and the completion of God's purpose for the world. How would you describe the Christian hope? What do you believe God's purpose is for the world?

Engaging All Ages

How do we understand difficult moments in our lives, especially when we believe in a God who is in control—a God who loves us? This week's passages might bring up some difficult questions for young and old and a definitive answer might not be the best response to the question of what these passages "mean." Instead, arm some children or teenagers with reporter notebooks and pencils. Their assignment: go into the congregation and get to know people. Let them report their findings for the entire parish to hear, perhaps at a fellowship event. The goal: to remind us that God knows us and—even when we have big questions—being known allows us to further know the God of graciousness, compassion, and truth.

Hymns for the Day

The Hymnal 1982
As Jacob with travel was weary one day 453 [SC]
Lord, thou has searched me and dost know 702 [SC]
Eternal light, shine in my heart 465, 466 [GR]
Immortal, invisible, God only wise 423 [GR]
My God, how wonderful thou art 643 [GR]
O day of God, draw nigh 600, 601 [GR]
The Lord will come and not be slow 462 [GR]
Come, thou almighty King 365 [GR]
Praise to the living God 372 [GR]
To God with gladness sing 399 [GR]
All my hope on God is founded 665
Christ is the world's true Light 542
Come with us, O blessed Jesus 336
Creator of the stars of night 60
Almighty God, your word is cast 588, 589
Come, labor on 541
Come, ye thankful people, come (vs. 2–4) 290
Father, we thank thee who hast planted 302, 303
For the fruit of all creation 424

Lift Every Voice and Sing II
We are climbing Jacob's ladder 220 [SC]
One bread, one body 151

Wonder, Love, and Praise
God the sculptor of the mountains 746, 74

Pentecost

Weekday Commemorations

Monday, July 24
Thomas à Kempis, Priest, 1471

He was born Thomas Hammerken in the Duchy of Cleves (about 1380) and educated by the Brethren of the Common Life. He joined its order (1399) in Zwolle, where he took his vows (1407), was ordained (1415) and made sub-prior (1425). The order, founded by Gerard Groote, comprised laity and clergy. The Brethren cultivated biblical piety, more practical than speculative, and stressed living the inner life and practicing virtue. The members supported themselves by teaching (Erasmus was a pupil) and copying manuscripts. Thomas is renowned for *The Imitation of Christ*, which Thomas composed, or compiled; the work has been widely translated, nearly as often as the Holy Scriptures.

Tuesday, July 25
Saint James the Apostle

James' familiar name, James the Greater, distinguishes the brother of John from the other apostle named James (commemorated with Philip) but also from the other James, "the brother of our Lord." This James was the son of Zebedee, a prosperous Galilean fisher; with his brother John, James left his home and business to follow Christ's call. He seems to have belonged among those chosen for the privilege of witnessing the Transfiguration, the raising of Jairus' daughter, and the agony in the garden. Jesus called the brothers "Sons of Thunder" because of their boiling tempers. James was the first apostle to die for Jesus.

Wednesday, July 26
The Parents of the Blessed Virgin Mary

Their names, Joachim and Anne, are apocryphal, and little is known about either of the parents of the mother of Jesus. Anne, thought to have descended from David, was presumably brought up in a good Jewish family that longed for the kingdom of God. In the second century an apocryphal gospel, *Protevangelium of James,* appeared to tell legendary stories of Anne and Joachim. In 550, the Emperor Justinian I built the first church to St. Anne, but not until the twelfth century was her feast day known in the West. The Roman Catholic Church joined Joachim's several dates with Anne's in 1969.

Thursday, July 27
William Reed Huntington, Priest, 1909

Born in 1838 in Massachusetts, Huntington served his church not only as ecumenist and statesman but also as a liturgical scholar. When the church faced schism in the late nineteenth century, Huntington encouraged reconciliation from his position as a member of the House of Deputies (1871 to 1907). His passion for unity resulted in *The Church Idea* (1870); the grounds he laid were accepted by the House of Bishops in Chicago in 1886. The sixth rector of Grace Church, New York City, he guided with breadth and generosity. He exemplified boldness in 1871, when he moved to support women's roles in the church by reviving the ancient order of deaconesses, which was met with resistance until 1889.

Friday, July 28
Johann Sebastian Bach, Composer, 1750

Born in Eisenach, Germany, in 1685, into a family of musicians, Bach achieved an enviable reputation as a composer and performer by early adulthood. In 1708, he became organist and chamber musician for the Duke of Weimar. In 1723, he was appointed cantor of the St. Thomas School in Leipzig and parish musician at both St. Thomas and St. Nicholas churches, a post he held until he died. Bach's music expressed his deep Lutheran faith. He not only interpreted the Bible in his "Passions," but he also wrote music for eucharists, perhaps the most renowned being "Mass in B Minor."

Saturday, July 29
Mary and Martha of Bethany

According to the Gospels of Luke and John, Jesus loved these sisters and their brother Lazarus. Luke's account tells the story of the sisters' hospitality, styling Martha as active and Mary as contemplative. Such symbolism has caused tension in interpretation through the ages. John's gospel reveals more about the women's characters as juxtaposed against Lazarus' death. Jesus arrives post-mortem. Martha meets him, trusting that Jesus will heal their brother, demonstrating her profound faith in Jesus as Messiah. John also describes Mary's anointing Jesus' feet with perfumed salve then wiping them with her tresses, a gesture of love that roused the disciples' criticism. The sisters symbolize faithful friendship.

The Ninth Sunday after Pentecost: Proper 12

July 30, 2023

The hidden power of the kingdom of God.

Color — Green

Preface — Of the Lord's Day

Collect

O God, the protector of all who trust in you, without whom nothing is strong, nothing is holy: Increase and multiply upon us your mercy; that, with you as our ruler and guide, we may so pass through things temporal, that we lose not the things eternal; through Jesus Christ our Lord, who lives and reigns with you and the Holy Spirit, one God, for ever and ever. *Amen.*

Readings and Psalm

Genesis 29:15–28

Today's reading describes how Jacob acquires Rachel as his wife so that God's promises to Abraham might be continued. Like Isaac before him, Jacob seeks a wife from the family of Laban, the brother of Rebekah. He is immediately smitten with Rachel, however Laban requires that he show his commitment through seven years of service. After seven years of service to Laban, Jacob expects to be able to marry Rachel. But Laban gives him Rachel's older sister Leah, explaining that it is their custom that unless the older sister is married first, the younger one cannot be married. Driven by his love for Rachel, Jacob agrees to seven more years of service. When they are ended, Jacob finally is able to marry his beloved Rachel.

Psalm 105:1–11, 45b

This hymn praises God who promised the land of Canaan to the covenant people and then kept the promise.

or

Psalm 128

The psalmist predicates the ancient understanding of the prosperous life—fruitful labor, a thriving family, and peaceful, long life in an abundant land—on following God's commandments.

or

1 Kings 3:5–12

Today's reading comes from the beginning of the narrative of Solomon's reign, based largely upon the "Book of the Acts of Solomon" (11:41). During a time of worship, Solomon has a dream. Solomon expresses a due sense of humility before the Lord and is already prudent enough to ask for "an understanding mind," the grace of practical and judicial wisdom, rather than for wealth or long life.

Psalm 119:129–136

The psalmist recognizes how valuable God's words/commands are and how much comfort there is in governing one's life by them. Knowing God's commands is a light for the mind and the way to the fullness of life.

Romans 8:26–39

The Spirit cooperates to bring the Christian's prayer before God and compensates for our weakness. The Spirit intercedes for us, implying a full sharing in our suffering and longings. God, "who searches the heart," (Proverbs 20:27) and the Spirit have one will and purpose (1 Corinthians 2:10–11). In the activity of prayer God is on both sides, both immanent and transcendent.

Matthew 13:31–33, 44–52

Today's reading puts together a sequence of three parables of the kingdom that are found only in Matthew. These parables begin with the customary phrase, "The kingdom of heaven is like . . . ," but the meaning is more, "It is the case with the kingdom of heaven as with . . . ." Thus the focus of the comparison can be shifted from one particular item to the pattern of the whole story, especially its conclusion.

Prayers of the People

Sisters and brothers, give thanks to the Lord and call upon God's name! Let us pray to God, saying, "Spirit, help us in our weakness. *Intercede for us.*"

God of the Church, may your people be as persistent as the mustard shrub. May we spread your love and grace to all people and in all places. May we do our kingdom work with the confidence that nothing can separate us from your love.

Silence

Spirit, help us in our weakness.

Intercede for us.

God of the world, make known your deeds among the peoples. Bring peace in places of conflict and violence.

Silence

Spirit, help us in our weakness.

Intercede for us.

God of creation, all of your works are marvelous. Everything in creation with which you have surrounded us speaks to your goodness. Give us eyes to see your fingerprints in our world.

Invite the congregation to add their thanksgivings, followed by silence

Spirit, help us in our weakness.

Intercede for us.

Present God, you did not withhold your own Son, but gave him up for all of us. May we all come to know and experience the depths of your love. By your love, transform hearts and change lives.

Silence

Spirit, help us in our weakness.

Intercede for us.

God of wholeness, neither hardship nor distress can separate anyone from your love. Assure the suffering and sick, the hurt and sorrowful, that you care for them. May they remember that you are God who does marvelous things.

Invite the congregation to add their petitions, followed by silence

Spirit, help us in our weakness.

Intercede for us.

God of our ancestors, you have always been mindful of your promises. You promise that not even death can separate us from your love. May all those who have died grow in your eternal love.

Silence

Spirit, help us in our weakness.

Intercede for us.

Images in the Readings

The parables are full of images that raise many questions. The **mustard seed** actually grows into a straggly annual bush, not the monumental Tree of Life (see for example Ezekiel 31:2–9) that is paradoxically evoked in the opening parable. In Jewish religious symbolism, the preferred sex is the man, the holy minister is a priest, and the holy bread is unleavened; yet in the parable the woman adds **leaven** to three measures of flour. The man sells "all that he has" to gain a **treasure**, and we think of Solomon's dream, for whom the preferred treasure was wisdom that comes only from God. The **net** that catches all kinds of fish is a commonplace symbol for the church. Yet by "the kingdom of heaven" Matthew does not mean merely "the church."

The first reading is one of the several biblical tales about the **wisdom of Solomon**, a phrase come into our language to signify immense and deep understanding. According to the monarchical myths of the ancient Near East, the king was anointed by God, next in power to God, God's servant, even God's son. Yet the later stories in 2 Kings describe Solomon as having been as prone to foolishness and error as any other king, as having given in to many temptations that separated him from the love of God. For Christians, Christ himself is wisdom.

Ideas for the Day

- Mustard seeds are not really the smallest of all seeds, and neither do they make champion trees. Most might be referred to as a bush, but hardly a tree. There are varieties that do grow taller, and woodier, but certainly not a tree for climbing or a packed aviary. The parable leans into the outrageous, garners the attention of the hearers who knew the plants well: Why in the world, what huh? What is Jesus doing with this one? Jesus is illustrating the reign of God and therefore his mission as a tremendous life-hosting tree that is connected to that ancient Tree of Life in the garden of Eden as well as the one of Proverbs 3 saying, "Wisdom, she is a tree of life to those who embrace her."

- Here is a different kind of parable. There was a person who wanted to do everything according to the desires of God. This person needed to paint the bedroom, and there were two colors of paint— red and blue. On the first night, the person asked God, what color should I paint my room? There was no answer. On the second night, the person asked God, what color should I paint my room? Again, no answer. On the third night, with a bit of frustration, the person asked God, what color should I paint my room? And on this night God answered, "I don't care, just do something!" In all the parables we hear today, the character began by just doing something.

- The thread in today's readings seems to be about trust. Jacob trusts in God (and Laban) that the promise will be fulfilled for him to marry Rachel, even following more years of work than he had anticipated. In Paul's letter to the Romans, we recognize that God's love and care supports us in our weakness through the Holy Spirit's intercession. We know and trust that Christ is at God's right hand, acting and speaking on behalf of our desires and needs.

Making Connections

What is prayer? It is a gift, often hidden, that can yield more than we can ask or imagine if we put it to use. Like a mustard seed, yeast, hidden treasure, a fine pearl, or a net, we cannot know what can come of it until we tap into its "purpose." Presiding Bishop Michael Curry's call to follow the Way of Love asks us to pray daily.

How might we blossom, grow, and be found if we take up the practice to pray every day? How might our lives be changed when we recognize that Jesus is our prayer partner in our conversation with God?

Engaging All Ages

"The kingdom of Heaven is like . . ." is one of the most familiar parts of scripture. Even our modern ears are trained to hear something different, something new and unexpected. This week, consider doing an "unexpected" themed worship service or formation hour. A couple of options: dueling sermons (two preachers, rotating back and forth), doing the scripture readings in a dramatic form or fashion, have people come up with their own "The kingdom of Heaven is like . . . " metaphors.

Hymns for the Day

The Hymnal 1982
If thou but trust in God to guide thee 635
Not here for high and holy things 9 [SC]
Be thou my vision, O Lord of my heart 488 [GR]
Eternal light, shine in my heart 465, 466 [GR]
God, you have given us power to sound 584 [GR]
Open your ears, O faithful people 536 [GR]
Eternal Spirit of the living Christ 698
God moves in a mysterious way 677
God of grace and God of glory 594, 595
Jesus lives! thy terrors now 194, 195
Like the murmur of the dove's song 513
Spread, O spread, thou mighty word 530
The Christ who died but rose again 447
Seek ye first the kingdom of God 711
The Lord will come and not be slow 462
"Thy kingdom come!" on bended knee 615

Lift Every Voice and Sing II
Children of the heavenly father 213

Wonder, Love, and Praise
Even when young, I prayed for wisdom's grace 906 [GR]

Pentecost

Weekday Commemorations

July 31
Ignatius of Loyola

Ignatius was born into a noble Basque family in 1491. In his autobiography, he tells us, "Up to his twenty-sixth year, he was a man given over to the vanities of the world and took special delight in the exercise of arms with a great and vain desire of winning glory." An act of reckless heroism at the Battle of Pamplona in 1521 led to his being seriously wounded. During his convalescence at Loyola, Ignatius experienced a profound spiritual awakening. Following his recovery and an arduous period of retreat, a call to be Christ's knight in the service of God's kingdom was deepened and confirmed.

The fact that Ignatius was an unschooled layman made him suspect in the eyes of church authorities and led him, at the age of thirty-seven, to study theology at the University of Paris in preparation for the priesthood. While there, Ignatius gave the *Exercises* to several of his fellow students; and in 1534, together with six companions, he took vows to live lives of strict poverty and to serve the needs of the poor. Thus, what later came to be known as the Society of Jesus was born.

August 1
Joseph of Arimathaea

Little is known of the life of Joseph of Arimathaea beyond the stories of Jesus' burial in the gospels. John speaks of Joseph as a secret disciple and couples him with Nicodemus, also part of the Jewish Sanhedrin drawn to Jesus. Later legends describe them as leaders in the early church. One of the loveliest legends, which cannot be dated earlier than the 1200s, tells of Joseph's bringing the Holy Grail with him to the ancient Church of Glastonbury in Britain. More concrete, though, is Joseph's boldly stepping forward—unlike the cowering disciples—to do what Jewish piety demanded: to offer his own tomb to prevent further desecration of Jesus' crucified body.

August 3
Joanna, Mary, and Salome, Myrrh-bearing Women

These three bear the tradition of the women who came to anoint Jesus' body with myrrh after his crucifixion only to find his tomb empty after resurrection. The faithful disciples were known for their unwavering devotion to the Christ in his earthly ministry. Joanna was healed by him, after which she served him loyally. Salome may have been related to Mary, Jesus' mother. Mary Magdalene is often conflated with Mary, the mother of James, and Mary, the wife of Cleopas. The Holy Myrrh-bearers are celebrated in the Orthodox Church on the second Sunday after Easter.

The Transfiguration of Our Lord Jesus Christ

August 6, 2023

Jesus' compassion for the people leads him to respond with food for mind and body. The feeding of the five thousand expresses the significance of the Holy Eucharist.

Color   Green

Preface   Of the Lord's Day

Collect

Let your continual mercy, O Lord, cleanse and defend your Church; and, because it cannot continue in safety without your help, protect and govern it always by your goodness; through Jesus Christ our Lord, who lives and reigns with you and the Holy Spirit, one God, for ever and ever. *Amen.*

Readings and Psalm

Exodus 34:29–35

Today's account explains the purpose of Moses' regular practice at the tent of meeting. Moses had asked to see God's glory (33:18–23); apparently his ongoing communion with the Lord imparted a continuing revelation of divine glory. That vision of glory so transfigured Moses' face that he had to wear a veil. Moses' experience became a type of the glory of the new covenant. Unlike Moses' radiance, which would fade, believers behold the Lord's glory and are being transformed into the Lord's likeness with a glory that always increases.

Psalm 99 or 99:5–9

Psalm 99 is a hymn celebrating God's kingship. It's three stanzas each close with a refrain about God's holiness.

2 Peter 1:13–21

The author writes in response to anxieties about different teachings in the community and about the delay of the second coming. He appeals to the tradition of apostolic testimony, particularly to his experience as a witness to the transfiguration. The transfiguration manifests Christ in his power, confirming the messianic prophecies of the Hebrew Bible and pointing toward his return in glory.

Luke 9:28–36

Luke's account of the transfiguration points back to the Hebrew Bible parallels and forward to Jesus' death, resurrection, and ascension. Moses and Elijah, who represent the law and the prophets—both fulfilled by Jesus—speak with Jesus "of his departure," literally his exodus, the new exodus he will lead through his death. The new exodus is accomplished through Jesus' death, resurrection, and ascension. Jesus' glory is his own (9:32), not a reflected glory as Moses' was. God's voice confirms what it proclaimed at Jesus' baptism: Jesus is the Son, the Chosen, fulfilling the roles of Moses, of the Davidic king and of the servant.

Prayers of the People

Friends, God our Savior is our refuge! So let us pray to God, saying, "Incline your ear to us; *hear our words.*"

God our Savior, show us your face. Satisfy your Church in your presence. Reveal to us your ways so that we might walk in the light of your truth.

Silence

Incline your ear to us;

Hear our words.

O God, your eyes are fixed on justice. We pray for all victims of war and violence and famine. Give heed to the cries of those in need throughout the world.

Silence

Incline your ear to us;

Hear our words.

God of abundance, you have blessed the earth to bring forth plenty. May we recognize the abundance in our own lives, so that those with little may also have their fill.

Silence

Incline your ear to us;

Hear our words.

O God, have compassion on the people of our region. Show us your marvelous loving-kindness so that trust in your goodness might replace our fears.

Silence

Incline your ear to us;

Hear our words.

God of blessing, we call upon you, for you answer us in our need. We pray this day for all those desperate for your blessing. Moved by compassion, heal the sick and suffering ones we hold in our hearts this day.

Invite the congregation to add their petitions and thanksgivings, followed by silence

Incline your ear to us;

Hear our words.

God our vindicator, justify the dead through the mercy of your Messiah. We pray that in the fullness of time, they may awake, beholding your likeness.

Silence

Incline your ear to us;

Hear our words.

Images in the Readings

Once again the readings include the central biblical images of **light** and **mountain**.

Yet God is not only brilliant light: important for the readings is the image of the **cloud**. Although contemporary people tend to think of clouds as relating to weather conditions, in the Bible the cloud is a sign of the presence of God. It is as if God covers the earth, brings life, effecting much yet suddenly vanishing. Christians can add that from God as cloud rains down the waters of baptism.

We are so accustomed to the language of being children of a God who is like a Father that we miss the astonishment of the early church, when this imagery was a religious surprise. Christ is to God as a **son** is to a father, and we are not pitiful creatures struggling to live in a hostile environment, but rather children cared for by a beneficent God. "Son of man," on the other hand, is the biblical name for the apocalyptic judge, thus only paradoxically the beloved Son of God.

Ideas for the Day

◆ Jealousy and greed are powerful motivators as any two-year-old already knows. In the novel *Sense and Sensibility* by Jane Austen, it is the manipulation of a brother by covetousness and bitterness that sets the downfall of the Dashwood women in motion. Like Joseph, they didn't do anything to garner the ire of their own relations, but the father's extraordinary love for the younger half-siblings was too much to take. Is there a way to restore such terribly fractured family relationships? As people called to act for a healed world, this is a moment to examine where we need to be reconciled and open to new possibilities. We encounter crisis after crisis, and yet, over and over God provides support as we gain perspective and new partners in pursuing the common good.

- Do you know that you can sing the words of "Amazing Grace" to the tune of the *Gilligan's Island* theme song? Try it up to the line "was blind, but now I see." It might have been a good song for the disciples to be singing; they might not have been so afraid. There are two phrases we might think about today that are often said in the gospels. The first one is "Come," and the second is "Do not be afraid." We all know how scary life can be. Sometimes the event is beyond our imagination. But the promise of Jesus is always there, even in the midst of a great storm. Can we listen and hear the invitation to come? Can we listen and hear the comfort of a declaration to not be afraid?

- A small boy offers a few loaves and fish to be shared with the crowd. The idea of making an offering of our possessions in faith is conveyed in this story. Often we fail to respond to Christ because we feel that what we have to offer cannot make any difference. "I know world hunger is a problem," we say, "but the problem is so big, what difference is my little sacrifice going to make?" In the hands of Jesus, the small and insignificant offering of the boy became enough to feed the crowd. When we offer the risen Christ our time, talent, and commitment, he can make it capable of bringing about the kingdom.

Making Connections

The story of Jesus' Transfiguration is all about change. It is an event that calls us to change into people who live with a sense of expectation and hope, who can act powerfully for the sake of the good and face opposition in life and not be overcome. And it's scary.

The change they witness produces so much fear in the disciples that they literally fall on their faces. This is perfectly natural; when we become used to things being a certain way, and they go a different way, it disorients us.

There may be comfort in avoiding change, sticking to received tradition instead. Just remember Peter in this story. He thinks that he can contain the change by boxing it in three little tents up on the mountain. When we slide into that sort of nostalgia, we're in trouble. We must respond to change; we can begin in fear, but remember that we are empowered for bravery.

Engaging All Ages

For some, these stories in the Bible can seem fantastic—mythical. And that's not a bad thing! One of the goals of scripture is to increase our religious imaginations, to see the world as God sees the world. And perhaps more importantly, to live in a way that believes and hopes in and for the miraculous. For some, this will cause a serious case of eyes rolling. For others, it's the bedrock of their faith. Either way, spend this week encouraging families and other members of your community to engage your religious imagination. Have parishioners write a new version of this well-known and loved story. Where would Jesus appear? How could we call something a miracle today? What is it that Jesus is calling us to walk out into on faith alone?

Hymns for the Day

The Hymnal 1982
O Zion, tune thy voice 543
Christ is the world's true Light 542
Christ, whose glory fills the skies 6,7
From God Christ's deity came forth 443
When morning gilds the skies 427
Yo soy la luz del mundo / I am the world's true light 75
Christ upon the mountain peak 129,130
O Light of Light, Love given birth 133,134
O wondrous type, O vision fair 136,137

Lift Every Voice and Sing II
Let the heav'n light shine on me 174
Jesu, joy of our desiring 75

Wonder, Love, and Praise

Pentecost

Weekday Commemorations

Monday, August 7
John Mason Neale, Priest and Hymnographer, 1866

Neale, born in London in 1818, is best known as a hymnodist, for a glance to the bottom of many pages of *The Hymnal 1940* and *1982* finds his name as composer or translator. As scholar and poet, Neale composed hymns and transposed Latin and Greek hymns into English spoken syntax in such turns of phrase as "Good Christian men, rejoice" and "Come, ye faithful, raise the strain." He was also a priest of the Oxford Movement, which revived medieval liturgical forms, and a humanitarian; as such, he founded the Sisterhood of St. Margaret to relieve the suffering of women and girls. A gentle man of good humor and modesty, he lived "unbounded charity."

Tuesday, August 8
Dominic, Priest and Friar, 1221

Dominic, who was born in Spain around 1170, founded the Order of Preachers known as the Dominicans. In England, they were the Blackfriars, a reference to the black mantles worn over their white habits. Legend has Dominic, in searching for a life of apostolic poverty, selling all his possessions to help people hungry from the 1191 famine. He was ordained in 1196. In 1203, he began preaching tours in France, and in 1214, he manifested his idea for a preaching order, granted by Honorius III about 1216. The Dominicans' Constitutions, formulated in 1216, set a priority of intellectual rigor: "In the cells, they can write, read, pray . . . and stay awake at night . . . on account of study."

Wednesday, August 9
Edith Stein (Teresa Benedicta of the Cross), Philosopher, Monastic, and Martyr, 1942

Stein became a Christian in 1921 after having been born a Jew in 1891 and becoming an atheist at fourteen. She nursed during WWI, then earned her doctorate at twenty-five and taught at the University of Freiburg. Discouraged from a monastic life, Stein taught at a Catholic school while studying Catholic philosophy and theology. Forced by Nazis to quit teaching, she entered a Carmelite community. In 1933, she beseeched the pope to condemn the Third Reich. When the Nazis ordered Christians of Jewish origin killed, Stein was gassed in Auschwitz. She was made a Roman Catholic saint in 1998.

Thursday, August 10
Laurence, Deacon, and Martyr at Rome, 258

The Emperor Valerian started persecuting upper-class clergy and laity in 257. Properties of the Church were confiscated; Christian worship was forbidden. On August 4, 258, Pope Sixtus II and his seven deacons were apprehended in catacombs and executed, except for the archdeacon, Laurence, who was martyred on August 10, roasted alive on a gridiron. Legend has Laurence presenting the sick and poor to the prefect, who demanded to see the Church's treasures. The Emperor Constantine erected a shrine and basilica over Laurence's tomb. For Laurence, to die for Christ was to live with Christ; a small, round, glass medallion, probably from the fourth century, now in New York's Metropolitan Museum, reads, "Live with Christ and Laurence."

Friday, August 11
Clare of Assisi, Monastic, 1253

The daughter of a wealthy family, and a noted beauty, Clare was inspired by Francis' words with the desire to serve God and to give her life to the following of Christ's teachings. She sought out Francis and begged that she might become a member of his order, placing her jewelry and rich outer garments on the altar as an offering. Francis could not refuse her pleas and placed her in a nearby Benedictine convent. Despite her family's attempts to remove her, she was adamant and other women joined her. She became Mother Superior of the order, which was called the "Poor Ladies of St. Damien," governing and caring for the sisters for forty years.

Saturday, August 12
Florence Nightingale, Nurse, 1910

Nightingale, born in 1820, was named Florence for the city of her conception. She remained unmarried in order to attack with single-mindedness her calling to the service of the Lord. She manifested that calling from a vision, first through nursing, considered unseemly for a woman of her class. She showed her mettle as superintendent of a London sanitorium, which was desperate for her organizing skills. Conditions in the military hospitals of the Crimea, where war raged, were just as deplorable; by 1856, Nightingale had set things straight there. Although best known for her role in health care reform, equally important to Nightingale was her commitment to a form of religion that was both personal and mystical.

The Eleventh Sunday after Pentecost: Proper 14

August 13, 2023

God's infinite mercy far surpasses our understanding. God's power is revealed as Jesus controls the waters.

Color Green

Preface Of the Lord's Day

Collect

Grant to us, Lord, we pray, the spirit to think and do always those things that are right, that we, who cannot exist without you, may by you be enabled to live according to your will; through Jesus Christ our Lord, who lives and reigns with you and the Holy Spirit, one God, for ever and ever. *Amen.*

Readings and Psalm

Genesis 37:1–4, 12–28

Today's reading is from the long cycle of Joseph stories in chapters 37–50 of Genesis. In this early section, we learn of the plot of his brothers, who resent the special love that Jacob has for him because he is the firstborn of Rachel, while they have other mothers. At the request of Jacob, Joseph journeys to check up on his brothers as they pasture the flocks. But the brothers see him coming, plot his death, and throw him into a pit. Only the influence of the eldest, Rueben, prompts them to sell him into slavery to a passing caravan rather than murder him. Though the situation seems bleak, God's providence, as always, guides the events. Joseph's presence in Egypt will turn out to be the means of rescue and reconciliation with his brothers.

Psalm 105:1–6, 16–22, 45b

This hymn praises God who promised the land of Canaan to the covenant people and then kept the promise.

or

1 Kings 19:9–18

Today's passage follows Elijah's demonstration that Yahweh is in control of the forces of nature (17:1) and is mightier than Baal (18:20–39). Elijah then flees the vengeance of Jezebel (19:1–3). An angel strengthens him on his journey to Horeb (an alternate name for Sinai). Verses 11b–12 are interpreted by commentators in various ways: as a sign that God works not in the external wonders of nature but through internal communication with servants of the Lord; or as a lesson to the fiery Elijah that God works in a quiet way as well as through miracle-working (18:38); or as a private inspiration for a public mission. The Lord's commands indicate God's sovereignty over history; the nations are God's to dispose.

Psalm 85:8–13

The psalmist both celebrates and prays for the Lord's gracious favor, forgiveness, deliverance, and justice.

Romans 10:5–15

In this passage, Paul compares the right relationship to God ("righteousness") that comes through a strict adherence to the Mosaic law to that which comes by faith. In contrast to a slavish adherence to this law, which is ultimately futile, the righteousness that comes by faith is entirely attainable. It requires no superhuman effort such as ascending into heaven or descending into the abyss. Such feats have already been accomplished by God in Jesus' incarnation and resurrection. People need to accept the "word of faith" proclaimed by the apostle. This acceptance is manifested both through inner conviction and outer profession. These signs of faith are rooted in the work of God, affirming that Jesus is God incarnate and that Jesus now lives.

Pentecost

Matthew 14:22–33

In today's reading, Jesus demonstrates his mastery over wind and sea (which, in the Old Testament, symbolized the powers of chaos and death) and is near to rescue the disciples when they desperately need help. He identifies himself by using the words, "It is I," which echo God's own self-description that became the proper name for God in the Old Testament (Exodus 3:14; Isaiah 43:10–13).

Prayers of the People

Sisters and brothers, the word of faith that we proclaim is near you, on your lips and in your heart! So let us pray to God, saying, "Be generous to all who call on you; *Lord, save us.*"

Lord God, capture our hearts. May your Holy Spirit prepare a way upon which the beautiful feet of your servants can bring good news to all those who are wearied by too much bad news.

Silence

Be generous to all who call on you.

Lord, save us.

Lord of all, your love makes no distinction between peoples or nations. We pray that wars and violence cease. May your reign of peace and justice come quickly.

Silence

Be generous to all who call on you.

Lord, save us.

Holy God, your Son walked on the water even as your Spirit moved over the face of the waters in creation. May we learn to respect the beauty and mystery, the power and goodness, of all you have made.

Silence

Be generous to all who call on you.

Lord, save us.

Strong God, give us wisdom like your servant Joseph that this congregation may be a symbol of hope and integrity to the leaders of our city.

Silence

Be generous to all who call on you.

Lord, save us.

Lord Christ, you bid your people be not afraid. You have promised that all who call on your name shall be saved. And so make your deeds known among the people—especially those in trouble, sickness, and pain.

Invite the congregation to add their petitions and thanksgivings, followed by silence

Be generous to all who call on you.

Lord, save us.

God of our ancestors, by your strength you rescue life even from the depths of the pit. You raised your Son from the grips of death and through him have promised to give new life to all who have died. May the dead rest in peace, even as they await the day of resurrection.

Silence

Be generous to all who call on you.

Lord, save us.

Images in the Readings

The disciples are nearly drowned by the storm of **wind and waves**. Many poetic passages in the Bible speak of wind and waves as though they are harbingers of death and of a sea monster as embodying chaos.

Watch once again the film *Titanic*. In the tale of Jonah, God both sends the storm and calms it. The theophany in Job 38 credits God with having control over the sea, and the authors of Genesis 1, in praising God's creative power, report that God created the sea monsters.

Mount Horeb, where Elijah meets God, is Mount Sinai. According to Exodus, God had appeared in earthquake, wind, and fire, but Elijah encounters only **silence**. This story comforts many of the faithful, for whom there seems to be more sheer silence than powerful wind from the Spirit.

Much Christian iconography has drawn the church as the **boat** from which Jesus, the I Am who is God, brings calm to the waters experienced by the faithful. We assemble weekly in the nave—think "navy"—to receive the peace of Christ.

Ideas for the Day

♦ Not everyone receives the chance to be reconciled as Joseph and his brothers are. The lectionary skips how Joseph rises from jail cell to right-hand advisor of the ruler. We know very little of what life was like for his father and brothers and their wives and households. We can only guess that the winds of change were not prosperous. Perhaps you imagine regrets rising up in the brothers, or could they have been haunted but silent about the whole incident? The way of steadfast love is one of seeking the sometimes long slow path to forgiveness and reconciliation. In the life of your community are there stories of fracture and then healing that become a way of good news?

♦ We are going to have to deal with the reality that even Jesus had to grow in his practice to love, just as each of us have to do. Can you think of a time when you really set someone apart, and then for whatever reason were able to see the person (or community) as completely human (created in the image of God)? It was an honest conversation between Jesus and the Canaanite woman that allowed Jesus to expand his notion of love. It was her willingness to speak in powerlessness and his willingness to listen while in power. When this happens, we then find healing surrounding us all.

♦ Paul speaks as a missionary to the Gentiles, still seeking to save some of his fellow Jews. If rejection of Jesus Christ meant the reconciliation of the world, their acceptance of him would be like life from the dead. How do we evangelize to those we are alike and in community with as well as those who may be different from us?

Making Connections

Jesus tells the disciples not to be afraid. And Peter challenges Jesus to prove his presence with an impossible task—walking on water. Peter finds he can't do it. What Peter can do is something much more important, something that any one of us can do: ask for help.

Jesus walks with us in love. When we step into that kind of relationship with God, we will find that it is easier to accept our helplessness and put our faith in God's care. This kind of faith is not about being particularly certain; it's all about love.

This story might have ended differently. Peter might have walked out on the water without any trouble at all and it would have made a very cool story. But it would not have been good news. We have a little faith, and we sink. And the little faith we have frees us to say, "Save me!"

Engaging All Ages

"Lord, help me." Is there a more powerful statement in all of scripture? It is a moment of shocking faith and vulnerability—something that, for many of us, might be uncomfortable if we experienced such a display of faith or were called upon to make a similar proclamation. Consider asking families to create a "Lord, help me" chart that can hang in a public place in the house. Encourage people to write down prayers—anonymous is fine—and when you see the poster, take a moment to pray for your friends and family. You could also post multiple posters in your church space, encouraging the same displays of public faith and prayer.

Hymns for the Day

From deepest woe I cry to thee 151 [SC]
Out of the depths I call 666 [SC]
Dear Lord and Father of mankind 652, 653 [GR]
Praise the Spirit in creation 506, 507 [GR]
The Lord will come and not be slow 462 [GR]
At the Name of Jesus 435
In Christ there is no East or West 529
Commit thou all that grieves thee 669
Eternal Father, strong to save 608
Give praise and glory unto God 375
How firm a foundation, ye saints of the Lord 636, 637
I sought the Lord, and afterward I knew 689
Jesus, Lover of my soul 699
Lead us, heavenly Father, lead us 559
O all ye works of God, now come 428
O God, our help in ages past 680
O worship the King, all glorious above 388

Lift Every Voice and Sing II
In Christ there is no East or West 62
Love lifted me 198
Jesus, Lover of my soul 79
Take my hand, precious Lord 106
Stand by me 200

Wonder, Love, and Praise
O all ye works of God, now come 884
Precious Lord, take my hand 800

Pentecost

Pentecost

Weekday Commemorations

Monday, August 14
Jonathan Myrick Daniels, Martyr, 1965

Jonathan Myrick Daniels was born in Keene, New Hampshire, in 1939. From high school in Keene to graduate school at Harvard, like many young adults Jonathan wrestled with vocation, until his discernment was clarified by a profound conversion on Easter Day 1962 and subsequently entered seminary. In March of 1965, the televised appeal of Martin Luther King Jr. to come to Selma to secure for all citizens the right to vote touched Jonathan's passions for the well-being of others, the Christian witness of the church, and political justice. Going to Selma he found himself in the midst of a time and place where the nation's racism and the Episcopal Church's share in that inheritance were exposed. After seminary he returned to Alabama to resume his efforts assisting those engaged in the integration struggle. Jailed on August 14 for joining a picket line, Jonathan and his companions resolved to remain together until bail could be posted for all of them, as it was six days later. Released and aware that they were in danger, four of them walked to a small store. As sixteen-year-old Ruby Sales reached the top step of the entrance, a man with a shotgun appeared, cursing her. Jonathan pulled her to one side to shield her from the unexpected threats and was killed instantly by the 12-gauge blast.

Tuesday, August 15
Saint Mary the Virgin, Mother of Our Lord Jesus Christ

Mary has been honored as the mother of Jesus Christ since the beginnings of the Church. Two gospels tell the story of Christ's birth to a virgin; Luke's gospel glimpses Christ's childhood in Nazareth under the care of his mother and earthly father, Joseph. During Jesus' ministry in Galilee, Mary often traveled with the women who followed Jesus, ministering to him; at Calvary, she stood with the women who kept watch at the cross. After the Resurrection, she accompanied the twelve in the upper room. She was the person closest to Jesus, having humbly accepted God's divine will. Later devotions lay many claims for Mary that cannot be proved by Holy Scripture.

Friday, August 18
William Porcher DuBose, Priest, 1918

DuBose spent most of his life as a professor at the University of the South, at Sewanee, Tennessee. He became well known at the age of fifty-six when he published the first of several books on theology Fluent in Greek and other languages, doctrine and life were always in close relationship with DuBose, who treated them as if they were always in dramatic dialogue, fusing contemporary thought and criticism with his own inner faith.

The Twelfth Sunday after Pentecost: Proper 15

August 20, 2023

Faith brings salvation to Jews and Gentiles alike.

Color Green

Preface Of the Lord's Day

Collect

Almighty God, you have given your only Son to be for us a sacrifice for sin, and also an example of godly life: Give us grace to receive thankfully the fruits of his redeeming work, and to follow daily in the blessed steps of his most holy life; through Jesus Christ your Son our Lord, who lives and reigns with you and the Holy Spirit, one God, now and for ever. *Amen.*

Readings and Psalm

Genesis 45:1–15

Today's reading describes Joseph's revelation of his identity to his brothers. Joseph, who had recognized his brothers, had planted a silver cup in his youngest brother Benjamin's food bag. When the cup is conveniently "found," Joseph demands that the boy remain as a slave in Egypt. The brothers are filled with sadness because they know that if anything happens to Benjamin, the aged Jacob will certainly die of sorrow. Joseph is so overcome with emotion when he perceives the repentance of his brothers that he reveals to them that he is their long-lost brother. He also explains that he knows that his enslavement in Egypt was God's way of ensuring their survival from the famine and thus also making sure that God's promises would be fulfilled.

Psalm 133

The psalmist offers a blessing for the covenant people that is also appropriate for families trying to live in unity.

or

Isaiah 56:1, 6–8

Today's reading continues many earlier themes, but with a change of focus. The terms "justice" and "right," previously applied to God's acts of deliverance, are here meant to be human qualities. In looking to the messianic age, Isaiah encourages those formerly regarded as hopelessly outside the covenant bond. Since God's "house" is intended to be open for "all peoples," no outcast should be downcast. Entrance into the covenant community will no longer be a matter of physical birth, ritual cleanness, or national identity, but rather a matter of individual choice and fidelity.

Psalm 67

This psalm is a thanksgiving for a good harvest. In opposition to the Canaanite fertility religions, the Israelites centered their praise directly upon God and God's relationship to the peoples of the world rather than upon the processes of nature.

Pentecost

Romans 11:1–2a, 29–32

In chapters 9–11 Paul has been wrestling with the problem of the rejection of Jesus by those whose whole history and relationship with God was a preparation for the Messiah. On the surface this looked like a frustration of God's purpose, but Paul establishes God's sovereignty in the working out of salvation history. Israel, not God, is responsible for its own rejection of the gospel, for Israel has failed to understand the meaning of its own tradition. Paul sees Israel's history as fulfilled in Christ (10:4, 9), but Israel has insisted on righteousness by works (9:31–32). Nonetheless God has foreseen and provided for this, too. Israel's failure is partial, for a remnant has believed (11:5); and it is temporary, for it is not irremediable (11:11). Because of the Jews' resistance, the gospel has been taken to the Gentiles, but this mission's success will lead to the Jews' restoration (11:25–26).

Matthew 15:(10–20) 21–28

Jesus' encounter with a Canaanite woman (vv. 21–28) foreshadows the offer of salvation beyond Israel to the Gentiles. The center of interest is not the miracle but Jesus' attitude toward Gentiles. A distinction is made between Jesus' mission and his response to individual faith wherever found. Matthew emphasizes for his Jewish Christian audience that God has been faithful to Israel but that Gentile faith cannot be denied.

Prayers of the People

Sisters and brothers, there's a wideness in God's mercy like the wideness of the sea! Therefore let us come before our loving God, saying, "Hear us, we humbly pray; *Lord, help us.*"

Loving God, you have shown your Church such great mercy. Through the witness of your Church, may those beyond our walls also experience the goodness of your mercy.

Silence

Hear us, we humbly pray;

Lord, help us.

Lord of all peoples, you have created us to live together. Help us to see that our common life depends on each other's work and goodwill. Cause wars to cease and generosity to prevail.

Silence

Hear us, we humbly pray;

Lord, help us.

Abundant God, you make the earth bring forth good food. As you provided for the children of Israel, we pray you will also provide for all those suffering from famine or need.

Silence

Hear us, we humbly pray;

Lord, help us.

Caring God, how good and pleasant it is when your children live together in unity. Pour out a spirit of reconciliation in our community.

Invite the congregation to add thanksgivings, followed by silence

Hear us, we humbly pray;

Lord, help us.

Lord Christ, may those who call out to you in great faith find your heart open to their cries. We ask for healing for the sick and suffering, the desperate, and disturbed.

Invite the congregation to add their petitions, followed by silence

Hear us, we humbly pray;

Lord, help us.

God of blessing, bless your people with life forevermore. May the dying find comfort; may the dead rest in your peace.

Silence

Hear us, we humbly pray;

Lord, help us.

Images in the Readings

That Jesus obliquely refers to the Canaanite woman as a **dog** has inspired much creative interpretation over the centuries. Traditionally the sentence was explained away as the technique Jesus employed to test the woman's faith. Some contemporary exegesis reads the exchange seriously and thus credits the woman with instructing Jesus about the breadth of God's mercy. Both of these explanations assume that the story is accurate historical reporting. The story also suggests that if our faith is strong enough, our wishes will be granted. Like the Jesus of Matthew's narrative, we too think of the other as a dog. Like the storyteller, we hope that our faith will bring us instant healing. It is a difficult story to proclaim and expound.

Despite our knowledge of anatomy, the **heart** continues over the millennia to be an image for the source and center of human intention.

Ancient temples were understood to be **houses of the deity**. Architecturally similar to the Lincoln Memorial, an open structure housed a statue of the god or goddess, and sacrifices were offered before the image of the divine. After the exile, strict traditionalists urged hierarchical regulations about how close to the presence of God each type of person could come. But Third Isaiah rejects this understanding of worship, saying the house of God will welcome all peoples. Christians have thought about their churches as in some way houses of God for all peoples. Yet for Christians, God dwells in the community and in word and sacrament, not in a house, and church buildings are less like temples and more like meeting places for the communal prayer of all peoples.

Ideas for the Day

♦ This psalm has a walking rhythm that isn't entirely lost in translation. Could it perhaps be shared by a group of pilgrims, making their way to a festival? Or is there another setting that it calls to mind—a hike or a campout? The imagery certainly suggests Passover and the Exodus: enemies rising, water that could have overwhelmed, but did not. It is a shared lyric of reorientation, of having had the experience of being under the thumb of real enemies and knowing real relief. Is there a song that sings to you that we are never left alone by God in pain and fear and panic?

♦ Do any of us think that Peter responded, "Yay, I get to be the judge for all eternity and decide who is in or out"? Do any of us think that if we were offered control of the keys to the kingdom of heaven that this would be a good thing? There is a powerful moment in the book *The Shack* when God offers the father, Mack, the ability to be the judge. God says, "You have already proven yourself very capable [of judging], even in our short time together. And besides, you have judged many throughout your life. You have judged the actions and even the motivations of others, as if you somehow knew what those were in truth. You have judged the color of skin and body language and body odor. You have judged history and relationships. You have even judged the value of a person's life by the quality of your concept of beauty. By all accounts, you are quite well-practiced in the activity."[1] Mack was scared to death. The God option, if we are to judge, turns out to be love—only love—always love.

♦ Peter is a symbol of leadership for the Church. What are Peter's qualities that give him this distinction? We are called to build our faith on a solid foundation so we can follow in Christ's footsteps, as well as all those who have come before us in recognizing the true nature of Jesus. Who has also shown the traits that we can model ourselves after (in our world today or in the past)?

Making Connections

The Canaanite woman is a prophet. She stands in the long line of those who argue with God and find that God is willing to change for our sakes. She puts her trust in God's promise of righteousness. She knows that God's property is always to have mercy—something more than just being nice to us.

Too often we want God to be another piece of technology that makes our lives easier. The Canaanite woman shows that faith is sticking to God, even when every sign says we shouldn't. She knows that our attempts at being good to get God's favor are bound to failure. God wants to transform us right now, not when we think we're ready.

Jesus has learned from the prophet Hosea the same lesson we must learn: "I desire mercy, not sacrifice." God operates out of mercy for us even when we don't believe it.

---

1 William P. Young, *The Shack* (Thousand Oaks, CA: Windblown Media, 2007), ch. 11.

Pentecost

Engaging All Ages

Today's passages are largely about transition, one thing becoming another thing—both physically and mentally. At this time of year, many people are also making transitions into new jobs, lifestyles, and of course schools. Consider planning some sort of acknowledgement or rite of passage for these big and small transitions. Blessing of the backpacks, hands, work bags, and other similar tools of work or play can be meaningful—especially when it is inclusive of all stages and ages of life.

Hymns for the Day

The Hymnal 1982

God moves in a mysterious way 677 [SC]
From all that dwell below the skies 380 [GR]
God of mercy, God of grace 538 [GR]
How wondrous and great thy works, God of praise!
    532, 533 [GR]
My God, thy table now is spread 321 [GR]
Only-begotten, Word of God eternal 360, 361 [GR]
We the Lord's people, heart and voice uniting 51 [GR]
In your mercy, Lord, you called me 706
Praise, my soul, the King of heaven 410
Sing praise to God who reigns above 408
There's a wideness in God's mercy 469, 470
O Spirit of the living God 531
O Zion, haste, thy mission high fulfilling 539
Thou, whose almighty word 371

Lift Every Voice and Sing II

Pass me not, O gentle Savior 139

Wonder, Love, and Praise

Weekday Commemorations

Thursday, August 24
Saint Bartholomew the Apostle

One of the twelve apostles, he is known to us only by being listed among them in the synoptic Gospels. His name means "Son of Tolmai," and he is often identified with Nathanael, the friend of Philip. Some sources credit Bartholomew with having written a Gospel, whose existence was known to Jerome and Bede, but which is lost today. There is a tradition that he traveled to India, bringing "the Gospel according to Matthew" in Hebrew there.

Friday, August 25
Louis, King, 1270

Louis IX of France was canonized by the Church in 1297. A man of unusual purity of life and manners, he was sincerely committed to his faith and to its moral demands. Courageous and fearless in battle, patient and uncomplaining in adversity, he was an impartial, just, and compassionate sovereign. He died while on crusade in Tunis. Because of his determined effort to live a personal life of Franciscan poverty and self-denial in the midst of worldly power and splendor, Louis is honored as a patron saint of the Third Order of St. Francis.

The Thirteenth Sunday after Pentecost: Proper 16

August 27, 2023

The foundation of faith.

Color   Green

Preface   Of the Lord's Day

Collect

Grant, O merciful God, that your Church, being gathered together in unity by your Holy Spirit, may show forth your power among all peoples, to the glory of your Name; through Jesus Christ our Lord, who lives and reigns with you and the Holy Spirit, one God, for ever and ever. *Amen.*

Readings and Psalm

Exodus 1:8–2:10

The Exodus account of God's liberation of the Hebrew people from their slavery in Egypt begins as the Egyptian Pharaoh plots to subject the slaves to greater forced labor and kill all their newborn males, which would mean the end of God's promise to Abraham of numerous descendants. The story moves from the general situation to the particular story of Moses. To avoid the Pharaoh's death sentence, Moses' mother hides him in a basket near the river, where he is found by the Pharaoh's daughter. She makes arrangements that the child be raised by a Jewish woman until he is old enough to be raised as her son.

Psalm 124

This is a psalm of thanksgiving that recalls that the existence of the people of Israel depends upon God, who saved them from the various enemies that threatened them.

or

Isaiah 51:1–6

In today's reading, Isaiah calls upon the disheartened exiles to remember God's acts in the past so as to be prepared for their deliverance in the future. "Rock" is a description for God, but here the author may be stressing instead Israel's fundamental character or solidarity in time with the patriarchs. As the Lord fulfilled the promise to Abraham against all hope, so God will redeem Israel now. Isaiah cries out against the lack of justice and righteousness in Judah (1:21, 5:7), but repeats his hope (2:1–4) that Jerusalem will be the center from which God's instruction and justice will be offered to the Gentiles (42:4).

Psalm 138

Although all creation is under God's care, the Lord's intimate love is available to each individual.

Romans 12:1–8

Paul begins the next section of his letter with a "therefore" that depends upon the whole of chapters 1–11. Paul has set forth God's act of redemption in Jesus Christ and has explained the outworking of salvation history. Now he turns to the Christian response. Paul exhorts the Romans not to "be conformed," to the pattern of "this world," the present age that is slipping away. Rather, by the renewal of their minds, Christians are to live now as if in the age to come. Thus they are being "transformed" from within. No longer bound by the external law, Christians discover whether their behavior accords with the will of God by proving or testing it in relation to the image of Christ being formed within.

Matthew 16:13–20

Today's reading recounts Peter's confession of Jesus as the Christ (Mark 8:27–29; Luke 9:18–20; John 6:67–69), and Jesus' proclamation of Peter as the rock. The common expectation was that the Christ, the Davidic Messiah, would reestablish kingly rule in some final way (24:3; Acts 1:6). Jesus radically reinterprets this expectation by joining it immediately to the charge to his disciples not to use this term and to the prediction of his suffering, death, and resurrection.

Prayers of the People

I appeal to you, brothers and sisters, by the mercies of God, to present your bodies as a living sacrifice, holy, and acceptable to God, which is your spiritual worship. Therefore let us come humbly before God, saying, "Our help is in your name, O Lord; *deal well with us.*"

Generous God, you have graciously given the members of your Church diverse gifts: may we, who are many, function in this world as the one body of your Son Jesus Christ.

Silence

Our help is in your name, O Lord;

Deal well with us.

God of the nations, mysterious and unexpected are the instruments of your salvation. Give us eyes to see your work in the lives of the most humble servants and the grandest royalty. Bless all those who put their trust in you.

Silence

Our help is in your name, O Lord;

Deal well with us.

Great God, the maker of heaven and earth, bring forth fruits in due season. May all the people of the world experience the blessing of sun and rain and harvest.

Silence

Our help is in your name, O Lord;

Deal well with us.

Caring God, give to the people of our region sober judgment. May each member of our community live in light of the great mercy you have shown us.

Invite the congregation to add thanksgivings, followed by silence

Our help is in your name, O Lord;

Deal well with us.

Lord God, be on the side of those in need of our prayers. May the sick and sorrowful not be overwhelmed but, instead, find freedom in you.

Allow the congregation to add their petitions and thanksgivings, followed by silence

Our help is in your name, O Lord;

Deal well with us.

Almighty God, you have promised through your beloved Son that not even the gates of Hades will prevail against the people of your redeeming. May all of the dead find comfort in your heavenly kingdom.

Silence

Our help is in your name, O Lord;

Deal well with us.

Images in the Readings

Rock is an image for the day. The psalms speak of the safety accorded by the rock; the prophet likens his religious heritage to a rock; Simon gets the name Peter, "Rocky." The Sermon on the Mount speaks of Jesus' teaching as a rock on which we are to build, and Paul writes in 1 Corinthians 4 that the rock from which water flowed was Christ. According to Jewish legend, the miraculous rock followed the Israelites throughout their nomadic decades, perpetually providing water. For Christians, the water of baptism follows the body of Christ, watering us throughout our journey. According to the worldview of the New Testament, **Hades,** the lowest of the three levels of the universe, housed the dead. Matthew uses the category Hades to indicate the challenge that confronts the Christian community: to fight against the power of death. Eastern Orthodox Christians especially recall this worldview in their beloved icon of the resurrection, in which Christ is standing on the broken doors of Hades and is raising from death into his arms both Adam and Eve.

The Isaiah reading includes the image of the **arm of the Lord**. In the Old Testament, God is described in terms humans know: God has ears, eyes, a mouth, fingers, hands, and strong arms. In the story of Noah's flood, God even smells the pleasant odor of the animal sacrifices. Our task is to ensure that these bodily images do not demote the divine into merely a superman. Christians can apply these very images to **the body** of Christ.

Ideas for the Day

♦ Two crucial skills of servant leadership are being able to listen, and the willingness to trust. To listen with true attentiveness is listening that is observant and patient and does not jump to conclusions, especially regarding what people are capable of—even ourselves. Moses is invited into so much more than he knew—a deep listening to God's intention and presence. He has to let go and trust God to be with him; he has what is needed in this moment. This is the kind of servant leadership that God sends to interrupt suffering and desperation.

♦ If we read the scripture carefully, we discover that the name of God is I AM and not I AM WHO I AM. When we struggle with trying to figure out who God is and what God is up to, it might be best to simply return to God's name, I AM. At some point, we might actually believe the name. At some point, we might even trust the name; we might even base our faith on the name. God simply IS. On one hand, it is the simplest reality to grasp and on the other hand it is the deepest, most mysterious, most profound truth we will ever experience.

♦ People are truly formed as Christians when they are part of a congregation that lives out Paul's words, "Rejoice with those who rejoice, weep with those who weep." How do you invite individuals in the congregation to fully take on this role of hospitality, listening, and walking alongside others in all times and circumstances?

Making Connections

This story from Matthew talks about how we gain spiritual insight, and what it can do to prepare us to take up God's work in the world: at the intersection of choice and action, you have to trust your gut.

Similarly, we stand at an intersection where we must respond to the destructive powers that seek to corrupt and destroy the creatures of God. Some days, it seems like the challenges we face are greater than our abilities. But we stand on the solid rock of God's presence in our lives.

When it seems like there's nothing we can do, remember that rock. When it looks like there is too much dread on the horizon, remember that rock. When it seems like we have run out of ideas to face the days ahead, remember that rock. Nothing can overpower it. Nothing can break it apart. Nothing can take it away.

Engaging All Ages

This week, have your kids practice yelling, "Get behind me, Satan!" Kidding. (Unless the mood strikes and, in that case, go with God!) In all seriousness, it can be powerful to reflect on our stumbling blocks—places and things that stretch us. It isn't sexy or fun, but sometimes a reminder of the importance of our weekly, corporate confession and the role of passing the peace as a reconciling way to prepare for communion can be helpful. Perhaps you might consider organizing a fellowship event—a potluck, perhaps—where the theme is community and reconciliation, complete with prompts at each table to start and continue conversations.

Pentecost

Hymns for the Day

The Hymnal 1982

I come with joy to meet my Lord 304
Our Father, by whose Name 587
Praise the Lord, rise up rejoicing 334
Put forth, O God, thy Spirit's might 521
Thou, who at thy first Eucharist didst pray 315
The God of Abraham praise 401 [GR]
To God with gladness sing 399 [GR]
God is Love, and where true love is 576, 577
Holy Spirit, font of light 228
Like the murmur of the dove's song 513
Lord, you give the great commission 528
O Holy Spirit, by whose breath 501, 502
Take my life, and let it be 707
Where charity and love prevail 581
From God Christ's deity came forth 443
Glorious things of thee are spoken 522, 523
The Church's one foundation 525
You are the Christ, O Lord 254

Lift Every Voice and Sing II

Wonder, Love, and Praise

Come now, O Prince of Peace 795
Unidos/Together 796
The desert shall rejoice 722 [GR]
Gracious Spirit, give your servants 782
Lord, you give the great commission 780
Muchos resplandores / Many are the lightbeams 794
Ubi caritas et amor 831

Weekday Commemorations

Monday, August 28
Augustine of Hippo, Bishop and Theologian, 430
Called "the greatest theologian in the history of Western Christianity," Augustine, born in 354 in North Africa, became a Christian in 386 under the guidance of his mother, Monnica. He was baptized by Ambrose, bishop of Milan, in 387. He returned to North Africa in 391, whereupon he was chosen by the people of Hippo to be a presbyter; four years later, he became bishop of Hippo. About 400, he wrote his spiritual autobiography, *The Confessions*; the extended prayer became a classic. Augustine wrote reams of treatises, letters, and sermons, thereby providing a rich source of insights into Christian truth. In 410, he wrote his greatest work, *The City of God*.

Tuesday, August 29
The Beheading of Saint John the Baptist
John baptized Jesus. John's preaching foretold Jesus' ministry and his death. All four Gospels describe John the Baptist as the prophet and preacher who created the advent of expectation and who awakened the repentance that leads to baptism. Herod demanded John's beheading out of fear of a leader among the people. Two Sundays in Advent focus on John's preaching; the First Sunday of Epiphany celebrates Jesus' baptism as fulfilling Christ's humanity and revealing his divinity. John's ministry had been integral to the start of Jesus' work: John's death marked a turning point toward Jerusalem and Jesus' death on a cross.

Wednesday, August 30
Margaret Ward, Margaret Clitherow, and Anne Line, Martyrs, 1588, 1586, and 1601
Ward, Clitherow, and Line were among victims of anti-Catholic violence on the part of Anglicans when armed Catholics and Protestants shamefully pursued the righteousness of Christ. Ward, "the Pearl of Tyburn," helped a Roman Catholic priest so was hanged. Clitherow, "the Pearl of York," was condemned for converting to Roman Catholicism and crushed to death on Good Friday. Line converted, also, and kept a house of refuge for fugitive priests; her house was raided on Candlemas. She, too, was hanged, declaring her only regret was that she could not offer sanctuary to a thousand more priests.

Thursday, August 31
Aidan, Bishop, 651

After the see-sawing of Christianity and paganism in Northumbria in Northern England, Oswald regained the throne and restored the Christian mission begun in 627 when his uncle, Edwin, was converted by a mission from Canterbury. During his exile, Oswald had lived at the monastery of Iona, where he had been converted and baptized, so he sent to Iona for missionaries. Gentle Aidan, head of the new mission, set his work on the distant island of Lindisfarne. He and his monks and their trainees restored Christianity in Northumbria, extending the mission through the midlands and as far south as London. According to the Venerable Bede, Aidan delighted in giving to the poor whatever kings gave to him.

Friday, September 1
David Pendleton Oakerhater, Deacon, 1931

Known as "God's warrior" among the Cheyenne Indians of Oklahoma, Oakerhater was originally a soldier who fought against the US government with warriors of other tribes in the disputes over Indian land rights. Upon his capture in 1875, he learned English, gave art and archery lessons to other prisoners in Florida, and had his first encounter with the Christian faith. This led to his call to transform his leadership in war into a lifelong ministry of peace. Baptized in 1878, he was ordained to the diaconate in 1881 and returned to Oklahoma where he was instrumental in founding schools and missions through great personal sacrifice.

Saturday, September 2
The Martyrs of New Guinea, 1942

Christians began evangelizing on New Guinea in the 1860s and 1870s, to little effect; Anglicans, specifically, began their mission there in 1891. Their first bishop was consecrated in 1898. This mission field still offers challenges because of the difficult terrain on the second largest island in the world and because the indigenes speak some five hundred distinct languages. During World War II, missionaries and native peoples were sorely tried. This feast day marks the witness of eight missionaries and two Papuan martyrs, betrayed by non-Christians to the Japanese invaders. The day remembers the faith and devotion of Papuan Christians, who risked their own lives to save the lives of others.

Pentecost

The Fourteenth Sunday after Pentecost: Proper 17

September 3, 2023

Pentecost

The cost of discipleship.

Color Green

Preface Of the Lord's Day

Collect

Lord of all power and might, the author and giver of all good things: Graft in our hearts the love of your Name; increase in us true religion; nourish us with all goodness; and bring forth in us the fruit of good works; through Jesus Christ our Lord, who lives and reigns with you and the Holy Spirit, one God for ever and ever. *Amen.*

Readings and Psalm

Exodus 3:1–15

This passage records Moses' life-changing encounter with God. Here God's name and character are revealed as Moses is commissioned as God's agent. The fiery bush signifies God's presence and activity. In response to God's presence, Moses hides his face, for in Hebrew thought it was fatal to see the Lord directly. God is revealed as the transcendent Other who chooses to be in a relationship of commitment and even intimacy with God's people. God is One who sees, hears, knows, and has come down to deliver. God's transcendent holiness does not preclude divine immanence and compassion.

Psalm 105:1–6, 23–26, 45c

This hymn praises God who promised the land of Canaan to the covenant people and then kept the promise.

or

Jeremiah 15:15–21

Jeremiah's proclamation to the people in exile—that Babylon was the instrument of God's judgment upon the people and that Judah should not resist—caused him to be regarded as a traitor by his own people. He has prayed for his enemies (14:7–11), but they have not listened to God's message. Now the prophet's concern for them is exhausted and he cries out for the Lord to take vengeance upon them. He affirms that he has been nourished on God's word (1:9), but protests that God's hand, usually a figure of inspiration and blessing, has become an intolerable burden. God responds that if Jeremiah will return again, assurance of support will also be renewed (1:18–19). The reward for Jeremiah's faithful service is not relief from suffering but more service.

Psalm 26:1–8

This psalm is an expression of innocence, perhaps as a ritual purification before entering the temple or participating in worship.

Romans 12:9–21

Love for one another must be without hypocrisy, characterized by humility, generosity, and sympathy. Christians should earn a reputation for meekness, moral uprightness, peacefulness, and patience. They should recoil with loathing from evil and embrace all that is good. Their passion for prayer and service should not diminish over time, but continue to result in blessing and a willingness to give themselves in humility to whatever tasks God presents. Revenge belongs to God alone. In verse 20, Paul quotes Proverbs 25:21–22 to illustrate the overcoming power of kindness. Such acts of goodness may or may not lead to the enemy's repentance, but they have an intrinsic power that is stronger than evil and will, finally, prevail.

Matthew 16:21–28

The anticipation of suffering and death was totally at odds with what was expected for and of the Messiah. Peter expresses this, once again speaking as the disciples' representative. Matthew makes Peter's response more vivid than Mark did by putting it into direct speech (Mark 8:32). Jesus responds to Peter's rebuke as a continuation of Satan's temptations in the wilderness (4:10). As Peter has been called the rock of foundation for the Church (16:18), so here he is a "stumbling block" because he has his mind set on human goals and priorities. Jesus also teaches the disciples that, as suffering is the price of messiahship, so it is also the cost of discipleship. The disciples must "deny themselves"—renounce all human things that keep them from following the example of Jesus.

Prayers of the People

My sisters and brothers, be kindly affectioned one to another with love. And let us come before God, saying, "We glory in your holy name, *and offer to you our prayer, O Lord.*"

Lord Jesus, you bid your disciples take up their cross and follow you: may your holy Church desire, above all, the things of God that we might overcome evil with good.

Silence

We glory in your holy name,

> *And offer to you our prayer, O Lord.*

Lord God of our forebears, you know the sorrows of the afflicted: Deliver those who are being oppressed. And grant your peace to all the world.

Silence

We glory in your holy name,

> *And offer to you our prayer, O Lord.*

Good Lord, you make known your wondrous works: reveal yourself in the works of your hands as you did to Moses our forebear on the holy mountain.

Invite the congregation to add their thanksgivings, followed by silence

We glory in your holy name,

> *And offer to you our prayer, O Lord.*

O Lord, grant that the people of our land be given to hospitality. May we abhor that which is evil and cleave to that which is good and, in so doing, may we live peaceably one with another.

Silence

We glory in your holy name,

> *And offer to you our prayer, O Lord.*

Strong Lord, make us weep with those who weep. Reveal your strength to the weak and lowly that they may rejoice in all your marvelous works.

Invite the congregation to add their petitions, followed by silence

We glory in your holy name,

> *And offer to you our prayer, O Lord.*

Almighty God, you reward each one according to their works: Give to the dead rest from their labors and life everlasting.

Silence

We glory in your holy name,

> *And offer to you our prayer, O Lord.*

Images in the Readings

That believers are to deny themselves, take up their **cross,** and follow Jesus has been a commonplace message throughout Christian centuries. Care must be taken that more privileged persons do not mouth these words to the less privileged, to those with minimal power to affect their own situation, as if what Jesus meant was to suffer in silence. All the baptized have been marked by the cross, and in the mystery of the resurrection, this cross is the way to life. Perhaps the cross we are called to carry is someone else's, which we willingly help to carry. One possibility is that Matthew was referring to the Tau, the sign of the end time for those who await the return of Christ.

Jesus calls Peter **Satan,** the one who opposes God. Ancient Israel knew no supernatural power of evil. In the Book of Job, the Satan is in God's throne room, goading God and accusing the righteous. By the time of Jesus, largely through influence of their Zoroastrian neighbors, Jews had come to believe in a supernatural being who personified evil and who, like the medieval devil, tempted persons to immoral behavior. Yet Christian theology has always resisted the popular dualist idea that there is a good god and a bad god and that human life is the battlefield between God and the devil. According to the New Testament, evil, although still present, has already been conquered in Christ's resurrection. Satan is behind us. Watch the remarkable film *The Apostle*, in which during the final sermon the Holiness preacher calls out to the devil, "Get behind me! Get behind me!"

The **burning coals** is an image for the shame that evildoers will experience when they encounter Christian forgiveness and generosity. In Romans 12:20, Paul is quoting Proverbs 25:21–22, an example of the degree to which Christian ethics repeats the teachings of the Hebrew scriptures.

Ideas for the Day

◆ Wicked is the most common English translation of the Hebrew *rasha*. However, the likely origin of the word "wicked" in English is connected to people, usually women, who were accused of witchcraft. While it has come to mean something closer to what the Hebrew word meant—corrupt, profane, wrongful—today we are subject to all sorts of reframing of such judgments. Does the prophetic witness urge us to have more candor about the wickedness: corruption, profanity, and victimization that is laying waste to God's creation and our neighbors?

◆ The Jewish ritual of Passover begins with a loaf of bread that is blessed and shared. The ritual concludes with the final cup of wine that is blessed and also shared by each person. In between the first action and the final action is what the Jewish people know to be the complete story of salvation. On Sundays, when we celebrate the Eucharist, might it be a good practice to be aware of the space found in between the paragraphs during the Words and Institution, and consider *that* space holds the entire story of salvation for us as well? Jesus certainly did.

◆ We have a responsibility to confront the evil that we see in ourselves, in one another, and in our society. On the other side of confrontation is forgiveness. We do not confront to destroy a person. We confront to lead a person into a deeper relationship with God and with neighbor.

Making Connections

I received an email from a new Episcopalian asking when they were to make the sign of the cross in the liturgy. I wrote a reply saying that people make the sign of the cross all the time, for all sorts of reasons.

But Jesus tells his followers that the sign of the cross is for one reason. It isn't as much about blessing yourself, or claiming protection, or an outward sign of piety; Jesus tells his followers that the sign of the cross is about giving up illusions and becoming real.

Jesus' words are a counter-narrative to everything that we hear in the world around us. What I hear around me are messages about minimizing risk and preventative care, safe boundaries and burrowing ever more deeply in my personal silo of security. Jesus is making a completely opposite claim: deny your own safety so that you can become fully alive. More than anything making the sign of the cross is an outward commitment to life in Jesus, life beyond the fear of death.

Engaging All Ages

Jesus provides protocols for handling troublesome church members. Interestingly, it is also good instruction on how to be an ally and an advocate for church members. For instance, the care of each child and youth in your church is important. Being the most loving, trusting, and forgiving of God's creations, young people can find themselves used and abused by others. Are there ways you can act as an ally and advocate to prevent such things? What protocols does your church implement to care for young people? In what ways can you talk about this with adults, youth, and children?

Hymns for the Day

The Hymnal 1982

Lord, dismiss us with thy blessing 344
We plow the fields, and scatter 291
What wondrous love is this 439 [SC]
The God of Abraham praise 401 [SC]
We sing of God, the mighty source 386, 387 [SC]
When Israel was in Egypt's land 648 [SC]
If thou but trust in God to guide thee 635 [GR]
Surely it is God who saves me 678, 679 [GR]
God is Love, and where true love is 576, 577
Holy Spirit, font of light 228
Like the murmur of the dove's song 513
Lord, whose love through humble service 610
O Holy Spirit, by whose breath 501, 502
Take my life, and let it be 707
Where charity and love prevail 581
Where true charity and love dwell 606
Day by day 654
New every morning is the love 10
Praise the Lord through every nation 484, 485
Take up your cross, the Savior said 675

Lift Every Voice and Sing II

Go down, Moses 228 [SC]
Where He leads me 144
I have decided to follow Jesus 136

Wonder, Love, and Praise

When from bondage we are summoned 753, 754 [SC]
Cuando el pobre nada tiene /
    When a poor one who has nothing 802
Gracious Spirit, give your servants 782
Put peace into each other's hands 790
The church of Christ in every age 779
Ubi caritas et amor 831
Will you come and follow me 757
You laid aside your rightful reputation 734

Weekday Commemorations

Monday, September 4
Paul Jones, Bishop, 1941

As bishop of Utah, Paul Jones (1880–1941) did much to expand the church's mission stations and to strengthen diocesan institutions. At the same time he spoke openly about his opposition to war. At a meeting of the Fellowship of Reconciliation in 1917, Bishop Jones expressed his belief that "war is unchristian," for which he was attacked with banner headlines in the Utah press. Yielding to pressure, Bishop Jones resigned in spring 1918. In his farewell to the Missionary District of Utah, he said, "Where I serve the Church is of small importance, so long as I can make my life count in the cause of Christ . . . but no expedience can ever justify the degradation of the ideals of the episcopate which these conclusions seem to involve."

Tuesday, September 5
Katharina Zell, Church Reformer and Writer, 1562

Zell, a Strasbourg Protestant (b. 1497), chose the holiness of marriage in 1523 over celibacy. Martin Zell was a priest when religion frowned on clergy for marrying. However, his outspoken bride defended the wedding of clergy in a pamphlet explaining to her fellow laity the biblical basis for marriage and for women to speak out—both acts of love, she claimed. The Zells welcomed eighty Christians driven from their homes for their beliefs; her refugees included John Calvin when he fled France. She also visited those sick with the plague and syphilis. Persistent, her last publication commented on the Psalms.

Wednesday, September 6
Hannah More, Religious Writer and Philanthropist, 1833

More, born in 1745 and raised in the Church of England, began writing as a child. Her first works were poems and women-centered plays for performance in girls' schools. In the 1780s, the abolitionist James Oglethorpe befriended her and influenced her. Her antislavery poems, though not always elegant, reached a public more interested in poetry than politics. More also published works on religion: *Practical Piety*, *Christian Morals*, and *The Character of St. Paul*. A philanthropist, More established twelve schools for the poor, donated money to Bishop Philander Chase for Kenyon College, and set up Sunday schools.

Pentecost

Thursday, September 7
Kassiani, Poet and Hymnographer, 865

The only woman whose writing appears in official liturgies of the Orthodox Church, Kassiani was born wealthy before 810 and well educated. She entered the monastic life as a nun and exploited her distinct talents for music and literature. She courageously defended veneration of icons and also founded a new convent. Unafraid to enter theological controversies, she declared: "I hate silence when it is time to speak." By 843, she'd built a convent on Xerólophos, the seventh hill of Constantinople, and become its first abbess. Hundreds of her poems are extant; about fifty of her hymns are still sung.

Friday, September 8
The Nativity of the Blessed Virgin Mary

Little is known of Jesus' mother—not her home or family. She may have descended from David's line and been brought up in a Jewish family that cherished the hope of Israel for the coming kingdom of God in remembering the promise to Abraham and the forebearers. In the second century, a devout Christian cobbled an account of Mary's birth in an apocryphal gospel, *The Nativity of Mary*. It included legends about Mary's parents, Joachim and Anne, a childless couple rewarded with the birth of a girl. The story goes that they dedicated her life to the service of God.

Saturday, September 9
Constance, Thecla, Ruth, Frances, Charles Parsons, and Louis Schuyler, Martyrs, 1878

The Sisters of the Community of St. Mary came to Memphis in 1875 in the middle of a yellow fever epidemic; instead of opening a girls' school as planned, the women cared for the sick. When the plague hit again in 1878, many professionals fled. But a few doctors stayed alongside Episcopal and Roman Catholic clerics and nuns, among other religious. Sisters Ruth and Helen came from the order's motherhouse. Within three weeks, Sister Constance died (September 9), followed by Sisters Thecla, Frances, and Ruth, doctors and clerics, and a devoted laywoman, in addition to twelve Roman Catholic clerics and thirty-four nuns. Many witnesses to the Great Physician—winners for their orders of an "imperishable renown"—share burial plots. They have ever since been known as the "Martyrs of Memphis."

The Fifteenth Sunday after Pentecost: Proper 18

September 10, 2023

The church is vested with Jesus' authority. Guidelines for discipline and other aspects of church life.

Color   Green

Preface   Of the Lord's Day

Collect

Grant us, O Lord, to trust in you with all our hearts; for, as you always resist the proud who confide in their own strength, so you never forsake those who make their boast of your mercy; through Jesus Christ our Lord, who lives and reigns with you and the Holy Spirit, one God, now and for ever. *Amen.*

Readings and Psalm

Exodus 12:1–14

Today's reading interrupts the narrative flow of the exodus story to give the community detailed instructions for celebrating the Passover. This meal is to be an annual memorial recalling the pivotal experience of the community's rescue by Yahweh from their slavery in Egypt. Celebrating the Passover ritual makes the exodus experience present to each generation, who in turn must attune their lives to the covenantal responsibilities that emerged from their relationship with Yahweh. Situated at the start of their year, the Passover ensures that each year will be consecrated by the memory of the community's founding experience of liberation.

Psalm 149

This psalm is a hymn of triumph celebrating God's mighty deeds in Israel's salvation history and imagining the establishment of justice on earth.

or

Ezekiel 33:7–11

Ezekiel's prophetic ministry to his people extended from before the fall of Jerusalem in 586 BCE to the time of the exile in Babylon. Today's reading harks back to Ezekiel's concern for individual responsibility. The sentinel or watchman, chosen by the townspeople, was responsible for warning them of the approach of an enemy. They then could come in from the fields and take refuge. In this passage, God both chooses the watchman and sends the awaited enemy in judgment. There is an implicit tension between the punishment of the wicked and the desire that they repent and live. Israel believed that mere membership in the community of God's people guaranteed salvation; here God declares that the individual is responsible for his or her own choices.

Psalm 119:33–40

The psalmist asks God to help understand and observe the commands of Torah and so follow the path of goodness and justice.

Romans 13:8–14

Paul concludes this section of moral exhortation (chaps. 12–13) with the principle that underlies his specific directions: love of neighbor. This is the obligation we always owe, summed up in the "royal law" (Leviticus 19:18; James 2:8). For Paul, love of neighbor is the direct overflow of our experience of God's love poured into our hearts. This gift is now to be poured into the lives of those around us. Since the gift we have been given by God cannot be directly repaid, we direct the repayment to others. As we become channels of grace, we discover that we are fulfilling God's law by loving others as God does.

Pentecost

Matthew 18:15–20

Today's reading speaks of discipline within the community of disciples, who are the Church. The responsibility of seeking out the erring member, based on Old Testament precedent, was an early part of the Christian community's behavior. If the member refuses to respond, even to the pleas of the assembled congregation, he is to be treated as "a Gentile and a tax collector" (v. 17), that is, by inviting him to enter the community through faith. Jesus models this treatment in his ministry by eating with tax collectors and "sinners" (9:9–13) and praising the faith of Gentiles.

Prayers of the People

Our Lord Jesus has promised that, when we gather in his name, he is here among us. Let us pray saying, "We are gathered in your name; *accept our prayers.*"

O Lord, you take pleasure in your people: May your Church be a community of honesty and humility. Help us to love each other—especially when love is a challenge.

Silence

We are gathered in your name;

Accept our prayers.

O Lord, you adorn the poor with victory: be with the hungry and the oppressed. Comfort the grieving. Give peace to all whose lives have been upset by natural disaster and war.

Silence

We are gathered in your name;

Accept our prayers.

O Lord, you have caused grapes to grow on the vine and wheat to grow in the fields so that we might celebrate this festival today. Bless the land to grow enough that all people may celebrate its bounty.

Invite the congregation to add their thanksgivings, followed by silence

We are gathered in your name;

Accept our prayers.

O Lord, your Law is summarized, "Love your neighbor as yourself." Help us to love our neighbors so that we might do no wrong by anyone.

Silence

We are gathered in your name;

Accept our prayers.

O Lord, may all those who now lament see the day when they shall sing to you a new song—a song of joy and praise. May those who weep, dance for joy. May the anxious rest on their beds in peace. And may all know that it was you, the Lord, who did this.

Invite the congregation to add their petitions, followed by silence

We are gathered in your name;

Accept our prayers.

O Lord, care for the dead as they await the great day of resurrection. May all who have died rest in your peace.

Silence

We are gathered in your name;

Accept our prayers.

Images in the Readings

We are **bound**, we are **loosed**: these are strong images describing the powers that hold us captive and the gift of God's Spirit that frees us for a life of love. The responsibility for correction, discipline, and forgiveness belongs to the community.

Tax collectors were despised collaborators who were infamous for cheating. Mercifully, Jesus is described as eating with tax collectors. This is good news for all of us.

Ezekiel calls us to be **sentinels**, those assigned to watch from the city walls for both any approaching dangers and any welcome visitors. The life of the Christian is an active life, watching in the world for the bad and the good and reporting to the community what we see.

Paul calls us to wake up; the **day** has come; get dressed, wearing Christ, for today there might be a battle.

In his mixing of metaphors, Paul blends the robe of baptism with the **armor** of a warrior. It's a dangerous world out there, everywhere affected by human sin.

Ideas for the Day

+ The exodus narrative is a central image of salvation history in the Old Testament. It is used to underscore the witness of real rescue from terrible forces of evil and it is also a metaphor for liberty from more obscure oppressions. Yet perhaps the words bring you pause, because you or someone near to you has served in the military. Hearing that warriors are being extinguished can be alarming. It is possible to feel both united to the liberation and sympathy for the soldiers who are thrown down. Learning how to be creative and compelling witnesses to the love of God when our feelings are complex is part of the lifelong journey of life together.

+ We all seem to like winning. We all seem to enjoy the party that often follows. Sometimes there is music, dancing, and cheers. So here is a challenge to us all: We know that God was with the people of Israel on the other side of the Red Sea. But if we believe that God is everywhere, then wouldn't it be true that God might also have been consoling the hearts of the widows, mothers, and daughters of Egypt? Can we imagine that God's love might ever extend beyond the winners? Can we imagine that God's mercy can override the political breaks in our world and in our society? It might be interesting for us to take a look and see what God is doing on the "other" side.

+ The passing of the peace is an acting-out of a forgiveness principle. God's forgiveness must be passed on to others if it is to be realized in our own lives. So when you are offering your gift at the altar, if you remember that your brother or sister has something against you, leave your gift there before the altar and go; first be reconciled to your brother or sister, and then come and offer your gift (Matthew 5:23–24).

Making Connections

Any time the Gospel talks about sin, it is in the context of God's loving forgiveness. In the Gospels, Jesus doesn't show a lot of interest in people's morality, but he is always restoring people to relationships of love and forgiveness.

We need to remember this to live as the community of Jesus. Our love is a decision. And we need the community's support for loving the unlovable because, without that support, no one can hope to live in service to others. To be faithful, we must take up the hard work of love with others.

This is one of those instances where it really is more important to be religious than it is to be spiritual. It's great to have your own private spiritual experience. But loving others, practicing your spiritual life in a place where people might challenge you, or confront you, or need you is hard. And it is the reign of God come to earth.

Engaging All Ages

How do we learn to forgive? Or maybe forgiveness is innate, the fingerprints of the divine touching our bodies even now after generations and generations. Forgiveness is a word that is used a lot in church, so it has the opportunity to lose some of its punch. Forgiveness is radical! For kids and youth, a take on the youth ministry game "Honey, I love you but I just can't smile." (See: You can't possibly forgive me again, right? I love you, and yes I forgive you again) might work well to unpack this week's readings. And maybe don't limit it to kids and youth! Let adults have some of that youth group fun as well!

Pentecost

Pentecost

Hymns for the Day

The Hymnal 1982

At the Lamb's high feast we sing 174 [SC]
The Lamb's high banquet called to share 202 [SC]
From deepest woe I cry to thee 151 [GR]
Lord Jesus, think on me, and purge away
    my sin 641 [GR]
'Tis the gift to be simple 554 [GR]
Awake, my soul, and with the sun 11
Awake, my soul, stretch every nerve 546
Awake, thou Spirit of the watchmen 540
Eternal Ruler of the ceaseless round 617
For the fruit of all creation 424
Jesu, Jesu, fill us with your love 602
All creatures of our God and King 400
Blessed Jesus, at thy word 440
Christ is made the sure foundation 518
Father, we thank thee who hast planted 302, 303
"Forgive our sins as we forgive" 674
God is love, and where true love is 576, 577
Joyful, joyful, we adore thee 376
Lord, make us servants of your peace 593
Singing songs of expectation 527
Where charity and love prevail 581
Where true charity and love dwell 606

Lift Every Voice and Sing II

Come, ye disconsolate 147 [GR]
Jesu, Jesu 74

Wonder, Love, and Praise

Lord Jesus, think on me, and purge away
    my sin 798 [GR]
Come now, O Prince of Peace 795
Unidos / Together 796
We all are one in mission 778

Weekday Commemorations

Tuesday, September 12
John Henry Hobart, Bishop, 1830

Buried beneath the chancel of Trinity Church in
New York City, lies John Henry Hobart, a staunch,
devoted, missionary-minded American Churchman
of the Episcopal Church. Hobart, born September
14, 1775, graduated from Princeton in 1793, and
was ordained a priest in 1801, having become an
assistant minister at Trinity the year before. He was
consecrated assistant bishop of New York in 1811;
five years later, he became diocesan bishop and rector
of Trinity. Within his first five years as bishop, Hobart
doubled the number of clergy and quadrupled the
number of missionaries. He planted a church in almost
every major town of New York State and served as
missionary among the Oneida Indians. He was a
founder of General Theological Seminary.

Wednesday, September 13
Cyprian, Bishop and Martyr of Carthage, 258

Cyprian so declared: "You cannot have God for your
Father unless you have the Church for your Mother."
Cyprian was born rich and lived an aristocratic and
cultivated life in North Africa before converting to
Christianity about 246. He was chosen bishop of
Carthage two years later. His hiding in 249 during
a persecution led to criticism; despite absence, he
continued to lead the church with compassion.
His sympathy continued after the persecution in
his handling of other lapsarians who fled, and his
moderate position prevailed. In another time of
persecution under Emperor Valerian, Cyprian, while
under house arrest in Carthage, was beheaded. Many
of his writings—on the Lord's Prayer, on unity in the
Church—have been preserved.

Thursday, September 14
Holy Cross Day

Supervision over the work of erecting a building complex in Jerusalem to mark the site of Christ's resurrection was entrusted to the empress Helena, mother of Emperor Constantine. Under Helena's direction, the excavation discovered a relic, believed to be of the "true cross." Calvary stood outside the city in Jesus' time; when *Aelia Capitolina* succeeded Jerusalem, the hill was buried under construction fill. Constantine's magnificent shrine included two main buildings: a basilica and a round church known as "The Resurrection." The buildings were dedicated on September 14, 335, the seventh month of the Roman calendar; the date was suggested by the account in 2 Corinthians of the dedication of Solomon's temple hundreds of years before.

Friday, September 15
Catherine of Genoa, Mystic and Nurse, 1510

Catherine (b. 1447) married at sixteen to ward off family feuds. Husband and wife were miserable: he was profligate with sex and money, which depressed her. On March 22, 1473, Catherine had a mystical, lifechanging experience of God's overwhelming love. Afterwards, she combined an intense, contemplative life with an active dedication to caring for the sick. Amazingly, her husband joined her in this good work, and the two became close, eventually moving into a large hospital in Genoa to devote themselves as caregivers. There, Catherine dictated works of mystical theology, which were published forty years after her death.

Saturday, September 16
Ninian, Bishop, c. 430

The Venerable Bede wrote about Ninian in *Ecclesiastical History*; otherwise, little verifiable information is available. Ninian, a Romanized Briton, was born late in the fourth century in Scotland, and may have been educated and ordained in Rome. He spent much time with and was heavily influenced by Martin of Tours in forming ideals of an episcopal monastic structure for missionary work. Candida Casa, Ninian's base, which is dedicated to Martin, sits in Galloway. Ninian's work may have covered the Solway Plains and the Lake District of England. He serves, with Patrick, as a link between the ancient Roman/British Church and the developing Celtic churches of Scotland and Ireland.

Pentecost

The Sixteenth Sunday after Pentecost: Proper 19

September 17, 2023

Living in community under God's dominion over evil and sin.

Color   Green

Preface   Of the Lord's Day

Collect

O God, because without you we are not able to please you, mercifully grant that your Holy Spirit may in all things direct and rule our hearts; through Jesus Christ our Lord, who lives and reigns with you and the Holy Spirit, one God, now and for ever. *Amen.*

Readings and Psalm

Exodus 14:19-31

This reading recounts the most exciting and dramatic event in the exodus story. It also demonstrates as no other event both God's power over our world and God's care for the covenant people. Having departed from Egypt, the Hebrews joyously begin their trek to the new land. Pharaoh, however, changes his mind about letting them go and leads his army and chariots in pursuit. Pinned between the sea ahead and the Egyptian chariots behind, the Hebrews cry to God for help. God comes to their aid first by sending a cloud to hide them and then by empowering Moses to part the waters of the sea. The Hebrews are "saved" by passing on dry ground through the wall of waters. When the Egyptian army follows, they bog down in the mud and, when the waters return to normal, are all drowned.

Psalm 114

This hymn of praise recalls God's care for the people on their exodus journey through the wilderness to the promised land. Extraordinary events illustrate God's power over nature, in particular over sea and river, and signify God's presence in their midst.

or

Exodus 15:1b-11, 20-21

This canticle derives from songs celebrating the climactic image of the exodus story: the destruction of Pharaoh's army in the Red Sea and the liberation of the Israelites from bondage in Egypt. It opens with a portion of the Song of Moses, a longstanding canticle in the Christian tradition, and concludes with the brief response of Miriam, Moses' and Aaron's sister.

or

Genesis 50:15-21

This reading concludes the Joseph cycle of stories. Joseph's brothers fulfill the dream with which the stories began (37:5-11; 42:6; 44:14). The author repeats the theme that God used the brothers' wickedness, the Egyptian slavery, and the injustice of Potiphar's household to accomplish good for Joseph, his family, and even for the Egyptians. Joseph remains in a right relationship with God, trusting God's purposes, yielding to God's sovereignty, and recognizing God's authority to judge. He saw the years of suffering and alienation from his family as God's plan: "God sent me" (45:5, 7-8).

Pentecost

Psalm 103:(1-7), 8-13

This hymn of thanksgiving is cast in very general terms, perhaps a recovery from illness. The psalmist affirms the Lord's steadfast love for the covenant people and invites all of creation to join his song of praise. The basis of God's call to forgiveness is found in God's mercy and generosity for humankind, who deserve only judgment (v. 10).

Romans 14:1-12

Today's reading is from a longer section (14:1–15:13) dealing with those who maintain various practices (such as abstinence from certain foods and the observance of special days) and those who do not. Paul's counsel centers around the motive for the behavior. Life and death are equally subject to Christ's Lordship. By his death, resurrection, and complete obedience, Jesus is Lord over all. As Lord, he deserves our service and worship. The choice to eat or to abstain, as every choice, must be made in light of Christ. Christ alone will judge the person's acts and intentions.

Matthew 18:21-25

Today's gospel reading concludes the discourse on discipline in the Church. Matthew presents the material as Jesus' response to a question by Peter. The servant's debt is huge. His promise of repayment is impossible to fulfill, thereby representing humankind's position before God. God's response to limitless debt is limitless forgiveness. The scene is repeated between the slave and his fellow slave, except that the debt is small and repayment feasible. But the wicked slave's response is totally different. The master's question (v. 33) is also posed to the Christian community.

Prayers of the People

Each of us is finally accountable to God. So let us pray, saying, "Lord, we are in need of your mercy; *have patience with us.*"

Lord, we acknowledge that we all sin against our brothers and sisters in Christ. Forgive us even as we forgive each other. Help us to be merciful to each other in the Church.

Silence

Lord, we are in need of your mercy;

Have patience with us.

Lord, we acknowledge that we desire to repay violence with violence. Open our hearts to forgive even those who commit evil acts towards us and those we love. Help us to live mercifully in our world.

Silence

Lord, we are in need of your mercy;

Have patience with us.

Lord, we acknowledge we do not always appreciate the diversity of your creation. Teach us to live in peace with each other and with your creation. Help us to live mercifully with our world.

Silence

Lord, we are in need of your mercy;

Have patience with us.

Lord, we acknowledge that we do not love our neighbors as you love us. Forgive us for placing ourselves as judge over others when judgment belongs to you alone. Help us to accept the great mercy you choose to show others.

Silence

Lord, we are in need of your mercy;

Have patience with us.

Lord, we pray for those whose lives are broken by evil. Because of your mercy we believe that whatever befalls them, they belong to you; you care for the brokenhearted. Help us to share your love with all those who are hurting.

Invite the congregation to add their petitions and thanksgivings, followed by silence

Lord, we are in need of your mercy;

Have patience with us.

Lord, we remember those who died in violence. We remember those men and women of the armed services, innocent bystanders, first responders, and even those we have called enemies. The dead belong to you, O Lord. Even as we seek your mercy for ourselves, judge all those who have died with mercy.

Silence

Lord, we are in need of your mercy;

Have patience with us.

Images in the Readings

Seventy-seven plays with the ancient idea that seven is the number of fullness and perfection, because seven combines three, a number that suggests divinity, and four, recalling the corners of the flat earth. So with seventy-seven, Jesus multiplies the number of total perfection.

Matthew's allegory utilizes imagery from the economic system of the first century: a **lord** was the owner of land and of all those who work the land, and a **slave** was one perpetually in the service of another.

In our English-language Bibles, Hebrew and the Greek words that denote such a masculine societal authority figure are translated as "lord." Christian faith in Christ's resurrection occasions the claim that "Jesus is Lord." "Lord" is the usual circumlocution used in our Bibles to render YHWH, God's first name. That we are slaves of God is New Testament imagery, albeit not a currently popular metaphor.

By the mysterious design of God, **Joseph** brought life to his people. Early Christian preachers saw in the Joseph story a parallel to Jesus, who was first brought low but was then raised to power and authority so as to forgive everyone and to feed the world.

Ideas for the Day

+ The movie *42* is less interested in baseball and more interested in the relationships of Jackie Robinson and Branch Rickey: two people who were led to prophetic action against the racial divide in professional baseball. Whether it is the historic characters or the screenwriters, there is unavoidable evidence of deep Christian formation in the movie conversations about the choice to step up, stand by, and follow through a difficult witness. As offered in the film, the daring action and the strength to weather the storm is evidence of a people who have a whole lot of gumption and plenty of organized Christian study, conversation, and prayer. These are the practices that can prepare believers to lead lives worthy of the gospel they claim to as their own.

+ In the second story of creation, God says to Adam and Eve that they are able to enjoy everything found in the garden with the exception of eating of the fruit of the Tree of Knowledge. Turns out that going for the Tree of Knowledge and eating its fruit was the same as attempting to be like God. It can be said that all sin is our attempt to be like God. God says we should stop trying that. Jonah had a hard time learning this lesson because he thought he knew better than God. Do any of us ever believe and act like that as well?

+ This Sunday begins a four-week, semi-continuous reading of Philippians. In today's portion, he begs them to live worthily of the gospel in unity, harmony, and generosity without grumbling or complaining, keeping always before themselves Jesus Christ as the supreme model for any moral action. How do we stay firm in the faith?

Making Connections

We get so used to transactional relationships, that it is hard to imagine those that are completely gratuitous. This may extend to our understanding of forgiveness. When we talk about forgiveness, if we speak with conditions, then our talk is no longer about forgiveness but a transactional relationship. If we insist on life being fair, we haven't fully realized the hell of living in a world that operates by judgment and by strict repayment of debts.

We betray our understanding of God's forgiveness to the extent that we do not forgive others. If we believe, teach, and proclaim that God forgives sin but then we do not, we haven't believed what we teach and proclaim.

Our challenge is to forgive others in the exact same manner that God forgives us, which is totally, unconditionally, freely, and in love. If we don't forgive, then we're still bound by the violence done to us.

Engaging All Ages

What does radical generosity look like? Who or what might it threaten? Encourage church attendees, young and old, to ponder these questions. A brainstorming session centered around ways they can be generous in their lives and communities might yield some great ideas—especially if you can establish a culture of "Yes, and . . ." that is used by many improv comedy groups. The general idea is: how can we take this one step further? Or to put it in more church-like language: How can we imagine God's kingdom right now? Another option could be a play on the youth group game "Bigger and Better." How can you receive generosity and then turn it into an act of generosity that's bigger and better?

Hymns for the Day

The Hymnal 1982

Guide me, O thou great Jehovah 690 [SC]
Praise our great and gracious Lord 393 [SC]
Sing now with joy unto the Lord 425 [SC]
When Israel was in Egypt's land 648 [SC]
All my hope on God is founded 665 [GR]
God moves in a mysterious way 677 [GR]
O bless the Lord, my soul 411 [GR]
Praise, my soul, the King of Heaven 410 [GR]
Praise to the Lord, the Almighty, the
　　King of creation 390 [GR]
Creator of the stars of night 60
Crown him with many crowns 494
Jesus, our mighty Lord, our strength in sadness 478
All creatures of our God and King 400
"Forgive our sins as we forgive" 674
Go forth for God, go to the world in peace 347
God is Love, and where true love is 576, 577
Joyful, joyful, we adore thee 376
Lord, make us servants of your peace 593
Most High, omnipotent, good Lord 406, 407
Praise the Lord, rise up rejoicing 334
Where charity and love prevail 581
Where true charity and love dwell 606

Lift Every Voice and Sing II

Go down, Moses 228 [SC]

Wonder, Love, and Praise

Wisdom freed a holy people 905 [SC]
Bless the Lord my soul 825 [GR]
No saint on earth lives life to self alone 776
Come now, O Prince of Peace 795

Weekday Commemorations

Monday, September 18
Edward Bouverie Pusey, Priest, 1882

Pusey led the Oxford Movement, which revived High Church teachings and practices in the Anglican Communion. Pusey, born August 22, 1800, spent his scholarly life at Oxford as professor and as canon of Christ Church. With John Keble and John Henry Newman, he produced *Tracts for the Times* in 1833 (thus, the movement is also known as Tractarianism). He proved most influential through sermons catholic in content and evangelical in zeal, but dangerously innovative to some (Pusey was suspended from preaching for two years). Pusey influenced many to remain in the Anglican Church after Newman defected to the Church of Rome in 1845. With his money, he built churches for the poor; with his time, he established the first Anglican sisterhood since the Reformation.

Tuesday, September 19
Theodore of Tarsus, Archbishop
of Canterbury, 690

Although Theodore was sixty-six when ordained archbishop of Canterbury in 668, he provided strong leadership for a generation. He was a learned monk from the East who had been residing in Rome when he began his episcopate. The Church was split between Celtic and Roman customs. When Theodore arrived in England, he set up a school excellent in all disciplines, and he unified Anglo-Saxon Christians, including regularizing Chad's episcopal ordination. He defined boundaries of English dioceses, presided over reforming synods, and laid foundations of parochial organizations. According to Bede, Theodore was the first archbishop whom all English obeyed. He was buried in the monastic Church of Saints Peter and Paul at Canterbury.

Pentecost

Wednesday, September 20
John Coleridge Patteson, Bishop of Melanesia, and His Companions, Martyrs, 1871

Patteson, who was stabbed five times in the breast, and his companions died at the hands of Melanesian islanders—the very people they had tried to protect from slave traders. As a result, the British government took serious measures to prevent pirates from hunting humans in the South Seas. Their martyrdom seeded the vigor of the Melanesian Church today. Patteson, born in Long (1827), was ordained in 1853 after travel in Europe. While a curate in Devonshire, near his family home, he answered a call in 1855 for help in New Zealand, where he established a boys' school on Norfolk Island. He learned, some say, to speak twenty-three of the languages of the Melanesian people.

Thursday, September 21
Saint Matthew, Apostle and Evangelist

A disciple of Jesus the Christ, Matthew left everything to follow the Master at his call. Matthew was identified with Levi, a tax collector, when tax collectors were seen as collaborators with the Roman state and, thus, spurned as traitors. Matthew was hardly the sort of person a devout Jew would associate with, yet Jesus noticed Matthew, rather than someone more pious. The disciple himself probably did not write the gospel of his name, given as author in homage. Through this gospel and its parables, Jesus speaks of faith and eternal life; of duty to neighbors, family, and enemies. Matthew is venerated as a martyr although circumstances of his death are unknown.

Friday, September 22
Philander Chase, Bishop, 1852

Ordained a deacon in 1798, he began mission work on the northern and western frontiers among the pioneers and the Mohawk and Oneida peoples. In 1799, at the age of twenty-three, he was ordained a priest and served as a rector in Poughkeepsie, New York, before moving to New Orleans where he established a church, then to Connecticut, followed by Ohio. In 1818 he was elected the first bishop of Ohio and continued to found new congregations while organizing the diocese. He also established Kenyon College and Bexley Hall Seminary. He served as the presiding bishop from 1843 until his death.

Saturday, September 23
Thecla of Iconium, Proto-Martyr Among Women, c.70

According to tradition, Thecla was a disciple of Paul. After hearing him preach the Gospel, Thecla abandoned marriage plans to follow him. Her legend is found in the second-century *Acts of Paul and Thecla*: Condemned to burn at the stake, she was saved by rain; thrown to beasts in an arena, she was protected by a lioness; baptizing herself in a pool, Thecla saw lightening kill hungry seals therein. Freed by the governor, this proto-martyr proceeded to preach the Word and become one of the most popular saints in the early Church, exemplifying freedom to teach and baptize.

The Seventeenth Sunday after Pentecost: Proper 20

September 24, 2023

God's gracious compassion for all people extends beyond human understanding.

Color   Green

Preface   Of the Lord's Day

Collect

Grant us, Lord, not to be anxious about earthly things, but to love things heavenly; and even now, while we are placed among things that are passing away, to hold fast to those that shall endure; through Jesus Christ our Lord, who lives and reigns with you and the Holy Spirit, one God, for ever and ever. *Amen.*

Readings and Psalm

Exodus 16:2–15

Today's reading recounts one of the many instances of the people's murmuring during the time of the exodus. The Israelites long for the meat and bread they ate in Egypt. The Lord responds by providing for them both flesh and bread, but on God's own terms, one day at a time. Thus God may "test" their faith. God acts, saying: "You shall know that I am the Lord your God" (v. 12). This statement of recognition occurs in the priestly writings, in Isaiah and in Ezekiel. God's actions disclose, to believer and unbeliever, the Lord of our world and life. God provides from nature's bounty for the Israelites, reliably supplying the needs of an unreliable people.

Psalm 105:1–6, 37–45

This hymn praises God who promised the land of Canaan to the covenant people and then kept the promise.

or

Jonah 3:10–4:11

Unlike the other prophetic books, the book of Jonah is not a collection of oracles, but a didactic story about a prophet. It illustrates the principle of human accountability and God's freedom and is a reminder of the availability of God's mercy to all through Israel's mission to the nations. Jonah feels that the meaning of his life has been taken away. He may fear that God's kindness to these Gentiles means the end of Israel's privileged status with God. He forgets that Israel, too, deserves only destruction but receives compassion. And although Jonah received mercy personally, he wants justice untempered by any reprieve for Nineveh. The concern he exhibits for the withered plant is a pale shadow of the care God has for the inhabitants of heathen Nineveh, for both human and beast.

Psalm 145:1–8

This is an acrostic psalm, each verse beginning with a successive letter of the Hebrew alphabet. It invites praise for God's greatness, love of the people, justice, and presence.

Philippians 1:21–30

The church in Philippi was Paul's first congregation formed on European soil, and his relationship with it remained consistently warm and close. In today's selection, Paul meditates upon the possibility of imminent execution. For Paul, both life and death are under the rule of Christ. Though life means communion with Christ, death will bring even fuller communion. Life, however, includes the opportunity to serve Christ further.

Matthew 20:1–16

The parable of the laborers in the vineyard is found only in Matthew. The point of the parable lies in the landowner's actions and is thus sometimes called the parable of the generous employer. The question "Are you envious because I am generous?" (v. 15) may be more literally translated, "Is your eye evil because I am good?" An "evil eye" indicates a jealous, ungenerous, envious attitude. It stands as a reminder to disciples that the first may again become last if they grumble at the reward the Lord gives to others, even to latecomers. The strength of Jesus' message is found in his words about God's generosity. God, as supreme Judge, has the right to say, "I grant mercy to whom I will."

Prayers of the People

Sisters and brothers, turn for help to the Lord your strength and constantly seek God's presence. Let us pray to our generous God, saying, "Lead us with gladness, O God; *cover us with shouts of joy!*"

Generous God, you have chosen us to do the work of your kingdom; you have called us to labor in your vineyard. With grateful hearts, we offer to you the best of what we have.

Invite the congregation to add their thanksgivings, followed by silence

Lead us with gladness, O God;

> *Cover us with shouts of joy!*

Generous God, you hear the cry of the hungry. Give bread to all those who face starvation. Use us, as you will, to relieve suffering in our world.

Silence

Lead us with gladness, O God;

> *Cover us with shouts of joy!*

Generous God, you make rivers run in dry places. You have blessed this earth with bountiful resources. Open our eyes to see your hand at work in the world about us.

Silence

Lead us with gladness, O God;

> *Cover us with shouts of joy!*

Generous God, there is enough kingdom work for everyone. Give us eyes to see the opportunities in our own neighborhood. Guide us that we may live in a manner worthy of the gospel of Christ.

Silence

Lead us with gladness, O God;

> *Cover us with shouts of joy!*

Generous God, you hear the cries of the desperate. Marvelous are your works, O God. May the sick and suffering rejoice in you. May the sorrowful call upon your name.

Invite the congregation to add their petitions, followed by silence

Lead us with gladness, O God;

> *Cover us with shouts of joy!*

Generous God, living is Christ and dying is gain. May those who now rest from their labors find their comfort in you. Let light perpetual shine upon them.

Silence

Lead us with gladness, O God;

> *Cover us with shouts of joy!*

Images in the Readings

The **vineyard** is a common biblical metaphor that designates the religious community. In biblical times wine was not only usually safer to drink than water, but it also symbolized the shared joy of the community. Its production relies on both the blessing of the Creator and the long-term joint efforts of growers and vintners, and its alcohol transforms our very bodies. Yet many congregations are quite stingy with the cup.

The Jonah story provides many allegorical images: **Nineveh** is the powerful enemy; **Tarshish** is for Jonah the farthest destination in the opposite direction away from Nineveh, across the Mediterranean Sea; the **bush** suggests personal comfort; the **worm** suggests God's correction to our selfishness; the **wind** is the breath of God; **Jonah** himself is a comic depiction of our very selves and of the church when we live out of typical human emotions. We too often do not know our right from our left hand. It is a great story.

The **spirit** of the Risen Christ will bring us into the unity expressive of a mutually forgiving community.

Ideas for the Day

- Every congregation is in some sort of transitional time, whether you know it or not, and whether you like it or not. Many are built on memories of a church-going bubble, and now we find ourselves anxious and thirsty for anything except this unsettling experience. We crave the old sense of security and we wonder how we can dare to live into the mission of Jesus we promised ourselves to. Whether we are like Moses in the desert, Ezekiel in exile, or the Jesus movement of the letters—we are called to unselfish humility and courageous love to meet the difficulties of a transitional time.

- Ezekiel offers a pastoral reminder that life towards God is better than life away from God. Again we find ourselves in yet another attempt to be God and attempt to control life for ourselves. Ezekiel is not the nicest prophet but at least he tries to tell the people the truth. Maybe it is just the way we have translated the words. Ezekiel says "repent" and maybe we should hear "turn around." It certainly is not as judgmental. Consider this, if you will; sometimes the whole world is taking a picture of something very special. Try turning around and then take that picture. You might be surprised with the image you capture.

- Paul describes the humility of Jesus Christ in the words of an ancient hymn that extols the saving work of Christ. If the hymn is about Christ, it is also about God, making clear the true nature of God. God's true nature is not selfishly to seize but openhandedly to give. Paul is appealing to the Philippians who were acting selfishly, living with a grasping attitude. Paul appeals to them to bring their conduct into harmony with the conduct of Christ. How does this "hymn" from today's epistle speak to us today?

Making Connections

Parables are not analogies; the vineyard owner in this parable is not God. Just notice how little he pays the workers: a denarius. That's the amount that a family can just hope to subsist on. These wages keep people poor. The vineyard owner is not doing much to help them out. He's giving them just enough to survive in their precarious lives.

This is the opposite of God. God doesn't just give us enough to scrape by. God gives us the full abundance of every good gift. The vineyard owner turns out to be the same old boss: a human model of grasping after more. He's the one who keeps people poor. This isn't the God of Jesus Christ.

The God of Jesus Christ makes himself known as the least and the last among mortals, bringing with him the blessing of eternal life. This is the one on whom we are called to pattern our lives.

Engaging All Ages

Today's Gospel passage never gets played for the humor that is so obviously found in the text. On that note, how can humor be something that brings revelation? Grace? Healing? Consider organizing an improv night. There are tons of resources available online that require little to no setup—only people willing to have fun. A fun twist could be picking out well-known Bible verses and using them as the prompts, asking participants to act out the different parts of the story.

Pentecost

Pentecost

Hymns for the Day

The Hymnal 1982

Glorious things of thee are spoken 522, 523 [SC]
Guide me, O thou great Jehovah 690 [SC]
How sweet the Name of Jesus sounds 644 [SC]
Lamp of our feet, whereby we trace 627 [SC]
Lord, enthroned in heavenly splendor 307 [SC]
O Food to pilgrims given 308, 309 [SC]
Shepherd of souls, refresh and bless 343 [SC]
Give praise and glory unto God 375 [GR]
God, my King, thy might confessing 414 [GR]
O bless the Lord, my soul 411 [GR]
Praise, my soul, the King of heaven 410 [GR]
We will extol you, ever-blessed Lord 404 [GR]
Eternal Ruler of the ceaseless round 617
For thy dear saints, O Lord 279
God be in my head 694
My God, accept my heart this day 697
Singing songs of expectation 527
Christ the worker 611
Come, labor on 541
For the bread which you have broken 340, 341
From glory to glory advancing, we praise thee,
     O Lord 326
Lord of all hopefulness, Lord of all joy 482
Not here for high and holy things 9
O Jesus, I have promised 655
O Master, let me walk with thee 659, 660
Rise up, ye saints of God 551
Strengthen for service, Lord 312

Lift Every Voice and Sing II

Jesus in the morning 76

Wonder, Love, and Praise

All who hunger gather gladly 761 [SC]
God be with you till we meet again 801 [SC]
We all are one in mission 778

Weekday Commemorations

Monday, September 25
Sergius of Radonezh, Monastic, 1392

Sergius' name is familiar to Anglicans from the
Fellowship of St. Alban and St. Sergius, the society
dedicated to promoting relationships between
Anglican and Russian churches. To the people of
Russia, Sergius serves as their patron saint. Born
in 1314, he was twenty when his brother and he
secluded themselves in a forest and developed the
Monastery of the Holy Trinity, a center for reviving
Russian Christianity. There, Sergius remained, a
simple servant, mystical in temperament and eager
to see his monks serve their neighbors. Sergius'
support of Prince Dimitry Donskoi rallied Russians
against Tartar overlords, thereby laying a foundation
for independence. Pilgrims visit his shrine at the
monastery of Zagorsk, which he founded in 1340.

Tuesday, September 26
Lancelot Andrewes, Bishop of Winchester, 1626

Andrewes' sermons, witty and grounded, made him
King James I's favorite preacher. Andrewes (born
1555 in London) was also a fine biblical scholar, able
in Hebrew and Greek, who served as a translator
for the Authorized (King James) Version of the
Bible. As dean of Westminster and headmaster of
its school, he influenced the education of many
churchmen, including poet George Herbert. *Preces
Privatae* illustrates his piety. He strongly defended the
catholicity of the Church of England against Roman
Catholic critics. He was a model bishop, even when
bishops were not esteemed. T. S. Eliot was inspired by
Andrewes' Epiphany sermon for the opening stanza of
"The Journey of the Magi."

Wednesday, September 27
Euphrosyne / Smaragdus of Alexandria,
Monastic, 5th century

Although her father planned her future with a
handsome husband, Euphrosyne rebelled, ran away,
cut her hair, donned men's clothing, and presented
himself as Smaragdus. He entered a monastic
community outside of Alexandria, progressing
in prayer and wisdom. When Smaragdus' father
Paphnutius visited the monastery to grieve his
daughter, the abbot sent father to son for spiritual
direction. Paphnutius failed to recognize his child in
his director for years. Only when Smaragdus lay dying
did the father see his daughter in his spiritual guide.
After Smaragdus' death, Paphnutius became a monk,
living in his child's cell the rest of his life.

Thursday, September 28
Paula and Eustochium of Rome, Monastics
and Scholars, 404 and c. 419

Paula (b. 347) and her daughter Eustochium (b. 386)
served as calming companions to the irascible scholar
Jerome, whom Paula met in 382. The two women
often recalled him to the image of Christ as mild
and humble. Eustochium vowed to remain a virgin,
instructed by Jerome's *De custodian virginitatis.* The
women, fluent in Greek, mastered Hebrew under
Jerome's tutelage. They followed him to the Holy
Land, where they settled in Bethlehem. There, Paula,
a Desert Mother who surrendered her wealth to the
service of God, built four monasteries, presiding over
them for twenty years, followed by Eustochium.

Friday, September 29
St. Michael and All Angels

Of the many angels spoken of in the Bible, only
four are called by name: Michael, Gabriel, Uriel,
and Raphael. The archangel Michael is the powerful
agent of God who wards off evil from God's people
and delivers peace to them at the end of this life's
mortal struggle. "Michaelmas," as his feast is called in
England, has long been one of the popular celebrations
of the Christian year in many parts of the world. The
archangel Michael is the patron saint of countless
churches.

Saturday, September 30
Jerome, Priest and Scholar, 420

Jerome was the foremost biblical scholar of the
ancient Church. His Latin translation of the Bible
from the original Hebrew and Greek texts known as
the Vulgate version, along with his commentaries and
homilies on the biblical books, have made him a major
intellectual force in the Western Church.

The Eighteenth Sunday after Pentecost: Proper 21

October 1, 2023

Society's outcasts are often more righteous before God than those who consider themselves righteous.

Color   Green

Preface   Of the Lord's Day

Collect

O God, you declare your almighty power chiefly in showing mercy and pity: Grant us the fullness of your grace, that we, running to obtain your promises, may become partakers of your heavenly treasure; through Jesus Christ our Lord, who lives and reigns with you and the Holy Spirit, one God, for ever and ever. *Amen.*

Readings and Psalm

Exodus 17:1–7

This is the second story about thirst and water in Exodus (see also 15:22–27). The stories are probably variants of the same tradition. The geographical differences in the accounts led to the later rabbinical story that the miraculous rock, source of providential water, followed the Israelites in their wandering. For people living in an arid land, thirst was a powerful metaphor for a human's need for God. Moses uses the staff that made the Nile foul to bring forth clean water. Israel's murmuring is a constant feature of the Exodus narratives. This incident at Massah (meaning "proof") and Meribah (meaning "find fault") became a byword for Israel's faithlessness.

Psalm 78:1–4, 12–16

This psalm is a long recital of the story of Israel's relationship with God. It encourages the audience to learn the lessons from their history and respond more appropriately to God's choice of them as covenant partners.

or

Ezekiel 18:1–4, 25–32

Ezekiel defends God's honor and righteousness and offers comfort and hope to the exiles. He draws upon the slowly emerging idea of individual responsibility, as found in the call to a personal examination of conscience in the liturgical rite for access to the temple and in other prophetic warnings. Israel's injustice blinds its understanding of God's ways. Yet God is free to promise life even to the wicked if they repent. They are called to a renewal of covenant with the Lord and a new life. Only God's purposes define true fairness.

Psalm 25:1–8

This acrostic psalm, each verse beginning with a successive letter of the alphabet, is a personal lament.

Philippians 2:1–13

Paul follows his exhortation to steadfastness in relation to the outside world (1:27–30) with an exhortation to harmony and to humility within the community of believers. Verses 6–11 of today's passage are generally considered to be a pre-Pauline hymn to Christ that Paul adopted to make his own point. The first stanza (vv. 6–8) recounts Jesus' own action. His "equality with God" is not a prize "to be exploited" for his own advantage. The second stanza of the hymn (vv. 9–11) stresses God's response to Jesus' obedience. The name God has bestowed on Jesus is Lord, (Greek, *Kyrios*), the circumlocution used by Jews as a substitute for speaking the Name of God, YHWH.

Matthew 21:23–32

The parable of the two sons is found only in Matthew and is the first of three parables on the judgment of Israel. Jesus insists that actions, not words, are the ultimate signs of obedience. Here Jesus defends his ministry of inviting into God's kingdom those outcast from Jewish society. Even though tax collectors and prostitutes live outside the law, they repent when the gospel of the kingdom is offered to them. They push ahead into the kingdom of God "ahead of" (v. 31; or even "instead of") the leaders who have sworn obedience to the law, but who will not accept the work of faith in the new law of Jesus.

Prayers of the People

Brothers and sisters, in humility regard others as better than yourselves. Humbly then, let us approach our God, saying, "To will and work for your good pleasure, *O Lord, enable us.*"

Christ Jesus, strengthen our tongues to declare you as Lord of our lives. May we, your Church, glorify your Heavenly Parent in word and deed.

Silence

To will and work for your good pleasure,

O Lord, enable us.

Christ Jesus, you chose not to exploit your equality with God, but humbled yourself to be with us. Give us your heart for the marginalized and poor. And may all people, especially those in power, follow your example of humility.

Silence

To will and work for your good pleasure,

O Lord, enable us.

Christ Jesus, by your birth in human likeness you blessed all of creation. Remind us that your feet have trod our soil and tasted our waters. Give us the will to care for this precious planet.

Silence

To will and work for your good pleasure,

O Lord, enable us.

Christ Jesus, you rule the world with love and compassion. Give to our local leaders compassion and vision that the people of our region might live as neighbors, looking out for each other's interests.

Silence

To will and work for your good pleasure,

O Lord, enable us.

Christ Jesus, you became obedient to the point of death that we might have abundant life. Work marvels in the lives of the sick and sorrowful. May they recount to generations the wonderful deeds you have done in their lives.

Invite the congregation to add their petitions and thanksgivings, followed by silence

To will and work for your good pleasure,

O Lord, enable us.

Images in the Readings

The parable speaks of a good and a bad **son.** Christianity lauds yet another son, the "only Son," who both answers yes and does the will of God. In the biblical worldview, a son is not understood as an independent agent, but is an extension of the father, owing the father everything. As well, according to the biological understanding of the time, it was the sperm that conveyed full humanity to the fetus. This sense of the child's connection with the parent is evident also in the reading from Ezekiel. Our culture thinks differently.

We are very distant from the first-century's horror at the image of the **cross.** The Roman government reserved this method of death by torture for the lowest criminals, and in Deuteronomy 21, even God is said to curse anyone executed by hanging on a tree. In the fourth century, the emperor Constantine outlawed crucifixion as a mode of execution, and since then jewels and gold, art and design have made of the cross an often beauteous sign of veneration. Some scholars suggest that "even death on a cross" is a Pauline interpolation into the hymn. The Good Friday liturgy invites persons to come forward to a full-sized roughhewn cross and bend the knee before it in praise of Jesus.

Pentecost

Pentecost

Ideas for the Day

- Why would someone abandon a vineyard? Even in the biblical era the cost of establishing a vineyard was considerable. There are two primary reasons: disease and changes in water availability. There are some vineyards that once made good wine and no longer do. That is good and healthy to name out loud for any organization. Love and keeping something going forever are not the same thing. Is a healthier more authentic and kingdom bearing vineyard (and therefore wine) what God is calling us to? If we trust in the steadfast love of God, we must put on the confidence that God is helping us to let go and to plant vineyards that yield fine life-giving fruits.

- For many years, the actual tablets from the film *The Ten Commandments* were in the narthex at St. Stephen's Episcopal Church in Hollywood, California. They were large (and they didn't weigh very much). The Ten Commandments seem to be so important to people that they are often found in many other places etched in heavy stone. Rules must be followed. "So let it be written. So let it be done!" How many of us remember that four are on one tablet and six on the other? Jesus knew this. The first tablet shows how we are to love God with all our being. The second tablet shows we might love our neighbor as ourselves. Now where can we hang that?

- The concept of stewardship comes out strongly in today's readings. We are stewards, not owners, of the Lord's vineyards. We will be called to an accounting of the stewardship of our resources. Our responsibility to bring justice, to use our resources wisely, and to be concerned for the environment is a part of our stewardship. Stewardship is more than a financial pledge to the church. It is a way of life in which we all recognize our responsibility to be faithful stewards.

Making Connections

The Baptismal Covenant provides a way of assessing the church's stewardship of God's vineyard. The vineyard that we care for is not ours, but God's. What does this say about the way we should take care of our homes, our resources, and one another? How do we share and spread our resources for continuing the apostles' teaching and fellowship, proclaiming the Good News of God in Christ, seeking and serving Christ in all persons, and striving for justice and peace?

Engaging All Ages

We live in a world of rejected things. A lot of it has to do with a lack of creativity, not to mention a materialistic view of the world that tells us we need more, better, *bigger* things. However, our story is one of rejected things that are given new purpose— restored, reconciled, resurrected. This week, encourage people to look for something that's been rejected (something that's been thrown away, something donated to a thrift shop, a forgotten present or piece of clothing in a closet—be creative!) Bring these items to church as object lessons, or even use them to make new creations (think: repurposing t-shirts or turning old sweaters into potholders).

Hymns for the Day

The Hymnal 1982

Come, thou fount of every blessing 686 [SC]
Glorious things of thee are spoken 522, 523 [SC]
Guide me, O thou great Jehovah 690 [SC]
O Food to pilgrims given 308, 309 [SC]
O God, unseen yet ever near 332 [SC]
Rock of ages, cleft for me 685 [SC]
Shepherd of souls, refresh and bless 343 [SC]
Surely it is God who saves me 678, 679 [SC]
Before thy throne, O God, we kneel 574, 575 [GR]
'Tis the gift to be simple 554 [GR]
All hail the power of Jesus' Name! 450, 451
All praise to thee, for thou, O King divine 477
At the name of Jesus 435
Morning glory, starlit sky 585
O Spirit of the living God 531
Sing, ye faithful, sing with gladness 492
The head that once was crowned with thorns 483

What wondrous love is this 439
Deck thyself, my soul, with gladness 339
Lord, dismiss us with thy blessing 344
Lord, we have come at your own invitation 348
O day of God, draw nigh 600, 601

Lift Every Voice and Sing II
Come, thou fount of every blessing 111 [SC]
Trust and obey 205

Wonder, Love, and Praise
Gracious Spirit, give your servants 782
You laid aside your rightful reputation 734

Weekday Commemorations

Tuesday, October 3
John Raleigh Mott, Ecumenist
and Missionary, 1955

Mott connected ecumenism and evangelism, following his mission's motto: "the evangelization of the world in this generation." As a young man (b. 1865, Cornell Class of '88), Mott volunteered in many capacities. He thought Christian communities needed to cooperate in the mission field, and he presided over the broadest gathering of Christian missionaries to that point. He drove the founding of the World Council of Churches. He received the Nobel Peace Prize in 1946 for establishing and strengthening international organizations working for peace. Although Mott was a Methodist, the Episcopal Church made him an honorary canon of the National Cathedral.

Wednesday, October 4
Francis of Assisi, Friar, 1226

After a misspent youth, as well as encounters with beggars and lepers, Francis embraced a life devoid of material goods. In 1210, Pope Innocent II confirmed the Rule of the Order of Friars Minor, the name chosen by Francis to underscore the "least" of God's servants. The order grew so large and lax that, by 1221, Francis had lost control of it. He remained joyful in his last years despite grievous suffering in body and spirit. Near his death, Francis received the *stigmata*, marks of Jesus' wounds, in his own hands and feet and side. Pope Gregory IX canonized Francis in 1228. Francis is admired for his bond with animals, if not imitated for voluntary poverty.

Friday, October 6
William Tyndale, Priest, 1536

William Tyndale was born about 1495 near the Welsh border. With degrees from Oxford and having studied at Cambridge, he was ordained about 1521 and served as a chaplain and tutor. However, he was a man with a single passion—to translate the Holy Scriptures in English. Lacking official sanction, he went to Germany in 1524 only to have his work strongly opposed by King Henry VIII, Cardinal Wolsey, and others. Betrayed by a friend, Tyndale was strangled and burned at the stake in Brussels. Years later, in 1535, Miles Coverdale completed the first translation of the whole Bible into English. Archbishop Thomas Cranmer adopted Coverdale's translation of the Psalter for the Book of Common Prayer 1539.

Saturday, October 7
Birgitta of Sweden, Mystic, 1373

Birgitta Birgersdotter, born in 1303 to a noble family, discerned a religious vocation early but was married at thirteen and had eight children. She practiced asceticism secretly. She had visions as a child, hearing Christ, Mary, and saints' warning voices in Swedish. She was discomfited when the voices became political; still, she criticized the king as a symbol of aristocracy. Birgitta counseled popes, clergy, and rulers, finding fault with their extravagance. She founded the Brigittine order, based on earlier revelations, and worked tirelessly for the pope to return to Rome from Avignon.

Pentecost

The Nineteenth Sunday after Pentecost: Proper 22

October 8, 2023

In the parable of the vineyard, Isaiah and Jesus both warn God's people that they will be held accountable for the fruits of the covenant.

Color   Green

Preface   Of the Lord's Day

Collect

Almighty and everlasting God, you are always more ready to hear than we to pray, and to give more than we either desire or deserve: Pour upon us the abundance of your mercy, forgiving us those things of which our conscience is afraid, and giving us those good things for which we are not worthy to ask, except through the merits and mediation of Jesus Christ our Savior; who lives and reigns with you and the Holy Spirit, one God, for ever and ever. *Amen.*

Readings and Psalm

Exodus 20:1–4, 7–9, 12–20

The Ten Commandments set forth the duties of the Israelites to God (20:3–11) and to those within the community (20:12–17). The commandments are covenant demands founded on their special relationship to God. The commandments concerning human interrelationships have parallels in other ancient cultures, but those concerning the people's relationship to God are unique to the Hebrew Bible.

Psalm 19

The psalmist celebrates God's revelation, expressed universally in creation and especially in the law.

or

Isaiah 5:1–7

Today's prophetic parable, the song of the vineyard, celebrates the expectation of the harvest. The audience are invited to pass judgment on the vineyard, a frequent image for Israel. The grapes are more than merely wild, they are "rotten grapes." The vine grower devoted his best efforts only to reap decay. Only in verse 7 does Isaiah's audience discover it has judged itself. Judgment and justice grow out of the covenant bond between God and the people.

Psalm 80:7–14

This lament of the nation for deliverance probably comes from the northern kingdom, whose tribes are enumerated.

Philippians 3:4b–14

Chapter 3 discusses Paul's opponents in Philippi who thought that Christians ought to keep the Jewish law, especially circumcision. Using a commercial metaphor, Paul responds to this by drawing up a profit-and-loss statement. What once he counted as assets—his Hebrew genealogy, his upbringing, and his strict observance of the law—he now counts as loss in comparison to the "value of knowing Christ" (v. 8). Paul, once religiously affluent, has been bankrupted by Jesus. He experienced the annulment of all his former values. Righteousness, a relationship of intimacy with God, is humbly received as a gift.

Matthew 21:33–46

The parable of the wicked tenants is rooted in the economic life of Galilee. Landowners were often absentee foreigners, resented by the local peasantry. The estate of such a foreigner was regarded as ownerless if he died without an heir, and the occupants would then have first claim upon the property. Thus, in the parable when the son arrives, the tenants may assume that the father has died and hope to claim the vineyard after killing the son. Matthew strengthens the allegorical references in the parable. The slaves clearly stand for the prophets, for the landowner (Matthew's metaphor for God in 20:1) sends two groups of slaves, reproducing the Jewish distinction between the former and latter prophets. The fate of the slaves is that of the prophets.

Prayers of the People

Sisters and brothers, the law of the Lord is perfect and revives the soul! So let us appeal to our Lord God, saying, "Let the words of our mouths and meditations of our hearts be acceptable in your sight, *O Lord, our strength and our redeemer.*"

Lord our God, you command us to have no other gods before you: give your Church such singleness of mind that we might not be distracted by the rubbish of our lives, but may strive to know Christ and the power of his resurrection.

Silence

Let the words of our mouths and meditations of our hearts be acceptable in your sight,

O Lord, our strength and our redeemer.

Lord our God, you command us to bear not false witness against others: Help us to live in peace with one another. In a world of harmful rhetoric, may we use our words to encourage and love—especially those whom we consider different.

Silence

Let the words of our mouths and meditations of our hearts be acceptable in your sight,

O Lord, our strength and our redeemer.

Lord our God, you command us to keep a holy Sabbath: make us generous stewards of this planet that it may be renewed and refreshed.

Silence

Let the words of our mouths and meditations of our hearts be acceptable in your sight,

O Lord, our strength and our redeemer.

Lord our God, you command us to covet nothing that belongs to our neighbor: give us kind and generous hearts for those with whom we share our neighborhoods. May a loving spirit rule this region.

Silence

Let the words of our mouths and meditations of our hearts be acceptable in your sight,

O Lord, our strength and our redeemer.

Lord our God, you desire that your people be not afraid: Pour on the sick, suffering, and struggling the abundance of your mercy. Bless them with goodness and healing through Jesus the Christ.

Invite the congregation to add their petitions and thanksgivings, followed by silence

Let the words of our mouths and meditations of our hearts be acceptable in your sight,

O Lord, our strength and our redeemer.

Lord our God, you have made us your own: may we, and those who have run the race of faith before us, attain the resurrection from the dead through the abundant mercy of your Son.

Silence

Let the words of our mouths and meditations of our hearts be acceptable in your sight,

O Lord, our strength and our redeemer.

Pentecost

Images in the Readings

The importance of wine in the diet of biblical societies is evident in the Bible's continual use of the **vineyard** as an image of the people. Wine, suggesting the goodness of communal participation, serves as a corrective to more recent individualist interpretations of Christian faith. Vineyards grow from age-old roots and require dedicated tending. God owns the vineyard: we are only renters; we need to collaborate with one another to produce good wine.

The passage in the Psalms about the rejected stone becoming the **cornerstone** caught on in Christianity. In Ephesians 2:20 Paul calls Christ Jesus the cornerstone of the household of God; in Acts 4:11 Luke uses cornerstone as a metaphor for Christ, as does the author of 1 Peter in 2:7. It is yet another biblical image about the reversal of values that God intends. The idea is that a huge stone at the foundation is not merely a decorative marker but actually supports the weight of the building above.

Ideas for the Day

♦ For some of us it seems impossible that we turned over this new century, from the 1900s to the 2000s, almost a quarter of a century ago. We hear people say "at the end of the last century" and still think of the 1800s. As we become more interested in the idea of legacy, we find ourselves concerned that this generation is rushing ahead, ignoring the people, wisdom, and pain of what helped us reach our modern ideas about life together. We see schools, factories, and fields that were once marvelous contributors to communities, welfare, and beauty—now shuttered, abandoned, or plowed under. Today's readings feature vineyards in various states of repair, ownership, and stewardship. What happened, and why, and what is the lesson there?

♦ Dumbledore once said "The trouble is, humans do have a knack of choosing precisely those things that are worst for them."[1] Or they are afraid to choose at all. Why the hesitation to ask for what we need—from ourselves, others, or even from God? We fear rejection or are uncertain. Unwilling to loosen the myth of control to chart our course, even if only in small amounts. Afraid of failure or lack of confidence. Not wanting to be a burden. This morning's collect does a lovely job of crafting words to remind us that we aren't always the best

judge of what's best for us, and to trust that God truly has more in store for us than we even know to desire, let alone to ask.

♦ In keeping with the flood of modern-day movies about the end of the world, let's try an insane recasting of this ancient and oft-reworked allegory by asking the question—what if the creator of the garden was the natural universe—science—the big bang, and God was appointed the overseer of the tenants called to care for it? When the natural order came calling, in the throes of global warming and plague, demanding, "Show us how you have been stewards of science and order revealed to you, and kept the garden thriving," the people of God responded by burning the garden, ignoring pandemic safety, and intending to retain the severely compromised garden for themselves, in the name of God?

Making Connections

What if today's parable was not about poverty, taxes, ownership, or murder? What if it was about the dream of mutuality? What if the situation being explored via parable, with allusions to Isaiah, was used to simply lay bare the reality of those who have more, those who have nothing, and those in-between, leveraging what they can of the haves, to avoid being a have-not, and ask—what can be done? Today's political and environmental players include those who have power, those who have none, and brokers who claim to be working for both. The utopian dream of everyone somehow meeting in the middle, in full agreement over renewable energy, wealth, homelessness, recycling—a peaceable kingdom where the extremes are less , , , extreme, is worth working towards. This week's collect assures us that God's readiness, mercy, and forgiveness are abundant. We need not fear pushing for justice for all.

Engaging All Ages

" . . . in everything by prayer and supplication with thanksgiving let your requests be made known to God." In worship today, pay attention to the Prayers of the People. These are your prayers. They are prayers for you, others in your church, and for the world.

You ask God for good things and you give thanks for good things. If you can, read a copy of this Sunday's prayers. Is there a prayer you would like to ask to have included in next Sunday's prayers? If so, ask your priest or the person who maintains the prayer list.

---

1 J. K. Rowling, *Harry Potter and the Sorcerer's Stone* (New York: Scholastic Press, 1998), 297.

Hymns for the Day

The Hymnal 1982

Eternal Spirit of the living Christ 698
Only-begotten, Word of God eternal 360, 361
Help us, O Lord, to learn 628 [SC]
Most High, omnipotent, good Lord 406, 407 [SC]
Praise to the living God 372 [SC]
The stars declare his glory 431 [SC]
Open your ears, O faithful people 536 [GR]
Awake, my soul, stretch every nerve 546
Fight the good fight with all thy might
     (vs. 1–2) 552, 553
Jesus, all my gladness 701
Lo! what a cloud of witnesses 545
Not far beyond the sea, nor high 422
We sing the praise of him who died 471
When I survey the wondrous cross 474
Christ is made the sure foundation 518
Hail, thou once despised Jesus 495
Lord Christ, when first thou cam'st to earth 598
My song is love unknown (vs. 1–2, 5) 458
O love, how deep, how broad, how high 448, 449
The great Creator of the worlds 489
The head that once was crowned with thorns 483

Lift Every Voice and Sing II

Ev'ry time I feel the Spirit 114 [SC]
Leave it there 197
Higher ground 165

Wonder, Love, and Praise

God the sculptor of the mountains 746, 747 [GR]
Ev'ry time I feel the Spirit 751 [SC]
When from bondage we are summoned 753, 754

Weekday Commemorations

Monday October 9
Robert Grosseteste, Bishop, 1253

Distinguishing himself as a scholar in many disciplines, from law to science and languages, Grosseteste was appointed master of the Oxford School. He was first teacher of theology to the Franciscans. He translated and commented on Aristotle's works from Greek as well as figuring a scientific method based on Augustine's theories. He influenced both Roger Bacon and John Wycliffe. In 1235, he was consecrated bishop of Lincoln and executed his office efficiently and conscientiously, traveling to each rural deanery with alacrity to preach, confirm, convene, and answer doctrinal questions. Grosseteste opposed royal abuses of local prerogatives: "As an obedient son, I disobey, I contradict, I rebel . . . ."

Tuesday, October 10
Vida Dutton Scudder, Educator, 1954

Scudder's love of scholarship was matched by her social conscience and deep spirituality. As a young woman, Scudder founded the College Settlements Association, joined the Society of Christian Socialists, and began her lifelong association with the Society of the Companions of the Holy Cross, a community living in the world and devoted to intercessory prayer.

Thursday, October 12
Edith Cavell, Nurse, 1915

In 1896, at thirty-one, Cavell became a nurse, working at hospitals and infirmaries throughout England and as a private nurse. In 1907, she became matron of the new *L'École Belge d'Infirmières Diplômées* in Brussels. When World War I began, she served as a Red Cross nurse; following German occupation of Brussels, she collaborated with others to smuggle Allied soldiers out of Belgium into neutral countries (she confessed to smuggling more than 175 people out of Belgium). A committed Christian, she nursed soldiers on both sides of the war. That and her outspokenness caused her arrest and execution in 1915 by the Germans.

Saturday, October 14
Samuel Isaac Joseph Schereschewsky,
Bishop and Missionary, 1906

When Schereschewsky (born in 1831 in Lithuania) was studying for the rabbinate in Germany, he was enticed toward Christianity through his reading of a Hebrew translation of the New Testament and by missionaries of the London Society for Promoting Christianity Amongst the Jews. In 1854, he immigrated to Pittsburgh to train for ministry in the Presbyterian Church; after two years, he became an Episcopalian. He graduated from General Theological Seminary in 1859, whereupon he emigrated to China, learning to write Chinese enroute. He translated the Bible and parts of the prayer book into Mandarin. He was elected bishop of Shanghai in 1877; partially paralyzed, he resigned his see in 1883 but continued translating.

Pentecost

The Twentieth Sunday after Pentecost: Proper 23

October 15, 2023

God's coming reign will be like a great banquet (often referred to as the "messianic banquet"), but we must be ready to accept the invitation.

Color Green

Preface Of the Lord's Day

Collect

Lord, we pray that your grace may always precede and follow us, that we may continually be given to good works; through Jesus Christ our Lord, who lives and reigns with you and the Holy Spirit, one God, now and for ever. *Amen.*

Readings and Psalm

Exodus 32:1–14

Today's reading begins a longer section on Israel's sin and God's forgiveness (chaps. 32–34). It serves both as a narrative sequel to the giving of the law on Mt. Sinai and as a spiritual reflection upon Israel's repeated failure of faith from the exodus to the exile. The worship of the golden calf signified the acceptance of the Canaanite rites of Baal. In view of the Lord's anger, Moses intercedes for the people. He reminds the Lord that these are God's own people, that God's name is now bound up with theirs and that God had promised Abraham, not Moses, many descendants. God's course of action is then revised, not capriciously but in keeping with God's purposes.

Psalm 106:1–6, 19–23

This psalm is an affirmation of God's righteousness and favor toward those who love the Lord, and a confession of sins present and sins past.

or

Isaiah 25:1–9

Today's reading pictures the end time when the Lord will prepare a feast of rich abundance for all people. For Jews, all meals had religious significance; here a feast provided by God becomes an anticipated element of the last days. This theme of the end-time banquet later became part of the messianic expectations. Isaiah boldly appropriates the language of Canaanite mythology in which the god Mot (death) swallowed up all creatures. Isaiah asserts, however, that God will finally conquer death in a once-for-all-time event. Those who are preserved through God's judgment will celebrate God's faithfulness.

Psalm 23

This psalm celebrates God's loving care for us under the guise of a good shepherd who provides food, security, and protection from all dangers.

Philippians 4:1–9

In closing his letter, Paul expresses his appreciation for the community's generosity in supporting his ministry. Apparently they had sent Paul certain gifts, presumably including money. God enables Paul to remain content in every situation. Paul's contentedness derives from God, the source of his strength. Paul joyfully accepts the provision of the Philippians, for their need then provides another opportunity for God to demonstrate generosity.

Matthew 22:1–14

The parable of the wedding banquet addresses God's initiative to open the reign of God to all. Matthew structures the story to illustrate salvation history. The first group of servants were like the prophets and the second group the Christian apostles and missionaries. The proper wedding clothing probably represents a new life marked by the fruits of repentance in good deeds. Since in Judaism good works were expected to act as "intercessors" before God (Acts 10:4), the guest without the garment is "speechless" (v. 12). Christians are cautioned not to rely on the calling, but to respond by living their baptism in daily life.

Prayers of the People

Rejoice in the Lord always; again I will say, Rejoice. Let us humbly approach our God, saying, "Remember us with favor, O Lord; *visit us with your saving help.*"

God our Savior, strengthen your Church to stand firm in your love. May we struggle not *with* one another, but instead struggle *beside* one another in the work of the gospel.

Silence

Remember us with favor, O Lord;

Visit us with your saving help.

God our Savior, you make happy those who act with justice. May the leaders and people of the nations dedicate themselves to pure and honorable dealings. Let your justice reign on this earth.

Silence

Remember us with favor, O Lord;

Visit us with your saving help.

God our Savior, you are good to us. You have blessed us with a rich creation and a beautiful planet for our home. May we cherish the gifts you have given us.

Invite the congregation to add their thanksgivings, followed by silence

Remember us with favor, O Lord;

Visit us with your saving help.

God our Savior, deliver our community from worry. Make us a people of prayer, a congregation who intercedes for our neighbors.

Silence

Remember us with favor, O Lord;

Visit us with your saving help.

God our Savior, you are always near. Assure the lonely; heal the sick; do mighty acts in the lives of the downcast. With thankful hearts, trusting in your mercy, we make our requests known to you.

Invite the congregation to add their petitions, followed by silence

Remember us with favor, O Lord;

Visit us with your saving help.

God our Savior, your mercy endures forever. May those who have died glory in your inheritance and feast at your heavenly banquet for all eternity.

Silence

Remember us with favor, O Lord;

Visit us with your saving help.

Images in the Readings

Here is a listing of only some of this Sunday's images. Matthew's parable merges several biblical images that describe our life with God. The **wedding** suggests lifelong love, commitment to the other, and communal joy in the union as a description of God's choosing and caring for us. Especially in a culture in which food was not plentiful and cheap, the **feast** connotes communal participation and extraordinary fullness. God is likened to a **king**, to whom is due honor and service. We are **guests**: that is, the meal is God's, not ours. The **wedding robe** suggests the white garment of baptism. Since the Bible often describes God as light, **outer darkness** suggests life totally distant and apart from God. Paul calls the somewhat problematic Philippian assembly his **crown**. Another ten images fill the poem from Isaiah. God not only throws out the unprepared guest, God also **shelters** us from storm, removes the **shroud** that finally covers all humans, like some kind of monster **eats up death**, and like a lover or a parent **wipes away our tears.**

Pentecost

Pentecost

Ideas for the Day

- There is an immense difference between knowing about God and knowing God. Moses is giving voice to a broader experience of desiring to feel God's presence and assurance. We want to know for sure that God (or our loved ones) are not going to abandon us. The response of God to Moses' anxiety about God's steadfast presence is gracious, but it is also expectant that this intimacy is not a one-way relationship. What people and organizations do we desire the assurance of but regularly manage to be steadfast partners with?

- One of the critical points in the eucharistic celebration is when the presider takes the host, lifts it high so that the people can see, and then breaks it. God expressed wisdom in not allowing Moses to see the divine face. It would have been too much. So it seems there is also wisdom when we are only allowed to take a piece of the consecrated bread each week. A little bit of Jesus might just be what the doctor ordered. It also seems fitting that when we do it in this way, only taking a little bit of Jesus, we are also sharing the love of Jesus with one another.

- The church must acknowledge the ultimate allegiance to God. It is important for the congregation to know the stories of those who have witnessed to that ultimate authority with their lives. Dietrich Bonhoeffer, a German theologian killed by the Nazi regime, is an example of the witnesses we have in Christian history. Are there other martyrs of modern times that we can speak of today? (See *Lesser Feasts and Fasts* or *Holy Women, Holy Men*.)

Making Connections

We don't know why the first round of invitees to the wedding feast chose not to attend. Perhaps his son was a scoundrel? Or the king himself? But we do know that whatever it was, the invited guests went out of their way to insult and shame the king in their refusals to attend. We see Matthew noting, again, that those without power are at the mercy of those in power, by summoning them to appear at the feast. Many of us have had the experience of a command performance: an appearance at a work, family, or church function, and resented it. Maybe you dressed appropriately,

attended with grace and integrity, or maybe you pulled a little passive aggression and purposely showed up late, or in inappropriate attire. Seems only one of the forced guests used what little power they had to let it be known they would not honor this king.

Engaging All Ages

If you are using track two, the appointed Psalm is Psalm 23. This well-known psalm is poetic, theologically deep, and meaningful to many, many people. That's all to say, it can also quickly become cliché or lose its deep connection to God every time it gets slapped on a coffee mug or half-priced sweatshirt. Print out copies of the psalm, along with some instructions for how to "diagram" a sentence. Invite people to "diagram" the psalm prayerfully, looking into each line, each word, and asking themselves, "What does this mean to my life right now?" The next week, offer a time for sharing and discussion.

Hymns for the Day

The Hymnal 1982
God the Omnipotent! King, who ordainest 569 [SC]
O for a closer walk with God 683, 684 [SC]
Sing praise to God who reigns above 408 [SC]
Glory, love, and praise, and honor 300 [GR]
My God, thy table now is spread 321 [GR]
My Shepherd will supply my need 664 [GR]
The King of love my shepherd is 645, 646 [GR]
The Lord my God my shepherd is 663 [GR]
Christ, whose glory fills the skies 6, 7
Holy Ghost, dispel our sadness 515
Jesus, all my gladness 701
Rejoice, the Lord is King 481
Rejoice, ye pure in heart 556, 557
Savior, again to thy dear Name we raise 345
Come, my Way, my Truth, my Life 487
Deck thyself, my soul, with gladness 339
O Jesus, joy of loving hearts 649, 650
The Lamb's high banquet called to share 202
This is the hour of banquet and of song 316, 317
We the Lord's people 51

Lift Every Voice and Sing II
The Lord is my shepherd 104 [GR]

Wonder, Love, and Praise
As we gather at your table 763

Weekday Commemorations

Monday, October 16
Hugh Latimer and Nicholas Ridley, Bishops and Martyrs, 1555, and Thomas Cranmer, Archbishop of Canterbury, 1556

Cranmer (born 1489), the principal figure in the Reformation of the English Church, was primarily responsible for the first Book of Common Prayer in 1549. Compromising his political with his reformation ideals led to his death—despite his recanting. Ridley (born 1500) also adhered to reformation ideals as he served as chaplain to King Henry VIII. Unwilling to recant his Protestant theology, Ridley died with Latimer at the stake. Latimer (born about 1490) was installed as bishop of Worcester in 1535 under Henry VIII; he resigned his see in 1539 and refused to resume it after Edward VI was enthroned. Latimer was imprisoned and burned at the stake with Ridley under the crown of Mary on October 16, 1555.

Tuesday, October 17
Ignatius of Antioch, Bishop and Martyr, c.115

Ignatius' seven letters, written to churches while he sojourned across Asia Minor, offer insight to the early Church. In one, he cautioned against Gnostic teachings that underscored Jesus' divinity over his humanity; in another, he condemned biblical literalism, citing Jesus Christ as "the ancient document." Ignatius held that the Church's unity would rise from its liturgy by which all are initiated into Christ through baptism. Ignatius thought of the Church as God's holy order in the world; he was concerned, therefore, with ordered teaching and worship. In ecstasy, he saw his martyrdom as the just conclusion to a long episcopate as second bishop of Antioch in Syria.

Wednesday, October 18
Saint Luke the Evangelist

Luke's gospel serves not as a biography, but as a history of salvation; Luke did not know Jesus, but he was inspired by those who had. He wrote the book that honors the name of the disciple and its sequel, the Acts of the Apostles. Luke wrote in Greek, allowing Gentiles to read his stories. Only Luke presents the familiar stories of the annunciation to Mary, of her visit to Elizabeth, of the child in the manger, and the angelic host's appearing to shepherds. He cites six miracles and eighteen parables not recorded by the other gospel writers. In Acts, Luke tells of the coming of the Holy Spirit and the struggles of the apostles.

Thursday, October 19
Henry Martyn, Priest and Missionary, 1812

Martyn translated the scriptures and Book of Common Prayer into Hindi and Persian and served as an English missionary in India. Born in 1781 and educated at Cambridge, Martyn, influenced by Charles Simeon, Evangelical rector of Holy Trinity Church, Cambridge, changed his mind about becoming a lawyer and became a missionary. He traveled to India in 1806 as chaplain for the British East India Co. He was there but five years before dying at age thirty-one; however, in that time, he organized private schools and founded churches in addition to translating the Bible. He also translated the New Testament into Persian. He died in Tokat, Turkey, where Armenians honored him by burying him like one of their own bishops.

Pentecost

The Twenty-First Sunday after Pentecost: Proper 24

October 22, 2023

God's power and will can be revealed even among those considered enemies or aliens. Since God's power extends to everyone, ultimate authority belongs to God.

Pentecost

Color   Green

Preface   Of the Lord's Day

Collect

Almighty and everlasting God, in Christ you have revealed your glory among the nations: Preserve the works of your mercy, that your Church throughout the world may persevere with steadfast faith in the confession of your Name; through Jesus Christ our Lord, who lives and reigns with you and the Holy Spirit, one God, for ever and ever. *Amen.*

Readings and Psalm

Exodus 33:12–23

This reading demonstrates Moses' close relationship with God. Exhausted from the burden of leading the people through the wilderness, Moses complains that he does not have enough help to accomplish his task. God responds by promising to be present in person to make sure that Moses and the people will go in safety.

Psalm 99

Psalm 99 is a hymn celebrating God's reign. This hymn is written in three stanzas, each of which closes with a refrain about God's holiness.

or

Isaiah 45:1–7

Today's reading tells of the Lord's choice of Cyrus as God's agent. Cyrus, king of Persia (559–530 BCE), overthrew the Babylonian empire and let the Jews return from exile. Isaiah asserts that Cyrus unknowingly does God's will and calls him God's "anointed," messiah. This term did not yet mean what it would later in Judaism or in Christianity, but it was a title reserved for the Davidic king. Only here in the Hebrew Bible is it used for someone outside the covenant people. For the sake of both Israel and of all people the Lord has acted. As the Creator of all, God rules over all nations.

Psalm 96:1–9 (10–13)

Psalm 96 proclaims God's power over all creation and over all nations.

1 Thessalonians 1:1–10

In Paul's absence, his community were exposed to the attacks of local Jews and Gentiles. His concern for their welfare led him to send Timothy back to visit. His joy at Timothy's encouraging report occasioned Paul's letter. He adapts the common form of a Greek letter to his own purposes. After saluting the recipients, Paul proceeds to a thanksgiving that he expands to express his sense of God's activity among them. He knows that God has chosen them. The evidence of their election lay in the power wrought by the proclamation of the good news.

Matthew 22:15–22

The question on the payment of the Roman tax was designed to force Jesus to offend some group, for the Jewish people were bitterly divided on the issue. To advocate payment of the tax as legal, as did the Herodians (the supporters of the ruling family) whose policy was complete loyalty to Rome, would alienate the general populace. At the other extreme, to advocate nonpayment, as did the Zealots, would signal treason and reinforce all the nationalist hopes and fears aroused by the triumphal entry into Jerusalem. The Pharisees also hated the tax, which implied their submission to a pagan sovereign rather than to God. Taking the coin, Jesus counsels them to "give" (v. 21; literally to "give back") to the emperor what is his and to give back to God what is God's. Jesus refuses to take sides on the political issue but uses the situation to address their failure to repay God with what belongs to God.

Prayers of the People

Brothers and sisters, beloved by God: Grace to you and peace. Let us pray to the Holy One, saying, "Be gracious to us, O God; *show us your mercy.*"

We always give thanks to you, O God, for the Church, constantly remembering before you its work of faith, labor of love, and steadfastness of hope in our Lord Jesus Christ. Inspire us by the Holy Spirit.

Invite the congregation to add their thanksgivings, followed by silence

Be gracious to us, O God;

Show us your mercy.

Almighty God, make us more like your Son, Jesus, who did not regard people with partiality. May we love justice. May we be gracious with all people.

Silence

Be gracious to us, O God;

Show us your mercy.

God our King, the earth shakes in your presence. All that is belongs not to us, but to you. May we be good stewards of all you have created.

Silence

Be gracious to us, O God;

Show us your mercy.

Holy One, you answer those who call upon you. Hear the voices of the weak and wronged. May this city know and experience your presence.

Silence

Be gracious to us, O God;

Show us your mercy.

Great Lord, give your people rest. Cover the sick and sorrowful with your healing hand. May the lonely and forgotten find favor in your sight.

Invite the congregation to add their petitions, followed by silence

Be gracious to us, O God;

Show us your mercy.

Living God, you have rescued the dying and dead from the coming wrath through the death and resurrection of your Christ. May our voices blend with theirs as they proclaim your greatness and worship around your throne forever.

Silence

Be gracious to us, O God;

Show us your mercy.

Images in the Readings

Typically, a **coin** is impressed with an image of the authority upon which the coin relies. In the United States, coins and bills bear the picture of presidents who function as model representatives of the sovereign people. In baptism, it is the cross of Christ that has been impressed on our bodies: he is the authority to whom we owe allegiance. As to taxes: Christians in different countries have widely ranging views about how much of our days' wages is rightly owed to the government.

The Isaiah reading plays with the idea of one's **name**. God calls Cyrus by name; God's personal name is YHWH, represented in most English-language Bibles as "the Lord." In his encouragement to the Thessalonians, Paul writes of God the Father, the Lord Jesus Christ, and the Holy Spirit. In baptism, the candidates are first called by their secular name, after which this triune name of God is placed on them. Yet in the second century, Justin Martyr wrote that to imagine that we can know and speak the very name of the almighty God is madness. Perhaps the name of God that we are given in the Bible is like a potholder, a way to hold on to something that is far too hot for bare human hands.

Ideas for the Day

♦ There is a part of happy that is utter joy, warm-cookies delight. But there is also a side of how we use the word "happy" that is saccharine, shallow, and vapid. "Happy" can also be an unattainable goal that shames our doldrums and griefs and steals the good and the holy from the daily reality of life. What is translated in the prayer book as "happy" is elsewhere sometimes translated as "blessed." It is that wish or prayer for well-being we utter when we say "bless you." It is the naming of the glowing centeredness and glad purpose with which we leave the eucharistic liturgy. How is holy happiness or blessing experienced by the people in your life?

♦ A blessing is best defined as the willingness to name how one sees God working in and through another person at that very moment. Can you imagine a world where we did this more than degrading the humanity of one another? Joshua was most likely already filled with the spirit of wisdom, but it was the laying on of hands and the naming by Moses that allowed Joshua to know his truth. He was affirmed and he was loved. Chances are that you might know someone who is broken, who needs to hear that you see God working through them.

♦ Our response to God comes as we respond in justice and love to one another. The one cannot be separated from the other. For a different perspective, see 1 John 4:20–21 for the negative way of stating this.

Making Connections

A funny little trap Jesus set here—asking those in the group challenging him for a coin. Pharisees considered handling coins with graven images idolatrous. Even commiserating with a Herodian, like those employed to help entrap Jesus in this story, in possession of a coin would be deeply shameful to them. There's nothing new about people keeping a little something nearby they know they shouldn't, just in case. Be it the phone number of a toxic ex, a powerful but brutal ally, a fifth of booze, private social media accounts, damaging secrets. Hidden in shame. Modern psychology is introducing a whole school of thought on the upside of shame, and narcissism thrives where shame is absent. Shame motivates individuals, and

won Jesus the first point in this week's riposte. Being the emotion signaling the need for reconnection and reconciliation, it's potentially a powerful motivator of change for the better.

Engaging All Ages

Loving God with all your heart, all your soul, and all your mind is connected with loving your neighbor. There is a mutual, almost symbiotic relationship being addressed here. We are loved beyond measure. We, in turn, love God and our neighbor in the way that has been modelled for us. As we move into Advent, consider using "All your heart," "All your soul," and "All your mind" as buckets for reflection, discernment, and formation during the season of preparation. This could be a preaching focus (the following passages can match up!), an intergenerational formation opportunity (use one for each week leading up to Christmas), or something as simple as asking parishioners of all ages to reflect on one per week during worship.

Hymns for the Day

The Hymnal 1982

Holy, holy, holy! Lord God Almighty 362 [SC]
Immortal, invisible, God only wise 423 [SC]
Rock of ages, cleft for me 685 [SC]
All people that on earth do dwell 377, 378 [GR]
Before the Lord's eternal throne 391 [GR]
Earth and all stars 412 [GR]
Praise to the living God 372 [GR]
Sing praise to God who reigns above 408 [GR]
I sought the Lord, and afterward I knew 689
In your mercy, Lord, you called me 706
Jesus, our mighty Lord 478
Lord, we have come at your own invitation 348
O for a closer walk with God 683, 684
All my hope on God is founded 665
Father eternal, Ruler of creation 573
God of grace and God of glory 594, 595
Jesus shall reign, where'er the sun 544
Judge eternal, throned in splendor 596
O God of earth and altar 591

Lift Every Voice and Sing II

Wonder, Love, and Praise

Weekday Commemorations

Monday, October 23
Saint James of Jerusalem, Brother of Our Lord Jesus Christ

Saint James of Jerusalem is called the Lord's brother in the Gospel according to Matthew and the Epistle to the Galatians. However, other writers, following Mark's path, thought James was Jesus' cousin; certain apocryphal writings name him as Joseph's son by his first wife. After Jesus' resurrection, James was converted and eventually became bishop of Jerusalem. Paul's first letter to the Corinthians notes that James beheld a special appearance of the Lord before the ascension; later, James was cordial to Paul at Jerusalem. At the Council of Jerusalem, it was James who would impose "no irksome restrictions" (circumcision) on Gentiles turning to God. His success at converting many to Jesus perturbed factions in Jerusalem, so he was cudgeled to death.

Wednesday, October 25
Tabitha (Dorcas) of Joppa

Before Peter arrived in Joppa to preach the Gospel, Tabitha (Greek: Dorcas) was reputed to be a good woman of charity, benefitting widows by sewing their clothes. The widows' desire to show these clothes to Peter testifies to Tabitha's gifts—and perhaps her admirable level of craft as a seamstress. When Tabitha died, her friends called Peter to come see her, perhaps depending on the apostles' reputation as wonder workers. The story is similar to the one of Jesus' miraculously healing a girl (Luke 8:41–56). Basil of Caesarea also mentions Tabitha's good works as a model for widows.

Thursday, October 26
Alfred, King, 899

Alfred, born in 849, one of five sons of King Aethelwulf, lived during a time of murder as Vikings invaded and settled in Britain. At four, he was blessed by Pope Leo IV on a trip to Rome. Alfred became king in 871. He halted the invasions through heroic battles and stratagems, thus securing control of southern and parts of midland England. He persuaded his foe, the Dane Guthrum, to accept baptism after Alfred won the battle of Edington in 878. He sought to repair damage wrought by the Viking invasions, especially on culture and clergy. Because of his courage and virtue, Alfred is the only English ruler to be called "great."

Friday, October 28
Saint Simon and Saint Jude, Apostles

Little is known of either Simon or Jude. The gospels name Simon as one of the disciples, the "Zealot," but that adjective may refer to his enthusiasm as much as to his membership in the "Zelotes" faction. John mentions him as being at the Last Supper. The Epistle of Jude may have been written by the disciple Jude, who is mentioned by John as brother to James the Greater. By tradition, the two are associated with Persia; some stories characterize them as martyrs. Jude may be confused with another Jude, who was surnamed Thaddeus; still, he is prayed to as the patron of lost causes. More questions than answers ensnare these two.

Pentecost

The Twenty-Second Sunday after Pentecost: Proper 25

October 29, 2023

To be righteous before God means doing right to the neighbor, the sojourner, and the person in need. To love God is to love the neighbor.

Color   Green

Preface   Of the Lord's Day

Collect

Almighty and everlasting God, increase in us the gifts of faith, hope, and charity; and, that we may obtain what you promise, make us love what you command; through Jesus Christ our Lord, who lives and reigns with you and the Holy Spirit, one God, for ever and ever. *Amen.*

Readings and Psalm

Deuteronomy 34:1–12

Today's reading describes several transitions. The reading itself is the ending of the book of Deuteronomy, which describes the people's pause at the Jordan to rededicate themselves to their covenant obligations before entering the Promised Land. A second transition is the death of Moses. Though God had forbidden the original exodus generation from entering the new land, God does allow Moses a peek at the land before he dies. The final words sum up the special character of Moses and his unique relationship with God. The final transition is that of the leadership of the community. With Moses' death, the leadership passes to Joshua who will take the people across the Jordan and oversee their settlement in the land.

Psalm 90:1–6, 13–17

In this psalm, attributed to Moses, the shortness of human life is lamented, and God's presence is sought so that the people may rejoice in all their days.

or

Leviticus 19:1–2, 15–18

The holiness enjoined in these chapters is not achieved by the actions or qualities of human beings, but by God's act in separating out a people and binding them in a special covenant. Chapter 19 echoes the Ten Commandments. Special attention is given to the needs of the disadvantaged. The gleaning of field and vineyard is left for the poor and the resident alien. Each member of the community has the responsibility to correct a fellow-member in love.

Psalm 1

This psalm, with its call to a righteous life based on knowledge of the "law of the Lord," the Torah, serves as a fitting introduction to all the psalms. It springs from the wisdom tradition, which emphasized how to live in both material and spiritual prosperity.

1 Thessalonians 2:1–8

Paul reminds the Thessalonians of the circumstances of his mission among them. He distinguishes himself from the common itinerant religious and philosophical teachers. Paul does not promote heresy or immorality, use trickery or flattery, nor seek self-aggrandizement. He could have presumed on his apostolic authority, but instead, like a nursing mother, he supported their new life by sharing his very self.

Matthew 22:34–46

Today's reading contains the third of the controversy stories that show Jesus' ability to confute his opponents. The law of Moses as set forth in the first five books of the Bible had, over the passage of centuries, been codified into 613 commandments. The question was often raised whether they were all of equal weight. The first part of Jesus' answer quotes Deuteronomy 6:5, which began the Jewish morning prayer called the Shema (from the first word in the quote, "hear"). The inclusion of "mind" (v. 37) may be an alternate translation for Gentiles of "heart," which, in Jewish understanding, was the core of a person, the center of thought and will and emotion.

Prayers of the People

Friends, the Lord has been our refuge from one generation to another. Let us pray to our God, saying, "Show your servants your works, O Lord, *and be gracious to us.*"

We pray for the leaders of the Church. Give bishops, priests, deacons, and lay leaders gentle and loving hearts. Empower us to share the gospel and ourselves with those in need.

Silence

Show your servants your works, O Lord,

And be gracious to us.

We pray for all humankind. Prosper the work of our hands. May all those who work earn a fair wage. May those without work find strength and encouragement in your love. Give us hearts to respect the dignity of every human being.

Silence

Show your servants your works, O Lord,

And be gracious to us.

We pray for all creation. You brought forth the mountains. You gave birth to the land and the earth. Give us the desire and will to care for all you have made.

Silence

Show your servants your works, O Lord,

And be gracious to us.

We pray for the areas in which we live. O God, we want to obey what you command. Help us to love our neighbors as ourselves.

Silence

Show your servants your works, O Lord,

And be gracious to us.

We pray for the afflicted and the suffering. And we pray for those who weep and mourn. Nurse them back to health as a mother tenderly nurses her children.

Invite the congregation to add their petitions and thanksgivings, followed by silence

Show your servants your works, O Lord,

And be gracious to us.

We pray for those who have died. Though we are swept away like a dream in this mortal life, you promise to raise us to life immortal through your Son. May your graciousness, O Lord, be upon us.

Silence

Show your servants your works, O Lord,

And be gracious to us.

Images in the Readings

The term **law** is tricky for us. According to the covenant in the Old Testament, the law was graciously given by God to delineate the way toward communal happiness. However, Paul uses the term critically, teaching that keeping these 613 commands will not bring us to God. Luther uses the term far more broadly to refer to everything in the Bible that preaches our sin and announces our death. For many contemporary hearers, the term means governmental regulations. Our task is to make sure that the meaning of any particular use of the term is clear. Psychologists suggest, in accord with Luther, that confronting the truth of the human condition is, although sad, finally welcomed, but then as Christians we gladly take refuge in the gospel of God's love in Christ Jesus.

Probably in 1 Thessalonians 2:7 Paul is suggesting that evangelists are like a **nursing mother**, since the children are her own. So Paul offers a balance to Matthew's image of the late-first-century church leader as an exegetical authority. Both are helpful images.

Pentecost

Psalm 110, cited in Matthew 22, pictures the Messiah sitting at the **right hand** of God. In ancient Near Eastern courts, the prince or a kind of prime minister sat on the right side of the monarch. From the psalm the phrase made it all the way into our creeds. In the fifteenth century, the mystic Julian reminds us that the phrase is a metaphor: "But it is not meant that the Son sits on the right hand as one man sits by another in this life, for there is no such sitting, as to my sight, in the Trinity." She suggests that the metaphor means that the Son is "right in the highest nobility of the Father's joy."

Ideas for the Day

♦ By 2025 the self-help industry market value is estimated to reach $14 billion. The industry, which consists of live events and seminars, speakers, coaching, weight loss programs, and holistic institutes, appeals to boomers and now millennials cannot seem to get enough ideas and guidance on how they might live their best lives. Missing from among much of this product is the underlying question: *Why* should we live our best lives? As people of faith, we emphasize loving ourselves, loving one another, and loving God, which can often be pressed into some of the self-help language. It is dangerous to let our various scriptural commandments join that head space where we keep all of the other ways we "should be all over ourselves." This matters far beyond life-organization and health tricks.

♦ This is the week to introduce your congregation to the Code of Hammurabi, the ancient and fascinating laws in circulation about a thousand years before Moses was given the Ten Commandments. You can find public displays of the Code of Hammurabi and the Ten Commandments all over the United States. However, a short bit of research will show you that in many places people have challenged displaying the Ten Commandments, and demanded their removal, even in the US Supreme Court. The distinction between the two that seems to matter is whether or not they are pushing a religion. Where do you find public displays of laws, or suggestions for order, appropriate or not, and are there any on your current campus?

♦ After being challenged to name the greatest commandment, followed by questions about the lineage of the messiah, Matthew wrote "No one was able to give him an answer, nor from that day did anyone dare to ask him any more questions." Of course, this is not, strictly speaking, accurate. Well-timed and well-constructed questions, and answers, are a continued hallmark of Jesus' ministry, arrest, trial, and death. Even the angels at the empty tomb asked what is perhaps the most important question in the entire story: Why do you seek the living among the dead? Questions cause the learner to begin with what they know, and risk stepping off in new or different directions to see things afresh. How important are questions for you, as a leader, when exploring the gospel with others?

Making Connections

Can there be a greatest commandment, among the 613 Jesus knew from the Torah? There was a custom among biblical writers to provide summaries of the laws, or collapse them into a collective precept of sorts (Psalm 15, Isaiah 33:15, Micah 6:8, Amos 5:4). Even this morning's collect suggests that simply embracing an increase in the trio of faith, hope, and charity might bring us closer to God's promises, and cause us to love what God commands. It is natural to want things simplified. Boiled down to reasonably sized bites, as it were. But this is big. This is important. This matters far beyond organization and short cuts. Pick your favorite summation of God's claim on your life, be it today's collect trio of love, or one of the others listed here, and let that be the point from which you plot your days, work, relationships, hence, your life.

Engaging All Ages

The Baptismal Covenant repeats the commandments to love God and neighbor. To embody the covenant means responding to God in praise, seeking and serving Christ in others, striving for justice and peace (BCP, 305).

The Ten Commandments is a set of guidelines from God that were given so that people could be better and treat other people better. Where else do you find guidelines and rules? At home? No dessert before eating your vegetables. Going to bed at a certain time. At school or the office? Types of clothes you can and cannot wear in those places? Discuss all these rules and why you think they were made. Think how these rules demonstrate love for God and love for others. If not, could you suggest ways to change them so that they did?

Hymns of the Day

The Hymnal 1982

O God, our help in ages past 680 [SC]
Praise to the living God 372 [SC]
Before thy throne, O God, we kneel 574, 575 [GR]
Father all-loving, who rulest in majesty 568 [GR]
Give praise and glory unto God 375 [GR]
Thy strong word did cleave the darkness 381 [GR]
God of mercy, God of grace 538
Lord, make us servants of your peace 593
O Spirit of the living God 531
Take my life, and let it be 707
All hail the power of Jesus' Name! 450, 451
Come with us, O blessed Jesus 336
Jesu, Jesu, fill us with your love 602
Lord, whose love through humble service 610
O Spirit of Life, O Spirit of God 505
Rise up, ye saints of God 551
Where charity and love prevail 581

Lift Every Voice and Sing II

Jesu, Jesu 74

Wonder, Love, and Praise

Jesus said: The first commandment is this 815

Weekday Commemorations

Monday, October 30
Maryam of Qidun, Monastic, 4ᵗʰ century

Underneath the many fictionalized legends of Maryam, an inspirational woman of history serves as inspiration. Orphaned, she was raised by her anchorite uncle Abraham in Edessa; for twenty years, she lived an ascetic life, teaching through the window of her room and being admired by all who met her. Having been seduced by a monk and being afraid to face her uncle, Maryam ran away and prostituted herself, but her uncle found her and, with compassion and comfort, led her home. Legend says that Maryam pleased God by her repentance and commiseration with sinners more than by her virginity.

Thursday, November 2
All Souls / All the Faithful Departed

The New Testament uses the word "saints" to describe all members of the Christian community; in the Collect for All Saints' Day, the word "elect" is used similarly. From very early times, however, the word "saint" was applied primarily to people of heroic sanctity, their deeds recalled gratefully by succeeding generations. Beginning in the tenth century, the custom began to set aside another day on which the Church recognized the whole body of the faithful, unknown to the wide fellowship of the Church, a day to remember family and friends who have died. During the Reformation, observance of this day was abolished, but Episcopalians, redefining its meaning, include it as an optional observance on their calendar.

Friday, November 3
Richard Hooker, Priest and Theologian, 1600

Born in 1553 near Exeter, he was admitted in 1567 to Corpus Christi College, Oxford, of which he became a fellow ten years later. Ordained in 1581, he served in a number of parishes but is noted for his comprehensive defense of the Reformation settlement under Queen Elizabeth I. His masterpiece, *Laws of Ecclesiastical Polity*, states that all positive laws of church and state are grounded from scripture revelation, ancient tradition, reason, and experience. Book Five of the *Laws* is a massive defense of the Book of Common Prayer, directed primarily at Puritan detractors.

Pentecost

The Twenty-Third Sunday after Pentecost: Proper 26

November 5, 2023

Being ready for judgment means striving for justice and righteousness.

Color   Green

Preface   Of the Lord's Day

Collect

Almighty and merciful God, it is only by your gift that your faithful people offer you true and laudable service: Grant that we may run without stumbling to obtain your heavenly promises; through Jesus Christ our Lord, who lives and reigns with you and the Holy Spirit, one God, now and for ever. *Amen.*

Readings and Psalm

Joshua 3:7–17

Today's reading describes the entry of the people into their new land under Joshua's leadership. It echoes several themes that tie this event to the exodus experience. Joshua receives God's approval and the promise that God's presence will guide and support him. Joshua directs the priests to lead the people by carrying the ark of the covenant. This box, containing the covenant scroll, was the portable presence of God in their midst. With God leading them, the people could enter the land with confidence. As the priests' feet touched the water, the river stopped until all the people had passed into the Promised Land on dry ground. This experience relives the people's exodus through the Red Sea.

Psalm 107:1–7, 33–37

This psalm encourages those whom God has rescued to give praise.

or

Micah 3:5–12

Micah's first message is directed to the prophets who sold their spiritual guidance and molded the prophetic word of God to tickle the ears of the wealthy and deceive rich and poor alike. Because of their avarice, the word would be taken from them, and their calling to the solemn office of prophet would be revoked. Verse 8 serves as a transition to Micah's general condemnation of Israel's officials. In verses 9–11, he denounces the wholesale betrayal of every vocation in Israel's leadership. Money was the measure of the day. Micah's condemnation climaxes with the ultimate hypocrisy: the leaders take refuge in their spiritual heritage and fear no recriminations for their abuse of power. Their smug assurances imply that God is like them and condones their behavior. Because of such wickedness, Jerusalem would become prey to ruin.

Psalm 43

This psalm, probably written as a part of Psalm 42, reflects the psalmist's yearning for God's presence.

1 Thessalonians 2:9–13

In today's reading, Paul defends the manner of his work. Though he could claim their financial support, Paul preferred to care for them gently and selflessly, like a mother with an infant. Paul urges the Thessalonians to recognize their citizenship in God's kingdom and their inheritance in God's glory. Paul's separation from them caused grief and, in spite of repeated efforts to visit again, he couldn't. But Paul rejoices in the hope of standing before the returning Lord with the believers of Thessalonica at his side.

Matthew 23:1–12

Chapter 23 serves as a conclusion to the controversy stories and a climax to Jesus' public ministry. Jesus sums up his opposition to the scribes and Pharisees by comparing their practices with his expectations of the disciples and by pronouncing woes condemning the false practices of the religious leaders. Jesus' criticism of titles of honor leads into the heart of this teaching: the values of the kingdom reverse the values of this world. Instead of seeking honors for themselves, Christian leaders are to become servants rather than masters. Christlike leadership is shown in service.

Prayers of the People

My brothers and sisters, all who humble themselves will be exalted. So let us appeal to God, praying, "We cry to you, O Lord; *good Lord, deliver us.*"

Humbly we adore you, good Lord. Give to your Church humility. May our lives be pure, upright and blameless; may we, in word and deed, proclaim your gospel.

Silence

We cry to you, O Lord;

Good Lord, deliver us.

Humbly we adore you, good Lord. Give to this nation humility. May we find our greatness not in status or self-exaltation, but in service to others.

Silence

We cry to you, O Lord;

Good Lord, deliver us.

Humbly we adore you, good Lord. Teach us to handle your creation with humility. Bless the soil to bring forth a fruitful harvest for the hungry. Bless the springs to give drink for the thirsty.

Silence

We cry to you, O Lord;

Good Lord, deliver us.

Humbly we adore you, good Lord. Give to our city humility. You have blessed us with a good place in which to dwell. Renew the spirits of our languishing. Put songs of thanksgiving in our mouths.

Invite the congregation to add their thanksgivings, followed by silence

We cry to you, O Lord;

Good Lord, deliver us.

Humbly we adore you, good Lord. Give healing and strength to those who call to you from humble hearts. Lift the burdens of those who are heavy laden. Encourage the sick and sorrowful with your love.

Invite the congregation to add their petitions, followed by silence

We cry to you, O Lord;

Good Lord, deliver us.

Humbly we adore you, good Lord. Your mercy endures forever. Bring those who have walked through the waters of baptism into that place of eternal life and promise.

Silence

We cry to you, O Lord;

Good Lord, deliver us.

Images in the Readings

In the second reading and the gospel, God is likened to a **father**. First-century Jews did not address YHWH as father, but in Greco-Roman paganism, Jupiter was indeed "Father of fathers." The New Testament adopts this cultural title for God, yet distinguishes the one who is father of Jesus from the father Jupiter who blasts humankind with lightning, alienates men from each other, and rapes women at will. Especially fourth-century theologians wrote about what Christians mean by calling God Father, explicitly denying that any male sexuality is intended. The psalm for the day illumines "father" by praising God who gives strength, light, truth, joy, gladness, help. Our address Father tries to contain these ideas, and far more.

Throughout scripture, God talks. God's **word** is heard from the beginning of time, it is spoken through the mouths of prophets and preachers, and it is embodied in Jesus Christ himself. The power and authority vested in this Word challenges our culture's post-modern preference for relativism. The churches that take ordination with high seriousness hope that the authority of proclaiming the word is merged with a vocation to servanthood.

Yet again on this Sunday we are called to be **servants**. The extent to which this call is countercultural cannot be exaggerated.

Ideas for the Day

+ The lectionary editors have it precisely right in their paring of this gospel portion with Isaiah's good news. Being "salt of the earth" or "light of the world" is "the fast" that Isaiah delineates. These actions—freeing captives and undoing oppression and feeding the hungry and clothing the naked—are not behaviors at a remove, but immediate, risky, hands-on interventions done for the sake of another, whoever that other may be. In fact, these are just the sorts of things that Jesus did and that he commends to his hearers in his final encouragement concerning the sheep and the goats at Matthew 25.31ff.

+ Ministry is bringing Christ's light into the world in the daily life of each Christian and in the corporate witness of the Church.

+ What can God reveal to us through the Spirit? We like to think we have things so well figured out. In fact, our desire to pinpoint and control every waking moment of our life may be blocking what the spirit has to say to us. Spirit moves through people. Being active in our church provides opportunities for us to hear what the Spirit is saying in our lives. Active participation in a Sunday service gives you the chance to listen to the Spirit. Sing the hymns with gusto, read the prayers with intention, greet your fellow congregants with energy and a smile.

Making Connections

The standard of character and holiness reserved for religious leaders is high. We don't expect as much from our grocery store clerks, bank tellers, or weathercasters, their hypocrisies easily overlooked or dismissed. For example, obesity and smoking are substantially higher among healthcare workers than in the general population, suggesting we improve our health, and we seem to be okay with that. Yet we hold anyone who claims to be religious to a higher standard than others, and are quick to push them off their pews when they reveal themselves to be

selfish, afraid, resentful . . . basically all the things we are. That might be why many are reluctant to out themselves as faithful people. These expectations of us we are uncertain we can meet, however misinformed or unrealistic, so we're disinclined to fess-up. How can we work towards honest, authentic articulation of ourselves as broken and beloved children of God?

Engaging All Ages

At this point in the year, most kids and teenagers (parents too!) are officially tired of the homework and tests. So, a passage that seems to put more on us—to be humble students and followers—might make for some exhausted sighs in the pews. Yes, we are followers of Christ. But we are called to live life differently—to not seek out power or fortune. To show up in a new way. This week, consider doing a "show up differently" Sunday. Encourage families to show up in wacky clothing, strange hats, even their pajamas. Then consider creating a place in your worship area where kids can bring blankets or pillows. The only problem is . . . people might fight for those new, best, seats in the sanctuary!

Hymns for the Day

Awake, my soul, stretch every nerve 546
Fight the good fight with all thy might 552, 553
Lo! what a cloud of witnesses 545
Guide me, O thou great Jehovah 690 (SC)
Before thy throne, O God, we kneel 574, 575 (GR)
O God of earth and altar 591 (GR)
Christ is the King! O friends upraise 614
Lamp of our feet, whereby we trace 627
O Christ, the Word Incarnate 632
All my hope on God is founded 665
Lord, for ever at thy side 670
O Jesus Christ, may grateful hymns be rising 590
Strengthen for service, Lord 312
Tell out, my soul, the greatness of the Lord 437, 438

Lift Every Voice and Sing II
Great is thy faithfulness 189
Deep river, my home is over Jordan 8 (SC)
On Jordan's stormy banks 9 (SC)

Wonder, Love, and Praise
The church of Christ in every age 779
These three are the treasures to strive for and prize 803
From the dawning of creation 748

Weekday Commemorations

Monday, November 6
William Temple, Archbishop of Canterbury, 1944

As bishop and later as archbishop, William Temple committed himself to seeking "the things which pertain to the Kingdom of God." He understood the Incarnation as giving worth and meaning not only to individuals but to all of life. A prolific writer on theological, ecumenical, and social topics, his two-volume *Readings in St. John's Gospel*, written in the early days of the war, became a spiritual classic. Temple was appointed archbishop of Canterbury in 1942 and reached an even wider audience through his wartime radio addresses and newspaper articles.

Tuesday, November 7
Willibrord, Bishop and Missionary, 739

While studying in Ireland for a dozen years (678–690), Willibrord heard a call to missionary work. Born in Northumbria (about 658), he was educated at Bishop Wilfrid's monastery at Ripon. In 690, he set out with twelve companions for Frisia (Holland); the area, though pagan, was increasingly being dominated by Christian Franks. Bishop Wilfrid and a few English people had delved in this mission field unsuccessfully, but, aided by the Frankish rulers, Willibrord established a base at Utrecht. Thus, Willibrord prepared the way for Boniface's greater achievements. Pope Sergius ordained him a bishop in 695. Three years later, Willibrord founded the monastery of Echternach, near Trier, where he died.

Wednesday, November 8
Ammonius, Hermit, c.403

Stories about Ammonius, well recorded in his time, tell of his cutting off his ear so he wouldn't be ordained in a time when forced ordination was common. Ammonius, a monastic hermit in Scete in Northern Egypt, was said to have memorized the Bible—both testaments. He was well educated, but he did not want to be the bishop of his people. After attempts to drag him to the bishop for ordination, Ammonius threatened to sever his tongue; his people, fearing the loss of his preaching and guidance, finally left him alone. Ammonius died while visiting his friend, John Chrysostom.

Thursday, November 9
Richard Rolle, Walter Hilton, and Margery Kempe, Mystics, 1349, 1396, and c. 1440

Rolle, Hilton, and Kempe developed the English mysticism that influenced Anglican spirituality. Rolle (b. 1290), a hermit and spiritual director, wrote widely and was read widely on theology and spirituality. Hilton (b. c. 1340) was a hermit and then an Augustinian canon at a Nottinghamshire priory; in his great work, *The Scale of Perfection*, he addressed the "luminous darkness" between loving oneself and God. Kempe (b. 1373), an illiterate mother of probably fourteen with her husband John, dictated *The Book of Margery Kempe*, which explored her mystic visions as well as her pilgrimages (Canterbury, Santiago de Compostela), and her compassion for sinners.

Friday, November 10
Leo of Rome, Bishop, 461

Unanimously elected pope in 440, Leo's ability to preach is shown clearly in the ninety-six sermons that exist to this day in which he expounds doctrine, encourages almsgiving, and deals with various heresies, including the Pelagian and Manichean systems. His letter to the Council of Chalcedon in 451 dealt effectively with the doctrine of the human and divine natures of the One Person of Christ. With similar strength of spirit and wisdom, Leo negotiated with Attila when the Huns were about to sack Rome, as well as other barbarians who sought to pillage and burn this city.

Saturday, November 11
Martin of Tours, Bishop, 397

Martin, a patron saint of France, was born (c. 330) in Hungary; he grew up in Italy, where he served in the army. He finally settled in Poitiers because he admired Hilary, the bishop. Hilary ordained Martin to the presbyterate about 350. Inspired by the monastic movement stemming from Egypt, Martin established a hermitage near Ligugé. Elected bishop of Tours (372), he agreed to serve only if allowed to retain his asceticism. His monastery at Marmoutier, near Tours, influenced the development of Celtic monasticism in Britain. Martin was not popular among his fellow bishops partially because he opposed their violent repression of heresy. His shrine at Tours became a secure sanctuary for seekers of protection.

Pentecost

The Twenty-Fourth Sunday after Pentecost: Proper 27

November 12, 2023

Being ready for judgment means striving for justice and righteousness.

Color   Green

Preface   Of the Lord's Day

Collect

O God, whose blessed Son came into the world that he might destroy the works of the devil and make us children of God and heirs of eternal life: Grant that, having this hope, we may purify ourselves as he is pure; that, when he comes again with power and great glory, we may be made like him in his eternal and glorious kingdom; where he lives and reigns with you and the Holy Spirit, one God, for ever and ever. *Amen.*

Readings and Psalm

Joshua 24:1–3a, 14–25

The generation that has come into the Promised Land enters into a covenant with the Lord similar to that into which their ancestors entered at Sinai. The ceremony reported here may have been an annual renewal of the covenant. It follows the form of ancient Hittite political treaties of that time. The recitation of God's act of salvation forms the historical creed of the Israelites. It is followed by the presentation of a choice, the response of commitment, and the enumeration of requirements. Early monotheism was not a metaphysical denial of the possibility of more than one god, but rather a moral decision of commitment to serve one particular god in response to God's prior choice of the people.

Psalm 78:1–7

The psalmist invites the people to reflect upon their past and learn from their mistakes in relation to God.

or

Wisdom of Solomon 6:12–16

Written around 100 BCE, the book of Wisdom was probably composed by a Hellenistic (Greek-speaking) Jew who attributed his work to Solomon. The book offers a fresh presentation of much of the earlier Old Testament teachings on wisdom. Today's reading urges all those in positions of authority to pursue wisdom, personified as a desirable woman. Though the reader is commanded to "seek" (v. 12), "desire" (v. 13), "fix one's thoughts on" and be "vigilant" (v. 15) for wisdom, she is readily accessible, eager to reward the diligent student.

or

Amos 5:18–24

Although Amos was from Judah, his mission was to the northern kingdom of Israel around 760–750 BCE when, under Jeroboam II, the kingdom was at the height of prosperity. Its wealth and power rested, however, upon injustice. Amos hammers at this discontinuity between the external state of society, demonstrated by its confidence in the day of the Lord, and its internal decay. The day of the Lord was popularly anticipated as the time when the Lord would vindicate Israel against its enemies. Amos radically reinterprets this smug expectation; that day will be "darkness, not light" (v. 18), bringing unexpected judgment even for Israel.

Pentecost

Wisdom of Solomon 6:17–20

This canticle continues from the reading and outlines the growth of the student who is dedicated to becoming wise.

or

Psalm 70

The psalmist pleads for the Lord's speedy assistance in delivering him from his enemies.

1 Thessalonians 4:13–18

The expectation of the Lord's imminent return has raised a concern: What is the fate of Christians who die before Christ's second coming? Although the followers of Plato believed in immortality only for the soul, and the initiates of the mystery religions expected to survive death, most pagans did not believe in life after death. Paul claims that all Christians have been united with Christ in his death and resurrection. Those who are alive at the Lord's return do not "precede" (v. 15) or have any special advantage over, those who have died. Christian hope is centered in Christ and in union with him. "We will be with the Lord forever" (v. 17).

Matthew 25:1–13

In response to the disciples' questions about the destruction of Jerusalem and the end of our world, Jesus prepares the disciples for life without his earthly presence. His parable of the ten bridesmaids provides guidelines for Christian behavior until Jesus returns in glory. The wise bridesmaids and the foolish ones both slept, but the latter's lack of forethought betrayed their true character. Declaring that he didn't know the bridesmaids, the bridegroom reveals that they had never been his friends, though they were in the bridal party. Here Matthew again emphasizes his parallel themes of ethical consistency and personal relationship: words matter less than obedience, which demonstrates genuine love.

Prayers of the People

Alleluia! Let us join the countless throngs who sing God's praises, praying, "We bless, O Lord; *your praise is ever in our mouths."*

God of the pilgrim Church, you love us and call us your children: give your Church a hunger and a thirst for righteousness. Continue to nurture us by the example and fellowship of those saints who have journeyed before us.

Silence

We bless, O Lord;

Your praise is ever in our mouths.

God of all people, you love us and call us your children: In a world of violence and war, you bless the peacemakers. Make us instruments of healing and peace.

Silence

We bless, O Lord;

Your praise is ever in our mouths.

God of creation, you love us and call us your children: you have given this earth to the meek. May our steps be gentle and leave a small footprint on our earth. As it has been handed on to us, may we carefully preserve this creation for future generations.

Silence

We bless, O Lord;

Your praise is ever in our mouths.

God of the city, you love us and call us your children: bless the poor with good things. Visit our impoverished neighborhoods with hope, mercy, and relief. Give us hearts for the poor in our region.

Silence

We bless, O Lord;

Your praise is ever in our mouths.

God of the mournful and suffering, you love us and call us your children: comfort and heal those in need. Hear them in their affliction and save them from their troubles.

Invite the congregation to add their petitions, followed by silence

We bless, O Lord;

Your praise is ever in our mouths.

God of the Church at rest, you love us and call us your children: we praise you for the faith and witness of all the saints. May their prayers and presence continue to strengthen us. It is with their triumphant voices that we join our own prayers and praises. Alleluia!

Invite the congregation to add their thanksgivings, followed by silence

We bless, O Lord;

Your praise is ever in our mouths.

Images in the Readings

The **wedding feast** is a biblical image for our life with God, and Christians have used the image as one way to describe holy communion. Philipp Nicolai's hymn "'Sleepers, wake!' A voice astounds us" (*Hymnal 82*, 61 and 62), is a fine example of the use of marriage imagery. In biblical times, a wedding was not about personal choice and lavish expense but about the communal celebration of the promise of new life and commitment.

Christians have used the **lamp** as an image for the word of God, with which we see God's way. Many Christians use oil as part of the ritual of baptism.

When Amos writes of the **waters** and "everflowing stream," Christians think of the water of baptism, which means to carry us, in the ship of the church, into a life of justice and righteousness.

Many Christians have literalized Paul's eschatological imagery of Christ's **appearance** in the skies, an **archangel**, a **trumpet**, and **clouds**. Recall that for Paul, this picture fit scientifically with his understanding of the universe. For us it does not, and to be Christian does not mean to hide in archaic thinking. Thus we need to use care when citing this first-century picture of the end of all things. We repeat Martin Luther: "What is this? What does this mean?"

Ideas for the Day

+ There are formal church seasons, like Advent and Easter. They get colors and festivals. Then there are the informal church seasons . . . like fall. During this "ordinary time" we typically hear lessons about property and stewardship, lessons about what we own and what owns us. This parable asks questions: What are you going to do? What are you going to trust, when everything else is pushed out of view? It seems judgmental, but this is a kingdom parable; a reign of God parable, a radical invitation to live into the last things which is going to demand some deciding. God wants to know our passion for God's estate, our generosity to God's creation, and wants to know of our love and trust in the Owner in the testimony of how we lived.

+ At one time you may have tried to read the Bible from beginning to end. Certainly the first two books are a fairly easy read. We know the stories and we have seen the movies. Then it gets somewhat boring (for many). There are a lot of lists and a lot of laws. And then we get to the book of Judges. We find a lot of fighting and a lot of what is called unfaithfulness. Worst reading EVER! Then we come to chapter 4 and the women, Deborah and Jael, are introduced. For two whole chapters we are shown the power of two women (not men) who are intentional about doing what is right. We need to pay attention to the final verse at the end of chapter 5 where it says, "and the land had rest for forty years."

+ We have the responsibility to use our talents to mirror God's creative action in the world. What we do shows forth the glory of God, no matter how insignificant we think our actions might be.

+ We must face the consequences of our failure to mirror God's creation, whether through our fear or rebellion. We face these consequences individually and as a nation and society.

Making Connections

Sometimes called "the parable of the closed door," this story is in the final discourse of Matthew's gospel, which emphasizes distinctions between those who are, and those who are not, ultimately included among faithful followers of Jesus: apparent in his separating sheep from goats, deciding who is included or excluded from the wedding banquet, and even his characterization of the last judgment. Expecting high standards for readiness in cultural, theological, and political aptitudes from the disciples is not bad in and of itself. But the major premise of Jesus' authentic parables was the breaking down of any social barriers. Today's story runs counter to the true message of Jesus. We should exercise caution, and not confuse discipline, which certainly strengthens our lives with God and in community, with faith itself. Our failure to get it right, and our judgment of others, attempts and failures, does not dictate or direct God's love.

Engaging All Ages

This week we are in the midst of changing seasons, both in terms of weather and in the church calendar. The rhythms of the church are a beautiful way to order our lives and not simply our worship. As we move into Advent, set up an opportunity for people of all ages (children especially) to watch as the liturgical colors of the church change. To ask questions. To help! For a more immediate idea (this one is kind of future-oriented, granted) have a "person on the street" style event at church who goes around interviewing members about what they do and don't know about the liturgical year. Show the video sometime in the future.

Hymns for the Day

The Hymnal 1982
O heavenly Word, eternal Light 63, 64
Guide me, O thou great Jehovah 690 [SC]
O God of Bethel, by whose hand 709 [SC]
Praise our great and gracious Lord 393 [SC]
Before thy throne, O God, we kneel 574, 575 [GR]
Judge eternal, throned in splendor 596 [GR]
The Lord will come and not be slow 462 [GR]
Jerusalem, my happy home 620
Jesus came, adored by angels 454
Jesus lives! thy terrors now 194, 195
Let all mortal flesh keep silence 324
Lo, he comes with clouds descending 57, 58
Rejoice, the Lord is King! 481
Lift up your heads, ye mighty gates 436
Once he came in blessing 53
Rejoice! rejoice, believers 68
"Sleepers, wake!" A voice astounds us 61, 62

Lift Every Voice and Sing II

Wonder, Love, and Praise
Even when young, I prayed for wisdom's grace 906 [GR]
Signs of ending all around us 721 [GR]

Weekday Commemorations

Tuesday, November 14
The Consecration of Samuel Seabury, 1784
Seabury could not—would not—swear allegiance to the English crown. He had sailed for England in 1783 after the American Revolution to seek episcopal consecration in England, but as an American citizen, he refused to swear. He turned to the Non-juring bishops of the Episcopal Church in Scotland: he was consecrated on November 14, 1784, as the first American bishop of the Episcopal Church. When he returned to these shores, he was recognized as bishop of Connecticut, and with Bishop William White he helped organize the Episcopal Church at the General Convention of 1789. He kept his promise to persuade the American church to adopt the Scottish form for the celebration of Holy Eucharist.

Pentecost

Wednesday, November 15
Herman of Alaska, Missionary, 1837

Known in the Russian Orthodox Church as Saint Herman: Wonderworker of All America, Herman (b. 1756) was the first saint to be canonized by the Orthodox Church in America. In 1793, he emigrated from St. Petersburg to Alaska. He defended the native Aleut against authorities with commercial interests, caring compassionately for all who sought him (they called him their North Star). Herman baked cookies for children. Though not formally educated or ordained, he earned a reputation as a teacher and sage. He wrote: "From this day forth, from this hour, from this very minute, let us love God above all."

Thursday, November 16
Margaret of Scotland, Queen, 1093

Scotland's most beloved saint was an English princess when King Malcolm married her about 1070. She devoted her queenly life to country, church, and family (this conscientious wife bore eight children). She considered practices among Scottish clergy to be old-fashioned and sloppy: Lent should start on Ash Wednesday not on the following Monday; the Lord's Day was for applying "ourselves only to prayers." She encouraged the founding of schools, hospitals, and orphanages, and she provided opportunity for her servants to worship. She influenced Malcolm, who trusted her political judgment, to reach out to isolated clans, although she was not successful in ending their bloody warfare. Malcom and Margaret rebuilt the monastery of Iona.

Friday, November 17
Hugh of Lincoln, Bishop, 1200

Born into a noble family at Avalon in Burgundy (France), Hugh become a canon regular at Villard-Benoit near Grenoble. About 1160 he joined the Carthusians, the strictest contemplative order of the Church and later became their procurator. Reluctantly, he accepted the invitation of King Henry II to come to England as prior of a new Carthusian foundation, and later reluctantly accepted King Henry's appointment to the see of London in 1186. Respected for his humility and tact, his total lack of self-regard, and his cheerful disposition, he was loved for his constant championship of the poor, the oppressed, and outcasts, especially lepers and Jews.

Saturday, November 18
Hilda of Whitby, Monastic, 680

Born in 614, Hilda lived chaste and respected for twenty years at the court of her great-uncle, King Edwin. Bishop Aidan was so impressed with her holiness of life that he recalled her to her home country in East Anglia and the next year appointed her abbess of Hartlepool. There, Hilda established the rule she had been taught by Paulinus, a companion of Augustine of Canterbury, and by Aidan. She became renowned for her wisdom, eagerness to learn, and devotion to serving God. Later, she founded the abbey at Whitby for nuns and monks to live by her strict rule. Hilda was sought by royalty and public servants for her advice and counsel.

The Twenty-Fifth Sunday after Pentecost: Proper 28

November 19, 2023

Being ready for the final judgment.

Color Green

Preface Of the Lord's Day

Collect

Blessed Lord, who caused all holy Scriptures to be written for our learning: Grant us so to hear them, read, mark, learn, and inwardly digest them, that we may embrace and ever hold fast the blessed hope of everlasting life, which you have given us in our Savior Jesus Christ; who lives and reigns with you and the Holy Spirit, one God, for ever and ever. *Amen.*

Readings and Psalm

Judges 4:1–7

Today's reading describes the way that God continues to actively intervene in the life of the covenant people after they have taken up residence in the Promised Land. When their sinfulness provokes God's anger, God allows them to be oppressed by the Canaanite king Jabin and his military leader Sisera. But then, as before in Egypt, the people cry out for God's help and God empowers their leader Deborah, a prophetess who speaks God's message, to summon the army under Barak, who will lead them to victory because God will be with them. True to the covenant obligations that God has assumed, God once again delivers the people from their enemies.

Psalm 123

This psalm is a lament in which the psalmist expresses confidence in God by the analogy of an attentive servant watching a master and hoping for a favor to be given.

or

Zephaniah 1:7, 12–18

The introductory verse to the book of Zephaniah sets his ministry during the reign of Josiah (640–609 BCE), probably during the early period before the king's reforms. Zephaniah's primary criticism is Judah's apostasy. He calls his audience to solemn silence before Judah's judgment. Searching the hearts of the people, the Lord finds only indolence and indifference. The figure is taken from the process of making wine. The wine must be poured off from the sediment and mixed or it will become syrupy and tasteless. Zephaniah builds upon the work of Amos to describe the day of the Lord as a battle scene. The silver and gold idols of the people will not save them.

Psalm 90:1–8 (9–11), 12

This psalm faces squarely the dark realities of the human condition within the context of faith.

1 Thessalonians 5:1–11

Paul responds to another of the Thessalonians' concerns, the desire to know the "times and the seasons" (v. 1), the persistent human wish to have an end-times timetable. Paul replies that such knowledge is not needful for Christians. The "day of the Lord" (v. 2), now identified with Jesus' second coming, will happen as unexpectedly as a thief's entry. False assurances leave people unprepared for "sudden destruction" (v. 3), final separation from God. The Thessalonians should not concern themselves so much with the imminence of the second coming as with its immediacy to their lives, which acts as a call to vigilance and freedom from excess.

Pentecost

Matthew 25:14–30

The second of Matthew's three end-time parables concerns the gift of talents and how they are used. Here the demand is to use one's gifts in order to participate fully in the reality of God's coming kingdom. The focus is on the last slave who does not put to use what he has been given. The question is not uncertainty about the date of the return, but about what reckoning will be required. According to rabbinical law, a man who buried property entrusted to him had taken the safest course and was not liable for its loss. Whereas the first two servants take the risk of losing their talents, the last servant shows that his primary interest is in his own security. The master, however, expects fruitfulness from his servants no matter how long his return is delayed.

Prayers of the People

Brothers and sisters, in love let us encourage one another and build each other up. Let us pray saying, "Have mercy upon us, O Lord, *have mercy.*"

Lord God, you have destined us not for wrath but for obtaining salvation through our Lord Jesus Christ: strengthen your Church to confidently share your gospel throughout the world.

Silence

Have mercy upon us, O Lord,

Have mercy.

Lord God, have mercy on all who are shown contempt and scorn: Hear the cries of the needy and lift up the downtrodden and lowly.

Silence

Have mercy upon us, O Lord,

Have mercy.

Lord God, you rule the day and the night: Bless and sustain the works of your hands. Restore your creation.

Silence

Have mercy upon us, O Lord,

Have mercy.

Lord God, you are enthroned in the heavens: may we trust not our own schemes but lift up our eyes to you. Lead and guide our city and its leaders in all justice and truth.

Silence

Have mercy upon us, O Lord,

Have mercy.

Lord God, you are a merciful God: hear the prayers of those who cry out to you for help. Be present with the suffering in their waking and their sleeping.

Invite the congregation to add their petitions and thanksgivings, followed by silence

Have mercy upon us, O Lord,

Have mercy.

Lord God, your Son Jesus died for us that we might dwell in your light forever: give to the dying and the dead the hope of salvation.

Silence

Have mercy upon us, O Lord,

Have mercy.

Images in the Readings

It is interesting that our English word **talent**, meaning ability, comes from interpretations of this parable. Christians believe that God's creation is ongoing, that every human capability is a gift from the Creator, and that we are called to use all of God's creation wisely.

Zephaniah's litany describing a **day of wrath** continues in our time especially in popular disaster movies. Humans continue to be fearful of an unknown future. When Christians gather on Sunday before an image of the crucified Christ, we acknowledge our fears, and protecting ourselves with the breastplate and helmet of the faith, we join together hoping for God's mercy.

Paul likens the coming of the end to **labor pains**. With the pregnant woman, we hope that the pains will lead to life. The infant will come into the light.

Ideas for the Day

- There are formal church seasons, like Advent and Easter. They get colors and festivals. Then there are the informal church seasons, like fall. During this "ordinary time" we typically hear lessons about property and stewardship, lessons about what we own and what owns us. This parable ask questions: What are you going to do? What are you going to trust, when everything else is pushed out of view? It seems judgmental, but this is a Kingdom parable, a reign of God parable, a radical invitation to live into the last things, which is going to demand some deciding. God wants to know our passion for God's estate, our generosity to God's creation, and wants to know of our love and trust in the Owner in the testimony of how we lived.

- At one time you may have tried to read the Bible from beginning to end. Certainly the first two books are a fairly easy read. We know the stories, and we have seen the movies. Then it gets somewhat boring (for many). There are a lot of lists and a lot of laws. And then we get to the book of Judges. We find a lot of fighting and a lot of what is called unfaithfulness. Then we come to chapter 4 and the women, Deborah and Jael, are introduced. For two whole chapters we are shown the power of two women (not men) who are intentional about doing what is right. We need to pay attention to the final verse at the end of chapter 5 where it says "and the land had rest for forty years."

- We have the responsibility to use our talents to mirror God's creative action in the world. What we do shows forth the glory of God, no matter how insignificant we think our actions might be. We must face the consequences of our failure to mirror God's creation, whether through our fear or rebellion. We face these consequences individually and as a nation and society.

Making Connections

The gospel this week is problematic, and fascinating to explore for many reasons. Prosperity Gospel folks hold it up as marching orders for accumulating wealth, and judging those who don't. Modern self-help-bent Christian writers use it to bolster the faithful to lean-in to their innate abilities. Liberation theologians refer to it as the parable of the whistle blower, where the third slave is the hero. A version of it in the Gospel of the Nazarenes reveals punishment for the one who most-mimicked his greedy master, instead of doing what was "right," and the one who buried the talent was shown compassion, and only lightly rebuked. Milton pondered: ". . . Thousands at his bidding speed and post o'er land and ocean without rest: They also serve who only stand and wait." We are conflicted by the possibilities for what this story suggests to be true about us.

Engaging All Ages

Today's Collect addresses how God continues to speak to us through the Bible. In "An Outline of the Faith, commonly called the Catechism" (BCP, 853), we have the church's explanation of what we believe the Bible to be—the Word of God.

Hymns for the Day

The Hymnal 1982

O Christ, the Word Incarnate 632
Word of God, come down on earth 633
Open your ears, O faithful people 536 [SC]
Before thy throne, O God, we kneel 574, 575 [GR]
O God, our help in ages past 680 [GR]
The Lord will come and not be slow 462 [GR]
Awake, O sleeper, rise from death 547
Eternal Ruler of the ceaseless round 617
Hark! a thrilling voice is sounding 59
I want to walk as a child of the light 490
From glory to glory advancing, we praise thee,
    O Lord 326
Lord Christ, when first thou cam'st to earth 598
Not here for high and holy things 9
O Jesus, I have promised 655
Once he came in blessing 53
Rise up, ye saints of God 551
Strengthen for service, Lord 312

Lift Every Voice and Sing II

Wonder, Love, and Praise
With awe approach the mysteries 759 [SC]
Signs of ending all around us 721 [GR]

Pentecost

Weekday Commemorations

Monday, November 20
Edmund, King, 870

At fifteen, Edmund ascended the throne of East Anglia and ruled as a Christian for fifteen years before Danish armies invaded England in 870. The Danes burned monasteries and churches, among other murderous atrocities. The leaders confronted Edmund and demanded he acknowledge their supremacy and forbid the practice of Christianity. Edmund refused. His army fought bravely against the Danes, but King Edmund was eventually captured; according to the account by Dunstan, Archbishop of Canterbury ninety years later, Edmund was tortured, beaten, shot with arrows, and beheaded. His remains were enshrined in a Benedictine monastery now called Bury St. Edmunds; this place of pilgrimage honors a saint steadfast in faith and to his people.

Tuesday, November 21
Mechthilde of Hackeborn and Gertrude the Great, Mystics and Theologians, 1298 and 1302

This pair of Benedictine nuns lived at St. Mary's Monastery in Helfta, known for encouraging the sisters' knowledge. Mechthilde (b. 1240) grew up pious and noble in Germany. Impressed with her abbess sister's convent library, Mechthilde refused to return home. She was well educated there and came to direct the choir and the library, illuminate manuscripts, and write (*Book of Special Grace*). Gertrude was given as a child to Mechthilde to raise at Helfta. Gertrude's writing, including *The Herald of Divine Love*, manifests her education with fluent Latin and extensive familiarity with scriptures and Christian authorities.

Wednesday, November 22
Clive Staples Lewis, Apologist and Spiritual Writer, 1963

"You must make your choice," C. S. Lewis wrote in *Mere Christianity*, "Either this man was, and is, the Son of God, or else a madman or something worse. You can shut Him up as a fool, you can spit at Him and kill Him as a demon, or you can fall at His feet and call Him Lord and God." Lewis did not always believe this. His conversion inaugurated a wonderful outpouring of Christian apologetics in media as varied as popular theology, children's literature, fantasy and science fiction, and correspondence on spiritual matters with friends and strangers alike. Lewis died at his home in Oxford on November 22, 1963.

Thursday, November 23
Clement of Rome, Bishop, c.100

Little is known of the life of Clement, and what is known is contested. He is said to be the third bishop of Rome, after Peter and Linus, or the fourth, after Jerome. Clement, it is also said, was consecrated by Peter himself. Clement governed from 88 to about 100. As a disciple of the Apostles, he was active in the early church. He is generally regarded as having written a letter about 96 from the Church in Rome to the Church in Corinth. A younger group at Corinth had deposed the elder clergy, jeopardizing the Church. In response, Clement organized a hierarchical structure of Church authority, interchanging the terms "bishop" and "presbyter." This letter was rediscovered in 1628.

Friday, November 24
Catherine of Alexandria, Barbara of Nicomedia, and Margaret of Antioch, Martyrs, c. 300

Popular as Catholic saints, Catherine, Barbara, and Margaret attracted even Anglican devotion after the Reformation. The waxing and waning of their popularity parallel interest in female martyrdom, including recasting trauma so devotees may want to remember them. Catherine, a young scholar who rebuked the emperor for cruelty, was tortured on a spiked wheel that broke so was beheaded. Beautiful Barbara, locked in a tower, was available only to her pagan tutors so was educated; when she confessed to being Christian, she was executed. Margaret embraced Christianity at her nurse's breast; for her faith, Margaret was sorely persecuted and eventually executed.

Saturday, November 25
James Otis Sargent Huntington, Monastic and Priest, 1935

Huntington, committed to active ministry based in the spiritual life, founded the first permanent Episcopal monastic community for men in the United States on those commissions. He was born in Boston (1854), graduated from Harvard, and studied theology in Syracuse, New York. He was ordained deacon and priest by his father, the first bishop of Central New York. Upon receiving a call to religious life, he resolved to found an indigenous American community. Beginning his common life at Holy Cross Mission on New York's Lower East Side, Huntington made his life vow on November 25, 1884. He increased his social witness to the Church by working with immigrants and for the single-tax and labor union movements.

Thanksgiving Day

November 23, 2023

The church recognizes the traditional Thanksgiving holiday as a holy day for our land, life, and heritage.

Color White

Preface of Trinity Sunday

Collect

Almighty and gracious Father, we give you thanks for the fruits of the earth in their season and for the labors of those who harvest them. Make us, we pray, faithful stewards of your great bounty, for the provision of our necessities and the relief of all who are in need, to the glory of your Name; through Jesus Christ our Lord, who lives and reigns with you and the Holy Spirit, one God, now and for ever. *Amen.*

Readings and Psalm

Deuteronomy 8:7–18

In the lesson from the Hebrew Bible Moses addresses the people as they prepare to enter Canaan, a productive and rich land where they will lack for nothing. As the people experience abundance they must not forget God, who has given them all things, nor imagine that it is only by their own strength that they prosper. The people must recall the lessons of the past, the commandments of the Lord, and the covenant they have sworn.

Psalm 65

A psalm of praise and thanksgiving to the savior, the mighty Lord, who creates the earth and causes it to bring forth abundantly.

2 Corinthians 9:6–15

In this epistle lesson Paul encourages believers at Corinth to be generous in giving toward a collection that he is gathering for the relief of the church in Jerusalem, mindful of how God has provided for the physical and spiritual needs of the Corinthians. A farmer who is stingy in sowing seed does not see great yield, but one who scatters seed freely enjoys a large harvest. In the same way free and joyful giving will bring reward. This summons to ministry is a test of their confidence in God, who will supply all things.

Luke 17:11–19

In the gospel story Jesus' command brings about the cleansing of ten lepers, but only one, a Samaritan, returns to give thanks. Jesus is on the way to his destiny in Jerusalem. The narrative illustrates the power of the reign of God to give a new lease on life. The lepers, who were formerly outcasts, would not be allowed to return home. Only a despised Samaritan recognizes that a life of gratitude and faith is now possible. Physical healing is but a first step. He becomes whole and finds salvation.

Pentecost

Pentecost

Prayers of the People, A Litany of Thanksgiving

Let us give thanks to God our Father for all his gifts so freely bestowed upon us, saying, *"we thank you, Lord."*

For the beauty and wonder of your creation, in earth and sky and sea,

> *We thank you, Lord.*

For all that is gracious in the lives of men and women, revealing the image of Christ,

> *We thank you, Lord.*

For our daily food and drink, our homes and families, and our friends,

> *We thank you, Lord.*

For minds to think, and hearts to love, and hands to serve,

> *We thank you, Lord.*

For health and strength to work, and leisure to rest and play,

> *We thank you, Lord.*

For the brave and courageous, who are patient in suffering and faithful in adversity,

> *We thank you, Lord.*

For all valiant seekers after truth, liberty, and justice,

> *We thank you, Lord.*

For the communion of saints, in all times and places,

> *We thank you, Lord.*

Above all, we give you thanks for the great mercies and promises given to us in Christ Jesus our Lord;

> *To him be praise and glory, with you, O Father, and the Holy Spirit, now and for ever. Amen.*

Images in the Readings

We are **lepers**, this is true: our very bodies are dying, little by little. Most of us are also **Samaritans**, this is true: we are seen by at least some others as not religiously pure enough. So in this worship service and with our entire lives, we are to praise God with a loud voice.

Paul's use here of the image of the **seed** can be applied to the New Testament's metaphor of the Word of God as seed. God provides the seed in the hearts of the baptized, and that seed grows in order for its fruit to be shared with others.

The **good land**, as the Deuteronomy passage calls the Promised Land, has been interpreted in the church as our life together in the faith. The land with the flowing streams, vines, and wheat: these can have not only literal reference to a contemporary life of plenty, but to the gifts of God that are realized in faith. But millions of people in the world, including many Christians and perhaps some worshippers present, are not eating their fill (Deut. 8:10).

Ideas for the Day

- All the lessons push into our lives with the word of God and ask revealing questions. Have we lived as if we know that all is God's and all goes back to God? The fall decor and game times only sort of block the darker truths that also come to our tables. Truths about our un-generosity and un-forgiveness and the terror of religious dissenters who risked the wild unknown rather than stay at home and the trauma that caused for indigenous peoples. What is it about the holidays that are supposed to be beautiful but somehow seem to bring out the broken in us?

- Thank you. *Gracias. Grazie.* It is easier in Spanish or Italian to see the word "grace" in the word for thank you. The Eucharistic Prayer is a Prayer of Thanksgiving. Every time we express our thanks to God, we start the glorious cycle of a holy conversation and dance with God. We say thank you and we see grace. If we do it enough, it turns out it can be the same thing, the same action.

Making Connections

Pushing Jerusalem into the story, certain that was Jesus' destiny, the geographical placing here doesn't make sense. But Luke was keen on foreigners being a part of this new thing. It's tempting to yoke that interest of "foreigners" into the myth of this American holiday, until the truth of colonization violently turns the question of "Who is the foreigner?" on its head. Ancient celebrations of harvest, and the abundance brought forth from this earth, are appropriate. Giving thanks, and returning thanks by caring for the earth and one another, is also appropriate. Tangible outreach actions and targeted formation/conversations pull us through the fog and bog of this particular holiday observance, including the exploration of reparations to indigenous and slave populations (especially those whose ancestors belong to/are us and our neighbors), and environmental steps we can and must take to return our planet to health, as faithful people.

Engaging All Ages

God gives abundantly. This is the theme in all the scriptures today. It is Thanksgiving after all. A holiday when people gather with their families. There is often a moment when you are told, "Say something you are thankful for." The response may come easy or it may come with a groan. Sometimes overflowing and sometimes a quick one-word answer. In the United States, it is really a holiday that seems to celebrate the success of the American Dream. But are there things in your life you can only attribute to God's blessing? Name them.

Hymns for the Day

The Hymnal 1982
All people that on earth do dwell 377, 378
As those of old their first fruits brought 705
Come, ye thankful people, come 290
For the beauty of the earth 416
From all that dwell below the skies 380
Glory, love, and praise, and honor 300
Now thank we all our God 396, 397
Praise to God, immortal praise 288
We gather together to ask the Lord's blessing 433
We plow the fields, and scatter 291
When all thy mercies, O my God 415
For the fruit of all creation 424
I sing the almighty power of God 398
Let us, with a gladsome mind 389
O all ye works of God, now come 428
Seek ye first the kingdom of God 711
Sometimes a light surprises 667
Holy Father, great Creator 368
To God with gladness sing 399
By gracious powers so wonderfully sheltered 695, 696
Commit thou all that grieves thee 669
Jesus, all my gladness 701
Joyful, joyful, we adore thee 376

Lift Every Voice and Sing II
Give thanks to the Lord for he is good 93
God is so good 214

Wonder, Love, and Praise
Let all creation bless the Lord 885
O all ye works of God, now come 884

Pentecost

The Last Sunday after Pentecost: Christ the King

November 26, 2023

This day is often referred to as the Sunday of Christ the King, or the Reign of Christ, meaning that Jesus stands above all earthly power and authority.

Color White

Preface Of the Lord's Day

Collect

Almighty and everlasting God, whose will it is to restore all things in your well-beloved Son, the King of kings and Lord of lords: Mercifully grant that the peoples of the earth, divided and enslaved by sin, may be freed and brought together under his most gracious rule; who lives and reigns with you and the Holy Spirit, one God, now and for ever. *Amen.*

Readings and Psalm

Ezekiel 34:11–16, 20–24

Ezekiel reveals God's nature as one of both compassion and judgment. God's mercy extends to the lost and injured—those who have suffered from the injustices of others as well as from their own wrong choices—and God's judgment reaches the sheep as well as the shepherds. As the shepherds have been judged, so also the sheep must be judged for their behavior to one another (vv. 17–22).

Psalm 100

Psalm 100, a hymn of praise to God, is a joyous affirmation of the people's loyalty to and dependence upon God.

or

Psalm 95:1–7a

A call to worship the Lord our God.

Ephesians 1:15–23

Today's reading is a prayer of thanksgiving. Paul shows by example the importance of making requests of God in prayer—that the baptized may cooperate with God in the working out of God's plan. Paul prays that his readers may be enlightened to understand the surety of their hope, the privileges and responsibilities of their inheritance, and the dimensions of God's power available to them through the resurrection and ascension of Jesus.

Matthew 25:31–46

Today's reading, the last of Matthew's three end-time parables, is more a vision of the last judgment than it is a parable. Here the Son of Man, Jesus' title for himself, is clearly identified as the King and Judge of all people, roles traditionally attributed exclusively to God. The King offers only one criterion of judgment: deeds of compassion. Here is Jesus' unmistakable revelation of God's true nature. As Son of Man, Jesus associates himself not with the brilliant, the pious, the famous, or the powerful, but with the least—the hungry, thirsty, lonely, sick, naked, and imprisoned. Jesus clearly delineates the values of the kingdom of heaven. Those who suffer are close to the heart of God. Those who minister to the suffering receive the Father's blessing. Good intentions are insufficient; what counts are actions, not words.

Prayers of the People

Serve the Lord with gladness and come before God's presence with a song. Let us pray together, saying, "We give you thanks, O Lord; *and call upon your Name.*"

Christ the King, you have been made head over all things for the Church: may we worthily live as your body in our world. Work your great power in and through us.

Silence

We give you thanks, O Lord;

And call upon your Name.

Christ the King, you gather all the nations of the world to yourself: bless the world's suffering with your everlasting mercy. May the oppressed be fed with your justice.

Silence

We give you thanks, O Lord;

And call upon your Name.

Christ the King, it is from your hand that all are fed: inspire righteousness in all people that the hungry may be fed and the thirsty given clean water to drink.

Silence

We give you thanks, O Lord;

And call upon your Name.

Christ the King, you care for those in prison: give us hearts for all those who are incarcerated. Where there is crime and violence in our city, offer your peace.

Silence

We give you thanks, O Lord;

And call upon your Name.

Christ the King, you are good: we pray you seek the lost, bind up the injured, and strengthen the weak.

Invite the congregation to add their petitions and thanksgivings, followed by silence

We give you thanks, O Lord;

And call upon your Name.

Christ the King, your faithfulness endures from age to age: may all your saints, at work and at rest, know the hope to which you have called us and the riches of your glorious inheritance.

Silence

We give you thanks, O Lord;

And call upon your Name.

Images in the Readings

Calling this Sunday Christ the **King** may elevate that image above all others. Currently on the world scene some nations have rejected monarchies, some maintain figurehead monarchs, and some, while not using the term king, maintain heads of state with absolute, even ruthless, power over the people. The Bible promises that God's power and majesty differ radically from the reign of most human monarchs. Thus we need to use the image of King as correcting the image of king.

Several hymns do a splendid job of playing the image against itself. As an example of how God's reign differs from that of human monarchs, the baptized saints receive riches and power from God. Some churches prefer the phrase "the Reign of Christ" as stressing the activity, rather than the status; unfortunately English has the problem of the homonym "rain."

In the Bible, written within a culture that treasured its pastoral past, **sheep and goats** are images of the life God gives to the people. Like sheep and goats, we are created by God to live together and offer ourselves for others. It is an urban prejudice to defame sheep as dirty and stupid.

Matthew's parable was depicted in sculptures over the main doorway and in wall paintings over the chancel of countless Christian churches, and one can imagine the fun that artists had in shaping the monsters on the left side of Christ the **judge**. As this imagery becomes less important for some Christians, it is important not to lose the biblical call that we saints are to live out the justice that God intends, serving each needy person who is Christ-for-us.

As the first-century decades progressed, **saints** became an increasingly common term for the baptized people of God. The usual English translation of "being personally holy," the word "saint" is used differently by the several Christian branches. In Ephesians, everyone who is enlightened is called saint, the meaning most Protestants have retained.

Pentecost

Pentecost

Ideas for the Day

- It isn't simple to follow the lead of God, to acknowledge our relatedness and reliance as well as our dependence. Especially for people who enjoy the blessings of the status quo, it may be hard to relinquish one's self-determination. However, it is this letting go that prepares us for the season that comes next, that expectant desire for Jesus' full and glorious incarnation. Giving our allegiance over to the reign of Christ is being in solidarity with the weak, exiled, persecuted, and challengers of evil across time and place. It is putting our heart, soul, and faith in solidarity with God's ways and prerogatives, rather than our own.

- We have spent a little more than six months making our way through Matthew's gospel. We discovered a lot of teaching, some parables, and conflicts with authority. The twenty-fifth chapter of Matthew is the cornerstone for many as what a life with Jesus is all about. We can say that we are followers of Jesus, but unless we are actually reaching out and naming the humanity of every human being, we have simply missed the point. We don't have to like everyone, but we do need to love them. The journey is about figuring out the infinite number of ways to love.

- The earliest Christian creed, "Jesus is Lord," means that Jesus stands above all other earthly power and authority. All through history and into the present moment, choosing God above earthly authority has caused persecution and conflict in the life of the church. The congregation and wider church must witness always to the authority of Jesus Christ, realizing that there will be times when conflict will be the direct result of such a witness.

Making Connections

Some of the traditions in the Episcopal Church have their origins in the royal court. For example, purple—the color for Advent and Lent—was the color associated with royalty and became linked to the coming of Christ as king. We seek the kingdom of God, where we will feast at the banquet table of the Lord. In the age to come, Christ will reign, and God's will will "be done on earth as it is in heaven."

Engaging All Ages

The use of "King" and "kingdom" language in the church often comes with hesitancy. It's highly gendered and promotes colonial and imperial ideas that the world could do well with abandoning. However, in the church the claim of Christ the King should come with different connotations, namely that Christ is the center of our lives. This week, encourage your parishioners to pray the ancient "Jesus Prayer" throughout the week. It goes: "Lord Jesus Christ, Son of God, have mercy on me." A simple email or letter to the congregation works. However, if you want to go the extra mile consider printing off small prayer cards with an icon on one side and the prayer on the other. If you want to really go the extra mile, set up a book club to discuss the spiritual classic *The Way of a Pilgrim*.

Hymns for the Day

The Hymnal 1982

Alleluia, sing to Jesus (vs. 1, 3–5) 460, 461
All praise to thee, for thou, O King divine 477
At the Name of Jesus 435
Hail to the Lord's Anointed 616
Jesus shall reign where'er the sun 544
King of glory, King of peace 382
Lead on, O King eternal 555
Let all mortal flesh keep silence 324
Ye servants of God, your Master proclaim 535
All people that on earth do dwell 377, 378
Before the Lord's eternal throne 391
Jesus, our mighty Lord 478
To God with gladness sing 399
All hail the power of Jesus' Name 450, 451
Crown him with many crowns 494
Hail, thou once despised Jesus 495
Lord, enthroned in heavenly splendor 307
Rejoice, the Lord is King 481
Christ is the King! O friends upraise 614
Father eternal, Ruler of creation 573
Lord, whose love through humble service 610
Praise the Lord through every nation 484, 485
Where cross the crowded ways of life 609

Lift Every Voice and Sing II

Soon and very soon 14
He is King of kings 96

Wonder, Love, and Praise

Cuando el pobre nada tiene /
    When a poor one who as nothing 802

Weekday Commemorations

Tuesday, November 28
Kamehameha and Emma,
King and Queen of Hawai'i, 1864, 1885

Within a year of ascending the throne in 1855, King Kamehameha IV and Queen Emma (each twenty years old) solicited funds to build a hospital in response to a smallpox epidemic. The people of Hawai'i, more accustomed to pomp than to humility in royalty, came to revere Emma and Kamehameha. In 1860, the king and queen petitioned the bishop of Oxford to send missionaries to establish the Anglican Church in Hawai'i; the priests arrived in 1862 to confirm the queen and king. Kamehameha translated the Book of Common Prayer and the Hymnal. He died a year after his little boy. Emma declined to rule alone but chose to end her days in a life of good works.

Friday, December 1
Charles de Foucauld, Monastic and Martyr, 1916

De Foucauld influenced revival of desert spirituality in the early twentieth century; he inspired the founding of new religious communities for women and men. Brother Charles of Jesus (b. 1858) mixed laxity with stubbornness as a young man. He served as an army officer before becoming an explorer in Morocco, where he encountered Muslims. Their faith inspired him to study his own: in 1886, he found God. He was ordained in 1901 and lived "a ministry of presence" in the Sahara. After being shot to death by bandits in 1916, he was beatified as a Roman Catholic martyr in 2005.

Saturday, December 2
Channing Moore Williams,
Bishop and Missionary, 1910

Bishop Williams was born in Richmond, Virginia, on July 18, 1829, and brought up in straitened circumstances by his widowed mother. He attended the College of William and Mary and the Virginia Theological Seminary. Ordained deacon in 1855, he offered himself for work in China; two years later he was sent to Japan and opened work in Nagasaki. Williams translated parts of the prayer book into Japanese; he was a close friend and warm supporter of Bishop Schereschewsky, his successor in China.

Pentecost

Index of Seasonal Rites